Corporate Actions

For other titles in the Wiley Finance Series
please see www.wiley.com/finance

Corporate Actions

A Guide to Securities Event Management

Michael Simmons and Elaine Dalgleish

John Wiley & Sons, Ltd

Telephone (+44) 1243 779777

Email (for orders and customer service enquiries): cs-books@wiley.co.uk
Visit our Home Page on www.wiley.com

Other Wiley Editorial Offices

John Wiley & Sons Inc., 111 River Street, Hoboken, NJ 07030, USA

Jossey-Bass, 989 Market Street, San Francisco, CA 94103-1741, USA

Wiley-VCH Verlag GmbH, Boschstr. 12, D-69469 Weinheim, Germany

John Wiley & Sons Australia Ltd, 42 McDougall Street, Milton, Queensland 4064, Australia

John Wiley & Sons (Asia) Pte Ltd, 2 Clementi Loop #02-01, Jin Xing Distripark, Singapore 129809

John Wiley & Sons Canada Ltd, 22 Worcester Road, Etobicoke, Ontario, Canada M9W 1L1

Wiley also publishes its books in a variety of electronic formats. Some content that appears in print may not be available in electronic books.

Library of Congress Cataloging-in-Publication Data

Simmons, Michael, 1951–
Corporate actions : a guide to securities event management / Michael Simmons & Elaine Dalgleish.
p. cm.
ISBN 13 978-0-470-87066-2
ISBN 10 0-470-87066-4
1. Securities industry. 2. Corporations—Finance—Management. I. Dalgleish, Elaine. II. Title.
HG4521.S573 2006
658.15′224—dc22

2005027085

British Library Cataloguing in Publication Data

A catalogue record for this book is available from the British Library

ISBN 13 978-0-470-87066-2 (HB)
ISBN 10 0-470-87066-4 (HB)

Typeset in 10/12pt Times by TechBooks, New Delhi, India
Printed and bound in Great Britain by Antony Rowe Ltd, Chippenham, Wiltshire
This book is printed on acid-free paper responsibly manufactured from sustainable forestry in which at least two trees are planted for each one used for paper production.

Contents

Introduction

Historically, within the securities industry the topic of corporate actions has been regarded as a specialist subject, yet one involving relatively few specialist people. In addition, Corporate Actions Departments have traditionally been manually intensive, with a low-level of *Straight Through Processing* (STP). However, organizations within the industry have increasingly recognized the risks (and indeed some organizations have suffered losses directly) and as a result a much greater level of attention is now being given to this topic. This includes the automation of many aspects of corporate actions processing.

Such an important and diverse topic requires a very good level of understanding, if those who hold securities positions are to ensure they receive the assets due to them, whilst controlling the numerous risks that inevitably exist in the processing of corporate actions.

This book aims to demystify the topic of corporate actions and to make the subject more easily understood by a broad audience.

The authors' intention is to explain the topic from first principles, and to take the readers to a point where they have a very good (but not expert) understanding of the subject. Readers will gain an understanding of the topic from a practical operational use perspective, enabling the application of such principles to specific market and workplace situations; in addition, the book is intended to be used as a reference of corporate action terms.

It is important to note that prior to reading the book, readers will need to possess a good fundamental understanding of securities settlement practices and associated operational procedures. It is intended that this book will build upon the basic settlement and operational principles described within *Securities Operations: a Guide to Trade and Position Management* (ISBN 0-471-49758-4), published in spring 2002 by Michael Simmons, one of the authors of this book.

This book is aimed at the following audiences:

- those who are new to the securities industry and who wish to gain a thorough understanding of a major aspect of securities operations (such readers are recommended first to read *Securities Operations: a Guide to Trade and Position Management* in order to gain a sufficient background understanding of the topic of corporate actions);
- those who work within securities industry firms (including investment banks, broker/dealers, institutional investors, retail and agency brokers, etc.) who have had no direct involvement with the subject of corporate actions, and who wish to (or are required to) broaden their

knowledge. This category includes traders, salespeople, risk controllers, auditors, compliance officers, static data personnel, settlement staff, reconciliations staff, accountants, etc.;
- those who work within a corporate actions department and wish to broaden their knowledge.

Additionally, the target audience also includes those who provide services to the securities industry, such as:

- software vendors
  - facilitating meaningful discussion with clients, increased understanding of business requirements by software designers and engineers when developing software and appropriate testing of software
- corporate action data providers (vendors)
  - allowing a greater appreciation of managing corporate action events, after the event data have been supplied to their clients
- management consultants
  - enabling peer-level discussion with clients and a greater understanding of clients' aims in this business area, particularly in light of the increased focus on financial reporting via the Sarbanes Oxley act
- custodians
  - providing assistance in understanding the processes their clients undergo in the successful management of corporate action events.

In order to provide a viewpoint enabling the reader to appreciate more easily the connectivity between the various sub-topics, the book is written primarily from the perspective of a Securities Trading Organization (STO).

We define an STO as operating in the following manner:

- It buys and sells securities for its own account.
- It typically maintains proprietary trading positions (whether positive or negative).
- It borrows and lends securities.
- It borrows funds to cover its positive trading positions.
- It undertakes repo transactions to minimize the cost of borrowing cash.

Furthermore, an STO may provide safe custody services to its clients, requiring the STO to hold securities (and possibly cash) in safekeeping on behalf of the client. The STO will need to ensure that it protects the interests of its clients (as well as itself), in relation to the management of corporate actions.

The majority of the concepts contained within the book, and the perspective from which the book is written, are applicable to any individual or organization (such as investment banks and fund managers) that owns securities or manages securities on behalf of others.

The book contains the following attributes and features:

- Structured development of reader understanding through logical and sequential explanation.
- Chapter topics restricted to easily digestible portions of information.
- Focus on corporate action event lifecycles and their components, in order to build a practical operational understanding of the management and impact of corporate actions.
- Explanation of industry terminology.
- Description of generic market practices and common conventions.
- Illustration of subject matter by use of diagrams, examples and analogies.

- Depiction of the full event lifecycle by use of detailed and sequential worked examples.
- Identification of the operational points of risk, control, STP and automation.

Rather than cover the practices within specific locations around the globe, we have attempted to convey concepts that will be applicable to the majority of locations. The intention is for the reader to apply these concepts in any location, as each of the major points covered within the book are typically practised within each market, but there is every possibility that each market has its own nuances in dealing with a particular point.

In compiling the information contained within this book, the authors have listed those types of events that they consider to be fundamental and the most common of corporate actions; not every conceivable event has been stated, nor will every possible variation of those events that are included, be covered. Nonetheless, we believe that readers will find that the method of explaining concepts will allow such concepts to be applied to variations of, and new types of, corporate action.

We have in general attempted to develop the reader's knowledge gradually by describing the various components of a topic conceptually, providing examples and making forward reference to later topics, and backward reference to earlier topics. Our objective has been to enable the reader to gain a complete overview of corporate actions, subsequently enabling communication with other people on any and all of the topics covered.

Due to the cumulative effect within the book, the chapters (particularly in the second half of the book) make numerous references to points covered within previous chapters; consequently it is recommended that the book is read sequentially, chapter-by-chapter (although as far as possible we have designed chapters to be read on a standalone basis).

Words and terms explained within the Glossary of Terms are highlighted in *italics* within the main text.

We have written this book entirely independently and not for and on behalf of any organization, for whom we have been an employee or for whom we have worked in a consulting capacity.

Although every effort has been made to remove errors from the text, any that remain belong to the authors! If the reader has observations on the style and content of the book, we would appreciate being informed of such comments, via the following website: www.info@mike-simmons.com.

Elaine Dalgleish and Michael Simmons

Disclaimer

The authors of Corporate Actions occasionally refer to well known organisations within the financial community in order to illustrate the context of typical trading and corporate actions scenarios. The scenarios created and the relationships and transections referred to are for illustrative purpose only and have no factual basis.

The authors accept no responsibility for any loss that purports to be incurred as a result of the content of this book.

Acknowledgements

We would like to express our gratitude for the contributions of the following:

Jon Foord
Harvey Colborne
Mark Rigby
Colin Baker
Sue Woods.

We would also like to thank Viv Wickham and Sam Hartley at the publisher John Wiley & Sons, for their help in the production of the book.

In particular, we would like to say a special thank you to Ailean Maclean and Graham McCormack, who have dedicated their time to the review of the entire book, ensuring both accuracy and continuity throughout. Without their input and efforts it would not have been possible to complete this book.

Finally we would like to say thank you to Allyson Simmons and Paul Andrews for their patience, support and objective comment during the writing of this book.

About the Authors

Michael Simmons has spent the majority of his working life within the operational areas of international investment banks, most notably within the S.G. Warburg group in London. Having gained a detailed understanding of various back office tasks through many years of hands-on experience, he assumed managerial responsibility for a number of operational areas.

In recent years, Michael has worked as head of business consultancy within a global computing services firm, and is now an independent analyst and trainer. Michael's areas of expertise include all aspects of the trade lifecycle and related activities including operational risks and control. Recent assignments include the offshoring of operational activities to India and operational risk analysis (the Sarbanes Oxley act). In addition, he creates and delivers training courses on the workings of the securities industry and associated operational aspects to audiences around the world.

Michael is author of *Securities Operations: A Guide to Trade and Position Management* published by John Wiley & Sons, which describes the fundamental components of operational activities from a first-principles perspective.

Elaine Dalgleish has spent her working life within the operational areas of investment banking and stock broking, working directly for international banking firms and financial software providers. Elaine's hands-on experience spans various middle and back office operational disciplines in multiple markets. Whilst working directly in investment banking and stock broking, this has ultimately included the managerial responsibility for a number of operational areas.

The focal point of Elaine's working history is the consistent involvement with Corporate Actions operations, initially with the manual processing of events as a custodian, and subsequently working as a Senior Business Analyst, specializing in Corporate Actions, analysing client requirements, and consulting in process re-engineering for Tier 1 and Tier 2 investment banks.

As a consequence, Elaine has both observed and been directly involved in the evolution of global market practices of Corporate Actions operations and the move to automation.

Observations on the style and content of this book can be conveyed to the authors by e-mail: info@mike-simmons.com

Part I
Introductory Elements

1

Basic Corporate Action Concepts

1.1 INTRODUCTION

For any holder of *securities*, whether an organization or individual, remaining in control of securities and cash positions is fundamental to the efficient management of its investment portfolio. This is not simply a matter of recording *trading* and *settlement* activity, but also the accurate processing and recording of the impact of *corporate action events* on those securities and cash positions.

This chapter serves to introduce the fundamental concepts and terminology associated with the processing and management of corporate actions.

1.2 DEFINITION OF CORPORATE ACTIONS

A corporate action is an event in the life of a security (typically) instigated by the *issuer*, which affects a position in that security.

If and when the issuer of an existing security distributes benefits to *shareholders* or *bondholders* (referred to throughout this book as *position holders*), or chooses to change the security's structure, such events are commonly known as corporate actions.

Many types of corporate action events exist, often with subtle variations, but it is possible to define and group these events based upon a combination of:

- the issuer's purpose;
- the impact of the event from the position holder's and market place's perspectives; and
- the lifecycle of the event.

The term 'lifecycle' is used in the context of this book to refer to the series of logical steps in the processing of a corporate action. Such lifecycles are determined by the nature of the corporate action. Note that detailed descriptions of numerous corporate action types are contained within Chapter 2, 'Event Description and Classification'.

1.3 PURPOSE OF CORPORATE ACTIONS

The purpose of a corporate action is (typically) driven by the aims of the issuer, and will vary according to the specific type of corporate action. Purposes include:

- **Distribution of Income**
  This relates to the distribution of profits on equities and the payment of interest on bonds, by the issuer. Profits (or earnings) are distributed to shareholders in the form of *dividend* payments, whilst interest is distributed to bondholders via *interest* payments (commonly known as *coupon* payments). Note that the payment of a dividend is dependent upon a

decision by the issuer's board of directors (dividend payments are not guaranteed), whereas coupon payments are made at pre-stated intervals and (for fixed-rate bonds) at the specified coupon rate in accordance with the terms of issue of the bond.

- **Raising of Capital**
  When the issuer wishes to raise further *capital* it may do so either by the issue of new equity via shares, or alternatively via the issue of *bonds* (also known as debt). The market place as a whole may be permitted to purchase either the new shares or debt, or the issue may be restricted to existing position holders only. In those instances where the issue of new equity at a price is offered to existing position holders only, then the event is considered to be a corporate action.
- **Restructuring of Issued Capital**
  From time to time the issuer may choose to restructure or re-organize the *issued capital* of the company. The issued capital is the total value of issued shares in the company; the total value is calculated by multiplying the *par value* of each share, by the quantity of shares issued.

  From time to time the issuer may choose to change the quantity of shares issued and/or the par value of those shares, for example by way of *share splits* or *buy-backs*.

  Many reasons exist for restructuring, including:
  - the reduction or increase of the total value of issued capital;
  - the reduction or increase of the current market price of the shares.
- **Redemption of Debt**
  In accordance with the terms of individual debt issues (in the form of bonds), the issuer will redeem the bonds at the *maturity date* (or prior to the maturity date if the issue terms permit).

  Upon issuance of bonds, the debt will appear as a liability in the *balance sheet* of the issuer; at redemption the liability will be reduced accordingly.
- **Restructuring of Debt Liabilities Against Issued Capital**
  From time to time an issuer may choose to restructure its balance sheet, by the conversion of debt liabilities to issued capital (where the bond issue terms permit). Such conversions will simultaneously reduce the debt liabilities of the issuer, whilst increasing the capital in issue.
- **Assuming Control of Another Organization**
  One organization, in this case not the issuer, may wish to gain control of (i.e. takeover) another organization, in order to, for example:
  - control competition in the same market;
  - control either supplier or distribution networks in the same market;
  - extend or diversify product range or market.
- **Dissemination of Information to Shareholders**
  The board of directors of an issuer is obliged to inform shareholders of various activities that affect the operation and profitability of the company, and in some cases will also need to seek the shareholders' approval of such activity before it is undertaken. Such information includes notification of company year-end results, capital investment programmes, notification of an *A.G.M*.

Figure 1.1 illustrates the various aims of the issuer (as described above), whilst also showing that in each case the corporate action event information is intended to be communicated to the position holder (the owner of the underlying security).

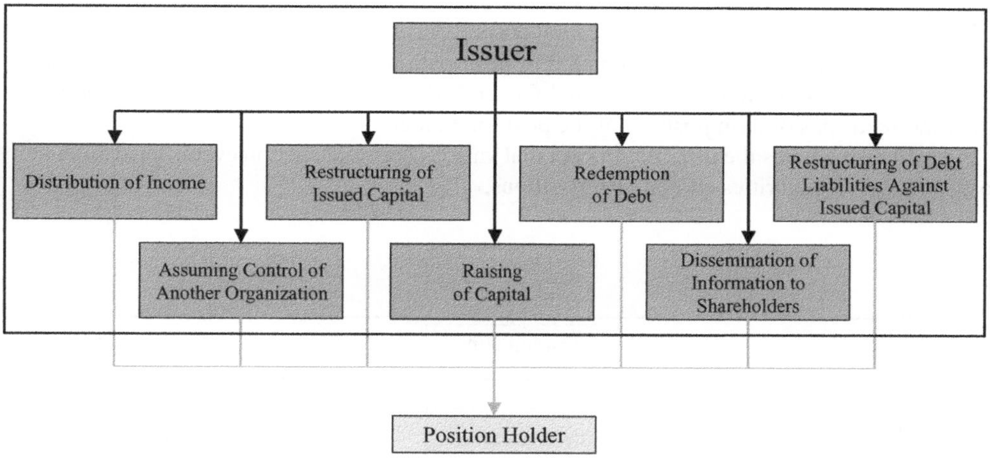

Figure 1.1 Purpose of corporate actions.

1.4 IMPACT OF CORPORATE ACTIONS

A corporate action event may be categorized in terms of its impact to the position holder, and in addition may be more broadly reflected in the market place by the change in price of the underlying security.

1.4.1 Impact from the Position Holder's Perspective

As a *position holder* the impact of a corporate action is measured in terms of its impact to securities and/or cash positions; consequently corporate action events can be categorized as follows.

Benefits

These are events that result in an increase to the position holder's securities or cash position, without altering the underlying security; for example, a bonus issue.

Re-organizations

These are events that re-shape or re-structure the position holder's underlying securities position, possibly also combining a cash element. For example:

- An *equity restructure* which results in, for example, the exchange of a security of one par value with a security of a different par value.
- A *conversion* where one type of security such as a convertible bond is exchanged for a different type of security, such as an ordinary share.
- A *subscription* where one type of security such as a Nil Paid Right is exchanged for a different type of security such as an ordinary share, upon the payment of a cash amount.

Issuer Notices

These events are used for the dissemination of information from the issuer to position holders (for example the notification of an Annual General Meeting), which results in no change to either the securities or cash position of the position holder.

Figure 1.2 illustrates the different impact that various corporate action events have upon the position holder's securities and/or cash positions.

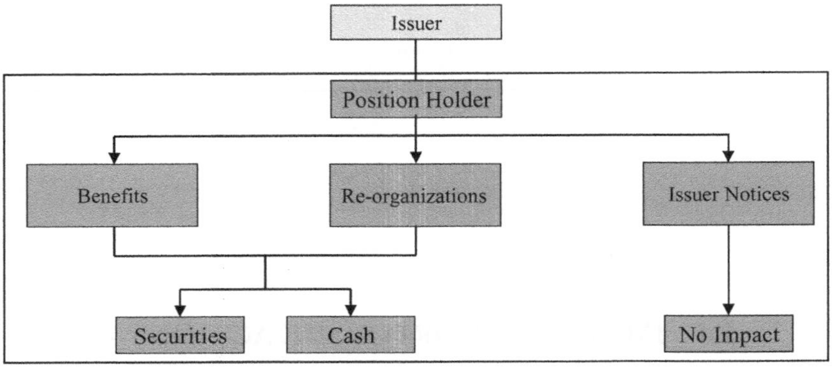

Figure 1.2 Impact from the position holder's perspective.

1.4.2 Impact on the Price of the Underlying Security

As well as directly impacting the *balance sheet* of the issuer and the securities and/or cash positions of position holders, a corporate action may also have an impact on the *market price* of the security to which it applies (known as the *underlying security*).

The demand for a security reflects many things; for example the supply, the perceptions of the market place as to the profitability of the issuer, the perceptions of the issuer's solvency and the state of its *capital reserves* and debts. Therefore, when an event occurs to alter any of these, the perception of the market place and the change in the demand for the security will be reflected in its price.

Therefore the event can also be considered to impact potential buyers and sellers of the underlying security, as the price a buyer may pay and a seller may receive may change.

1.5 THE LIFECYCLE OF A CORPORATE ACTION

Across the range of specific types of corporate actions a number of different lifecycles can apply from their initial announcement until the actual receipt and distribution of securities and/or cash *resultant entitlement* (where applicable). As previously indicated the term 'lifecycle' is used in the context of this book to refer to the series of logical steps, predominantly determined by the nature of the corporate action.

These different lifecycles can be categorized as follows:

- Mandatory
- Mandatory with Options

- Voluntary
- Multi-stage
- Issuer Notices

Each of these is described below.

1.5.1 Mandatory (Generic) Lifecycle

For those events that are defined as mandatory, the position holder has no choice as to whether and/or how it participates in the event. The event will be applied to all position holders, and the securities and/or cash positions of each position holder will be impacted in the same fashion. The logical steps of the mandatory lifecycle are common to all event lifecycles (with the exception of the Issuer Notices lifecycle), and therefore in the context of this book they form the generic lifecycle. Mandatory events are detailed in Chapters 6–15.

1.5.2 Mandatory with Options Lifecycle

By contrast to standard mandatory events, these events will offer the position holder a choice as to how it participates in the event. The position holder will be given two or more alternatives as to the combination of securities and/or cash that it will receive as a result of the corporate action. The lifecycle of this event will incorporate the steps of the mandatory (generic) lifecycle, and will in addition incorporate steps to manage the position holder's choice as to the securities and/or cash it wishes to receive. Mandatory with Options events are detailed within Chapters 16 and 17.

1.5.3 Voluntary Lifecycle

For voluntary events, participation in the event is purely based upon the choice of the position holder. This is in contrast to the two lifecycles introduced above, where participation is mandatory. The position holder will be given the option to 'take no action' (or not to participate), and in addition may also be given a choice as to the combinations of securities and/or cash it receives should it choose to participate. The lifecycle of voluntary events is very similar to that of the mandatory with options lifecycle, supporting the management of the position holder's choice. Voluntary events are detailed within Chapters 16 and 18.

1.5.4 Multi-Stage Lifecycle

These are complex events that combine two or more stages (lifecycles) in their overall life. From the issuer's perspective each of these events is a single action, nonetheless from the position holder's perspective the event can be viewed as containing many interdependent lifecycles. Furthermore, each lifecycle can be categorized as being mandatory, mandatory with options or voluntary. Multi-stage events are detailed within Chapters 19–21.

1.5.5 Issuer Notices Lifecycle

These events are used for communication purposes only to position holders, and do not involve any securities and/or cash entitlements. Therefore these events have a significantly shorter operational lifecycle than those previously mentioned, as there is no impact to the position holders securities and/or cash positions as a result of the event. Issuer Notices events are detailed within Chapter 26.

Figure 1.3 illustrates the different lifecycles described above.

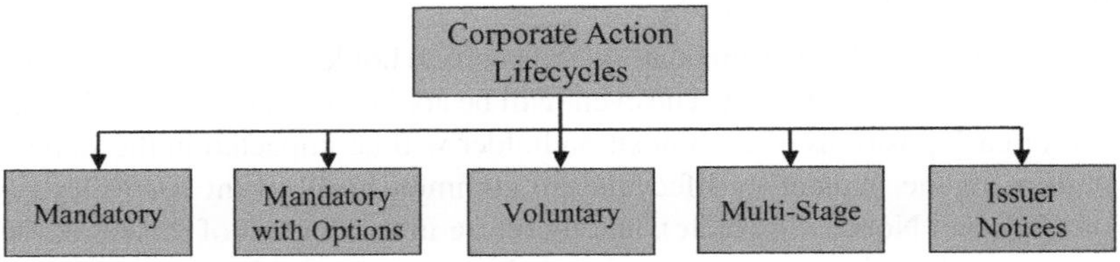

Figure 1.3 Corporate action lifecycles.

1.6 SUMMARY

It is important to appreciate that issuers of securities and their advisers will continue to find inventive ways of raising further capital, offering income options to their shareholders and re-organizing their capital structure.

Understanding the basic principles of a corporate action, i.e. the issuer's aim, the impact on securities and/or cash positions, and the lifecycles, provides a fundamental structure that can be applied to the current and future corporate actions environment. In this way practitioners are well equipped to deal with this ever-evolving area of the securities industry.

2
Event Description and Classification

2.1 INTRODUCTION

This chapter provides an informal description of the common corporate action event types. The descriptions utilize the concepts introduced in the previous chapter, and additionally events are classified based on the following:

- the *issuer's* purpose;
- the impact on the *position holder*;
- the lifecycle of the event.

It is important to note that this is not intended to be an exhaustive list of events, but rather is intended to provide an introduction to the most common types, which will be referred to throughout later chapters.

In the previous chapter the following concept of grouping events from the position holder's perspective was introduced:

- *Benefits*
- *Re-organizations*
- *Issuer Notices*

This chapter introduces a further breakdown of grouping so as to provide a more specific indication as to the issuer's primary intent in announcing the event. For example, when focusing on re-organization events, they can be further broken down into the following sub-groups:

- Equity (Issued Capital) Restructure
- Debt Restructure against Equity (Issued Capital)
- Debt Redemption
- Raising of Capital
- Re-organization of Company Structure

Despite this more specific grouping it is important to remain flexible when considering such events. Whilst for some events the sub-grouping is straightforward and rather obvious, in other cases it is far more arbitrary. In the main, this is because by means of a single type of event, the issuer may be able to achieve a number of objectives simultaneously. For example, whilst typically a Rights Issue would be considered primarily as the raising of capital, it also results in the restructuring of the issued equity of a company.

Therefore the sub-groups (described in the following section) have been created to reflect the authors' view of the issuer's primary intent.

2.2 EVENT DESCRIPTIONS

The events described within this chapter are placed within the following sub-groups:

- Payment of *Interest* Due
- Payment of *Income* Earned

- Distribution of *Capital* Reserves
- Equity Restructure
- Debt Restructure against Equity (*Issued Capital*)
- Debt *Redemption*
- Raising of Capital
- Re-organization of Company Structure
- Issuer Notices

Note that all event titles are expressed from an international perspective, unless indicated otherwise. Variations in event titles and their treatment are described further in Section 2.5 of this chapter.

2.2.1 Payment of Interest Due

Coupon Payment

This is the payment of interest in cash against the *face value* (i.e. the quantity, also known as nominal value) of a bond (whether it be *fixed-rate bonds* or *floating rate notes*), to the holder.

The cash amount payable is based on the face value of the bond, the interest rate, and the period (e.g. annual or semi-annual (twice yearly)) to which the interest payment relates. Note that each *coupon payment* is regarded as an individual corporate action event.

For example, a position holder may hold USD 1,000,000 face value of XOX AG, 8.25% bonds, maturing 1st June 2020. When the issuer makes a coupon payment (in this example annually) on 1st June each year, the position holder will be entitled to receive USD 82,500.00 cash (prior to tax).

Two variations of the coupon payment event exist:

- Coupon Payment – a mandatory event where the payment of interest occurs in a single designated currency.
- Coupon Payment with Currency Option – a mandatory with options event where payment of interest may occur in any of a number of currencies (as offered by the issuer), with the position holder having to *elect* at least one currency.

In addition, the payment of coupon to *position holders* may include a capital portion representing the redemption or repayment of part of the capital value of the debt. This may be known as a coupon payment with capital or *amortized coupon*.

2.2.2 Payment of Income Earned

Dividend Payment

This is the distribution of the company's earnings for a defined *earnings period*, to *equity* position holders.

Dividend payments are entirely tied to company earnings and therefore have no guaranteed payment. When paid, payments are often made at regular intervals (e.g. quarterly or semi-annually), according to the convention in the specific market place. The distribution of income may occur in a number of forms, e.g. cash, securities or scrip. In addition, the position holder may be offered options as to the form in which the payment is received (i.e. a choice of currency, or the ability to elect to receive the income as securities, rather than cash).

For example, a position holder may hold 100,000 GBP1.00 ordinary shares, which represents a capital value of equity in the issuer of GBP 100,000.00. When the issuer announces a dividend at a rate of GBP0.15 per share, the position holder will be entitled to receive GBP 15,000.00 cash (prior to tax).

A number of varieties of dividend events exist:

- Cash Dividend – a mandatory event where the distribution occurs in a single designated currency.
- Stock Dividend – a mandatory event where the distribution occurs in securities.
- Scrip Dividend – a mandatory event where the distribution occurs in the form of scrip (temporary certificates). The scrip represents the issuer's promise to pay a cash dividend, at a time when earnings may be considered sufficient to distribute, but for the present time cash reserves are being conserved.
- Optional Dividend – a mandatory with options event where the distribution may occur in either the form of cash or securities, with the position holder having to elect at least one of these forms.
- Dividend Re-investment Plan (DRP or DRiP) – a mandatory with options event where the distribution may occur in either cash or securities (based upon the re-investment of the cash value in the purchase of further shares from the issuer at a published price), with the position holder having to elect at least one of these forms.

2.2.3 Distribution of Capital Reserves

Liquidation Distribution

This is the distribution of cash and assets to position holders as a result of the *liquidation* of the company.

The liquidators may make multiple distributions as assets are sold off over a period of time. Once the final distribution is made the position holder's security will cease to exist.

The event may be mandatory or mandatory with options (where on occasions the *position holder* may be offered a choice as to the form the distribution takes).

Bonus Issue (or Capitalization Issue, and in the US a Share Split (without change of par value))

This is the distribution of additional assets free of cost to position holders, in proportion to their existing holding.

The issue will result in an increase to the position holder's *underlying holding* where the issue is in the same security as that of the underlying holding, or alternatively may result in a holding of an additional security.

For example, a position holder may hold 100,000 GBP1.00 ordinary fully paid shares in company ABC. The issuer may distribute two new shares in ABC for every five already held. Therefore the position holder will receive a further 40,000 GBP1.00 ordinary shares, increasing its overall position to 140,000 GBP1.00 ordinary shares. Alternatively the *issuer* may distribute two *preference shares* in company ABC for every five ordinary shares held in ABC. In this case the position holder will receive 40,000 preference shares in ABC resulting in a new holding, while still retaining its original holding of 100,000 ordinary shares.

A Bonus Issue is a mandatory event.

2.2.4 Equity Restructure

Change in Security Ranking (or Assimilation)

Securities issued by way of other events, such as *bonus issues* and *rights issues*, may often be issued with different characteristics from existing issued securities, the most common of which may be their entitlement to future dividend payments.

This event occurs at the point in time when two such securities with different characteristics become identical in all respects, e.g. rank *pari-passu* for future dividends. The result to the *position holder* will be the exchange of its 'non-ranking' securities for ordinary securities.

For example, a position holder may have a position of 100,000 AUD1.00 ordinary shares and 50,000 AUD1.00 new ordinary shares received six months earlier as a result of a bonus issue (but which, at the time of issue, did not entitle the holder to the next dividend). When the *issuer* announces the Change in Security Ranking, the 50,000 new ordinary shares will merge with the ordinary shares, resulting in a combined holding of 150,000 AUD1.00 ordinary shares (all of which will *rank* for the next dividend).

A Change in Security Ranking is a mandatory event, and can often form part of a multi-stage event.

Share Split (or Sub-Division, and in the US a Share Split (with change in par value))

A share split is an increase in an issuer's number of issued shares proportional to a reduction in the capital (par) value of each existing share.

The result is no change in the *capital value* (i.e. the quantity of shares held multiplied by their *par value*) of the shareholder's equity, or to the total market value of the shareholder's position, at the time of the split; nonetheless the *market price* per share will normally reduce proportionally to the change in par value.

For example, a position holder may have a position of 100,000 AUD1.00 ordinary shares, which represents a capital value of equity in the issuer of AUD 100,000.00. The issuer announces a two for one share split with each AUD1.00 ordinary share being replaced by two AUD0.50 ordinary shares. As a result of the share split, the holder's holding will be 200,000 AUD0.50 ordinary shares. The quantity of shares held has increased to 200,000, whilst the capital value of equity remains unchanged as AUD 100,000.00.

A Share Split is a mandatory event.

Consolidation (or Reverse Split)

A consolidation is a decrease in an issuer's number of issued shares proportional to an increase in the capital (par) value of each existing share.

The result is no change in the capital value of the shareholder's equity or the total market value of the shareholder's position at the time of the consolidation, nonetheless the market price per share will normally increase proportionally to the change in par value.

For example, a position holder may have a position of 100,000 AUD1.00 ordinary shares, which represents a capital value of equity in the issuer of AUD 100,000.00. The issuer announces a one for two consolidation with every two AUD1.00 ordinary shares being replaced by one AUD2.00 ordinary share. As a result of the consolidation, the holder's holding will be 50,000 AUD2.00 ordinary shares. The quantity of shares held has decreased to 50,000, whilst the capital value of equity remains unchanged as AUD 100,000.00.

A Consolidation is a mandatory event.

Scheme of Arrangement

A Scheme of Arrangement is a broad term to describe an event where the issuer issues, to position holders, combinations of securities and/or cash in exchange for the existing underlying security.

The purpose, similar to that of a Share Split or Consolidation, is a restructure of the issuer's issued capital.

In the following example the issuer's aim is to increase the number of shares in issue at the same time as reducing the par value of each share. A *position holder* may have a position of 100,000 GBP1.00 ordinary shares in company ABC, which represents a capital value of equity in the *issuer* of GBP 100,000.00. The issuer announces:

- a reduction in the par value of the securities of GBP0.25, making the new par value GBP0.75;
- a distribution of one GBP0.75 share for every three original GBP1.00 shares held (*fractions* distributed as cash at GBP0.75 per share).

This will result in a total of 133,333 (based upon the original 100,000 shares, together with a distribution of 33.333 additional shares) GBP0.75 ordinary shares, representing capital value of equity in the issuer of GBP 99,999.75, together with the distribution of GBP0.25 cash (representing 1/3rd of a share).

Typically the event will be mandatory, but may be mandatory with options where the issuer offers position holders a choice as to the form of distribution to be received, e.g. a choice of securities or cash.

Capital Repayment (or Decrease in Value or Return of Capital)

This is a reduction in the capital (par) value of an equity, thereby reducing the position holder's ownership in the company.

The capital reduction is paid by the issuer to the position holder, and the original security is exchanged for securities appropriate to the new capital value, on a one for one basis. The quantity of the position holder's position does not change, whilst the capital value of the position holder's equity does change.

For example, a position holder may hold 100,000 EUR1.00 ordinary fully paid shares, which represents a capital value of EUR 100,000.00. A capital repayment by the issuer of EUR0.20 per share will reduce the capital value of each share to EUR0.80. The position holder will now hold 100,000 EUR0.80 fully paid ordinary shares. The total number of shares held has not changed, but the capital value of the equity is now EUR 80,000.00 and the position holder will receive EUR 20,000.00 in cash.

A Capital Repayment is a mandatory event.

Buy-Back (or Repurchase Offer or Issuer Tender Offer)

This is the repurchase of issued capital (equity) by the issuer at a published price.

The terms of the Buy-Back may relate to the entire issued capital or to a portion only. In addition, the 'price' paid per share may be the face value (par) or at a discount or premium to the face value (this being based upon prevailing market conditions at the time of the offer). The event results in the exchange of the Buy-Back quantity for cash, and therefore results in the removal (in the case of the entire issued capital) or reduction (in the case of a portion only) of the holding. In this way the Buy-Back differs from the Capital Repayment, as there is no change in the face value of each unit.

For example, a *position holder* may hold 100,000 EUR1.00 ordinary fully paid shares. The *issuer* offers to buy 20% of issued capital at a price of EUR0.70, which represents a discount of EUR0.30 to the face value of the equity. Therefore, if the position holder wishes to accept this offer against its entire holding it will receive EUR 14,000.00 in cash, in exchange for 20,000 shares, with its holding reducing to 80,000 shares.

A Buy-Back is voluntary event, as the position holder is under no obligation to sell any or all of its holding to the issuer.

Odd Lot Offer

This is the opportunity for position holders with *odd lot* holdings, to 'round' their holdings into tradable *lots*.

A 'lot' represents the normal tradable parcel of a security. The rounding of holdings is achieved by the issuer offering to sell additional securities to the position holder (i.e. the position holder will buy), at a published price, in order to 'top up' its holding. In some cases the issuer may also offer to buy (i.e. the *position holder* will sell) those holdings that are less than a lot.

For example, a 'lot' for company ABC may be 100 shares, and the issuer announces that it will buy at a price of GBP 7.50 per share any holdings under 100 shares. Therefore, if a position holder has 63 shares and accepts the offer, it will receive GBP 472.50 in exchange for its holding.

An Odd Lot Offer is a voluntary event, as the position holder may decide to take no action at all.

Warrant Exercise

Warrant Exercise is the opportunity for *position holders* to exchange ('exercise') their holding in warrants to another form of security (usually ordinary shares or common stock), at a fixed price, at or before a pre-specified date.

The initiator of the exercise is the position holder, rather than the *issuer*. The schedule and terms of exercise are set out upon issue of the warrant security; should warrants not be exercised by the final exercise date, the warrant security will *expire*.

For example, a position holder may hold 100,000 warrants. The terms of exercise allow the position holder to exercise 1000 warrants for 100 ordinary shares, at a cost of HKD 815.00. Therefore, in the event that the position holder chooses to exercise its holding, it would receive 10,000 ordinary shares, at a total cost of HKD 81,500.00.

An exercise is a voluntary event, as the position holder may decide to take no action at all.

2.2.5 Debt Restructure against Equity (Issued Capital)

Bond and Note Conversion

This is an opportunity for *position holders* to convert or to exchange their holding to another form of security (usually ordinary shares or common stock).

Typically, these are debt securities in the form of bonds or notes, but could also be convertible preference shares. The initiator of the conversion is the position holder, rather than the *issuer*.

From the issuer's perspective, such a conversion results in a change in its *balance sheet* from issued debt to *issued capital*. The conversion may additionally require the payment of a pre-stated price to the issuer. The schedule and terms of conversion are set out upon issue of the convertible security.

For example, a position holder may hold USD 10,000,000 face value of *convertible bonds*, represented by 10,000 bonds with a denomination of USD 1,000 each. The terms of the conversion allow the position holder to convert each USD 1,000 bond for 20 ordinary shares. Therefore, in the event that the position holder chooses to convert its holding, it would receive 200,000 ordinary shares.

A conversion is a voluntary event, as the position holder may decide to take no action at all.

2.2.6 Debt Redemption

Bond Redemption

This is the repayment of the capital value by the *issuer* to the *bondholder* on or before the *maturity date* of the bond.

The terms of repayment, i.e. capital value and final redemption date (also known as the maturity date), are known at the time of issue of the bond. Typically, the redemption of the bond is mandatory under the terms of its issue, nonetheless the issuer may decide to redeem the bond early in full or in part, in which case this will be a mandatory event. Some issues allow the holder to initiate redemption, in which case this will be a voluntary event. In all cases the position holder will exchange its holding for receipt of cash.

For example, a position holder may hold USD 1,000,000.00 face value of XOX AG, 8.25% bonds, maturing 1st June 2020. At final maturity of the bond on 1st June 2020, the issuer will pay 100% (in this example) of the bond's *face value*; the position holder will be entitled to receive USD 1,000,000.00 cash.

A number of varieties of bond redemption events therefore exist:

- Bond Redemption (or Final Maturity); the repayment of the debt in full at the maturity date as stated at the time of issue. This is a mandatory event.
- Partial Redemption (or Partial Call); the repayment of part of the debt value across all position holders prior to the published maturity date. This is a mandatory event.
- Early Redemption (or Full Call); the repayment of the full debt value prior to the published maturity date. This is a mandatory event.
- Voluntary Redemption (or Put Call); the repayment of debt at the request of the position holder prior to the published maturity date. This is a voluntary event.
- Drawing (or Lottery); the repayment of selected holdings of debt by the issuer prior to the published maturity date. This is a mandatory event, but differs from a partial redemption in that only the selected holdings are affected.

2.2.7 Raising of Capital

Rights Issue

This is the offer of new shares to existing *shareholders* in proportion to their existing holdings, at a specified price.

A rights issue is one mechanism by which an issuer can raise further *capital*. The right itself is typically issued as a security known as a *Nil Paid Right* but does not in itself represent any *equity* in the *issuer* and has a very short life span (typically expiring as little as two or three weeks after its initial issue). The distribution of the right to existing position holders is a mandatory event.

The nil paid right is *renounceable* (or saleable), meaning that the position holder may sell its nil paid rights in the market, or potentially purchase more.

Prior to expiry any holder of nil paid rights may convert them to the specified security, as detailed in the rights issue prospectus, upon payment of the specified price by the specified deadline. This is known as *exercise* or *subscription.* It is the position holder's choice as to whether it subscribes and pays the cost of subscription or not, and therefore this stage is a voluntary event.

Failure to subscribe the nil paid rights prior to the end of their life will result in their *expiry*, and this stage is therefore treated as a mandatory event.

For example, a *position holder* may hold 100,000 GBP1.00 ordinary fully paid shares in company ABC. The issuer may offer one new share in ABC for every five already held, at a price of GBP 6.75 per share. Therefore the position holder will receive the offer of a further 20,000 GBP1.00 ordinary shares, at a cost of GBP 135,000.00. The position holder may elect to subscribe to none, some or all the shares it is being offered. Should the position holder choose to subscribe to all the shares offered, its holding will increase by 20,000 GBP1.00 ordinary shares upon payment to the issuer (by the specified deadline) of GBP 135,000.00, thereby increasing its overall position to 120,000 GBP1.00 ordinary shares.

The overall life of the event comprises a number of stages, both mandatory and voluntary, and is therefore regarded as having a Multi-Stage Lifecycle. Note that this topic is explored in-depth in Chapter 21, 'Example of a Rights Issue'.

Entitlement Issue

This is the offer of new shares to existing *shareholders* in proportion to their existing holdings, at a specified price.

As with a rights issue this is a *capital* raising exercise. In all respects this event is the same as a rights issue, except that the right to subscribe is *non-renounceable* (i.e. non-saleable or transferable).

The overall life of the event comprises a number of stages, both mandatory and voluntary, and is therefore regarded as having a Multi-Stage Lifecycle.

Priority Issue

This is the offer of a new form of security or of a holding in a new company, to both the public and to existing position holders in proportion to their existing holdings (occasionally including a maximum quantity for which position holders may apply), at a specified price.

Existing position holders in the underlying company are given priority to apply over members of the public. The right to purchase is non-tradable.

A Priority Issue is a voluntary event, as the position holder may decide to take no action at all.

Equity Call (or Instalment Call)

This is the increase in capital (par) value of a *partly paid* equity by the payment of further *capital* by the *shareholders*.

The equity call applies only to those shares against which some capital has previously been paid, and therefore does not apply to *nil-paid* shares (where initial capital is paid as a subscription). For instance, a AUD1.00 ordinary share represents the ownership of AUD1.00 of capital value in the issuer, whilst a AUD1.00 ordinary share partly paid to AUD0.50 represents ownership of AUD0.50 of capital value. The issuer may *call* a further instalment of capital or the full balance from the position holder, resulting in the conversion of the partly paid share to a fully paid share.

The terms and timetable for calls is normally fixed at the time of issue of the partly paid share. This method of issuing securities and subsequently making further capital calls against them allows the issuer to spread the raising of revenue over a period of time.

For example, a position holder may hold 100,000 AUD1.00 paid to AUD0.75 ordinary shares. A call of AUD0.25 per share is due, which will make the shares up to AUD1.00 fully paid. In paying the call, the position holder will pay the issuer AUD 25,000.00 and its holding of 100,000 partly paid shares will be replaced by 100,000 AUD1.00 fully paid ordinary shares.

Equity calls are predominantly mandatory, with non-payment of the call resulting in forfeiture of the holding by the position holder. On rare occasions the call may be treated as voluntary, where it is an interim (not final) instalment. Under this circumstance the partly paid security may continue to trade without the call paid, but the final call will be mandatory, resulting in forfeiture if not paid.

2.2.8 Re-organization of Company Structure

Merger

A Merger is the exchange of securities in the merged companies, for securities in the new combined company.

A merger occurs when the assets of two companies are combined. The result is typically the exchange of securities in the merging companies, for securities in the new combined company, and may also include a distribution of cash to the *position holders*. Where multiple forms of distribution are available, the position holder may, in addition, be offered the choice as to the specific form it wishes to elect. Often the exact terms of the exchange will differ according to which *underlying security* a position is held in, as is illustrated in the following example.

For example, company ABC and company Z agree to merge and form a single company XYZ. The terms of the merger are:

- to replace shares in ABC with one share in the new company XYZ for every one share held in ABC; and
- to replace shares in Z with one share in the new company XYZ for every five shares held in Z.

A position holder may hold 100,000 GBP1.00 ordinary fully paid shares in company ABC, whilst another position holder holds 75,000 GBP1.00 ordinary fully paid shares in company Z.

The result of the merger will be that the position holder in ABC will have its holding replaced with 100,000 shares in XYZ, whilst the position holder in Z will have its holding replaced with 15,000 shares in XYZ.

The event is mandatory or may be mandatory with options (where a choice as to the form of distribution is offered).

Spin-off (or Demerger or Unbundling)

This is the distribution of securities in a subsidiary to the *shareholders* of the parent company, without the surrender of the original *underlying security.*

This event typically involves no cost to the *position holder* in the parent company. On occasions the position holder may be offered a choice as to the form of distribution to be received, e.g. a choice of securities, or cash.

For example, company ABC decides to spin-off a new company XYZ. The terms of the spin-off give the position holder a choice:

- to receive two shares in the new company XYZ for every five shares held in ABC; or
- to receive one share in the new company XYZ and GBP1.00 in cash for every five shares held in ABC.

A position holder may hold 100,000 GBP1.00 ordinary fully paid shares in company ABC. It may choose either option in the spin-off, with quite different results. If the position holder elects the first option it will receive 40,000 shares in XYZ. Alternatively, if it elects the second option it will receive 20,000 shares in XYZ together with GBP 20,000.00 in cash.

The event is mandatory or may be mandatory with options (where a choice as to the form of distribution is offered).

Takeover (or Acquisition or Tender)

This is the exchange of securities in the target company, for securities and/or cash offered by another organization.

A change in *controlling interest* is achieved via the accumulation of *issued capital* in the target company (known as 'the *offeree*') by the person(s) or organization launching the takeover (known as 'the *offeror*'). The reasons for takeovers can generally be categorized from their economical viewpoint to the offeror, as a desire to:

- control competition in the same market;
- control either supplier or distribution networks in the same market;
- extend or diversify product range or market.

A takeover could combine any or all of these desires.

Where the target of the takeover bid is a *listed company,* the accumulation of capital by the offeror will directly affect the *position holders* in the target company. Initially, there is a soft impact by way of affecting the *market price*, as the market price will increase, reflecting the increase in demand generated by the offeror. Once the offeror has accumulated a significant holding in the target company, it will be required by market regulations to state its intention, as to whether it wishes to launch a formal offer to gain control, or not. Where the intention is to make a formal offer, such an offer is made to the position holders of the target company, stating the percentage of issued capital that is to be acquired, which could be anything up to 100%, and the price per share that the offeror will pay, and the period for which the offer is open.

Position holders who accept the offer in exchange for their holding in the target company may receive either securities offered by the offeror, or cash, or a combination of both. At this time, acceptance of the offer is entirely voluntary on the part of the position holder. Nonetheless, in the event that the offeror acquires sufficient shares resulting in the target company no longer being able to remain listed, then any remaining minority of position holders will have their position *compulsorily acquired* by the offeror, and as such this is a mandatory event.

2.2.9 Issuer Notices

Issuer Meetings with Proxy Voting

This is the notification, to *position holders*, of a company meeting.

Typically, these meetings are the Annual General Meeting (A.G.M.) or Extraordinary General Meeting (E.G.M.). Issuer Meetings are often held to obtain shareholder ratification of company decisions, for example the adoption of financial statements, the sale of *capital*, the distribution of *income*, etc. In response to the notification of a company meeting, the position holder may choose to issue a *proxy vote*.

This event applies to all position holders, but will not directly impact the position holder's securities and/or cash position.

A company meeting is an Issuer Notice.

Information Only

This single term represents all instances where the *issuer* communicates specific changes in information pertaining to the securities in issue, or to the company itself.

Unlike Issuer Meetings, the notification is information only and does not require ratification by *shareholders* (though any changes it is communicating may have previously been the subject of a shareholder meeting). These notifications may in turn impact the terms or occurrence of future events in the security. Examples of notifications include:

- extension to the *maturity date* of a bond;
- advice of a bond in default of its *coupon payment*;
- adjustment of a bond *coupon rate*;
- a change in the identification of a security, e.g. name change or change in *ISIN* number;
- a change in the *lot* size of a security;
- changes to the trading status of a security, e.g. suspension or delisting;
- bankruptcy or impending legal action against the issuer.

This event applies to all position holders, but will not directly impact the position holder's securities and/or cash position.

An Information Only event is an Issuer Notice.

2.3 EVENT CLASSIFICATION

The advantage of being able to classify events in terms of their impact and lifecycle from an operational perspective is primarily to be able to develop sets of common operational procedures, which can then be applied to each category. Advantages also exist from an operational training perspective, in that it allows the trainee to view a set of events collectively, rather than being introduced to each event independently of each other.

Using the descriptions provided earlier in this chapter, it is now possible to classify the common events in terms of the impact and lifecycle categories introduced in the previous chapter.

This is illustrated via a matrix (Table 2.1), which identifies the impact of the event, both from the issuer's and the position holder's perspectives, versus the operational lifecycle of the event.

2.3.1 Impact

The impact is initially split between *benefit*, *re-organization* and *issuer notices*. It is then progressively broken down to reveal a more specific indication of the issuer's intent, together with the actual outcome to the position holder in terms of movements of securities and/or cash against its original position.

2.3.2 Lifecycle

With respect to lifecycle, the same categories introduced in Chapter 1 are used, these being Mandatory, Mandatory with Options, Voluntary, Multi-stage and Issuer Notices lifecycles. Similarly to impact, these have been broken down into more specific sub categories, where appropriate.

A selection of the events described earlier in this chapter has been included within the matrix, to illustrate how they can be classified.

For example, within the Impact Type of re-organization, Debt Redemption is shown. The impact on the *position holder* is always to remove its securities holding, and to receive cash (as *capital*) irrespective of the specific type of redemption. In this respect the five varieties of redemption described earlier in this chapter appear exactly the same. However this is not the case operationally, as illustrated when plotting these events against their respective lifecycles. It can now be seen that despite their common impact on the position holder, these events are a mixture of both mandatory and voluntary lifecycles. To the STO's Corporate Actions Department this will mean that the procedures to manage these events will differ somewhat between those that are mandatory and those that are voluntary. (These differences will be specifically explored throughout this book).

In summary, the classification matrix can be regarded as an analysis tool in identifying the high-level characteristics and lifecycle of both existing and new events that may be introduced by issuers.

2.4 EVENT COMBINATIONS

Issuers may combine multiple events to achieve the overall impact that they require. This is particularly common with respect to *re-organizations*, where an issuer aims to restructure the issued equity capital. For example, a *share split* by itself represents a restructure of issued equity capital, as does a *capital repayment*. Nonetheless the issuer could combine the two events to achieve the overall impact required.

Imagine that the issuer wishes to restructure its equity capital by increasing the number of shares in issue, and simultaneously reduce the total value of issued equity capital. For example, an issuer may have issued 2 million, USD1.00 fully paid ordinary shares to the public. Each USD1.00 ordinary share would be known as *fully paid*, which indicates that each share represents USD1.00 ownership in the issuing company, to the *position holder*. The issuer's financial records will show that there is a total of USD 2,000,000.00 of capital represented by equity issued to the public. The issuer's aim is to reduce the capital value of issued capital and increase the number of shares in issue.

Table 2.1

			Lifecycle							
			Mandatory			Mandatory with Options	Voluntary	Multi-Stage		Issuer Notice
Impact Type	**Issuer's Perspective**	**Position Holder's Perspective**						Mandatory	Voluntary	
Benefit	**Payment of Interest Due (Debt)**	Receive Cash (as Income)	*Coupon Payment*							
	Payment from Income Earned (Equity)	Receive Cash (as Income)	*Cash Dividend*							
		Receive Securities (as Income)				*Dividend Re-investment Plan*				
	Distribution of Capital Reserves	Receive Cash (as Capital)	*Capital Distribution*							
		Receive Securities (as Capital)	*Bonus Issue*					*Rights Issue*		
Re-organization	**Issued Capital (Equity) Restructure**	Remove Securities	*Share Split*	*Scheme of Arrangement*	*Mandatory Equity Call*		*Warrant Exercise*			
		Pay Cash			*Mandatory Equity Call*		*Warrant Exercise*			
		Receive Cash (as Capital)		*Scheme of Arrangement*						
		Receive Securities (as Capital)	*Share Split*	*Scheme of Arrangement*	*Mandatory Equity Call*	*Scheme of Arrangement*	*Warrant Exercise*			
	Debt Restructure against Issued Capital (Equity)	Remove Securities					*Convertible Bond Conversion*			
		Receive Securities (as Capital)					*Convertible Bond Conversion*			
	Debt Redemption	Remove Securities	*Bond Maturity, Early Redemption, Bond Call*				*Voluntary Redemption*			
		Receive Cash (as Capital)	*Bond Maturity, Early Redemption, Bond Call*				*Voluntary Redemption*			
	Raising of Capital	Remove Securities							*Rights Issue*	
		Receive Securities (as Capital)							*Rights Issue*	
		Pay Cash							*Rights Issue*	
	Re-organization of Company Structure	Remove Securities	*Merger*			*Merger*		*Takeover compulsory acquisition*	*Takeover*	
		Receive Securities (as Capital)	*Merger*	*Spin-off*		*Merger Spin-off*		*Takeover compulsory acquisition*	*Takeover*	
		Receive Cash (as Capital)	*Merger*	*Spin-off*		*Merger Spin-off*		*Takeover compulsory acquisition*	*Takeover*	
	Issuer Notice	No Impact to Securities or Cash Position								*A.G.M.*

Impact

A two for one share split of USD1.00 ordinary shares will result in each USD1.00 ordinary share being replaced by two USD0.50 ordinary shares. The total issued capital will still equal USD 2,000,000.00, but is now represented by a greater number of shares issued (4 million).

A capital repayment to position holders of USD0.20 per share immediately following the share split will reduce the capital value of each issued share to USD0.30, making them USD0.30 fully paid ordinary shares.

The result following both the share split and capital repayment will be 4 million USD0.30 fully paid ordinary shares issued, with a total issued capital of USD 1,200,000.00.

In this example the issuer could have simply reduced the capital value of issued capital to USD 1,200,000.00 by making a capital repayment of USD0.40 against each USD1.00 ordinary share. This would have reduced the capital value of each share to USD0.60, with 2 million shares remaining in issue. By implementing a share split immediately prior to the capital repayment the issuer has achieved the additional aim of increasing the number of shares in issue.

Issuers (and their advisers) can become very creative in order to achieve their aims. It is therefore not unusual to find successive events from the issuer within a limited timeframe, which will have a cumulative effect on the position holder's final position. In such situations failure of the STO to apply one event successfully or to apply events in the correct sequence may result in subsequent errors in applying successive events. Accurate diarizing of these events and identification of any event dependencies will enable the STO to reduce risk in such situations.

2.5 EVENT VARIATIONS AND TERMINOLOGY

Within the Event Descriptions section of this chapter (Section 2.2), reference was made to different names for certain events that are used in different markets. For example, a Bonus Issue is known in the US as a Share Split, but equally in some markets a Share Split may be known as a Sub-Division.

However, besides name differences it is important to note that in some cases the same event can be treated differently in different markets. For example, in terms of calculation of the result of an event, a 3 for 2 rights issue is interpreted one way in the US and in a different way within European and Asia Pacific markets.

Such differences are explored within Chapter 8 ('Event Terms Capture and Cleansing') and Chapter 11 ('Calculation of Resultant Entitlements').

In practice, from a corporate actions processing perspective, events are typically differentiated at a granular level in order to facilitate detailed processing (on an STP basis) of the many event variations that may occur in the market place. For example, *S.W.I.F.T.* supports a number of specific event types relating to information only events.

2.6 SUMMARY

In order to ensure that appropriate and timely action is taken by the operations areas of STOs (and other organizations that hold equity and bond positions), it is essential to understand the nature of each type of corporate action.

Furthermore, successful management of events can be aided by grouping like events and applying standard operational procedures wherever possible. The approach of identifying the key attributes of an event will also enable a timely response to the introduction, by issuers, of new variations of events, and the understanding of market variances of existing events.

3
The Securities (and Corporate Actions) Market Place

3.1 INTRODUCTION

The complete lifecycle of a corporate action, from announcement through to receipt of entitlement by the *position holder*, involves a number of parties. Such parties include those that are involved with trading and/or settlement of trades within the *secondary market*, namely:

- the position holders – individual investors, institutional investors and STOs;
- agents for investors – those organizations that act as intermediaries between investors and the market place; this includes brokers, Internet brokers, clearing banks, stockbrokers, etc.;
- CSDs, ICSDs and custodians.

It also includes those that are involved with the announcement and the supply of corporate action information, namely:

- *issuers*, and
- *data vendors*.

This chapter provides a description of such participants in the securities market place, and specifically their roles in relation to corporate actions.

3.2 THE SECURITIES MARKET PLACE – OVERVIEW

In order to appreciate the various participants' roles in a corporate actions context, it is essential to first understand the fundamental aspects of the securities market place.

The securities market place involves:

- the trading environment
- issuers (and their agents, such as registrars)
- securities
- investors
- agents for investors
- securities trading organizations (STOs)
- CSDs, ICSDs and custodians

and their inter-relationships. Figure 3.1 illustrates such relationships:

3.2.1 The Trading Environment

The market place is generally considered to be the environment within which *securities* are bought and sold. Central to some market places is the existence of a stock exchange, which acts as the primary meeting point for those wishing to buy and sell securities, while other

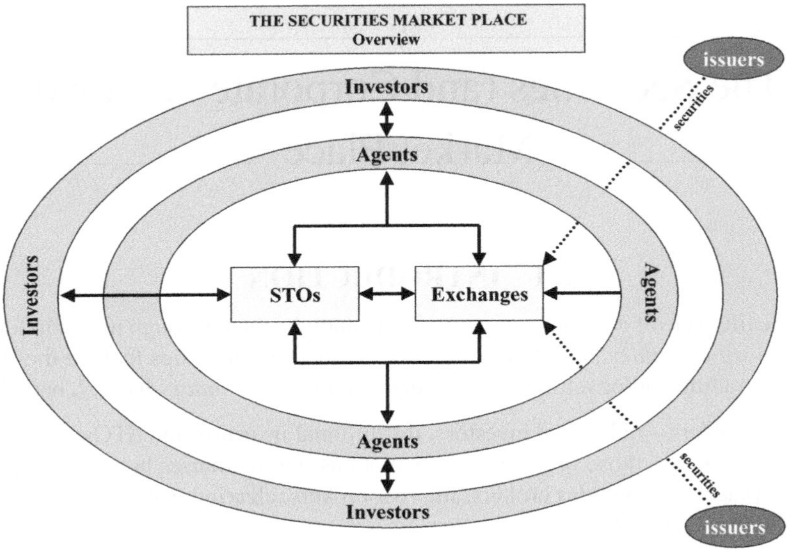

Figure 3.1 The securities market place: overview.

markets may exist without a stock exchange, with buyers and sellers contacting each other directly. Trades executed over an exchange are generally termed 'on-exchange', or 'exchange-traded', whereas other trades are executed by telephone on an OTC ('Over-the-Counter') basis. The evolution of these markets around the globe has involved the introduction of rules and regulations to ensure that an individual market is regarded as a fair and just place to conduct business.

The various markets developed their rules, regulations and methods of operation over many years to suit their local needs and in some markets national governments imposed rules. This resulted in, for example, strict dividing lines between the activities of the market participants and fixed commission amounts charged to clients for buying and selling securities. These rules, regulations and methods of operation affect not only trading and settlement, but also corporate actions.

However, in many markets the removal (or reduction) of controls imposed by governments has occurred in the last quarter of the 20th century, in order to promote competition between market participants and this has resulted in the removal of fixed commission charged to clients. The removal or reduction in controls is known as deregulation.

Each securities market has an associated and recognizable place for sellers and buyers to effect settlement of their trading activity, so that trading in a security within a specific market, such as trading HSBC shares on the Stock Exchange of Hong Kong, typically means settling the trade at the Central Clearing and Settlement System (CCASS), while trading French Government bonds in the Paris Bourse, typically means settling at Euroclear France.

The majority of securities have historically been traded only within their domestic exchange, but increasingly, popular securities can be traded over multiple exchanges. From an operational perspective, the exchange over which a trade has been executed may well affect the location of settlement.

3.2.2 Issuers

Those that raise *capital* through the creation and distribution of securities to investors are known as *issuers*. Table 3.1 lists the normal types of issuer with well-known examples of such organizations. It is important to note that only companies or corporations can issue shares, whereas all the issuer types listed can raise capital through the issue of bonds; the differences between equity and bonds, for both issuers and investors, are described below.

Table 3.1

Issuer Type	Typical Method of Raising Cash	Example Issuers
Companies or Corporations	Either by selling shares/equity (representing ownership) to investors, or by selling bonds (representing a borrowing of cash) to investors. Some issuers do both.	Colgate-Palmolive (USA) Cheung Kong (Hong Kong) Marks & Spencer (UK) Nestle SA (Switzerland) Qantas (Australia) SASOL (South Africa) Telebras (Brazil)
Sovereign Entities	Selling bonds to investors	Kingdom of Denmark New Zealand
Local Governments	Selling bonds to investors	City of Barcelona
Government Agencies	Selling bonds to investors	Federal National Mortgage Association
Supranational Organizations	Selling bonds to investors	International Bank for Reconstruction & Development (World Bank) Inter-American Development Bank

3.2.3 Securities

When organizations (issuers) need to raise capital, they have a number of alternatives; one option is to issue securities. Two main forms of securities exist, namely:

- equity, and
- debt.

Equity

Equity represents ownership in a company; the purchase of shares by an investor gives the investor partial ownership in that company (a 'share' in the company). The issuer effectively dilutes the ownership of the company by spreading ownership across hundreds or thousands of investors, dependent upon the size of the company and the number of shares in issue.

The issue of equity provides the company with 'permanent' cash; in other words when the company sells shares initially there is no intention to repay to shareholders the capital received (however, on an exceptional basis an issuer may decide to buy-back shares from shareholders).

If the company performs well, investors will reap the benefit through increases in the market price of the share as well as through greater profit distribution (for example through income [dividend] payments). However, a typical equity issue has no pre-defined amounts of income that are payable to the shareholders, or pre-defined points in time when income is payable.

Consequently, from the shareholders' perspective payments of income are neither guaranteed nor predictable (even if a company has paid dividends at regular intervals historically, there is no guarantee that this will be the case in future). If an investor wishes to sell its shareholding, the shares are not normally purchased by the issuer but are sold in the securities market place and ultimately purchased by another investor.

Table 3.2 shows examples of existing equity issues with the description of the share.

Table 3.2

Issuer	Description of Issue
Colgate-Palmolive (USA)	USD0.01 common stock
Cheung Kong (Holdings) Limited (Hong Kong)	HKD0.50 shares
Marks & Spencer PLC (UK)	GBP0.25 ordinary shares
Nestle SA (Switzerland)	CHF1.00 shares
Qantas Airways Limited (Australia)	AUD1.00 ordinary shares

Debt

A debt issue reflects a borrowing of a specific amount of cash by an issuer (such as a company, government or government agency) in a specified currency; the purchase of bonds by an investor is effectively an 'IOU' – a promise by the issuer to repay the capital to the investor at a future point in time and to make periodic payments of interest to the investor at pre-defined points in time and (normally) at a pre-defined rate of interest. Interest on bonds is commonly referred to as *coupon*.

From an issuing company's perspective, there is no dilution of ownership in the company as a result of issuing a bond; therefore investors in bond issues are not owners of the company. The issue of debt provides the issuer with a temporary receipt of cash, as it will be repaid at a future point in time (even if the period of the borrowing is as much as 30 years). Outgoing cash payments by the bond issuer are predictable throughout the life of the bond issue. The terms of the issue are set at the time of issue, including the date repayment of capital (also known as the maturity date) will be made, as well as the amount and dates for periodic payments of coupon. Note that there are some exceptions to such rules.

If an investor wishes to sell its bondholding, the bonds are not normally purchased by the issuer but are sold in the securities market place to another investor, as is the case for equities.

Examples of existing bond issues are shown in Table 3.3.

Table 3.3

Issuer	Description of Issue		
	Currency	Annual Coupon Rate	Maturity Date
Alliance & Leicester PLC	Pounds Sterling (GBP)	5.875%	14th August 2031
China (People's Republic of)	Japanese Yen (JPY)	4.65%	11th December 2015
France (Government of)	Euros (EUR)	3.0%	25th July 2009
Inter-American Dev. Bank	U.S. Dollar (USD)	7.125%	15th March 2023
Mexico (Government of)	Netherlands Guilder (NLG)	5.31%	31st December 2019
New Zealand Government	New Zealand Dollars (NZD)	6.5%	15th April 2013
Saskatchewan (Province of)	Canadian Dollars (CAD)	9.6%	4th February 2022
United Airlines	U.S. Dollar (USD)	8.65%	24th December 2009
Zurcher Kantonalbank	Swiss Francs (CHF)	3.25%	29th July 2005

3.2.4 Investors

In general there are two types of investor, the individual and the institutional investor.

Individual Investors

Most individuals invest in securities for their personal gain, whether their focus is capital growth through an increase in the market value of their investment, or regular income through the receipt of dividends on shares or coupon on bonds.

Individual investors visit the market place via agents (also known as intermediaries) such as stockbrokers and Internet brokers, through whom the buying and selling of securities is effected.

To buy or sell securities, an individual usually places with an agent a request (commonly known as an *order*) to buy or sell a specific quantity of a specific security (and may also state a specific price).

An individual may decide to operate one or more securities accounts; these are known as *portfolios* and may be used, for example, to distinguish between holdings in equities versus debt, or international versus domestic securities, thereby enabling separate assessment of profitability in a way that suits the investor. Similarly for cash accounts, an individual may require an income account to be maintained to reflect receipts of dividends on equities and coupon on bonds, whilst having a separate capital or investment account over which the cost of purchases is debited and sale proceeds are credited.

Following purchases of securities, an individual can choose whether to look after its portfolio of securities itself, or to have its portfolio held and managed by its agent for which a fee is normally charged to the individual. Historically, certificates representing an individual's ownership of shares or bonds would have been either held by the individual or by a stockbroker, bank or investment manager on behalf of the individual. In the present day, securities holdings may be represented by a certificate of ownership, or by an electronic (*dematerialized*) holding.

Institutional Investors

The terms *institutional investor* or institutional client are collective terms used to describe organizations (rather than individuals) that visit the securities market place and invest in securities. The type of organization that constitutes an institutional investor varies but includes companies in the capacity of:

- mutual fund managers (also known as unit trust managers)
- pension funds
- insurance companies
- hedge funds, and
- charities.

In parallel with individual investors, when wishing to buy or sell securities institutional investors place orders with an agent who typically charges a commission when a trade is executed. However, institutional clients may also trade on a net price basis (for instance, directly with an STO) where no commission is payable.

Institutional investors have the power to select the agents and STOs with whom they trade; the quantity and size of orders and trades originated by institutional investors forms a significant portion of business transacted across the world's various stock exchanges. They choose to trade with certain STOs on factors such as:

- execution performance: the speed of response to requests to buy and sell securities, and the competitiveness of prices;
- the research information provided: STOs employ analysts who study securities markets, companies and securities and provide forecasts and investment advice to institutional clients;
- operational performance including
  - the speed and accuracy of applying post-trade confirmation of trades to the institutional client within the agreed timeframe;
  - the timely and accurate processing of corporate actions on the client's securities that are held in safe custody by the STO.

Institutional clients demand a high quality service from STOs and if the service provided to the institutional client falls below an acceptable level, the institutional client may cease trading with a specific STO and take its business to a competitor.

3.2.5 Agents for Investors

There exists in the securities market place a type of organization that can be categorized as acting in an agency or intermediary capacity, in relation to buying and selling securities on behalf of its clients (not on its own behalf) who may be individuals only, institutions only, or a combination of both. Types of organizations operating business in this fashion are shown in Table 3.4.

Table 3.4

Agent	Description
Broker or Stockbroker	A company that specializes in fulfilling requests from its clients, to buy or sell securities
Retail broker	An alternative name for a stockbroker
Internet broker	An organization whose clients place requests to buy and sell securities via the Internet
Clearing bank	A bank that operates standard cash accounts for its clients and which typically offers a share dealing service
Financial adviser	An individual or organization that gives investment advice to its clients

Organizations acting as agents are required by law to pass on to their clients the price as executed by the third party within the market place; the agent's objective is to make profit by charging commission to the client placing the order, for successfully executing the client's order. Agents are not allowed to buy securities at one price and 'mark-up' (increase) the price before selling to the client so as to make profit on the traded price, or to decrease the price when the client is selling.

Besides providing a trading (or dealing) service to their clients, these companies may also operate as custodians of their clients' securities, for which the client may be charged a fee.

3.2.6 Securities Trading Organizations (STOs)

The term securities trading organization (STO) is a collective term that describes those who reside within the securities market place, namely traders and market makers, who sell securities to or buy securities from:

- agents acting on behalf of individual or institutional investors;
- institutional investors who have opted not to use an agent;
- other STOs such as traders and market makers.

(It does not refer to those who act as agents or intermediaries between investors and those who reside within the market place).

Unlike an agent who must pass on the price at which a trade has been executed, an STO sells securities at a price that may well be different from the price at which the securities were purchased. Where this is the case, the trader is carrying out securities trading (in the name of the STO) on a *proprietary* basis and is said to have traded 'as principal' or 'on a principal basis', whereas an agent conducts trading 'as agent' or 'on an agency basis'.

It is perfectly normal for STOs to invest for their own account and to maintain positive (also known as 'long') trading positions in hundreds or thousands of different securities at any one point in time. The trading position in some securities may have been acquired one minute ago, last month or even years ago and may be the result of one or many purchases and sales. In many markets around the globe, traders are allowed to sell securities that they do not own, with the intention of buying at a later time and at a lower price in order to generate profit for themselves. This is known as 'short selling' and results in a negative trading position.

Table 3.5 shows an example of a trader's current trading position of +23.50 million shares, made up of the following trades (assume today to be 14th December):

Table 3.5

Operation	Quantity	Trade Date	Trading Position
		6th January	zero
Buy	10,000,000	7th January	+10,000,000
Buy	5,000,000	2nd February	+15,000,000
Sell	13,000,000	21st July	+2,000,000
Buy	40,000,000	16th August	+42,000,000
Sell	6,000,000	14th September	+36,000,000
Sell	12,500,000	29th September	+23,500,000

Being in a positive securities trading position such as the example in Table 3.5 means that there will be a negative cash position (providing settlement of trades has occurred), but as STOs tend not to have a sufficient store of their own cash that can be used to pay for purchases and positive trading positions, the funds will need to be borrowed. The cost of borrowing cash has a detrimental impact on trading profit, so a vitally important activity is 'funding'; the borrowing of funds at the cheapest rate of interest.

Unlike arrangements made by some institutional investors regarding the use of global custodians, most STOs hold securities representing their positive trading positions directly with custodians located in the normal place of settlement of the security. Following purchases and sales of securities, the STO issues a *settlement instruction* to its relevant custodian to perform settlement on the STO's behalf. Following settlement, the resultant securities and cash positions will be updated by the custodian and reported to the STO. The STO will then need to update its internal books & records in order to maintain an accurate picture of outstanding trades with counterparties and settled securities and cash positions in the outside world, in turn enabling the STO to remain in control of its business.

3.2.7 CSDs, ICSDs and Custodians

With much of today's securities trading by investors, agents and STOs being executed in securities originating overseas, the services offered by custodians are normally used to provide greater efficiency and reduced risk in relation to trade settlement and the holding of securities in safe custody.

When securities are bought or sold, it is normal for institutional clients, agents for investors and STOs to utilize the services of their specific custodian in the financial centre relating to the traded security.

An STO, for example, is likely to have set-up arrangements with numerous custodians in various financial centres around the globe. When buying or selling individual securities, the STO will require the settlement of the transaction to be effected through its appropriate custodian within the relevant financial centre. This is illustrated in Table 3.6.

Table 3.6

Individual Security	Origin of Security	Relevant Financial Centre	Relevant Custodian
Sony Corporation Shares	Japan	Tokyo	Bank of Tokyo, Tokyo
Marks & Spencer Shares	U.K.	London	Crest, London
Qantas Shares	Australia	Sydney	ANZ Sydney
Italy 6.2% bonds 15th August 2010	Italy	Milan	Citibank, Milan
U.S. Treasury 5.0% bonds 1st May 2015	U.S.A.	New York	J.P. Morgan New York

Following execution of a trade, an STO must decide which of its custodians is appropriate in order to carry out the settlement of the trade, then issue a message (commonly known as a *settlement instruction*) to the relevant custodian.

The settlement instruction contains details of the trade, and tells the custodian to deliver or receive securities, and to pay or receive cash on the value date of the trade. The counterparty to the trade (typically an institutional client or another STO) will also need to issue a settlement instruction to its custodian within the relevant financial centre.

Having each received a settlement instruction, the seller's and the buyer's custodians will attempt to match the details. Once a match has been achieved, on value date the securities and cash are exchanged, and the resultant increase or decrease in securities and cash is recorded by the STO's custodian against the STO's securities and cash accounts maintained by the custodian. Note that although the intention is to settle trades on value date, *settlement failure* can occur.

Where the custodian holds securities and cash on behalf of the STO, the custodian is responsible for (among other services):

- holding the securities in safe keeping on behalf of the account holder;
- holding cash balances in safe keeping on behalf of the account holder;
- reporting of securities and cash positions to the STO;
- management of corporate actions falling due on the securities.

Various terms are used to describe those involved in the provision of trade settlement and custodial services on behalf of those who execute trades, and some are shown in Table 3.7. Each of these performs a specific custodian's role.

Table 3.7

Term	Description
Custodian	An organization that holds securities and (usually) cash on its client's behalf; and may effect settlement of trades on its client's behalf
Global custodian	As per custodian above, but has a network of local (or sub) custodians that hold securities and cash and effect settlement of trades on behalf of the global custodian
Local custodian	A custodian that operates within a specific financial centre
Sub custodian	A custodian within a global custodian's network of custodians
Central securities depository (CSD)	The ultimate storage location of securities within a financial centre, usually in *book-entry* form; settlement of trades may be provided as an additional service
National central securities depository (NCSD)	A CSD that handles domestic securities of the country in which it is located
International central securities depository (ICSD)	A CSD that handles international securities. Only two organizations are recognized as ICSDs, namely Clearstream (Luxembourg) and Euroclear (Brussels)
Settlement agent	An organization that effects the exchange of securities and cash on behalf of its clients; resultant securities and cash balances may or may not be held

A full description of the securities market place can be found within Chapter 2 of *Securities Operations: A Guide to Trade and Position Management.*

3.3 PARTICIPANTS – THE CORPORATE ACTIONS PERSPECTIVE

Further to the overview of the securities market place above, each participant-type will now be viewed from the perspective of corporate actions. Consequently, the participants will be described in the general sequence of their involvement with corporate actions, namely:

- Issuers
- CSDS and ICSDs
- Custodians
- Position holders
  - Individuals
  - Institutions
  - STOs

Figure 3.2 represents an overview of the above-mentioned parties involvement in corporate actions.

Step 1: the issuer may communicate corporate action information to CSDs and ICSDs (1a), to position holders (1b) or to custodians (1c).
Step 2: the CSD or ICSD may communicate with custodians (2a), or directly with the position holder (2b) (dependent upon which is the participant of the CSD or ICSD).
Step 3: the custodian will communicate directly with its client, the position holder.

Note that some corporate action events require one-way communication (from issuer to the ultimate position holder), whereas optional and voluntary corporate action events additionally require the position holder to advise its election decision to the issuer.

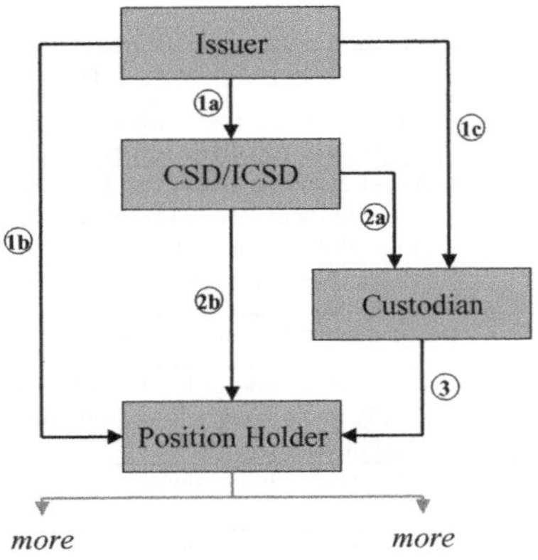

Figure 3.2 Corporate actions participants: overview.

3.3.1 Issuers

The issuer is the originating entity that issues securities to the market place in order to raise cash.

Issuers announce the details of corporate actions at the time of security issuance (usually bonds), or during the life of the security (typically equities).

The issuer will advise the details of a corporate action event to those individuals or organizations with whom the issuer has direct contact. Where a position holder's securities are held directly with a CSD or ICSD, it is the CSD or ICSD that has the direct contact with the issuer (rather than the position holder itself); the issuer will therefore communicate events directly to the CSD or ICSD. Alternatively, for those securities that permit registration of securities directly into the position holder's name, the issuer will have direct contact with the position holder.

3.3.2 CSDs and ICSDs

The Central Securities Depository (CSD) or International Central Securities Depository (ICSD) is the ultimate storage location of securities within a financial centre, in which the record of ownership is typically maintained electronically (by book-entry). The CSD/ICSD maintains a record of the total quantity of a security held, and reconciles this with the breakdown of holdings at individual participant level. CSDs and ICSDs usually have direct contact with issuers.

When a corporate action becomes due, the CSD/ICSD must ensure that it

- becomes aware of the existence of the event;
- gathers the correct details of the event;
- collects from the issuer the correct quantity of securities and/or cash value, at the appropriate date; and
- disburses to the relevant participants the correct quantity of securities and/or cash value at the appropriate date.

In addition, for elective events the CSD/ICSD must ensure that it

- advises its participants of the deadline by which the participant must make its decision;
- monitors responses from its participants; and
- communicates *election decisions* to the issuer, by the *issuer's deadline*.

3.3.3 Custodians

The custodian is an organization that specializes in holding securities and (usually) cash and effecting movements of securities and cash on behalf of its account holders. The custodian may hold securities with a CSD/ICSD or directly with the issuer. An STO that does not have direct membership of a CSD/ICSD will utilize the service of a custodian that has direct or indirect (via a sub-custodian) membership.

The custodian is in a similar position to CSDs and ICSDs from a corporate actions perspective, as it must ensure that it

- becomes aware of the existence of an event;
- gathers the correct details of the event;
- collects from the CSD/ICSD or issuer the correct quantity of securities and/or cash value, at the appropriate date; and
- disburses to the relevant account holders the correct quantity of securities and/or cash value at the appropriate date.

In addition, for elective events the custodian must ensure that it

- advises its account holders of the deadline by which the participant must make its decision;
- monitors responses from its account holders; and
- communicates election decisions to the CSD/ICSD or issuer, by the relevant deadline.

3.3.4 Position Holders

This is a generic term that describes individuals or organizations that hold a securities position. This specifically includes individuals, institutional investors, counterparties and STOs (as holders of proprietary positions).

Whether an individual, an institutional investor or an STO, the position holder will clearly wish to maximize any advantage that can be gained from corporate action events. This can be summarized as

- becoming aware of and gathering correct details of the event (although this is less likely in the case of an individual);
- collecting (from the issuer, CSD/ICSD or custodian) the correct quantity of securities and/or cash value, at the appropriate date; and
- being alerted to elective events well in advance of decision deadlines.

The position holder will be in communication directly with either the issuer (for those securities that permit registration of securities directly into the position holder's name), or with the CSD, ICSD or custodian.

Figure 3.3 illustrates the different types of position holder.

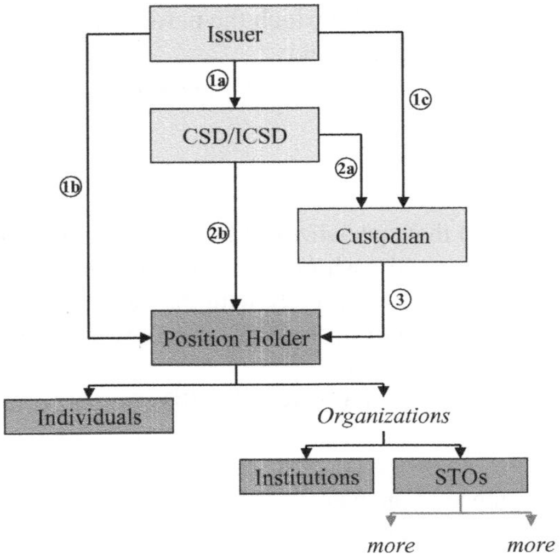

Figure 3.3 Securities position holders: overview.

3.3.5 Individuals

For those markets where it remains possible, individual investors may choose to maintain a direct relationship with the issuer, or to utilize the custodial services provided by organizations such as agents for investors, custodians and STOs. Note: individual investors wishing to become direct members of CSDs/ICSDs will be dependent upon the membership criteria of each CSD/ICSD.

The individual can expect to receive corporate action event information and resultant entitlements directly from whomever holds the securities.

3.3.6 Institutional Investors

This is a generic term given to investors that are organizations, as opposed to individuals; such investors include fund managers, hedge funds, insurance companies and pension funds.

As institutional investors can have their securities registered directly with issuers, held by CSD/ICSDs, or held and managed by global or local custodians, the institution can expect to receive corporate action event information and resultant entitlements from all such organizations. In the case of custodians, the provision of such information is normally part of the service the custodian provides to its account holders.

3.3.7 Securities Trading Organizations (STOs)

An STO is an organization that practises proprietary trading, involving the buying, selling and holding of securities for its own account. As well as holding its own proprietary positions, the STO may hold securities in safe custody on behalf of its clients, with obligations to service and protect its clients' interests, as well as its own.

For those STOs that operate a safe custody service, from a corporate actions perspective the STO has a dual role. It has obligations to

- itself, for events relating to its proprietary positions; and
- its clients (including institutions and individuals), for events relating to securities held in safe custody.

These obligations are represented in Figure 3.4.

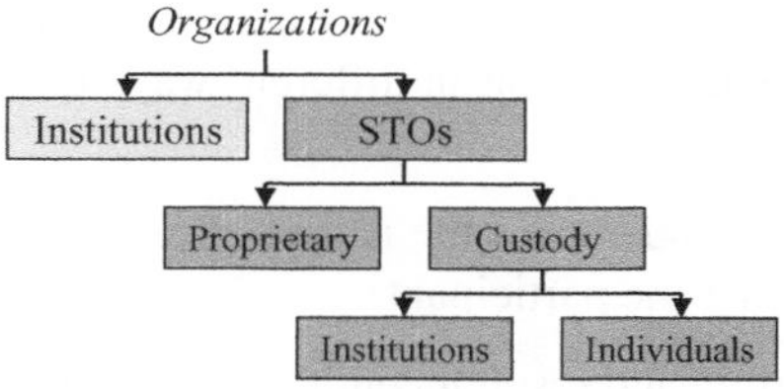

Figure 3.4 The STO's dual role.

The different types of holdings that the STO manages, i.e. proprietary and (potentially) custody, and the likely different types of custody clients, i.e. institutional and individual, will typically require differing methods of management throughout the lifecycle of the event, according to the STO's *service level agreements* with these types of position holders. It is essential for the Corporate Actions Department to distinguish at the highest level between such differing levels of service, and to incorporate this aspect of business into its day-to-day procedures.

Despite the fact that the STO's securities (whether solely proprietary positions or for proprietary plus safe custody positions) will be held by a combination of issuers, CSDs, ICSDs and custodians, rather than rely solely upon corporate action event information being provided by such organizations, the STO may well seek event information completely independently. Such a strategy allows the STO to take an objective view and to take control of corporate action event information, without being reliant upon a single source of information. This topic is explored further in Chapter 8, 'Event Terms Capture and Cleansing'.

Consequently, the STO is in a similar position to CSDs, ICSDs and custodians from a corporate action perspective, in that it must ensure that it

- becomes aware of the existence of an event;
- gathers the correct details of the event;
- collects from the CSD, ICSD or custodian the correct quantity of securities and/or cash value, at the appropriate date; and
- disburses to the relevant trading book (for proprietary positions) and clients (for safe custody positions) the correct quantity of securities and/or cash value at the appropriate date.

In addition, for events with elections the STO must ensure that it

- advises its trading books and safe custody clients of the deadline by which they must make a decision;
- monitors responses from trading books and safe custody clients; and
- communicates election decisions to the relevant CSD, ICSD or custodian, by the specified deadline.

3.4 SUMMARY

In order to ensure adequate controls in the processing of corporate action events, it is essential to understand and appreciate the various roles of the different participants within the securities market place, within the overall lifecycle of the event. For example, an appreciation

- that the issuer is the originating source of event information and resultant entitlements, but that a number of participants such as CSDs/ICSDs and custodians may exist between the issuer and the STO;
- of the different types of positions that the STO may hold, for example, proprietary and custody, which may require management in different ways throughout the lifecycle of the event.

In addition it is important to understand the nature of an STO's relationship with a given participant, for example, whether the participant

- is a source of event information and resultant entitlement in the eyes of the STO, such is the case in a custodian; or
- is a recipient of event information and resultant entitlement from the perspective of the STO, as is the case of parties for whom the STO holds positions.

ENDNOTE: within this chapter, certain figures, tables and text have been reproduced with permission from *Securities Operations: A Guide to Trade and Position Management*, ISBN 0-471-49758-4, author Michael Simmons, publisher John Wiley & Sons, Ltd.

4
Static Data

4.1 INTRODUCTION

'Static Data' is the commonly used term to describe a store of information that is used to determine appropriate actions necessary to achieve successful processing of its business; it is a significant factor in enabling an STO to achieve *STP*. Static data plays a vitally important role in the processing of *trades* and *settlements*, calculation of overnight *accruals* (relating to positions in bonds) and in the processing of corporate actions.

This chapter identifies the specific types of static data required for the STO to automate the processing of its business, highlighting corporate actions related data, and describes the value of accurate and timely set-up of such information, and the importance of ongoing maintenance of such data.

4.2 SECURITIES STATIC DATA

From a trade processing perspective, STOs need to hold the description, attributes and characteristics of securities allowing, for example:

- accurate trade cash value calculation; and
- accurate accrual calculation on bonds.

Securities static data is publicly available data. Each security has specific and unique attributes of which an STO must make itself aware, as financial losses may occur if information is not held accurately. Some of these attributes have a direct link with corporate actions; correctly set-up basic security information will not only result in correct trade cash value calculations, but also that associated corporate action resultant entitlement values will be correct.

4.2.1 Common Attributes of Securities Static Data

Whether for *equities* or *bonds*, it is normal for certain common aspects of securities static data to be set-up within the STO's systems for a variety of reasons, including:

- The identification of the specific security (within both trading systems and books & records systems) relating to the recording of trades and corporate action resultant entitlements.
- The communication of
  - *trade confirmations* to counterparties
  - *settlement instructions* to *custodians*, *CSDs* and *ICSDs*
  - *safe custody* position statements to clients
  - transaction reporting to regulators, and
  - corporate action communications to position holders.
- The reconciliation of
  - *trading positions* (between the trading area(s) and books & records), and
  - *settled custodian positions* (between *books & records* and custodians, CSDS and ICSDs).

These common aspects include:

- The full name and description of the security (avoiding ambiguity with any other security); this is normally used when the STO issues a communication to a client. For example
  - Colgate-Palmolive Inc., USD 1.00 Common Stock
  - New Zealand Government, 6.5% Bonds 15th April 2013 (NZD)
- The short name of the security; this informal description is typically used within the STO's organization in order to save space on internal reporting. For example
  - Colgate-Palm common
  - NZ Gov't 6.5% 150413
- External reference; the market-wide security identifier typically used within all communication to outside parties. The securities identification number that is used globally is *ISIN* (International Securities Identification Number), although local codes are often used in addition, such as Cusip (USA and Canada) and Sedol (in the UK). For example
  - ISIN: XS1234567893
- Internal reference; one or more security identifiers that are specific to the STO, typically used for communication between the STO's internal systems.
- Issued currency; the currency of issue of an individual security, whether the denominated currency of a bond that represents the cash received by the issuer, or the par value currency of an equity issue that represents the value of ownership in the issuer.

4.2.2 Detailed Attributes of Securities Static Data

In addition to the common securities static data mentioned above, a number of more detailed attributes are normally set-up within the STO's static data repository; such aspects facilitate the processing of trades and settlements, overnight accruals and corporate actions. The types of attributes will typically differ according to the specific type of security, at minimum distinguishing between debt and equity and potentially classifying security types at a more granular level.

Such aspects are primarily associated with debt issues as a bond begins its life with known and specified attributes that are applicable throughout its life, and which directly define the terms of corporate action events for the security (for example the schedule of coupon payments). The use of such data for corporate actions is explored within Section 8.2.

For example, the (fictitious) debt security XOX AG, 8.25% bonds maturing 1st June 2020 was issued on 1st June 2000. This security has a fixed coupon rate (8.25%) throughout its life, with coupons payable annually on the 1st June, starting in the year 2001 and ending in 2020. Table 4.1 shows the attributes (inclusive of the common attributes) that should be set-up within the STO's static data in order to maximize automation and *STP*.

The table reveals that extensive use of the same information can be made in the processing of trades, corporate actions and in the calculation of daily accruals.

The information contained within Table 4.1 will allow automation of:

- trade processing
  - accrued interest calculation[1]
  - validation of trade quantity versus denominational values
- corporate actions processing
  - the date of each coupon payment
  - the rate of each coupon payment

[1] Note that the concepts of accrued interest and daily accruals processing are explained within *Securities Operations: A Guide to Trade and Position Management* (accrued interest on pages 117–124; daily accruals on pages 393–394).

Table 4.1

Security Attribute	Example	Typical Uses: Trade Processing	Typical Uses: Corporate Actions Processing	Typical Uses: Daily Accruals Processing
Issuer	XOX A.G.	✓	✓	✓
Security full name	XOX A.G. 8.25% bonds 1st June 2020	✓	✓	
Security external reference	ISIN: XS1234567893	✓	✓	✓
Issued currency	USD	✓	✓	✓
Security group	Eurobond (USD)	✓	✓	✓
Coupon rate type	Eurobond fixed rate	✓	✓	✓
Coupon rate	8.25%	✓	✓	✓
Coupon frequency	Annual	✓	✓	✓
Day count	30/360	✓	✓	✓
Coupon payment dates	1st June	✓	✓	✓
Primary value date	1st June 2000	✓	✓	✓
First coupon payment date	1st June 2001	✓	✓	✓
Denominational values	USD 5000.00 and USD 20,000.00	✓		
Maturity date	1st June 2020	✓	✓	✓

  - the date of final maturity
  - the price payable on final maturity
- daily accruals processing
  - the daily value of accrued interest on long and short trading positions[2].

Equity issues typically have a limited number of detailed attributes by comparison with most debt securities. Unlike debt securities, because events throughout the life of an equity are not predictable (and do not form part of the conditions of the issue of the security), there is limited information that can be set-up within static data.

Consequently, the market place is completely reliant upon the accuracy of the event terms as announced and captured. Therefore, with respect to corporate actions, it is not possible to set-up within static data the details of such events, in advance of the *announcement*. Note that when such events are announced, the details may be held in an independent corporate actions repository, rather than within the STO's main repository of static data. This topic is explored in Chapter 8, 'Event Terms Capture and Cleansing'.

Table 4.2 lists the attributes (inclusive of the common attributes) of those characteristics of equities that are typically known and are able to be set-up within the STO's static data in order to maximize automation and *STP*.

Table 4.2

Security Attribute	Example	Typical Uses: Trade Processing	Typical Uses: Corporate Actions Processing	Typical Uses: Daily Accruals Processing
Issuer	CDE plc	✓	✓	n/a
Security full name	CDE plc, GBP1.00 Ordinary Shares	✓	✓	n/a
Security external reference	ISIN: GB9876543215	✓	✓	n/a
Issued currency	GBP	✓	✓	n/a
Security group	UK equity	✓	✓	n/a
Par value	GBP1.00 Ordinary Shares		✓	n/a
'Lot' sizes	500 shares	✓	✓	n/a
Ranking for dividend	Full Ranking		✓	n/a

[2] Note that the concepts of accrued interest and daily accruals processing are explained within *Securities Operations: A Guide to Trade and Position Management* (accrued interest on pages 117–124; daily accruals on pages 393–394).

Table 4.2 reveals that extensive use of the same information can be made in the processing of trades and corporate actions; however, daily accruals are not applicable to non-interest bearing securities.

The information contained within Table 4.2 will allow automation of:

- trade processing
  – validation of trade quantity versus *lot* sizes
- corporate actions processing
  – to what extent the security *ranks* for upcoming *dividends*.

4.2.3 Changeable Detailed Attributes of Securities Static Data

It is important to note that certain detailed attributes of securities may change or are variable during the life of the security; this is applicable to both debt and equities.

In the case of debt securities, unlike the fixed-rate bond stated previously, the following are examples of securities with changing attributes:

- floating rate notes
  – the *coupon* rate for each coupon period is calculated immediately prior to the coupon period according to pre-specified criteria, with the coupon payable at the end of each period
- mismatch floating rate notes
  – the same basic concept as for floating rate notes, but with the coupon payable at the end of multiple coupon periods
- flip-flop floating rate notes
  – the security is issued as a floating rate note, becomes a fixed interest security and then reverts to a floating rate note
- split coupon bonds
  – bonds issued as zero coupon bonds, but which during the life of the bond become coupon paying bonds
- step-up bonds
  – bonds that are issued with an initial lower than average coupon rate, and at some later point the rate is increased to a higher than average coupon rate
- amortizing bonds
  – bonds (such as mortgage backed-bonds) that pay coupons and partial repayment of capital to investors in instalments over a period of time in a specific manner. The *capital repayment* results in the *face value* of the bond remaining unchanged, but a percentage is applied to the bond price and to interest payments, in order to represent the decrease in cash owing by the *issuer*
- capitalizing bonds
  – bonds that have a percentage of their coupon payments converted into capital, resulting in the capital amount outstanding being increased in recognition that the cash amount will eventually be repaid by the issuer.

It is essential for the STO to maintain its static data in line with the outside world.

With regard to equities, the following will give rise to changes to static data:

- Issues not *ranking* for dividend
  - Some equities are issued (for example, as resultant entitlement from a *bonus issue* or a *rights issue*) without qualifying for the next dividend on the existing ordinary shares/common stock; such securities are named (e.g. New Ordinary Shares) in order to distinguish them from the ordinary shares/common stock. However, once the next dividend has been paid, the non-ranking shares and the ordinary shares/common stock usually become equal in all respects (they are said to rank *pari-passu*), at which point holdings in the non-ranking shares will become *fungible* with the holdings in the ordinary shares/common stock (and the non-ranking security will cease to exist).
- Par value
  - The impact of certain types of corporate action event will result in a change to the *par value* of an equity issue. For example, the outcome of a Share Split is the decrease in par value, while a Consolidation will result in an increase in par value.

4.2.4 Additional Corporate Actions Securities Static Data

Other corporate actions related information that is of value in setting-up within security static data includes:

- Securities Tax Status: different categories of securities attract different rates of taxation. For example, Eurobonds are (at the time of writing) tax exempt. (Refer to Chapter 25, 'Management of Income Tax').
- Rates of *Withholding Tax*: tax deducted in the issuer's country of residence, on income paid by issuers to investors, whether on equities or bonds. Investors resident in certain countries may be subject to a lower rate of withholding tax, if the issuer's country and the investor's country have a *double taxation agreement*. (Refer to Chapter 25, 'Management of Income Tax').
- Conversion/Exercise Schedules: details of the terms of conversion or exercise, as announced by the issuer at the time of issue of the security. (Refer to Chapter 8, 'Event Terms Capture and Cleansing').
- Country of Issue: the issuer's country of residence. This information is used to facilitate the calculation of withholding tax rates mentioned above.
- Registrars (or Issuer's Agent): the name and address of the registrar. For certain corporate action events requiring communication directly with the registrar or agent (e.g. subscription to rights issues), the name and address information is required to facilitate such communication.
- Issuers: for those exceptional cases where communication is required to be direct to the issuer (e.g. *proxy voting*), the name and address of the issuer itself.

4.3 PARTICIPANT STATIC DATA

Further to the description (in Chapter 3) of securities market place participants, certain participant static data is held by the STO to service its trades and the positions it holds (for itself and for its custody clients). This includes static data relating to:

- The STO: it is essential for information relating to the STO itself to be held within static data. This is commonly known as 'company static data'. For example, the STO will need to determine where it wishes to settle each trade, which is based primarily upon the security type (e.g. US equities are to be settled via the STO's US custodian, and Japanese Government bonds are to settle via the STO's Tokyo custodian). The information as to where the STO wishes to settle each security type is held within its static data repository. Associated with this information is the STO's settlement account number at each custodian.

- Counterparties: when the STO executes a trade, in order to automate its processing the STO must maintain a store of information relating to the specific counterparty's settlement details (e.g. account number 98765 at *Crest*, and account number 45678 at *Euroclear*), at security type level. Where the STO needs to issue a *trade confirmation* to the *counterparty*, the STO will need to maintain details of the required transmission medium (e.g. telex, fax, *S.W.I.F.T.)* and where appropriate, the number of copies required and the address for each.
- Position Holders: whether for holdings relating to its trading books or for its safe custody clients, the STO will need to hold details of how to disburse corporate action entitlements. For example, when a cash dividend is being processed, the STO must be aware whether to credit funds to a safe custody client's cash account with the STO, or to remit funds to an account of the client held externally. This topic is explored in Chapter 13 ('Collection/Disbursement of Resultant Entitlements').

The attributes of such static data can be categorized as follows:

- common attributes
- detailed attributes
- changeable detailed attributes
- additional attributes

Each of these is described below.

4.3.1 Common Attributes of Participant Static Data

In parallel with securities, certain common attributes of participant static data are normally set-up within the STO's static data repository for a variety of reasons, including:

- The identification of the specific trading book, counterparty or custody client (within both trading systems and books & records systems) relating to the recording of trades and corporate action resultant entitlements.
- The communication of
  - trade confirmations to counterparties
  - settlement instructions to custodians, CSDs and ICSDs
  - safe custody position statements to clients, and
  - corporate action communications to position holders.

  These common aspects include:
- the full name of the counterparty (avoiding ambiguity with any other counterparty); this is normally used when the STO issues a communication to a counterparty. For example
  - QRS Healthcare Growth Fund
- the short name of the counterparty; this informal description is typically used within the STO's organization in order to save space on internal reporting. For example
  - QRS Hcare Gth
- external references; the abbreviations and codes that are used by the industry community to identify the specific counterparty. For example
  - the S.W.I.F.T. 'BIC' (Bank Identification Code)

- ISMA's Trax code
- settlement account numbers at CSDs, ICSDs and custodians
- internal reference; counterparty identifiers that are specific to the STO, typically used for communication between the STO's internal systems, such as between the front office system(s) and the settlement system, and between settlement system and the *general ledger.*
- participant type; categories of participant such as
  - *trading book*
  - *counterparties* (potential further breakdown into market professionals and institutional clients) and
  - *custody clients*

  in order to provide management information (e.g. trading statistics) and automated updating of participant sub-sets within static data.

4.3.2 Detailed Attributes of Participant Static Data

In addition to the common participant static data mentioned above, a number of more detailed attributes are normally set-up within the STO's static data repository; such aspects facilitate the processing of trades and corporate actions.

For example, following trade execution, QRS Healthcare Growth Fund may require the issuance of multiple trade confirmations (by the STO) to multiple addresses:

(a) one original confirmation to the head office of QRS, plus
(b) two copy confirmations to QRS' settlement office, plus
(c) one copy confirmation to QRS' accountant.

Associated with this information must be a record of the trade confirmation transmission method required by QRS, for instance (in relation to the above list of trade confirmations):

(a) by telex
(b) by fax
(c) by paper (contract note)

A similar set of static data will need to be maintained by the STO in relation to communicating corporate action information such as;

- Event Terms Announcement
- Preliminary Entitlement Notice
- Final Entitlement Notice
- Preliminary Claim Notice
- Final Claim Notice

Note that each of these communication types is described in Chapter 10 ('Communication of Event Information').

In relation to the settlement of trades and corporate action entitlements, the STO will need to hold within its static data repository the precise CSD, ICSD or custodian and the associated account numbers that it (i.e. the STO) and its individual counterparties will use. Table 4.3 illustrates an example of such information held within the STO's static data.

The information in Table 4.3 is also fully utilized by the STO's Corporate Actions Department when managing an event; integral to the timely and accurate processing of a corporate

Table 4.3

	Example of the CSDs/ICSDs and Custodians Used in Each Location	
	STO	**Counterparty QRS Healthcare Growth Fund**
CSD/ICSD/Custodian names and locations	C1: Custodian A, Sydney C2: Custodian E, Tokyo C3: Custodian L, New York	C1: Custodian C, Sydney C2: Custodian G, Osaka C3: Custodian M, New York
Related securities account numbers	C1: Main account: 5023598 C2: Main account: A007880 C3: Main account: 111693XM	C1: Main account: 553289 C2: Main account: BB9096220 C3: Main account: 110242TP
Related cash account numbers (and currency)	C1: Main account: 5023598 (AUD) C2: Main account: A007880 (JPY) C3: Main account: 111693XM (USD)	C1: Main account: 553289 (AUD) C2: Main account: BB9096220 (JPY) C3: Main account: 110242TP (USD)

action is the knowledge of where trades have settled or are due to settle. This topic is explored within Chapter 11 ('Calculation of Resultant Entitlements').

4.3.3 Changeable Detailed Attributes of Participant Static Data

It is very important to note that participant static data may change at any time. Once static data has been set-up, the type of information that is most likely to change is:

(a) counterparty settlement location and associated account numbers
(b) communication transmission methods
(c) counterparty addresses

Points (a) and (b) may arise where the counterparty believes it can increase efficiency and/or reduce costs by changing its custodian in a specific market place.

It is normal for the counterparty to communicate the details of such changes to the STO, in advance of the effective date of the change; an example of a change to counterparty settlement location and associated account numbers is illustrated in Table 4.4.

Table 4.4

	Example of the CSDs/ICSDs and Custodians used by QRS Healthcare Growth Fund in Japan	
	Prior to 1st October	**From and including 1st October**
CSD/ICSD/Custodian names and locations	C2: Custodian G, Osaka	C2: Custodian T, Tokyo
Related securities account numbers	C2: Main account: BB9096220	C2: Main account: XBU57702X
Related cash account numbers (and currency)	C2: Main account: BB9096220 (JPY)	C2: Main account: XBU57702X (JPY)

It is essential that within the STO's operational environment, changes to static data be effected at (and not before) the date at which the change becomes effective. For example, if counterparty QRS Healthcare Growth Fund advises the STO on 15th September that, with effect from 1st October, trades in US equities are to be settled via a different custodian from that used presently, the effective date of changes to the STO's static data records must be actioned appropriately. Changes to static data actioned either in advance of or later than 1st October are likely to lead to unmatched settlement instructions and failed settlement; costs associated with failed settlement are likely to be chargeable to the STO, if the counterparty can prove that the STO was aware of the new information in good time, but failed to issue appropriate settlement instructions.

It is also possible for the STO to decide to change its custodian within a specific market place, in which case the STO must ensure it communicates such changes to its counterparties in good time, and that its static data is updated to reflect the change, to become effective at the appropriate date.

Entirely separately from changes to settlement location, a counterparty may choose to change the transmission method by which it requires trade confirmations or corporate action information to be issued by the STO. Relevant changes to static data by the STO will need to be effected efficiently, otherwise relationships with counterparties (in particular institutional clients) may be adversely affected.

4.3.4 Additional Corporate Actions Participant Static Data

Other corporate actions related information that is of value in setting-up within participant static data includes:

- Events with Elections Standing Instructions: when a corporate action event with elections falls due, some position holders may choose to provide standing instructions to the STO. Such standing instructions may state, for example:
  - always elect cash for Dividend Re-Investment Plans
- Rates of Holder's Residency Income Tax: tax on income deductible by the tax authorities in the position holder's country of residence, according to its tax status (e.g. individual, corporation or charity). Collectors of income on behalf of others (e.g. STOs collecting income on behalf of their safe custody clients) in some instances are obliged to deduct such tax prior to passing on the final disbursable amount to the position holder. (Refer to Chapter 25, 'Management of Income Tax' for a description of this topic). The set-up of the applicable tax rates within static data allows automated calculation and deduction of the taxable amount.
- Notification Medium and Addresses: the processing of corporate actions presents the STO with the opportunity to communicate with position holders on one or more occasion, for example, to inform holders of an impending event or of resulting changes to the position holder's securities and/or cash positions. In order to provide such communication in an efficient manner, the STO will need to hold the position holder's preferences for the medium of communication (e.g. fax, e-mail, S.W.I.F.T.) and the appropriate addresses. This topic is explored within Chapter 10 ('Communication of Event Information').

Note that each static data item listed in this section is also subject to change.

4.4 SOURCES AND MAINTENANCE OF STATIC DATA

For both securities and participants, static data is typically gathered (and maintained) from a variety of sources.

4.4.1 Securities

For those STOs that trade in numerous markets around the globe, the details of securities in which they trade will derive from many sources in numerous locations. The accurate collection of relevant data is a task that should not be underestimated. If losses are to be avoided, the accuracy of the information is paramount, as is the timeliness of setting-up the data.

When a security is being brought to the market place, it is normal for the issuer (or its agent) to produce a *prospectus* or offering circular; a document detailing the terms of the issue. The information contained in the prospectus is publicly available, at which point the relevant custodians, CSDs and ICSDs typically set-up the details of the issue in their own static data systems (enabling *STP* in their own environment).

Some STOs gather their securities static data directly from the prospectus, but this may not always be available within the urgent timeframes in which an STO typically requires the information. Another option is to request the necessary information from a custodian, CSD or ICSD. If the relevant information is gathered from such sources, the details of the security will be input to the STO's static data system manually, or automatically if a feed is available.

However, there is an alternative: a number of companies specialize in gathering and distributing securities static data to those who are prepared to subscribe to such a service. These companies are known as *data vendors* and include those listed in Table 4.5.

Table 4.5

Valorinform	Extel
Reuters	Standard & Poor's
Financial Information	Xcitek
Telekurs	Bloomberg

These companies typically provide data by electronic feed, or via the Internet.

Some STOs subscribe to one service provider; others subscribe to many to enable a comparison of data provided by two or more providers, in an effort to ensure that only completely accurate securities information is updated within the STO's own static data repository.

The provision of current securities prices and the details of corporate action events are associated with the supplying of securities data; corporate action events are covered in Chapter 8 ('Event Terms Capture and Cleansing').

In the case of Floating Rate Notes (FRN), it is essential that the STO has internal mechanisms to alert it to the fact that a specific FRN has an impending coupon rate announcement for the next coupon period (commonly known as 'rate re-fixing'). Such alerts allow the STO to maintain a continual history of coupon rates relating to individual FRNs. Rate re-fixing information is usually published within the financial press, in addition to being available from the STO's custodian and data vendors.

4.4.2 Participants

As mentioned in Section 4.3, the STO is normally concerned with participant static data for

- the STO itself
- counterparties, and
- position holders

and the source of such static data is described below.

- The STO: the overall *trading book* structure within the front office is typically the sole responsibility of trading management, and the books & records (managed by the operations areas) are usually required to match that structure. Periodically, trading management will decide to reorganize its trading book structure, resulting in the introduction, amendment or deletion of trading books. Such re-organizations should be instigated within both trading systems and books & records systems at the same time in order to prevent the mismatch of information (e.g. trading positions and P&L).

With reference to the STO's custodians, the custodian normally provides the specific account number(s) to the STO.

- Counterparties: When an STO trades with a *counterparty* for the first time (whether a market professional or institutional client), it is usual for the STO and the counterparty to swap custodian details directly, for each market in which trades may be executed between the two parties; better still, exchanging information in advance of the first trade between the two parties allows immediate *STP*.

  Additionally, the STO will need to gather all other appropriate pieces of information from the counterparty, in advance, in order to avoid halting processing of trades whilst the missing information is sought; this information, for example, would include counterparty membership numbers and the required medium of trade confirmation.

  Counterparty information should be considered as private information, whereas security information is publicly available information. Consequently, the information as to which custodian a particular STO or institutional investor uses for settlement of, for example, Swedish equity, is unlikely to be freely available. Consequently, it is normal that only when two parties have agreed that they will trade with one another, will information such as custodian details be swapped.

  Historically, the process of gathering this information has been a manual exercise. However, such information is nowadays available for those organizations (including STOs and institutional investors) that choose to subscribe to a service known as 'Alert'. Counterparty custodian details are available electronically via Alert; the advantage of this being that the updating of an STO's counterparty static data can be automated, thereby removing errors typically associated with manual input of data.
- Position Holders: much of the information required to be held by the STO in relation to safe custody holdings will be contained within the Service Level Agreement (SLA) that is drawn-up between the STO and its client. This typically contains details of
  - whether the account is to operate on an *actual settlement* or a *contractual settlement* basis;
  - the specific account(s) over which purchase costs and sale proceeds are to be debited or credited;
  - the client's residency status for tax purposes;
  - the specific account(s) over which income is to be credited;
  - the client's preferences for events with elections; and
  - the client's external bank account details.

4.5 SUMMARY

The very efficient processing of trades can result only from applying static data to trade data automatically. To facilitate this, the relevant static data must be populated within all relevant systems, from a reliable source, at the earliest opportunity.

Any situation that differs from that ideal is likely to result in fundamental problems impacting service levels to clients and the cost-effectiveness of processing trades.

As the window for the processing of trades becomes ever smaller, the timeliness and accuracy of static data will play an increasingly important role.

From a corporation actions viewpoint, similar sentiments apply. The STO is able to automate a number of components of the corporate actions lifecycle (and by so doing increase the efficiency and reduce the risk of corporate actions processing), if relevant static data is inserted and maintained accurately and in a timely manner.

ENDNOTE: within this chapter, certain figures, tables and text have been reproduced with permission from *Securities Operations: A Guide to Trade and Position Management*, ISBN 0-471-49758-4, author Michael Simmons, publisher John Wiley & Sons, Ltd.

5 Securities Position Management

5.1 INTRODUCTION

Accurate and timely record keeping is paramount for any organization, if it wishes to remain in full control of its goods and cash. Such standards of record keeping are equally as important for STOs.

For its normal (non-corporate actions) business, the STO will maintain records of the items shown in Table 5.1 in its books & records.

Table 5.1

Item	Description
Trades	A complete record of all trades executed
Trading book positions	The net sum (by quantity) of all trades in each security
Unsettled trades	Trades that have yet to settle and which are outstanding with counterparties
Settled trades	Trades that have settled at the custodian/CSD/ICSD and which are no longer outstanding with the counterparty
Settled custodian positions	The net sum of all settled trades in each security, held by a custodian/CSD/ICSD

Additionally, the STO may hold securities in *safe custody* for and on behalf of the STO's clients; such holdings do not belong to the STO and therefore the STO's *books & records* must reflect that fact. Nevertheless, the STO must maintain a full historic record of the clients' trading activity and the effect of such trading on the clients' positions.

The STO is able to prove that its books & records are accurate through the process of *reconciliation*, involving the comparison of each component (above) with external parties (including, for example, trading positions held within the front office).

For a complete explanation of the above, refer to *Securities Operations; a Guide to Trade and Position Management* by Michael Simmons (one of the authors of this book).

The relevance of such record keeping to the management of corporate action events is as follows. Once the STO is aware of an impending corporate action event, at the appropriate time the STO will assess whether any (*trading book* or *custody client*) positions are held. Furthermore, *unsettled trades* may need to be considered, even where zero *trading positions* exist. Note that these topics will be described fully in subsequent chapters.

When assessing whether such positions are held and whether any unsettled trades exist, the Corporate Actions Department within the STO will utilize the STO's basic books & records.

5.2 THE STO'S RISK

For the day-to-day management of its business, the STO is able to remain in control of its business where its books & records are updated accurately and in a timely fashion.

It is clearly essential for accuracy and timeliness to be achieved together, as one without the other will not result in a true record of the STO's business. The accurate recording of (for example) the details of a trade will not contribute to accurate books & records where that trade is not recorded on its trade date. Similarly, the timely updating of a trade with the details of settlement (as advised by the custodian) will not result in accurate books & records if (for example) an incorrect quantity of securities is posted.

Maintaining accurate and timely books & records from the outset enables the STO to reconcile all components of its business speedily and with the minimum of effort, thereby avoiding the sometimes huge manpower costs (and the associated time) of investigating and correcting discrepancies.

The condition of the STO's books & records will be reflected within its Corporate Actions Department, as it is the core information upon which that department relies.

If the STO's books & records are accurate, there is every possibility that the Corporate Actions Department will

- accurately ascertain whether trading books or safe custody clients are entitled to the event, and
- subsequently correctly calculate the entitlement amounts owed to the position holders.

Alternatively, should the STO's books & records be inaccurate, the Corporate Actions Department may

- fail to ascertain that a trading book or safe custody client is entitled to the event, or
- calculate *resultant entitlement* amounts based on incorrect positions, or
- expend a great deal of effort in ascertaining the correct positions.

In these cases, risks may be incurred by the STO that are very difficult to quantify, as the extremely diverse nature of corporate action events may result in cash losses on a small or a large scale, besides the possibility of losing clients (through a failure to service their safe custody positions).

5.3 FUNDAMENTALS OF SECURITIES POSITION MANAGEMENT

In order to achieve proper internal control over securities positions, STOs must adopt strict record-keeping regimes, and ensure that the regime is applied consistently and in a timely fashion. A common record-keeping regime is illustrated below, detailing:

- individual trades;
- the effect of those trades on *ownership positions* (trading book);
- open trades with *counterparties*; and
- *settled custodian positions*.

The three example trades listed in Table 5.2 will be used as the basis to calculate ownership versus location positions at various moments in time. All three trades are in the same security (Sony Corporation shares); there was no trading position prior to the first trade executed on 15th June and the time gap between trade date and value date is deliberate, to make the examples easy to follow.

The following series of tables (Tables 5.3–5.7) shows the ownership versus location position of Sony Corporation shares at various points in time, relating to the three trades listed in

Table 5.2

Trade Date	Value Date	Operation	Quantity	Trading Position
				Brought-forward 0
15th June	25th June	Buy	2000	+2000
1st July	10th July	Buy	6000	+8000
15th July	20th July	Sell	5000	+3000

Table 5.2. Note that the following convention is used in these tables:

- within 'ownership'
  - the STO's positive trading position is represented by a '+' sign, and consequently
- within 'location'
  - an open purchase due from a counterparty will be shown as a '–' sign
  - a settled purchase held at the STO's custodian will be shown as a '–' sign
  - an open sale due to a counterparty will be shown as a '+' sign.

Table 5.3 shows the position immediately after the first trade has been executed.

Table 5.3

Sony Corporation Shares (as at 15th June)			
Ownership		Location	
STO	+2000	–2000	Counterparty 'X'
	+2000	–2000	

This shows that 2000 shares are owned by the STO and that these shares have not yet been delivered to the STO's custodian by the counterparty, as the value date (the intended date of delivery) is in the future.

Up to and including one day prior to value date (i.e. 24th June), the ownership versus location position remains the same as above due to the fact there were no more trades executed as at that date and settlement has not yet occurred for the trade that has been executed.

Assuming that the trade settles on value date (at the custodian), the internal records will need to be updated as shown in Table 5.4.

Table 5.4

Sony Corporation Shares (as at 25th June)			
Ownership		Location	
STO	+2000	–2000	Custodian Bank of Tokyo, Tokyo
	+2000	–2000	

This shows that 2000 shares are owned by the STO and that these shares have been delivered by the counterparty to the STO's custodian, the Bank of Tokyo, Tokyo. It also shows that there are no open trades in this security.

If the ownership versus location position were now viewed after the second trade was executed on 1st July, the situation would be as shown in Table 5.5.

Table 5.5

Sony Corporation Shares (as at 1st July)			
Ownership		Location	
STO	+8000	–2000	Custodian Bank of Tokyo, Tokyo
		–6000	Counterparty 'Y'
	+8000	–8000	

This shows that as a result of the second trade, the ownership position has increased and that part of the position is held at the STO's custodian and the remainder is open with the counterparty.

Moving ahead to the 20th July, and assuming the second trade (for 6000 shares) has settled, Table 5.6 reveals that the ownership position has been reduced due to the sale on 15th July. It also shows that 5000 shares have failed to settle on the value date and are still owed to the counterparty, and that the securities that are owed to the counterparty are still held in the STO's Tokyo custodian.

Table 5.6

Sony Corporation Shares (as at 20th July)			
Ownership		Location	
STO	+3000	−8000	Custodian Bank of Tokyo, Tokyo
		+5000	Counterparty 'Z'
	+3000	−3000	

Table 5.7 shows the situation on 22nd July.

Table 5.7

Sony Corporation Shares (as at 22nd July)			
Ownership		Location	
STO	+3000	−8000	Custodian Bank of Tokyo, Tokyo
		+5000	Counterparty 'Z'
	+3000	−3000	

This shows that the sale is still outstanding and will remain so until settlement occurs at the STO's custodian.

In all cases above, the ownership position is equal to the sum of the location position. Providing that double entry book-keeping (see Generic Securities Accounting Principles below) methods are employed, it should not be possible for the ownership versus location position to become out of balance, whether using manual methods or a books & records system. Although the focus in the above examples has been on the quantity of securities, the same concepts are applicable to cash.

5.4 GENERIC SECURITIES ACCOUNTING PRINCIPLES

The information shown in Tables 5.3–5.7 utilizes certain basic principles and practices that are common in the accounting of any organization's business, including:

- double entry book-keeping
  - every entry recorded is effected using a minimum of two equal but opposite (debit versus credit) entries – this is known as 'double entry book-keeping', and is designed to provide control through offsetting entries;
- journal
  - a set of balancing debit and credit entries that are used to update account balances, and which may comprise various combinations of debit and credit entries (see Table 5.8).

Table 5.8

Number of Entries	
Debit	**Credit**
One	One
One	Many
Many	Many
Many	One

Note that each debit or credit entry will include:

- Who? – the party to whom the entry applies, for example in the case of a proprietary purchase
  – the specific trading book's updated securities position, and
  – the specific counterparty (so as to reveal securities due to the STO).
- What? – the security and the quantity pertaining to the entry; following-on from the previous example, the quantity and securities purchased.
- When? – the date(s) pertaining to the entry; following-on from the previous example, against the trading book
  – a trade date entry, reflecting the purchase date, and
  – a value date entry reflecting the intended settlement date.

Each entry will normally include a narrative that describes the main detail of the entry, for example 'buy 2000 Sony Corporation shares' and is likely additionally to include the trade reference number.

In order for the STO to maintain proper control over its business, journal entries will be passed:

- immediately after each trade has been executed;
- immediately after value date; and
- immediately after each trade has actually settled.

Thereafter the probability of successful reconciliation of the STO's books & records with the records of external entities is maximized.

5.5 EXTENDED SECURITIES POSITION MANAGEMENT

Under some circumstances, the nature of its business may demand that the STO maintains a greater level of detail than that represented above.

For example, for its safe custody business the STO may choose to maintain two accounts at its custodian within a specific market. For (*withholding*) tax reasons, safe custody clients that are resident of certain countries may have income on their holdings deducted at one rate (*treaty* rate), whereas all other clients will have income deducted at a higher rate (*non-treaty* rate). This topic is explored within Chapter 25 ('Management of Income Tax'). The STO must therefore ensure that securities are moved-in and moved-from the appropriate account at the custodian, according to the individual client (and its residency). It is therefore essential that the STO maintains accurate and timely books & records of individual client's trades and positions, and the associated account at the custodian.

Table 5.9 represents an example of the STO's books & records, in such a situation. Should Client L sell (say) 1000 shares, it is essential for the STO to instruct Custodian Z to remove securities from Custody Account 1, as the particular client qualifies for a treaty rate. By so doing, when the issuer pays income the custodian will deduct the appropriate rate of tax from the holding within each of the accounts, and the STO will in-turn disburse the correct payment to the client.

Table 5.9

DEF Corporation Shares			
Ownership			**Location**
Client L (A/C 1)	+2000	–5000	Custodian Z, Custody A/C 1 – treaty
Client M (A/C 1)	+3000	–1500	Custodian Z, Custody A/C 2 – non-treaty
Client N (A/C 2)	+1500		
	+6500	–6500	

Failure to remove the securities from the appropriate account would result in the situation shown in Table 5.10, where the ownership positions are not correctly represented within the custodian accounts.

Table 5.10

DEF Corporation Shares			
Ownership			**Location**
Client L (A/C 1)	+1000	–5000	Custodian Z, Custody A/C 1 – treaty
Client M (A/C 1)	+3000	–500	Custodian Z, Custody A/C 2 – non-treaty
Client N (A/C 2)	+1500		
	+5500	–5500	

In order for the STO to control such movements effectively, the books & records must be maintained at an appropriately granular level. This appropriate level is achieved by ensuring that the debit or credit entry that reflects the custody client (ownership) position includes a reference to the specific custody account at the custodian.

5.6 DISPARATE TRADE AND POSITION RECORDS

Within some STOs, certain aspects of its books & records may be maintained discretely from others, requiring additional effort to consolidate the STO's trades and positions. For example, the STO may operate two (or more) trading systems, requiring that the trading positions within the trading systems will require consolidating prior to attempting to reconcile with the STO's books & records.

A similar scenario exists even where the STO operates a single trading system, as the books & records may not necessarily be held within a single system. For instance, the records of

- trading book positions
- safe custody positions, and
- securities lending and borrowing activity

may be held individually, therefore requiring consolidation in order to gain a complete view of the position within a single security.

5.7 RECONCILIATION

As mentioned above, the STO's reconciliation process is designed to prove that its books & records are accurate, through the comparisons shown in Table 5.11.

Table 5.11

Item	Comparison	Purpose
Trades	To trading systems	To ensure that all trades captured by the traders are successfully captured within books & records
Trading book positions	To trading systems	To ensure that trade-dated securities positions within the trading system agree with the equivalent in books & records
Unsettled trades	To settlement instruction statuses received from custodians	To ensure that trade details are recognized and agreed by counterparties
Settled trades	To settlement instruction statuses received from custodians	To ensure that all trades reported by custodians as having settled have been updated within books & records
Settled positions	To position statements received from custodians	To ensure that positions reported by custodians agree with books & records

Furthermore, an STO's complete picture of an individual security can be reconciled internally by comparing:

- trading position (also known as the 'ownership' position), with
- the sum of open trades and the settled position (also known as the 'location' position).

The value in performing an ownership versus location comparison is that it is intended to confirm that the quantity of securities the STO owns as a result of trading (represented by the trading position) is

- held within the control of the STO (at the STO's custodian), and/or
- due to be delivered to the STO by counterparties from whom the STO has purchased securities, and/or
- due to be delivered by the STO to counterparties to whom the STO has sold securities

and also that its records balance internally.

The above-mentioned concepts are important as they form the basis for good operational management, proper control over assets and accurate calculation of corporate action entitlements.

5.8 SUMMARY

The accurate and timely record-keeping of trading and settlement activity provides the crucial foundation for risk-free and well-controlled corporate actions processing, the immediate impact of which can be seen in Chapter 9 ('Determining Entitlement').

In addition, the principles of securities position management (described here as applying to trading and settlement activity), apply equally to corporate action activity as described in Chapter 12 ('Passing of Internal Entries'), and Chapter 14 ('Updating of Internal Entries').

ENDNOTE: within this chapter, certain figures, tables and text have been reproduced with permission from *Securities Operations: A Guide to Trade and Position Management*, ISBN 0-471-49758-4, author Michael Simmons, publisher John Wiley & Sons, Ltd.

Part II

Mandatory Events

6
Overview of the Generic Corporate Action Lifecycle

6.1 INTRODUCTION

As introduced in Chapter 1, the Corporate Action Lifecycle comprises a number of significant operational elements almost irrespective of the category or type of corporate action, with the exception of Issuer Notices events. These common operational elements define the Generic Corporate Action Lifecycle, and their explanation forms the basis of Chapters 6 to 15.

The elements of the Generic Corporate Action Lifecycle can be presented as a series of logical steps. To enable the reader to navigate easily through the appropriate chapters, the diagram shown in Figure 6.1 will be used at the beginning of each of those chapters, re-presenting the overall logical flow of elements.

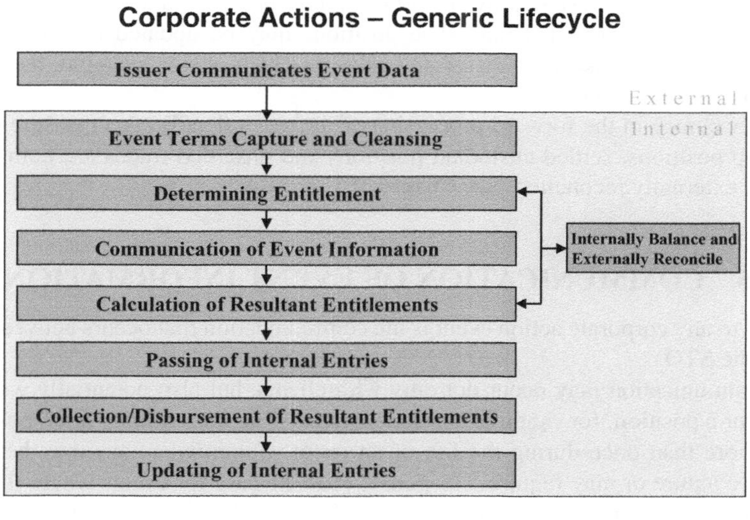

Figure 6.1 The generic corporate actions lifecycle.

From an operational standpoint, it is important to appreciate (despite illustrating the operational elements in a logical flow) that in reality some elements may be iterative in nature, or occur in parallel to others. For example the 'Collection and Disbursement of Resultant Entitlements' and associated 'Updating of Internal Entries' may occur sequentially or in parallel.

It is also important to note that the lifecycles of events with elections involve additional elements to those in the generic lifecycle. An example of this is the management of elections, necessitating the communication to holders of the available alternatives, and the monitoring of each holder's decision. These lifecycles are described in Chapter 16, 'Concepts of Events with Elections'.

6.2 ISSUER COMMUNICATES EVENT DATA

The *issuer* communicates the details and terms of an event. This may be upon the issue of the security itself, as is the case for *coupon* events on debt securities, or at any time throughout the life of the security as is the case for a *dividend payment* on equity. See Chapter 8.

6.3 EVENT TERMS CAPTURE AND CLEANSING

The capture and recording of *event data* is the first step in any corporate action lifecycle from the STO's perspective, even for those events that do not result in any impact to the *position holder's* securities and/or cash positions. This operational element encompasses the type of data necessary to record and the process of managing this information throughout the lifecycle. See Chapter 8.

6.4 DETERMINING ENTITLEMENT

Following on from the capture of event data, it is then necessary to determine against which positions the terms of the event are to be applied. Positions (including *ownership positions* and *location*, the latter represented by *settled custodian positions* and *unsettled trades*) will be determined using the event details. The positions may be updated throughout the life of the event in order to take account of any relevant changes, for example, as a result of further trading and settlement.

To ensure accuracy in the forward processing of the event details, as a measure of control the ownership positions, settled custodian positions and unsettled trades are both internally balanced and externally reconciled. See Chapter 9.

6.5 COMMUNICATION OF EVENT INFORMATION

Fundamental to any corporate action event is the communication that occurs between position holders and the STO.

Holder communication may occur not only with clients, but also potentially with anyone responsible for a position, for example the trader responsible for a *trading book* position, and may occur more than once during the life of an event. Communications may be purely of an informative nature or may require a response, as is the case for events where the position holders are required to indicate an action to the STO, such as events with elections. See Chapter 10.

6.6 CALCULATION OF RESULTANT ENTITLEMENTS

At the appropriate time, the entitled amount (of securities and/or cash) due to the holders is calculated. This involves applying the calculation terms of the event and any elections to the entitled positions (including unsettled trades) that result in the derivation of the final *resultant entitlement*. As a control measure, in parallel with positions, resultant entitlements are externally reconciled prior to settlement. See Chapter 11.

6.7 PASSING OF INTERNAL ENTRIES

Once the resultant entitlement is calculated and reconciled, internal securities and/or cash entries are passed. It is at this time that the expected impact of the event is reflected on the positions holder's securities and/or cash positions, and the differences between *benefit* events and *re-organization* events become apparent. See Chapter 12.

6.8 COLLECTION AND DISBURSEMENT OF RESULTANT ENTITLEMENTS

As a result of the corporate action event, actual changes to securities and/or cash positions will occur. This element encompasses the actual *collection* and *disbursement* of those resultant entitlements, including the variety of settlement methods and the impact on *unsettled trades* via *claims*, *compensations* and *transformations*. See Chapter 13.

6.9 UPDATING OF INTERNAL ENTRIES

Once actual receipt and disbursement of resultant entitlements has occurred, it is important to update the internal entries (made previously) to the position holder's accounts. See Chapter 14.

7

Straight Through Processing

7.1 INTRODUCTION

Straight Through Processing (commonly known as *STP*), is a securities industry wide term to describe the objective of managing trades throughout the trade lifecycle automatically and without human intervention.

All the steps involved in a trade, from the point of order receipt (where relevant) and trade execution through to *settlement* of the trade, are commonly referred to as the 'trade lifecycle'.

The management of all STOs require that trades are processed in the most proficient manner possible, and this is reflected in the desire to achieve STP; this is only achievable if the trade lifecycle is begun by recording the details of each trade in a timely and accurate fashion within the front office, and is handled efficiently, cost effectively and within the various deadlines in the operational areas of the STO.

A problem created early on in the trade lifecycle will cost more to correct the further it flows through the operational process, the effect of the error being replicated and magnified.

The trade lifecycle can be regarded as a series of logical steps, which are represented in Figure 7.1 (however it should be noted that some of these steps can occur in parallel, or in a different order to that stated below).

Historically, within many STOs there was little or no connectivity between the various systems, thereby necessitating re-keying (manual input) of individual trade details at various points. Even where connectivity existed between an STO's internal systems, a lack of consistent static data (primarily *security* and *counterparty* identifiers) prevented automatic passing of trade details from system to system.

From the STO's perspective, the objective is as follows: following trade execution, to input the details of individual trades once only, and from that point until the complete settlement of the trade, each of the steps should be managed in a fully automated fashion.

The trade lifecycle involves a series of steps, which includes both the internal and the external management of trades.

With regard to STOs communicating externally, similar concepts apply. For example, once a *settlement instruction* is transmitted by an STO, the management of the instruction by the custodian should ideally be effected on an STP basis.

In order to achieve STP, the STO is reliant upon two sets of information:

1. 'skeleton' trade details (which may be referred to as 'variable data') provided by the front office, and
2. supplementary trade details (which may be referred to as *static data*) provided by the operations area.

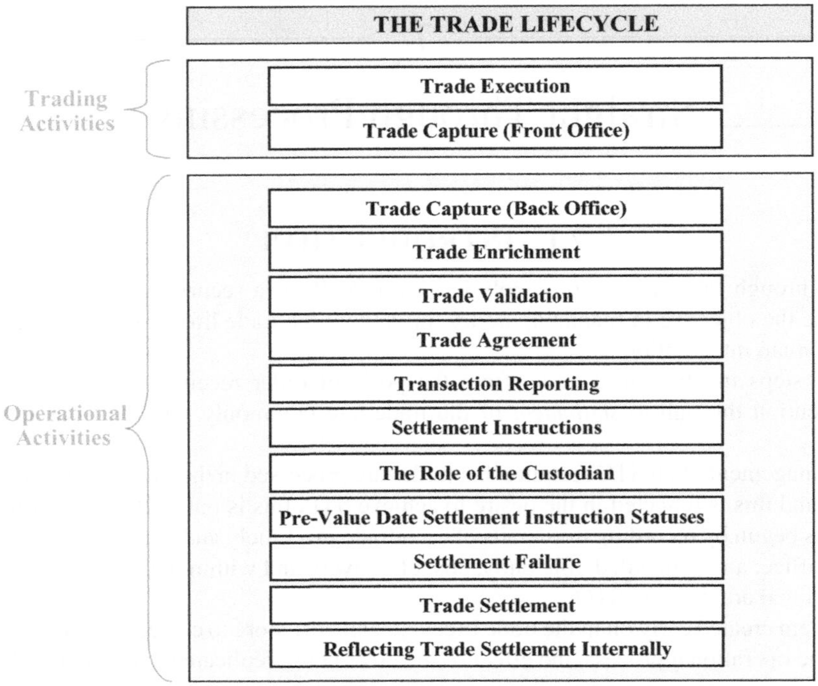

Figure 7.1 The trade lifecycle.

Providing the front office passes complete skeleton trade details to the operations area, STP may well be achievable if all the appropriate supplementary trade details can be attached to the skeleton trade details automatically.

The topic of Straight Through Processing of trades is discussed throughout the book *Securities Operations; a Guide to Trade and Position Management* by Michael Simmons (one of the authors of this book).

7.2 STP AND CORPORATE ACTIONS

STP in relation to the generic corporate action lifecycle components described in the previous chapter and illustrated in Figure 7.2, will be depicted at the appropriate points within the relevant chapters that immediately follow this chapter.

The value in managing its corporate actions processing in an STP fashion is that it allows the STO to focus its manpower on those steps that validly require human intervention (rather than to touch every single step of the process).

A meaningful example of this is the process of calculating *resultant entitlement* (Chapter 11). The STO may decide to operate on an STP basis for

- the calculation of resultant entitlement

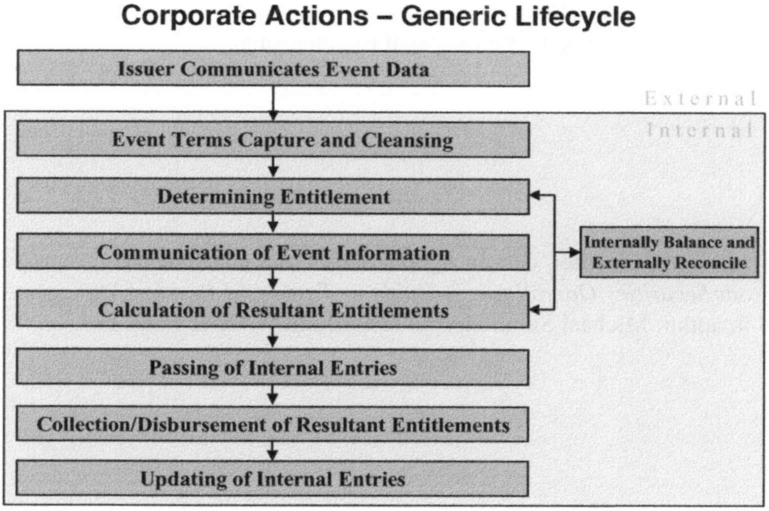

Figure 7.2 The corporate actions generic lifecycle.

which is determined by a set of rules that state 1) the securities *ratio*, 2) the treatment of *fractions*, and 3) the calculation sequence (each of which is fully described within Chapter 11). Following this calculation, however, the STO may opt to invoke a manual (and possibly occasional) check of such calculations, which may result in the need for the STO to adjust resultant entitlements manually where an imbalance has been identified (this is also described fully within Chapter 11).

However in reality, it is not unusual to find that within an STO's environment the successful management of corporate actions on an STP basis is reliant to a large degree on communication between the STO's various systems. The following are aspects of the STO's business that impact the processing and management of corporate actions:

- static data; a repository of security and counterparty data;
- trading systems; containing records of trades and trading positions at trading book level;
- settlement system; containing the detail of individual trades and their settlement status, plus *trading positions* and *settled custodian positions;*
- *safe custody* system; containing the detail of *custody clients'* holdings and whether trades are open with counterparties or settled at the *custodian*; and
- corporate actions event data; containing the details of events as supplied by one or more *data vendors*.

Each of these may supply one or more components of corporate actions into a discrete system:

- corporate actions system; containing the detail of individual corporate action events plus trading positions, *open trades* and settled custodian positions (for trading books and safe custody clients).

If the information contained within such systems is communicated correctly and in a timely manner, corporate actions-related STP may well be achievable.

ENDNOTE: within this chapter, certain figures, tables and text have been reproduced with permission from *Securities Operations: A Guide to Trade and Position Management*, ISBN 0-471-49758-4, author Michael Simmons, publisher John Wiley & Sons, Ltd.

8

Event Terms Capture and Cleansing

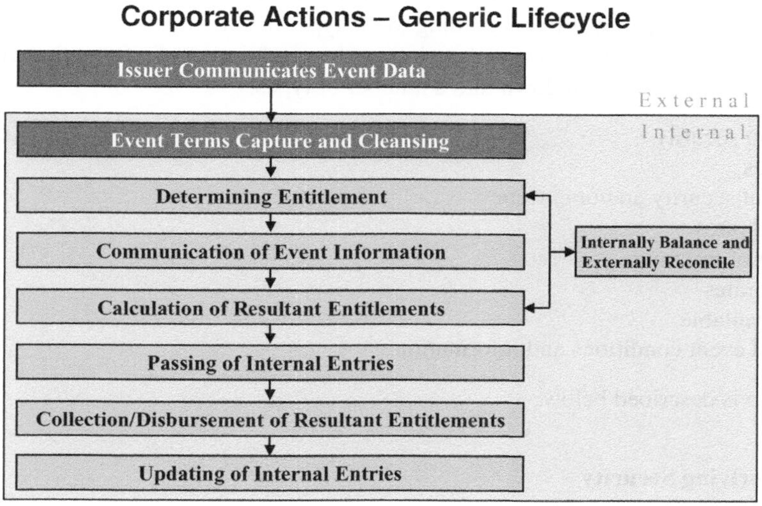

8.1 INTRODUCTION

The capture and recording of event terms is the first stage in any corporate action lifecycle, even for those corporate actions that do not result in any impact to the *position holder's* securities and/or cash positions. The purpose of this chapter is to describe the type of information necessary to record, and the process of managing this information throughout the lifecycle.

Event terms represents the collective conditions and information stipulated by the *issuer* pertaining to the *event*. The event terms will dictate which position holders and holdings are affected by the event, when they are affected and how the *resultant entitlements* applicable to those positions are calculated.

The accuracy and timeliness of capturing the event terms is critical to the STO's Corporate Actions Department. Errors in the information collected may result in the incorrect calculation of resultant entitlements, whilst delays may result in the STO missing critical dates in the application of the event to position holders.

'Cleansing' of event terms is a method of ensuring that the information captured is of the highest quality possible, thereby minimizing the risk of error in the calculation of resultant entitlements. It is the comparison and verification of event information from multiple sources.

Whilst this chapter will focus upon the capture and cleansing of event terms from the perspective of the STO, this stage equally applies to any holder of positions, custodians and investors alike.

8.2 EVENT TERMS

As stated previously, *event terms* refers to the collective conditions and information stipulated by the issuer pertaining to the event.

Generically the *event terms* set the conditions for which position holders are affected by the event, when they are affected, and the exact rules for the calculation of resultant entitlements. The exact type of information included may differ from event type to event type. The event examples, provided in Chapters 15 and 21, will serve to illustrate how the specific information included in event terms may differ according to the type (or classification) of event.

Generically, in addition to the event description, the conditions and information included in the event terms may be broken down into a number of types:

- Underlying security
- Event dates
- Entitlement security and/or currency
- Ratios and rates
- Treatment of fractions
- Exchange rates
- Options available
- Additional event conditions and information

Each of these is described below.

8.2.1 Underlying Security

The underlying security represents the security to which the event terms will be applied, resulting in the distribution of *benefits* to position holders in that security or the *re-organization* of their holding. Holders of the underlying security will be eligible for the event, pending the other conditions of the event.

An *issuer* may have at any point in time multiple types of securities in issue, with an event applying to one or many of those securities. It is therefore critical that the STO correctly identifies to which security(s) the event will apply. Failure to do so may result in the incorrect calculation of those positions and position holders to which the event applies with the end result being the incorrect calculation of *resultant entitlements*.

8.2.2 Event Dates

Fundamental to the terms of an event are the dates that apply to the event. Event dates include dates that set the conditions for *entitlement* to the event, due dates for the distribution of resultant entitlements or the effectiveness of the event, and deadline dates for those events where the position holder is required to communicate with the issuer.

Those dates that set the conditions for entitlement to the event are the Record Date and the Entitlement Date.

In the case of equities, the record date (also known as the 'Books Close Date' in some markets) is the date on which the issuer will close its books to identify registered *shareholders*. In the case of bonds, the record date is the date on which a *custodian* identifies its account holders to whom the event applies. The ways in which the record date is used are described more fully within Chapter 9, 'Determining Entitlement'. All events, irrespective of the type, normally have a record date. It is important to note that the closure of the books typically occurs after the close of business on the record date; therefore record date functions are normally performed after (and not before) this point. Consequently within this book, references to functions relating to record date are written from this perspective.

The entitlement date (also known as the Ex Date in some markets), applies predominantly to *benefit* events on equities. The entitlement date is the date used to determine whether a seller or buyer (irrespective of whether they hold a registered position as at the record date) is entitled to the benefit. How these dates combine to determine entitlement to an event is explored in detail in Chapter 9 ('Determining Entitlement').

Where an event results in the distribution of benefits or the re-organization of a holding, the event terms will also include a due date at which this will occur. This date may be known as the Payment Date or Distribution Date in the case of benefit events, and the Effective Date in the case of re-organizations.

For those events that offer the position holder a choice of options for its resultant entitlement, the event terms will also include deadline dates. At minimum will be a deadline date stipulated by the issuer, by which it is to receive communication of the position holder's election. The application of deadline dates and their impact to the management of an event is explored in more detail in Chapter 16 ('Concepts of Events with Elections').

As with all other information contained within the event terms, accuracy in the recording of the event dates is critical. Failure to ensure recording of correct event dates may result in the incorrect determination of entitled positions, errors in the timing of updating positions with the entitlement, or failure to communicate elections in a timely fashion. All such scenarios carry a risk of financial loss to the STO.

8.2.3 Entitlement Security and/or Currency

The Entitlement Security and/or Currency represent the security or currency that will:

- be distributed as a result of a *benefit*, or
- potentially replace the underlying security in the case of a *re-organization*.

The entitlement security may be the same as the *underlying security*, another existing security issued by the issuer, or a new security to be issued by the issuer. Some events may result in the distribution of multiple securities and/or currencies.

8.2.4 Ratios and Rates

This is a generic expression that refers to the amount of *resultant entitlement* in the entitlement security and/or currency that a position holder will receive as a result of the event, relative to its existing holding in the underlying security.

'Ratio' is often used where the event relates to an entitlement security. The ratio is made up of two numbers that state the quantity of the entitlement security, relevant to the underlying security.

In the majority of European and Asia Pacific markets:

- the first number will indicate the additional quantity of the entitlement security to be distributed, relative to
- the second number that indicates the quantity of the underlying security.

In the US market:

- the first number indicates the final holding after the event, relative to
- the second number that indicates the quantity of the original underlying security.

The impact of the differences in treatment of ratios according to market is most evident in benefit events where the entitlement security is the same as the underlying security, and is illustrated by the following example.

Assuming a rate of three for two, and an underlying holding of 10,000 XXX shares, the securities entitlement will be calculated as follows:

- In European and Asia Pacific Markets

  divide holding by 2 (10,000/2 = 5,000), multiply by 3 (5,000 × 3 = 15,000)

  which produces a resultant entitlement of 15,000 shares, which when added to the position holder's existing holding will result in a final holding of 25,000 (10,000 + 15,000) shares.

  The original holding has increased by 15,000 shares, as a result of the event.
- In US Markets

  divide holding by 2 (10,000/2 = 5,000), multiply by 3 (5,000 × 3 = 15,000)

  which produces a resultant entitlement of 15,000 shares, which replaces the position holder's existing holding and results in a final holding of 15,000 shares.

  The original holding has increased by 5,000 shares, as a result of the event.

In the above examples, note how the announcement using the same terms (i.e. a rate of three for two) produces dramatically different results due to the treatment within the different markets. Both the resultant entitlements and the resulting new holding in security XXX differ dramatically despite the original underlying holding being the same and the ratio appearing to be the same. It is essential to be aware of the different market treatments of ratios to avoid the incorrect calculation of resultant entitlements.

'Rate' is often used where the event is an entitlement to cash. The rate is made up of two numbers that state the quantity and units of the entitlement currency, relevant to the underlying security.

For example, '5 cents per share', or '150 pence per share'. Most commonly, a currency rate will be announced in the lowest unit of the entitlement currency. Nonetheless, this is not always the case. Failure to capture the correct units against the rate, i.e. putting the decimal point in the right place, will result in significant errors in the calculation of resultant entitlements. For example, assume a rate of GBP 150 is captured and applied to a holding of 10,000 XXX shares. This could represent either 150 pence per share, or alternatively 150 pounds per share. The first would result in an entitlement of GBP 15,000.00, whilst the second would result in an entitlement of GBP 1,500,000.00.

The application of Ratios and Rates is explored in more detail in Chapter 11 ('Calculation of Resultant Entitlements').

8.2.5 Treatment of Fractions

In addition to the announcement of Ratios and Rates, the event terms will also include conditions applying to the treatment of fractions in the calculation of resultant entitlements. This is because some rates may result in the creation of fractional entitlements, i.e. resultant entitlements that are not whole units of the underlying security.

For example, assume a rate of two new shares for every five shares held in security XXX, and an underlying holding of 99 XXX shares. To calculate the resultant entitlement the underlying holding will be divided by five, and then multiplied by two as follows.

To calculate the resultant entitlement

$$\text{divide holding by } 5\,(99/5 = 19.80),\ \text{multiply by } 2\,(19.80 \times 2 = 39.60)$$

which produces a whole number (39) plus a fractional amount (0.60).

The conditions pertaining to the treatment of fractions will indicate how the resultant entitlement is to be rounded to a whole unit.

Treatment of Fractions is explored in more detail in Chapter 11 ('Calculation of Resultant Entitlements').

8.2.6 Exchange Rates

As stated previously, the event may result in the distribution of an entitlement currency, or multiple currencies, and in these instances the event terms will include a rate for this distribution, together with specifying the entitlement currency itself.

It is possible that the distribution rate is specified in a currency other than that of the entitlement currency. This may occur when the issuer announces, for example, the distribution of income based upon an earnings per share rate in the issued currency ('par' currency) of the equity in question, but due to an excess foreign currency position on its books chooses to pay the income distribution in a currency other than the par currency. In this instance, the event terms will also include the announcement of the exchange rate between the par currency and the entitlement currency, in order to calculate *resultant entitlements*.

8.2.7 Options Available

As introduced in Chapter 1 ('Basic Corporate Action Concepts'), some events may be elective in nature, thereby offering the *position holder* a choice of how it participates, or whether it participates in the event at all.

The terms of such events will include the alternatives available to the position holder, known generically as 'options'. How options impact the Corporate Actions Department will be specifically explored in Chapter 16 ('Concepts of Events with Elections').

8.2.8 Additional Event Conditions and Information

The conditions and information contained within the event terms described so far can be considered quite generic to all types of events, with the exception of 'Options Available', which as previously stated applies only to events with elections.

Over and above these generic conditions and information, the event terms may include additional information, specific to the type of event or the market in which the event applies. This additional information may include:

- whether the event is taxable or non-taxable with respect to its immediate impact on the *position holder*, refer to Chapter 24 'Concepts and Management of Taxation';

- Shareholder Eligibility conditions, refer to Chapter 16, 'Concepts of Events with Elections;
- Directors Recommendations, for example recommendations in favour of acceptance of a Takeover.

8.3 SOURCES OF EVENT TERMS

The originating source of all *event terms* is the *issuer* of the underlying security to which the event applies (with the exception of Takeover terms, as described in Chapter 22 ('Concepts of Takeover Events'). The issuer will publicly announce the terms of the event to the market place (the timing of this is described in the following section). The terms will then be disseminated throughout the market place to interested parties. This will include:

- *CSDs/ICSDs*
- *Custodians*
- *Position holders*, including STOs, institutional and individual investors

In addition to the above, the event terms will be communicated to market regulators, and *data vendors*. Data vendors are organizations that provide the service of disseminating market data, which may include trading and price information, together with that of Corporate Actions Event Data to service subscribers, such as STOs and other market organizations. At the time of writing, examples of data vendors are Telekurs, Bloomberg, Reuters and Financial Information.

The potential flow of the event terms to market participants is illustrated by Figure 8.1, which also includes data vendors. As can be seen in the figure the event terms may take multiple routes before reaching their final destination. For example, the STO may capture the event terms directly from the issuer, via its CSD/ICSD or custodian (depending upon the location of the holding), and via a data vendor.

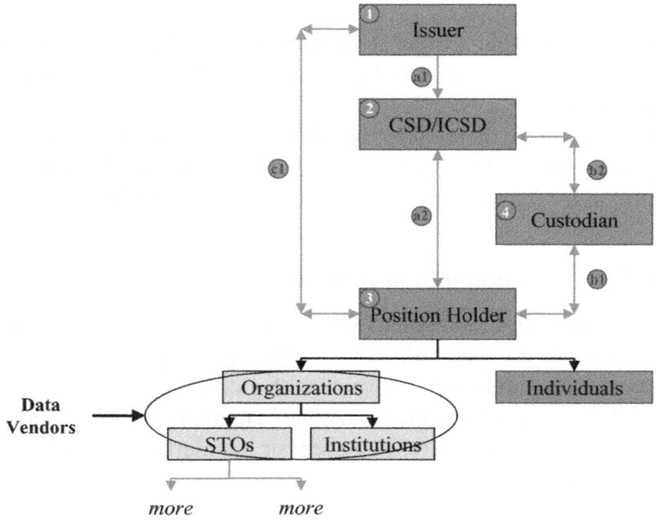

Figure 8.1 Flow of event terms.

The source of the event terms will normally dictate the timing of their availability, together with the recipient's perception of the reliability of the information captured. Both of these issues are explored in the following sections.

8.4 AVAILABILITY OF EVENT TERMS

As described in the previous section the originating source of all event terms is the issuer. The timing of the issuer's communication of event terms may occur either:

- upon issue of the security, or
- during the life of the security

Both of these are described below.

8.4.1 Upon Issue of the Security

Typically event terms available at the time of the issue of the security will apply to events on *bonds* and *warrants*, and therefore form part of the issue conditions of that security; for example, terms and schedule of the *coupon* (interest) payments due on the bond, together with details of the redemption (maturity) of the bond. This is because unlike *equities*, bonds represent debt (from the *issuer's* perspective), where the position holder lends *capital* to the issuer, and the terms of interest payable on that debt and the termination of that debt are legally required to be available at the issue of that debt (the same as any other cash borrowing situation).

Despite the terms of the event(s) being available at the time of issue of the security, they will not be acted upon by the STO (or other position holders) until a time closer to the appropriate dates of the event(s). For example, a bond may be issued with a commitment by the issuer to pay coupon interest on the same date each year throughout the 20-year life of the bond; clearly there is little purpose in calculating the resultant entitlement today, in relation to a coupon payment event scheduled to be paid (say) ten months from now.

It is important to note that despite the terms of the event being available at the time of the issue of the security making the event predictable, it may still not be guaranteed. It is possible for the issuer to be in default of coupon payments, or to allow, for example, the early redemption of the bond (should the terms of the issue permit it).

In addition, in specific circumstances, such as coupon payments on *floating rate notes* (where the interest rate changes on predetermined dates), it will be necessary to supplement the original announced terms with the coupon rate applicable to each coupon payment.

Care is therefore required to ensure that such terms are reviewed throughout the life of the security, when approaching forthcoming scheduled events. To assist in this process, many organizations employ the services of a *data vendor* despite the event terms having been known at the time of issue of the security.

8.4.2 During the Life of the Security

The majority of events falling within the category of 'announced by the issuer' during the 'life' of the security (hereafter referred to as 'announced events') apply to equities, and result from decisions made by the issuer's board of directors.

As such these events may be made at any time throughout the life of the security and are not predictable. These events include:

- Dividends
- Bonus Issues, and
- Share Splits.

Announced events, once approved by the board of directors and announced to the market place, are rarely withdrawn, and can therefore be considered as virtually guaranteed. The announcement of such events usually occurs a short period prior to the *record date* of the event.

Since announced events are not predictable and do not form part of the conditions of the issue of the security, the market place is completely reliant upon the accuracy of the event terms as announced and captured. Due to the increasing volumes and sometimes complexity of these events, recent times have seen increasing pressures on STOs and other organizations to ensure the timely and accurate capture of these event terms, in order to avoid the inevitable high costs associated with errors in this information.

8.5 CLEANSING OF EVENT TERMS

In order to ensure that information applied by the STO is of the highest quality possible, the cleansing of event terms compares and verifies event information from (potentially) multiple sources.

8.5.1 The Importance of 'Clean' Event Terms

The previous sections have highlighted the importance of capturing complete and accurate *event terms*. As stated previously, the event terms dictate which position holders and holdings are affected by the event, when they are affected and how the resultant entitlements applicable to those positions are calculated.

Failure to capture this information in a timely, complete and accurate fashion will expose the STO (and any other organization) to significant financial loss. In a less direct manner, such failure will have the inevitable impact on the efficiency of the STO's client service and consequent longer-term profitability.

To address these issues an increasing number of organizations are introducing the step of Cleansing of Event Terms within their operational flow. Despite this increased awareness there is still a significant absence of cleansing in many organizations, with complete reliance upon a single source of event terms (often from the custodian) to support the Corporate Actions Department.

Cleansing of event terms involves the comparison of all or some of the conditions and information pertaining to an event across a number of sources, and is applicable when the STO does not receive the information directly from the *issuer*, i.e. via other sources such as *data vendors*, CSDs/ICSDs and custodians. Cleansing may result in choosing one source over another for the entire event terms, or alternatively choosing one source over another for each piece of information within the event, thereby building a composite record of the event terms.

8.5.2 Approaches to 'Clean' Event Terms

A number of approaches are available to the STO in order to ensure 'clean' event terms, namely:

- Sourced from multiple External Data Providers;
- Sourced as pre-cleansed publicly available information; and
- Fully outsourced cleansing.

Sourced from Multiple External Data Providers (e.g. Bloomberg, FT) and CSDs/ICSDs and Custodians

In this approach the organization would assume the full responsibility for the cleansing step itself. It will collect the information from the various sources, compare individual pieces of information or entire announcements, and based upon a pre-defined set of rules select which information is deemed accurate to proceed with.

The advantage of this approach is that the STO may take full ownership of the operation in order to take responsibility for its own risk, whilst the disadvantage is that it is likely to require significant resource and/or automation investment on the part of the STO to support the process.

Sourced as Pre-Cleansed Publicly Available Information from External Data Providers (e.g. Fidelity), but Still Requiring Secondary Cleansing against Custodian Information

This approach involves the STO subscribing to a single external data provider that has previously verified the information being provided, prior to passing it on. The STO will then require only a secondary comparison against the information that its CSD/ICSD or custodian provides directly to it.

The advantages of this approach are the reduction in costs associated with the STO avoiding subscribing to multiple external data providers itself, with the STO still retaining some management of its own risk directly by being responsible for the cleansing against its own custodians' information. The STO still requires the investment to support the secondary cleansing, albeit on a potentially smaller scale than if it was responsible for the full cleansing operation.

Fully Outsourced Cleansing

In this approach the STO can completely outsource the cleansing operation to a third party. The third party would compare information from multiple external data providers, together with that information which the STO would normally receive directly from CSDs/ICSDs or custodians relating to their specific holdings.

The advantage of this approach is a significant reduction in cost for the support of the cleansing operation by the STO itself, as the third party would bare the brunt of all human resourcing and automation costs (although the cost of outsourcing needs to be considered). The perceived disadvantage to any operational outsourcing is the loss of control over the management of the operation.

8.5.3 Timing of Event Terms Cleansing

Where event terms are being captured from multiple sources and cleansing is employed in the operation, careful consideration is required as to the timing of the cleansing step. This is because it is highly likely that information will be received from different sources at different times between the initial announcement from the issuer and the point in time when the event comes into effect.

It would be possible to compare and cleanse progressively the event terms as received from each source, but this involves potentially unnecessary repetition of the process, and makes it unclear as to when a final clean set of event terms has been derived. The alternative is to choose a point in time offset and prior to the earliest event date (entitlement date or record date) as the date upon which cleansing takes place.

8.6 WHEN TO APPLY EVENT TERMS

Once a final set of clean event terms has been captured it is necessary to consider the timing of the next step within the corporate action lifecycle. This is the initiation of the true internal processing of the event, starting with the determination of entitlement, as described in the following chapter.

Timeliness is critical to ensure that all subsequent steps in the lifecycle can be adequately managed, for example the issuing of communications to position holders.

Typically it is expected that this will occur prior to the first of the event dates, either entitlement date (where applicable to the type of event) or the *record date*.

The exact timing of when to apply the event terms may differ according to the event type, the specific market to which the event applies and the level of automation which may be applied to the processing of the event, both internally and externally within the market place.

8.7 MANAGING CHANGES TO EVENT TERMS THROUGHOUT THE LIFECYCLE

Despite having captured and cleansed the event terms and being potentially part way through the lifecycle, updates or amendments to the event terms may actually be received throughout the lifecycle of the event. This may be because certain key pieces of information are not available until later in the event lifecycle, such as exchange rate, or simply because a correction to event information is received from one of the sources or even the issuer.

How the STO addresses such changes will depend upon the type of information and how far progressed through the lifecycle of the event is the operation. No such changes can be disregarded and must always be dealt with urgently. Some changes may impact steps in the lifecycle already undertaken therefore requiring a rework of that step, or alternatively may apply to a later stage in the lifecycle not yet commenced, therefore requiring an update to the event terms only.

For example, referring to the generic lifecycle shown in Figure 8.2, Table 8.1 illustrates some possible impacts of changes to event information on the STO's Corporate Actions Department, depending upon the type of change and where in the lifecycle it occurs.

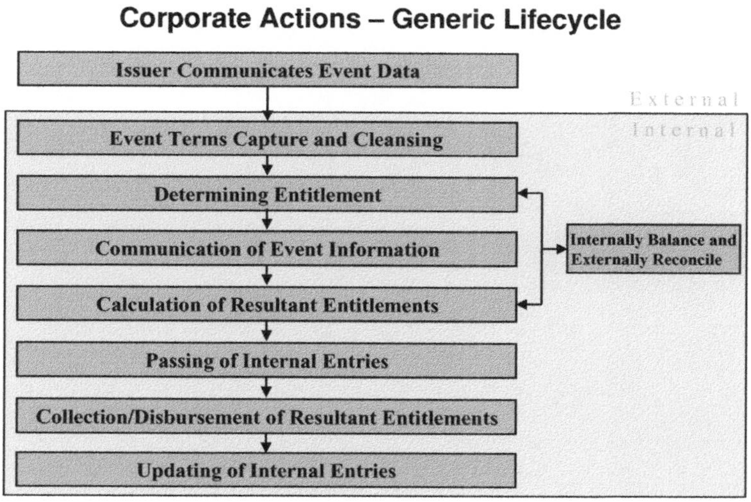

Figure 8.2 The corporate actions generic lifecycle.

Table 8.1

Change	Stage within Lifecycle Determining Entitlement	Communication to/from Position Holders	Calculation of Resultant Entitlements
Underlying Security	Rework	Rework	Rework
Ratio or Rate	No Impact	Rework	Rework
Record Date	Rework	Rework	Rework
Payment Date	No Impact	Rework	No Impact

8.8 SUMMARY

Many issues exist for the consideration of the STO in the capture and cleansing of event terms. The accuracy of the subsequent management of any event is heavily dependent upon this step, and the risks of financial loss due to inaccuracy are significant. Equally, the costs of resourcing and/or automating the process can be considerable.

The challenge is to achieve a balance between these two types of costs whilst not jeopardizing the efficiency or accuracy of the overall operation.

In addition, the issue of efficient integration of automated capture and cleansing to existing operations (which may also be automated) exists. Non-integration of these operational steps will increase potential re-keying of information across systems, thereby increasing the risk of error and decreasing the likelihood of achieving Straight Through Processing (*STP*).

9 Determining Entitlement

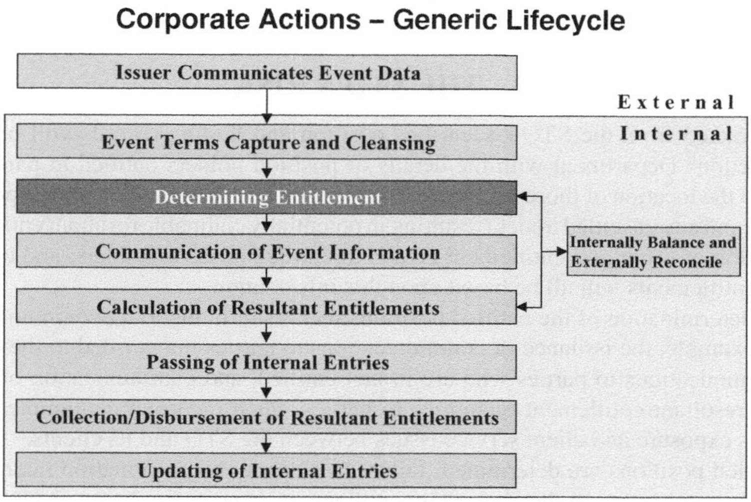

9.1 INTRODUCTION

Following on from Chapter 5 ('Securities Position Management'), which outlines the importance of securities position management to the Corporate Action process, it is now necessary to determine against which positions the terms of the event are to be applied, and to describe the process of ensuring that these position data are accurate and reconciled. In addition it is necessary to identify any *unsettled trades* that will result in *claims* and apply the terms of the event to these items. This is achieved by using conditions of the event terms and applying them to the STO's position, trading and settlement records.

Note: at this stage in the book the term 'claim' is being used in a generic sense to represent all situations where resultant entitlement of securities or cash are due to be received from or paid to *counterparties*.

The term, 'Determining Entitlement' therefore refers to the identification of accumulated trading and *settled custodian positions*, and unsettled trades (including securities loan/borrows and repos) that meet the conditions of the event terms. That is, such positions that are:

- in the *underlying security* of the event, and
- traded on an entitled (*cum*) basis.

This chapter describes the three steps involved in determining and managing entitled positions, including unsettled trades:

1. The methods of identifying such positions and trades based upon the conditions of the event terms and market conventions; the business principles are described separately for equity (Section 9.5) and bonds (Section 9.7) to illustrate the differences in these principles.
2. Proving the integrity of this information by ensuring that the total of the *ownership positions* is equal to the *location* sum.
3. Reconciliation of accumulated trading positions, settled custodian positions, and unsettled trades, with external parties (including reconciliation with other departments within the STO).

9.2 THE STO'S RISK

The data extracted from the STO's securities position and trading records will provide the Corporate Actions Department with the details of position holders entitled to participate in the event, and the location of those positions. The location is represented by settled positions at the custodian and any unsettled trades (resulting in potentially claimable resultant entitlements). Communication of event and entitlement details to entitled position holders, and calculation of resultant entitlements will all be based upon this information.

Incorrect determination of the entitled positions will result in incorrect communications to parties. For example, the issuance of communications to parties not entitled to the event, not issuing communications to parties who are in fact entitled, and communication of incorrect holding and resultant entitlement quantities to parties. Such incorrect communications can create serious exposure and client service issues between the STO and its clients.

Once entitled positions are determined, failure to balance this information internally may result in mismatches between those resultant entitlements expected to be received from locations, and those deliverable to position holders. Such an imbalance typically indicates an error in the determination of the entitled positions (including any unsettled trades).

Finally, failure to reconcile settled custodian positions with the custodian may result in the receipt of resultant entitlements other than those originally expected, again highlighting an error in the determination of entitled positions (including unsettled trades).

9.3 TYPES OF ENTITLED POSITIONS (INCLUDING UNSETTLED TRADES)

For the purposes of applying the corporate action terms, the Corporate Actions Department will identify entitled positions and trade information from the STO's position management records. This section is intended to describe the types of positions and trade information required to be identified and the reasons why. How the Corporate Actions Department will apply the terms of the event in order to perform this step is described in later sections of this chapter.

At the highest level the position and trade information can be categorized as:

- *Ownership Positions*, and
- The *Location* (of those positions).

(For details of how ownership positions and location are recorded and maintained refer to Chapter 5, 'Securities Position Management')

In order to manage the event efficiently, the Corporate Actions Department will, in addition, take a more granular view of the position and trade details extracted from the STO's securities position records and identify different types of ownership positions and different types of location positions, as described below.

9.3.1 Ownership Positions

Ownership positions represent those cumulative *trading positions* recorded on behalf of:

- *Trading books*, and
- *Custody clients*.

As described in Chapter 5 ('Securities Position Management'), the STO will record both the trade date and the value date of the trade, with the value date reflecting the date upon which the trade is intended to settle. As a consequence the STO will be able to identify cumulative positions based upon the trade date, as well as those based upon the value date.

In addition the STO will normally indicate 'long' trading positions with a positive sign, and 'short' trading positions with a negative sign. It is important when deriving entitled ownership positions that the Corporate Actions Department is able to identify long and short trading positions correctly. Where a trading position is long, this will result in the calculation of resultant entitlements to be disbursed to the position holder; whilst where a trading position is short, this will result in the calculation of resultant entitlements to be collected from the position holder.

When deriving entitled ownership positions for the purpose of applying the terms of the corporate action, the Corporate Actions Department will distinguish between those positions that are held on behalf of a trading book and those held on behalf of a custody client. This is because in many cases the operational procedures in managing communications, and the resultant entitlements, may differ between the two types of ownership.

As well as identifying the cumulative trading positions of position holders, the Corporate Actions Department may, according to the type of event, also identify within the cumulative trading position the portion of that position which is represented by:

- settled custodian positions, and
- unsettled trades.

This is a particular requirement to support the calculation of *resultant entitlements* for *re-organization* events. This topic is explored in more detail in Chapter 11 ('Calculation of Resultant Entitlements').

9.3.2 Location

The location of ownership positions will depend upon whether the constituent trade(s) that make up the position are settled or not as at the *record date* of the event. At the highest level therefore, the location may be represented by:

- solely settled custodian positions, or
- solely unsettled trades, or
- a combination of settled custodian positions and unsettled trades.

Settled Custodian Positions

Settled custodian positions reflect the cumulative settlements (both receipts and deliveries) which have taken place within the STO's accounts at its various custodians. The Corporate Actions Department will need to ensure that, as at the record date of the event, each settled position at each custodian account is identified for the purpose of applying the corporate action terms. Settled custodian positions will result in the calculation of resultant entitlements to be collected by the STO from the custodian.

Unsettled Trades

Unsettled trades will reflect both outstanding receipts and deliveries that are yet to settle (including those arising from *securities lending and borrowing*). In identifying unsettled trades, the Corporate Actions Department will identify each individual trade, not just the total (or sum) of unsettled trades. This is because each unsettled trade will result in an individual claimable situation either in favour of or against the STO for the resultant entitlement, with the counterparty of the unsettled trade.

Unsettled receipts of securities will result in the calculation of resultant entitlements to be collected by the STO from the trade *counterparty*, also known as claims 'in favour' of the STO.

Conversely, unsettled deliveries of securities will result in the calculation of resultant entitlements to be disbursed by the STO to the trade counterparty, also known as claims 'against' the STO.

It is imperative that the Corporate Actions Department correctly distinguishes between potential claims in favour or against the STO, in order to avoid subsequent errors in the collection and disbursement of resultant entitlements.

Combination of Settled Custodian Positions and Unsettled Trades

Of course, for an individual security it is entirely feasible that, as at the *record date* of the event, a combination of both *settled custodian positions* and *unsettled trades* (both due from and due to counterparties) may exist.

The view of *ownership positions* can be illustrated by the following series of tables.

Initially the STO's records reflect that as of 25th June (see Table 9.1):

- an ownership position of 2,000 Sony Corporation shares exists on behalf of Trading Book A, and
- an equal location position of 2,000 Sony Corporation shares exists at custodian Bank of Tokyo, Tokyo.

Table 9.1

Sony Corporation Shares (as at 25th June)			
Ownership		**Location**	
Trading Book 'A'	+2,000	−2,000	Custodian Bank of Tokyo, Tokyo
	+2,000	−2,000	

As at 25th June, if the terms of an event in Sony Corporation were to be applied to these positions, then the Corporate Actions Department would identify from this information the ownership position on behalf of Trading Book 'A' versus a single location (in this case the settled custodian position at custodian Bank of Tokyo). The resultant entitlement from the corporate action event would be collected by the STO from the custodian Bank of Tokyo, and disbursed to Trading Book 'A'.

Trading Book 'A' purchases a further 6,000 Sony Corporation shares on 1st July, from Counterparty 'X' (with a value date of 10th July). As a result of that purchase, the STO's records would appear as follows (see Table 9.2):

- an ownership position of 8,000 Sony Corporation shares exists on behalf of Trading Book A;
- the location is a combination of a settled custodian position and an unsettled trade
  - a settled custodian position of 2,000 exists at custodian Bank of Tokyo, Tokyo, and
  - an unsettled (purchase) trade of 6,000 exists with Counterparty 'X'.

Table 9.2

Sony Corporation Shares (as at 1st July)			
Ownership			**Location**
Trading Book 'A'	+8,000	−2,000	Custodian Bank of Tokyo, Tokyo
		−6,000	Counterparty 'X'
	+8,000	−8,000	

As at 1st July, if the terms of an event in Sony Corporation were to be applied to these positions, then the Corporate Actions Department would identify from this information the ownership position on behalf of Trading Book 'A' versus a combination of locations (in this case the settled custodian position at custodian Bank of Tokyo, and the unsettled trade with Counterparty 'X'). The resultant entitlement from the corporate action event would be collected by the STO from the custodian Bank of Tokyo and claimed from Counterparty 'X', and both disbursed to Trading Book 'A'.

Moving ahead to 10th July, when the purchase from Counterparty 'X' is due to settle, assuming that the trade settles, the STO's records would appear as follows (see Table 9.3):

- an ownership position of 8,000 Sony Corporation shares exists on behalf of Trading Book A, and
- an equal location position of 8,000 Sony Corporation shares exists at custodian Bank of Tokyo, Tokyo.

Table 9.3

Sony Corporation Shares (as at 10th July)			
Ownership			**Location**
Trading Book 'A'	+8,000	−8,000	Custodian Bank of Tokyo, Tokyo
	+8,000	−8,000	

As at 10th July, if the terms of an event in Sony Corporation were to be applied to these positions, then the Corporate Actions Department would identify from this information the ownership position on behalf of Trading Book 'A' versus a single location (in this case the settled custodian position at custodian Bank of Tokyo). The quantity of the ownership position on behalf of the trading book remains unchanged from 1st July, but the location now reflects the settlement (on 10th July) of the 6,000 shares purchased. The resultant entitlement from the corporate action event would be collected by the STO from the custodian Bank of Tokyo, and disbursed to Trading Book 'A'.

In the examples above, all positions and trades are assumed to qualify for the event. Nonetheless this is not always the case, according to the terms (applicable dates) of an event. This chapter will go on to describe these business rules, and their application to the STO's records, in order to identify which trading and settlement activity is entitled to participate in an event.

9.4 LINKS BETWEEN OWNERSHIP POSITIONS AND LOCATION POSITIONS

As described in Chapter 5 ('Securities Position Management'), under some circumstances the nature of its business may demand that the STO effectively maintains a direct link between ownership positions and their corresponding location (whether it be represented by a settled custodian position, or by an unsettled trade, or by a combination of both). Table 9.4 represents such a link.

Table 9.4

DEF Corporation Shares			
Ownership			Location
Client L (A/C 1)	+2000	−5000	Custodian Z, Custody A/C 1 – treaty
Client M (A/C 1)	+3000	−1500	Custodian Z, Custody A/C 2 – non-treaty
Client N (A/C 2)	+1500		
	+6500	−6500	

The benefits of this link are most significant to the Corporate Actions Department, in that it will provide them with the necessary information to:

- Manage exposure in the settlement of resultant entitlements, by ensuring that the disbursement of entitlements to the position holders occurs only once the entitlement is collected from the correct location for that ownership position. This approach to settlement is described further in Chapter 13 'Collection/Disbursement of Resultant Entitlements'.
- Accurately manage income tax liabilities between owners and locations (refer to Chapter 24 'Concepts and Management of Taxation').
- More easily identify the source of position reconciliation discrepancies if it is known which ownership positions constitute the location quantity that does not reconcile with the custodian.

Therefore, where the nature of the STO's business demands such record keeping, it is essential that the Corporate Actions Department ensures that where such a link exists that it is accurately reflected in the information associated with the entitled positions identified by them.

9.5 EQUITY EVENT ENTITLEMENT BUSINESS PRINCIPLES

Rather than utilizing all the conditions contained within the event terms, a subset is typically used in order to identify any entitled positions, including *unsettled trades* (using the STO's position management records). The positions and unsettled trades identified will be in the *underlying security* of the event, against which a set of business principles will be utilized when applying the event's *entitlement date* and *record date*.

The following sections describe the business principles that apply where both an entitlement date and a record date are applicable in determining entitlement; this is predominantly the case for equity benefit events. Note that determination of coupon entitlement on bonds is described in Section 9.7 of this chapter.

9.5.1 Entitlement Date

The Entitlement Date (also known as 'ex date') is the key date in determining whether a buyer or seller is entitled to participate in an event, and normally applies to *benefit* events, i.e. those events that result in an increase to the position holder's securities or cash position, without altering the underlying security. Note that the entitlement date does not usually apply to *re-organizations*, as for these events all positions and unsettled trades as at the record date will be impacted by the event.

For equity benefit events, the entitlement date normally precedes the record date in the event lifecycle and in theory allows sufficient time for those trades executed prior to the entitlement date to be settled by the record date of the event; i.e. the time between the entitlement date and the record date generally reflects the standard settlement cycle within the market. For example, in the Hong Kong equity market the standard settlement cycle is three days, and the usual gap between entitlement date and record date is two business days. Note that the entitlement date is usually set by the market, rather than by the issuer. However there are exceptions to the abovementioned sequence, for example UK *rights issues*, where the record date precedes the entitlement date.

Under normal circumstances, purchases prior to the entitlement date, known as *cum trading* will be entitled to participate in the event, whilst purchases on or after the entitlement date, known as *ex trading* will be excluded from participation in the event. The terms *cum* and *ex* are known as *trade conditions*. Refer to Section 9.5.3 of this chapter for further expansion of cum and ex trading.

Because of the change in entitlement status of trades before and after the entitlement date, the market price of the underlying security will normally reflect the value of the benefit to a buyer of the security. That is to say, that up to but not including the entitlement date of a benefit event, the security will become more attractive to a buyer as it will be entitled to receive the benefit and therefore the price paid for the security will increase to reflect this. Equally, on and after the entitlement date, when the buyer is no longer entitled to receive the benefit, the price of the security will drop.

The following example (Figure 9.1) illustrates the change in the market price of QANTAS Airways ordinary shares, as a result of the declaration of a *dividend* of AUD0.12 per share, reflecting the impact of the dividend only (and no other market influences).

Note that the prices and dividend used in this example are illustrative only.

Leading up to the announcement of the dividend, the shares are trading consistently in a price range of the low AUD3.20s. Upon the announcement of the dividend, the price of the share begins to rise to nearly AUD3.30 per share, illustrating the increased attractiveness of the security to investors as a result of the dividend.

On the entitlement date, 15th May, when purchases are no longer (under normal trading conditions) entitled to receive the dividend, the share price drops to reflect that the security is no longer as attractive, in terms of its entitlement to receive the dividend. Typically over the ensuing trading period the share price will revert to approximately that prior to the announcement of the dividend.

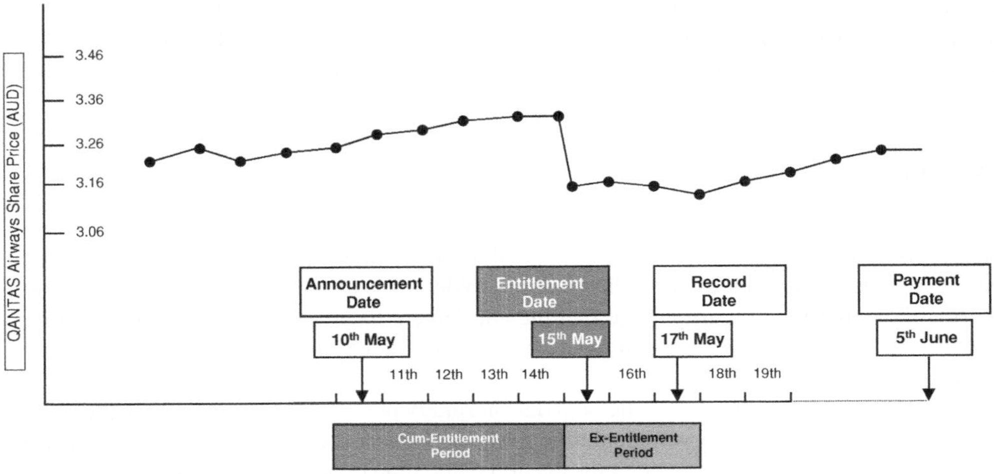

Figure 9.1 Example price change before and after entitlement date of a dividend.

The entitlement date is critical in identifying both entitled ownership positions as a result of trading, together with unsettled trades, i.e. those trades that are traded on a cum basis, but remain unsettled as at the record date of the event.

9.5.2 Record Date

The record date represents the date upon which the *issuer* or *custodian* identifies account holders of the underlying security. In practice, for *registered securities* such as *equities*, this will require the closing of the company *register* of shareholders on the record date.

The position at the issuer or custodian as at the record date will reflect all settlements that have taken place up to and including that date. It is against this position that it will disburse *resultant entitlements* or effect *re-organizations*.

However, in markets where paper registration remains in place, the STO will need to take account of the various stages of *settlement* and *registration*; that is, date settled, date sent for registration (in the case of a purchase) and date registered.

The issuer or custodian will not normally have any knowledge of the underlying trade conditions that make up the settled position, e.g. whether the trades were dealt cum or ex; or details of the *beneficial owners* to the trades, i.e. the trading book or client for whom the STO holds the position. Nonetheless, in some markets, the CSD/ICSD may take account of trade conditions as advised by the STO and its counterparty and adjust resultant corporate action entitlements accordingly.

The responsibility lies with the STO to identify entitled ownership as described in the previous section.

9.5.3 Normal Cum and Normal Ex Trading

Under normal trading circumstances the following rules of entitlement will apply.

During the *cum entitlement period*:

- the purchaser of a trade with a trade date prior to the entitlement date will gain entitlement to the benefit, and
- the seller of a trade with a trade date prior to the entitlement date will lose entitlement to the benefit.

During the ex *entitlement period*:

- the purchaser of a trade with a trade date on or after the entitlement date will not gain entitlement to the benefit, and
- the seller of a trade with a trade date on or after the entitlement date will retain entitlement to the benefit.

The above is illustrated in Figure 9.2.

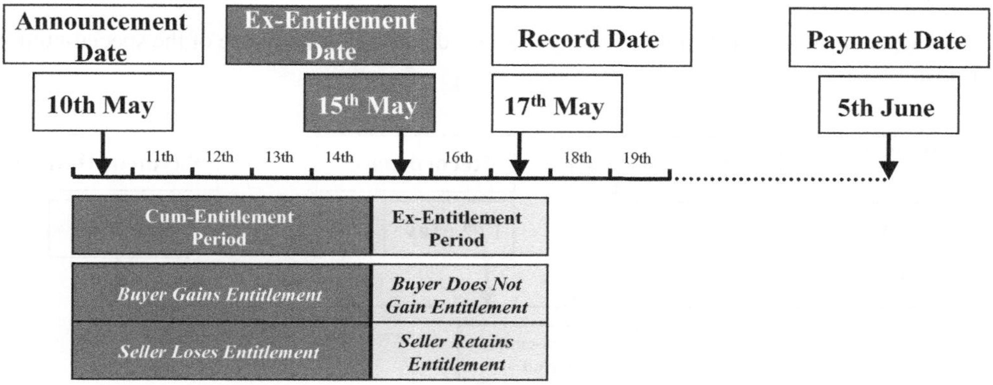

Figure 9.2 Rules of entitlement for normal cum and normal ex trading.

9.5.4 Special-Cum and Special-Ex Trading

As stated earlier in this section, during the cum entitlement period the market price of the underlying security will normally reflect the value of the benefit to a cum buyer, i.e. the underlying security will cost more during the cum entitlement period. This means that the buyer will pay more and receive the benefit, whilst the seller will receive a higher price but lose the benefit. The reverse occurs during the ex entitlement period.

In some markets, in addition to the normal trading conventions stated above, it is possible for a buyer and seller to agree to execute trades on a 'special' basis at prices outside of the normal cum and ex trading prices, and to reverse the normal entitlement rules. Trades executed under these circumstances are known as 'special trades'.

Two types of special trading exist. *Special-Ex trading* may occur during the cum entitlement period, whilst *Special-Cum trading* may occur during the ex entitlement period up to and including the record date (or payment date –1, according to market convention). The terms 'special-cum' and 'special-ex' are known as *trade conditions*; such trade conditions are the mechanism by which trades with unusual arrangements are communicated both internally within the STO, and externally between the STO and its client (usually on a *trade confirmation*).

Special-Ex Trading

- The purchaser of a special-ex trade with a trade date prior to the entitlement date will pay a lower price, and will not gain entitlement to the benefit, and
- The seller of a special-ex trade with a trade date prior to the entitlement date will receive a lower price, and will retain entitlement to the benefit.

Special-Cum Trading

- The purchaser of a special-cum trade with a trade date between the entitlement date and record date or payment date –1 (inclusive of these dates) will pay a higher price, and will gain entitlement to the benefit, and
- The seller of a special-cum trade with a trade date between the entitlement and record date or payment date –1 (inclusive of these dates) will receive a higher price, and will lose entitlement to the benefit.

The above is illustrated in Figure 9.3 (using the record date as the final date of the special-cum period).

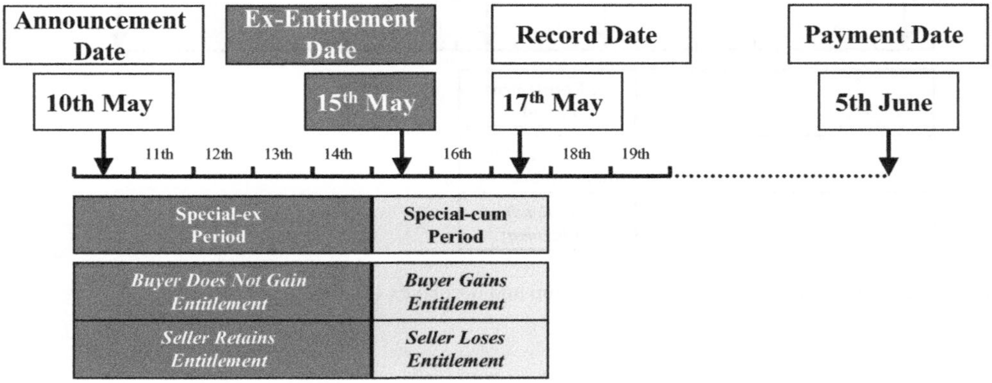

Figure 9.3 Rules of entitlement for special cum and special ex trading.

The procedure to determine entitled positions and to identify any *unsettled trades* must take into account any special trading. To ensure accuracy, the Corporate Actions Department will be reliant upon any special trades being easily identifiable by the use of the correct special trade conditions. This procedure will also include any repos and securities borrowing/lending transactions during the period in question.

9.5.5 Special Value Date

Where an ex entitlement period exists for an event, the length of that period is expected to mirror the normal *settlement cycle* for the particular market. Therefore any trades executed prior to the entitlement date typically have a *value date* on or before the record date, and trades executed on or after the entitlement date typically have a value date after the record date. Assuming perfect settlement, i.e. no *failed settlements* or early settlements, then only cum positions would be reflected in the settled custodian position.

This is illustrated in Figure 9.4;

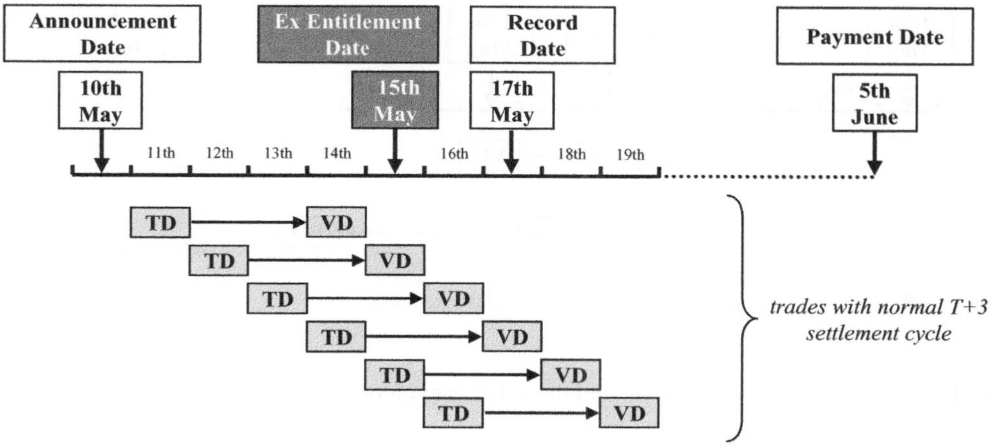

Figure 9.4 Relationship between a T+3 settlement cycle, entitlement date and record date.

However, in reality this is not always the case. It is possible to execute a trade on or after the entitlement date on an ex entitlement basis, but with a short value date (i.e. with a trade date to value date period that is shorter than the standard settlement cycle) which settles prior to the record date. In this case the buyer will receive the entitlement within its location position, as the custodian would not be expected to know that the trade was executed on an ex entitlement basis, but it will not be entitled to it. Assuming that the trade settles on the agreed short value date then this will result in a reverse claim, where the entitlement will be returned to the seller. Should settlement of the trade fail on or prior to the record date then no action is required.

Conversely it is possible to execute a trade prior to the entitlement date on a cum basis, but with a long value date (i.e. with a trade date to value date period that is longer than the standard settlement cycle) which settles after the record date. In this case the seller will receive the entitlement within its location position, as the custodian may not be aware that the trade was executed on a cum entitlement basis, but it will not be entitled to it. (Note that in some market places, custodians are able to recognize such special trades and can therefore adjust the location entitlement quantity. This topic is described in more detail in Section 9.5.6 of this chapter, and in Chapter 13, 'Collection/Disbursement of Resultant Entitlements').

Assuming that the trade settles on the agreed long value date then this will result in a claim, where the entitlement will be claimed by the buyer. Should settlement of the trade occur on or prior to the record date then no action is required (however, early settlement is unlikely).

Figure 9.5 illustrates two special value date trades, together with a description of the impact of settlement both prior to and after the record date, on the location of the entitlement.

Trade A

In cases where the STO has purchased securities (on behalf of a trading book) on a normal ex basis, with the trade date on or after the entitlement date (and therefore the trading book is not

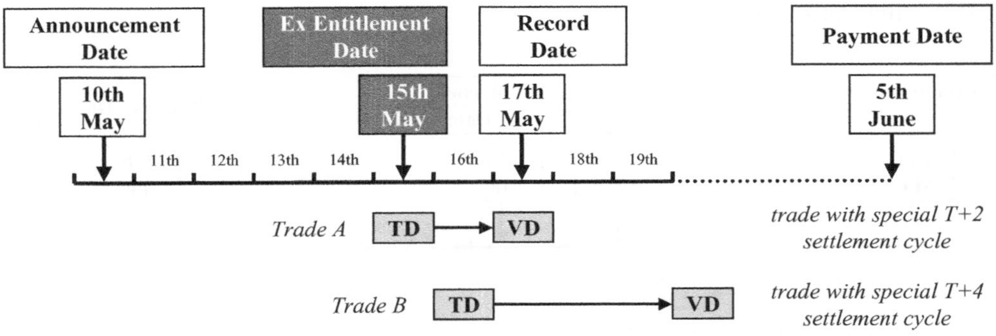

Figure 9.5 Rules of entitlement for trades with special value dates.

entitled to the resultant entitlement), and the value date on or prior to the record date, then

- where settlement occurs on value date (or prior to record date), the resultant entitlement will be received by the STO within its settled custodian position, but entitlement will be due to the selling counterparty. Consequently this will result in a claim against the STO.
- where settlement does not occur on value date (or by the record date), the resultant entitlement will not be received by the STO within its settled custodian position, and therefore will be received directly by the selling counterparty. Consequently no claim is applicable.

In cases where the STO has sold securities (on behalf of a trading book) on a normal ex basis, with the trade date on or after the entitlement date (and therefore the STO/trading book is entitled to the resultant entitlement), and the value date on or prior to the record date, then

- where settlement occurs on value date (or prior to record date), the resultant entitlement will be received by the buying counterparty, but entitlement will be due to the STO. Consequently this will result in a claim against the counterparty and in favour of the STO.
- where settlement does not occur on value date (or by the record date), the resultant entitlement will be received by the STO within its settled custodian position. Consequently no claim is applicable.

Trade B

In cases where the STO has purchased securities (on behalf of a trading book) on a normal ex basis, with the trade date on or after the entitlement date (and therefore the STO/trading book is not entitled to the resultant entitlement), and the value date later than the record date, then

- where settlement occurs on (or after) value date, the resultant entitlement will not be received by the STO within its settled custodian position. Consequently no claim is applicable.
- in the extremely unlikely circumstance of settlement occurring prior to value date and no later than the record date, the resultant entitlement will be received by the STO within its settled custodian position, but entitlement will be due to the selling counterparty. Consequently this will result in a claim against the STO.

In cases where the STO has sold securities (on behalf of a trading book) on a normal ex basis, with the trade date on or after the entitlement date (and therefore the STO/trading book is entitled to the resultant entitlement), and the value date later than the record date, then

- where settlement occurs on (or after) value date, the resultant entitlement will be received by the STO within its settled custodian position. Consequently no claim is applicable.
- in the extremely unlikely circumstance of settlement occurring prior to value date and no later than the record date, the resultant entitlement will be received by the buying counterparty, but entitlement will be due to the STO. Consequently this will result in a claim in favour of the STO.

9.5.6 Depot Adjustment Date/Compensation Date

Some markets, for example the US equity market, support a Depot Adjustment Date (also known as a Compensation Date). This date typically applies to *benefit* events and occurs after the record date and prior to the Payment or Distribution Date of an event.

Under normal circumstances (where this date does not apply), the STO's settled custodian position held at a CSD/ICSD will reflect all settlements that have take place up to and inclusive of the record date of the event (as described in the previous sections). Where the depot adjustment date does apply to an event, the CSD/ICSD will take account of *cum* trades (both normal and special-cum) that have settled past the record date and up to and inclusive of the depot adjustment date. In doing so, the CSD/ICSD will adjust the record date quantity against which the STO will receive entitlement, thereby avoiding the need for the STO (or the trade counterparty) to initiate claims for those cum trades that have been settled between the record date and the depot adjustment date.

Figure 9.6 has a record date of 13th March and a depot adjustment date of 16th March.

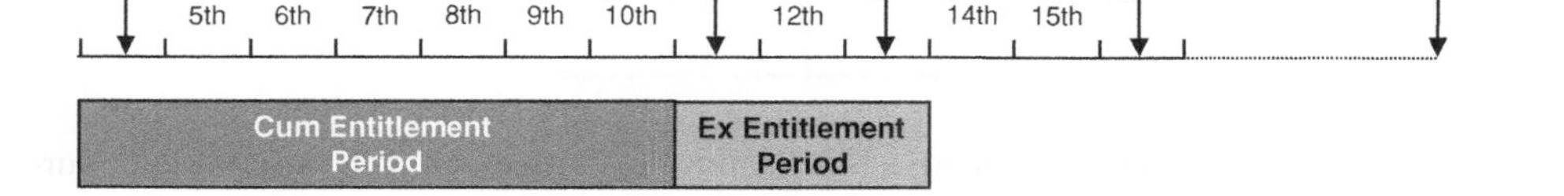

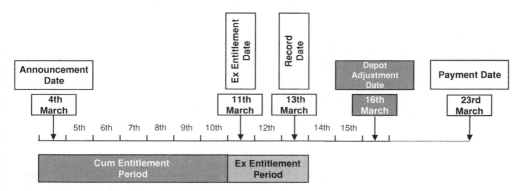

Figure 9.6 Typical event timeline with depot adjustment date.

As at 10th March, the STO's position records appear as shown in Table 9.5.

Table 9.5

Colgate-Palmolive Shares (as at 10th March)			
Ownership			**Location**
Trading Book 'A'	+9,000	–3,000	Custodian J.P. Morgan, New York
		–6,000	Counterparty 'X'
	+9,000	–9,000	

Between the 11th March and 13th March (record date) inclusive, the STO continues to trade and settle Colgate-Palmolive shares as follows:

- settle a purchase of 6,000 shares (with counterparty 'X') on a trade basis of 'normal cum', and
- Trading Book 'A' purchases 8,000 shares on a trade basis of 'special cum' from counterparty 'Y'.

As at the 13th March (record date) the STO's position records appear as shown in Table 9.6.

Table 9.6

Colgate-Palmolive Shares (as at 13th March)			
Ownership		Location	
Trading Book 'A'	+17,000	−9,000	Custodian J.P. Morgan, New York
		−8,000	Counterparty 'Y'
	+17,000	−17,000	

The result of the settlement of 6,000 shares purchased from Counterparty 'X' is a settled custodian position of 9,000 Colgate-Palmolive shares as at the record date of 13th March.

During the period 14th March to 16th March (Depot Adjustment Date) inclusive, the STO settles the following trade:

- purchase 8,000 shares (with counterparty 'Y') on a trade basis of 'special cum'.

As a result, the custodian will adjust the record date position of the STO (for the purpose of applying the corporate action event only), reflecting an increase of 8,000 shares as a result of the settlement of the special-cum purchase prior to and inclusive of the depot adjustment date. (In parallel, the selling counterparty's record date position will be reduced to reflect its delivery to the STO prior to and inclusive of the depot adjustment date.)

The final settled custodian position against which the STO will collect entitlement is 17,000 shares (9,000 settled as at record date and a further 8,000 settled after the record date and by the depot adjustment date). As a result, the STO will not need to claim the resultant entitlement against the special-cum purchase of 8,000 shares from the selling counterparty.

The final positions to which the terms of the event will be applied are as shown in Table 9.7.

Table 9.7

Colgate-Palmolive Shares – Final Entitled Positions			
Ownership		Location	
Trading Book 'A'	+17,000	−17,000	Custodian J.P. Morgan, New York
	+17,000	−17,000	

It is important to note that the effective 'backdating' of settlement of the special-cum purchase only affects the positions utilized by the Corporate Actions Department. The settlement and position keeping operations of the STO should record settlement of all trades (whether they be cum or ex) as at the actual settlement date.

9.6 EQUITY EVENT – ITEMIZED TRADING AND SETTLEMENT SCENARIOS

In order to enable the reader to gain a more detailed understanding of determining entitlement, the business principles described in Section 9.5 are brought together within Tables 9.8–9.11.

Table 9.8 Normal cum trading

Basis	Trading (from the STO's perspective) Operation	Trade Date	Value Date	Entitlement Due to?	Actual Settlement Date?	Holding in STO's Settled Custodian Position as at RD?	Claim Situation?
Normal Cum (normal VD)	Buy	Prior to Ent Date	On or prior to RD	STO	On or prior to RD	Yes	No claim applicable
Normal Cum (normal VD)	Buy	Prior to Ent Date	On or prior to RD	STO	Later than RD	No	Claim in favour of the STO
Normal Cum (normal VD)	Sell	Prior to Ent Date	On or prior to RD	Buying Counterparty	On or prior to RD	No	No claim applicable
Normal Cum (normal VD)	Sell	Prior to Ent Date	On or prior to RD	Buying Counterparty	Later than RD	Yes	Claim against the STO
Normal Cum (long VD)	Buy	Prior to Ent Date	Later than RD	STO	Later than RD	No	Claim in favour of the STO
Normal Cum (long VD)	Buy	Prior to Ent Date	Later than RD	STO	No later than RD (unlikely)	Yes	No claim applicable
Normal Cum (long VD)	Sell	Prior to Ent Date	Later than RD	Buying Counterparty	Later than RD	Yes	Claim against the STO
Normal Cum (long VD)	Sell	Prior to Ent Date	Later than RD	Buying Counterparty	No later than RD (unlikely)	No	No claim applicable

Table 9.9 Normal ex trading

Basis	Trading (from the STO's perspective) Operation	Trade Date	Value Date	Entitlement Due to?	Actual Settlement Date?	Holding in STO's Settled Custodian Position as at RD?	Claim Situation?
Normal Ex (normal VD)	Buy	On or after Ent Date	Later than RD	Selling Counterparty	Later than RD	No	No claim applicable
Normal Ex (normal VD)	Buy	On or after Ent Date	Later than RD	Selling Counterparty	No later than RD (unlikely)	Yes	Claim against the STO
Normal Ex (normal VD)	Sell	On or after Ent Date	Later than RD	STO	Later than RD	Yes	No claim applicable
Normal Ex (normal VD)	Sell	On or after Ent Date	Later than RD	STO	No later than RD (unlikely)	No	Claim in favour of the STO
Normal Ex (Short VD)	Buy	On or after Ent Date	On or prior to RD	Selling Counterparty	On or prior to RD	Yes	Claim against the STO
Normal Ex (Short VD)	Buy	On or after Ent Date	On or prior to RD	Selling Counterparty	Later than RD	No	No claim applicable
Normal Ex (Short VD)	Sell	On or after Ent Date	On or prior to RD	STO	On or prior to RD	No	Claim in favour of the STO
Normal Ex (Short VD)	Sell	On or after Ent Date	On or prior to RD	STO	Later than RD	Yes	No claim applicable

Table 9.10 Special-cum trading

Basis	Trading (from the STO's perspective) Operation	Trade Date	Value Date	Entitlement Due to?	Actual Settlement Date?	Holding in STO's Settled Custodian Position as at RD?	Claim Situation?
Special-Cum (normal VD)	Buy	On or After Ent Date	Later than RD	STO	Later than RD	No	Claim in favour of the STO
Special-Cum (normal VD)	Buy	On or After Ent Date	Later than RD	STO	No later than RD (unlikely)	Yes	No claim applicable
Special-Cum (normal VD)	Sell	On or After Ent Date	Later than RD	Buying Counterparty	Later than RD	Yes	Claim against the STO
Special-Cum (normal VD)	Sell	On or After Ent Date	Later than RD	Buying Counterparty	No later than RD (unlikely)	No	No claim applicable
Special-Cum (Short VD)	Buy	On or After Ent Date	On or prior to RD	STO	On or prior to RD	Yes	No claim applicable
Special-Cum (Short VD)	Buy	On or After Ent Date	On or prior to RD	STO	Later than RD	No	Claim in favour of the STO
Special-Cum (Short VD)	Sell	On or After Ent Date	On or prior to RD	Buying Counterparty	On or prior to RD	No	No claim applicable
Special-Cum (Short VD)	Sell	On or After Ent Date	On or prior to RD	Buying Counterparty	Later than RD	Yes	Claim against the STO

Note: the above table illustrates the entitlement rules applicable to special-cum trading, based upon the record date being the last date of the special-cum trading period. As indicated earlier, in some markets the last date of the special-cum trading period can be payment date −1.

Table 9.11 Special-ex trading

	Trading (from the STO's perspective)						
Basis	**Operation**	**Trade Date**	**Value Date**	**Entitlement Due to?**	**Actual Settlement Date?**	**Holding in STO's Settled Custodian Position as at RD?**	**Claim Situation?**
Special-Ex (normal VD)	Buy	Prior to Ent Date	On or prior to RD	Selling Counterparty	On or prior to RD	Yes	Claim against the STO
Special-Ex (normal VD)	Buy	Prior to Ent Date	On or prior to RD	Selling Counterparty	Later than RD	No	No claim applicable
Special-Ex (normal VD)	Sell	Prior to Ent Date	On or prior to RD	STO	On or prior to RD	No	Claim in favour of the STO
Special-Ex (normal VD)	Sell	Prior to Ent Date	On or prior to RD	STO	Later than RD	Yes	No claim applicable
Special-Ex (Long VD)	Buy	Prior to Ent Date	Later than RD	Selling Counterparty	Later than RD	No	No claim applicable
Special-Ex (Long VD)	Buy	Prior to Ent Date	Later than RD	Selling Counterparty	No Later than RD (unlikely)	Yes	Claim against the STO
Special-Ex (Long VD)	Sell	Prior to Ent Date	Later than RD	STO	Later than RD	Yes	No claim applicable
Special-Ex (Long VD)	Sell	Prior to Ent Date	Later than RD	STO	No Later than RD (unlikely)	No	Claim in favour of the STO

These tables are segregated by their basis:

- Normal cum trading
- Normal ex trading
- Special-cum trading
- Special-ex trading

Within each table, the effect of the actual settlement date (e.g. settlement date later than record date) is considered regarding whether the trade forms part of the STO's settled custodian position as at record date, and correspondingly whether a claim situation exists.

9.7 BONDS EVENT ENTITLEMENT BUSINESS PRINCIPLES

For *coupon payments* on bonds, in parallel with entitlement calculation on equities, a subset of the event conditions is typically used in order to identify any entitled positions, including *unsettled trades* (using the STO's position management records). The positions and unsettled trades identified will be in the *underlying security* of the event, against which a set of business principles will be utilized when calculating entitlement. The following sections describe the business principles that apply to coupon payments.

9.7.1 Determining Entitlement

The coupon payment date on *fixed rate bonds* is predictable as is the *record date*, which is normally a fixed number of days (commonly one business day) prior to the coupon payment date. In general, entitlement is determined by the *value date* of trades in relation to the coupon payment date (although different practices exist in different markets). It is recommended that the *accrued interest* section of *Securities Operations: A Guide to Trade and Position Management* (ISBN 0-471-49758-4) be read prior to or in conjunction with the following.

When buying an interest-bearing bond, the buyer compensates the seller for the proportion of coupon earned since the previous coupon payment date. In turn, that buyer will be compensated by either:

- selling the bond and receiving compensation from the (new) buyer; or
- retaining the bond beyond the entitlement date for the next coupon payment and receiving compensation from the issuer on the coupon payment date.

Figure 9.7 illustrates the principles of how to calculate entitlement to a coupon payment (where record date is payment date –1).

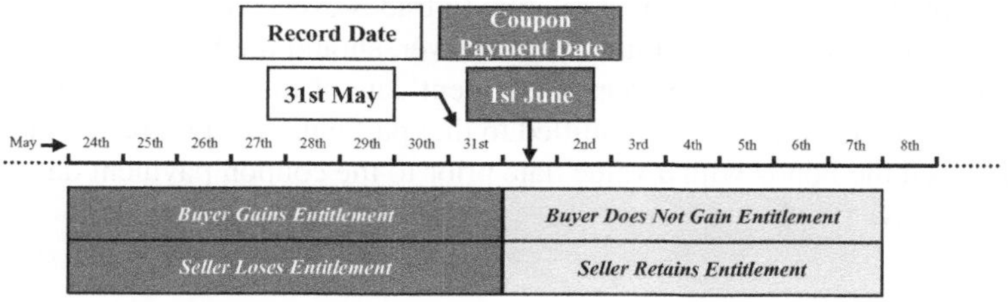

Figure 9.7 Calculation of entitlement to coupon payments (record date is payment date −1).

In essence (in the example stated in Figure 9.7), during the coupon period immediately prior to the coupon payment date:

- the purchaser of a trade with a value date on or prior to the record date will be entitled to the coupon payment; and
- the seller of a trade with a value date on or prior to the record date will lose entitlement to the coupon payment.

During the period immediately following the coupon payment date:

- the purchaser of a trade with a value date after the record date will not gain entitlement (to the coupon payment that is being made); and
- the seller of a trade with a value date after the record date will retain entitlement.

For example, using the dates in Figure 9.7, if an STO buys USD 1 million bonds on (trade date) 25th May, for value date 28th May (T + 3) from Counterparty G, the STO will need to pay the seller the cash value of 357 days of accrued interest. From the seller's perspective, he has received compensation (via the 357 days paid by the STO), so cannot also expect to receive the coupon payment of (in this case) a full year of 360 days. However, from the buying STO's perspective, it has paid out 357 days to the seller, and therefore does expect to receive the coupon payment for the full year, providing the STO does not sell with a value date prior to the record date.

Assuming that the STO executes no more trades on or before the record date, on 31st May the STO's books & records will be as shown in Table 9.12.

Table 9.12

ABC 8.25% Bonds 1st June 2020 (as at 31st May)			
Ownership		Location	
Trading Book 'A'	+1,000,000	−1,000,000	Custodian X Main Account
	+1,000,000	−1,000,000	

Having previously captured the detail of this particular coupon payment (within its static data repository, typically at the time of issue launch), the STO needs to assess whether it (or its safe custody clients) is entitled to the coupon payment, by viewing its books & records as at the record date. The STO is therefore entitled to the coupon for the entire coupon period (in this case one year), on USD 1 million bonds, which at a rate of 8.25%, equates to USD 82,500.00; the next task is to determine from whom the benefit will be received.

Note that where the number of days between record date and payment date is greater than one day, the purchaser of a trade with a value date during this period will gain entitlement.

Providing the STO continues to own the bonds, it will be entitled to future coupon payments. The above example looked at entitlement relating to trades executed immediately prior to the coupon payment date within a particular year, however, should the STO maintain its holding of USD 1 million bonds beyond the coupon payment date of the following coupon payment (due 12 months later), the STO will be entitled to that particular coupon payment as the STO will have purchased the bonds with a value date prior to the coupon payment date, more than 12 months previously.

9.7.2 Record Date

For *bearer securities*, payment of coupon by the issuer is made on the payment date, to those that present the relevant coupons (originally attached to the bond certificate) to the issuer's appointed *coupon paying agent*.

In parallel with registered securities, an entitled buyer will receive its benefit direct from the issuer, without having to claim it from the seller, providing the security is delivered to the buyer (or its custodian) on or prior to the record date. The buyer would then detach the relevant coupon from the bond certificate and present the coupon to the coupon paying agent who will first verify the authenticity of the coupon before paying the interest amount on the coupon payment date. The holder of a bond who fails to present the coupons by the coupon payment date will suffer a delay in receiving its benefit.

The majority of STOs use local custodians, *NCSDs* or *ICSDs* as custodians in order to hold their securities and to receive and deliver securities that have been purchased or sold. One custodian is likely to hold the securities on behalf of numerous account holders, and part of the service that custodians provide to their account holders is:

- the cutting of coupons;
- the presentation of coupons to the coupon paying agent;
- the collection of the benefit; and
- the distribution of the benefit to the appropriate holders.

For example, a custodian may be holding a total of USD 95 million face value of bonds, from which it cuts the relevant coupon, the latter being presented to the coupon paying agent. Typically, this occurs just prior to the coupon payment date, to ensure that the payment of the benefit is not delayed. The custodian will need to distribute the coupon payment on USD 95 million bonds, in proportion to the holdings of its account holders. This is achieved by the custodian adopting a record date method, where all holders of the security as at close of business on the record date will be credited with the coupon amount proportional to their record date holding. In the case of Clearstream Luxembourg and Euroclear, the record date is usually one day prior to the coupon payment date.

Therefore, providing the STO's books & records are up-to-date and accurate, the information held on the 'location' side of the books & records will tell the STO from whom the benefit is receivable. For instance, if the entire quantity of entitled securities was held within the STO's account at the custodian on or before the record date, this would tell the STO to expect the benefit to be received from the custodian (without needing to *claim* from a selling counterparty). Alternatively, if as at the record date the delivery of securities relating to the STO's purchase had not occurred, this shows that the benefit is due from the seller.

In a situation where the STO itself processes physical bearer bonds, adequate procedures should be in place (within the settlements department) to ensure that any receipts or deliveries of such securities are effected with the correct coupons attached. For example, a receipt of bearer bonds with previously collectible coupons attached is (under normal market practice) regarded as a bad delivery and as such should be returned to the deliverer without payment.

Note that when selling securities that are not delivered to the buyer prior to the close-of-business on record date, the STO will receive a benefit payment to which it is not entitled. The subject of claims is detailed within Chapter 13, 'Collection/Disbursement of Resultant Entitlements'.

9.8 APPLYING THE BUSINESS PRINCIPLES IN PRACTICE

The STO will endeavour to identify, as at the *record date* of the event, all:

- *Ownership positions*, comprising
  - *Trading book* positions, and
  - *Custody client* positions
- *Location* components, comprising
  - *Settled custodian positions*
  - *Unsettled trades* resulting in *claims* in favour of the STO
  - Unsettled trades resulting in claims against the STO

It does this using the terms and the conditions of the event (as described earlier in this chapter and in Chapter 8 ('Event Terms Capture and Cleansing'), these primarily being:

- the *underlying security*
- the event *entitlement date* (where applicable), and
- the event *record date*.

The purpose of this exercise is to identify all of those situations that will result in resultant entitlements to be collected and disbursed by the STO (refer to Chapter 11, 'Calculation of Resultant Entitlements', for details of the actual calculation).

In practice, the exercise of *determining entitlement* is not simply a matter of the Corporate Actions Department taking an extract of ownership positions and location components from the position keeping records of the STO, and applying the event terms to that information. The Corporate Actions Department must take this information and create its own view of it, based upon the business principles described earlier in this chapter, ensuring that only relevant trading and settlements are included.

As described previously, whilst the majority of *cum trading* takes place prior to the entitlement date, it is possible for further special-cum trading to take place up to and including the record date (or payment date –1) of the event. For this reason it is necessary to monitor trading until the record date (or payment date –1), using the business principles described previously.

The business principles described in the earlier section provide the STO with a set of rules with which to identify the entitled positions including unsettled trades in the underlying security of the event, from the securities position records. This section describes the application of these rules in practice. Note that for ease of understanding, the explanations and illustrations utilize the record date as the final date of the special-cum period.

Ideally the Corporate Actions Department will design a single process (whether this be manual or automated), which accurately identifies such positions and trades, accommodating:

- events with or without an ex period, and
- the identification of cum trading during the ex period (where applicable).

In addition, the Corporate Actions Department extracts position and trade data from the securities position records as at a single date, thereby ensuring stricter control on the integration of the data.

The business principles described in the earlier section can be translated into a number of rules that the Corporate Actions Department may apply, in order to satisfy this requirement and identify the different types of positions and unsettled trades. These rules, which are described below, cover:

- identification of ownership positions;
- identification of settled custodian positions;
- identification of potential claims.

9.8.1 When to Determine Entitlement

As stated previously, the STO will endeavour to identify as at the *record date* of the event all *ownership positions* and *location* components. In practice, this exercise will typically occur following the capture and cleansing of event terms, but prior to the actual record date of the event itself.

It is not necessary for the STO to wait until the actual record date of the event in order to determine *entitlement*, and in fact it is not recommended. Due to the nature of position keeping methods described earlier in Chapter 5 ('Securities Position Management'), the STO is able to 'project' (or identify positions as at a future date) based upon the trading and settlement activity known at the current date. This highlights the difference between the date when position information is extracted 'as at', and the date that the step is actually performed within the lifecycle of the event.

In reality, this means that at a time prior to the record date, for example on or prior to the *entitlement date*, the STO will be able to identify the expected ownership positions and location components as at the record date, based upon the trading and settlement information known at that time. This provides the Corporate Actions Department with an initial view of the ownership positions and location components against which the event terms will be applied, and allows sufficient time to process this information (including the issue of communications to position holders, the initial issue of *claim* notices, and the passing of internal *ex date accrual entries*) rather than waiting for the record date itself, which would allow the Corporate Actions Department very little time to process the ownership position and location components.

Any further trading and settlement activity that occurs up to and including the record date must constantly update the initial extract of information that the Corporate Actions Department takes from the STO's position keeping records.

The practical rules to identify

- ownership positions,
- settled custodian positions, and
- potential claims (in favour of and against the STO)

described in this section are based upon taking an initial view of the entitled positions (including location components) and then updating this information with further trading and settlement activity, based upon the business principles previously described, up to and including the record date of the event.

A simple illustration of the cycle to perform such identification is shown in Figure 9.8, based upon an example event lifecycle for Marks and Spencer plc.

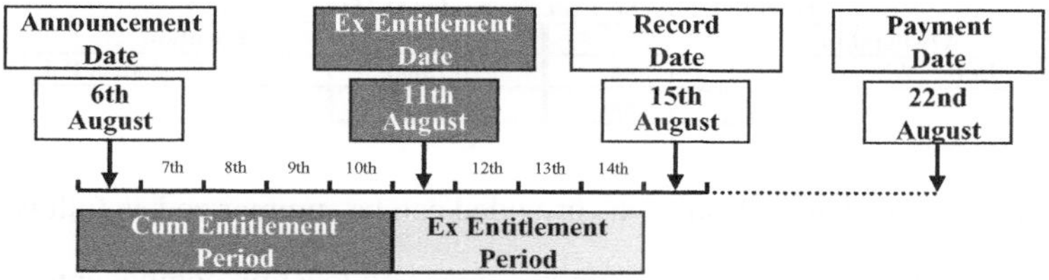

Figure 9.8 Typical benefit event timeline.

In the lifecycle diagram, the event has an entitlement date of 11th August and a record date of 15th August. The Corporate Actions Department will attempt to determine entitlement for those ownership and location components as at the record date of 15th August, but decides to perform this exercise initially on the 9th August. Therefore any further trading and settlement activity between 10th August and 15th August inclusive (that meets the entitlement conditions of the event) will need to be adjusted against the initial extract of information.

Assume the initial view of entitlement taken on 9th August, as at 15th August, is as shown in Table 9.13.

Table 9.13

Marks and Spencer plc Shares (projected as at 15th August)			
Ownership			Location
Trading Book 'A'	+12,000	−12,000	Custodian P, London
	+12,000	−12,000	

This reveals the Corporate Actions Department's view of the ownership positions and location components as at 15th August (to which the event terms would be applied) based upon trading and settlement activity known when the information was extracted on 9th August.

Assume that on 10th August, Trading Book 'A' purchases a further 5,000 shares (from Counterparty 'Z'), on a normal cum basis, with a value date of the 15th August.

At the time that this trade was executed on 10th August, the trade is unsettled, having a value date of the 15th August (record date). The projected view of the Corporate Actions Department will identify this trade at this time as a potential claim (in favour of the STO); this is because the Corporate Actions Department must assume a worst case situation (i.e. at the earliest point possible identify all potential claim situations, even including those that may still settle on or prior to the record date).

The updated view of entitlement will be as follows shown in Table 9.14.

Table 9.14

Marks and Spencer plc Shares (projected as at 15th August)			
Ownership			Location
Trading Book 'A'	+17,000	−12,000	Custodian P, London
		−5,000	Counterparty 'Z'
	+17,000	−17,000	

Assume that on 15th August, settlement of the purchase of 5,000 shares from Counterparty 'Z', takes place on value date. Accordingly the Corporate Actions Department will take account of this settlement activity and update its view of entitlement as shown in Table 9.15.

Table 9.15

Marks and Spencer plc Shares (as at 15th August)			
Ownership		**Location**	
Trading Book 'A'	+17,000	−17,000	Custodian P, London
	+17,000	−17,000	

The approach described and illustrations provided can be summarized as follows:

1. Take an initial view of entitled ownership positions and location components projected as at the record date of the event, but prior to the record date.
2. Update the view of entitled ownership positions location components with entitled trading and settlement activity between the time of the initial view and the record date.

In order to achieve the above, the STO could employ the following methods:

- take full extracts every day up to and including the record date, or
- take an initial full extract, and then add trade and settlement activity.

The choice the STO makes is likely to be dependent upon the system holding the data and the system receiving the data.

9.8.2 Identification of Ownership Positions

The business principles dictate that the accumulated position as a result of all trading up until the entitlement date of the event (where it applies) is entitled; but as mentioned previously a number of exceptions exist to this rule, including:

- the non existence of an entitlement period, as is the case for *re-organization* events;
- *special-ex trading* prior to entitlement date; and
- *special-cum trading* on and after the entitlement date.

The rules applied by the STO to identify entitled ownership positions must accommodate all of the above scenarios. Where an *entitlement date* applies to the event, either of two practical approaches to the requirement to identify the entitled ownership positions are available to the STO; each approach is described below.

Identify Cum Trading Relative to the Entitlement Date, Then Adjust

This approach involves the identification of all cum ownership positions on the basis of the trade date (and trade conditions) of the constituent trades, relative to the entitlement date of the event; thereafter the STO would identify any further special cum trading during the ex entitlement period, and adjust the entitled ownership position according to whether the special-cum trade is a purchase or sale.

This approach, whilst being a literal interpretation of the business principles described in the previous sections, introduces a number of practical issues for the STO:

- There are potential inefficiencies in operating a procedure (whether it be manual or automatic) to identify entitled ownership positions, which applies to those events that have an ex entitlement period (typically benefits only). Therefore, it requires a separate procedure to accommodate all event types that do not have an ex entitlement period.
- This procedure requires the identification of entitled ownership positions 'as at' the entitlement date of the event, whilst the identification of location positions (described in sections to follow) will be 'as at' the record date of the event. This will mean that the STO will effectively need to identify different types of position information 'as at' different times from the securities position records. As described in Chapter 5 ('Securities Position Management'), the integrity of position keeping is ensured by the value of *double entry book-keeping* principles, ensuring that 'as at' every date there is an equal and opposite entry, and thus the record must balance. By identifying ownership positions and location 'as at' different dates, this integrity is broken, potentially introducing both balancing and reconciliation issues to the process.

Identify Cum Trading Relative to the Record Date, Then Adjust

This approach involves the identification of all cum ownership positions on the basis of the value date (and trade conditions) of the constituent trades relative to the record date of the event, discounting any trades executed between the entitlement date and record date of the event, unless executed on a special cum basis.

As described in Section 9.5.3 of this chapter, any trade executed on a normal cum basis will typically reflect the standard settlement cycle of the market and therefore will have a trade date prior to the entitlement date and a value date on or prior to the record date of the event, thereby making the buyer automatically entitled to the event. As such, these trades will be automatically reflected in the value dated positions of the position holder as at the record date of the event, satisfying the basic business principles of entitlement.

This approach is by far the recommended approach to the STO for two main reasons:

- A single approach that can be applied to all types of events (whether they have an ex entitlement period or not) will provide the STO with efficiencies in both the design and application of the procedure, whether it is manual or automatic.
- The identification of entitled ownership positions 'as at' the record date of the event is consistent with the rules applied to the identification of location information, and therefore maintains the integrity of the position keeping as a result of double entry book-keeping.

Where an ex entitlement period does not apply (typically *re-organizations*) a single approach only is necessary to the identification of entitled ownership positions for the event. This is because all purchases up to and inclusive of the record date of the event are entitled, i.e. all trades are executed on a normal basis, and no special trades (special-cum or ex, and special value date) exist.

The following rule satisfies the business principles described previously in this chapter, together with the additional requirements to create a single set of rules to support all events, and identify all positions (both ownership and location) as at a single date. This is based upon the recommended approach, namely: identifying cum trading relative to the record date, and then adjusting. The rule is shown in Figure 9.9.

Using this rule, the Corporate Actions Department will initially identify entitled ownership positions as at the record date, but at some time prior to the record date, and then continue to

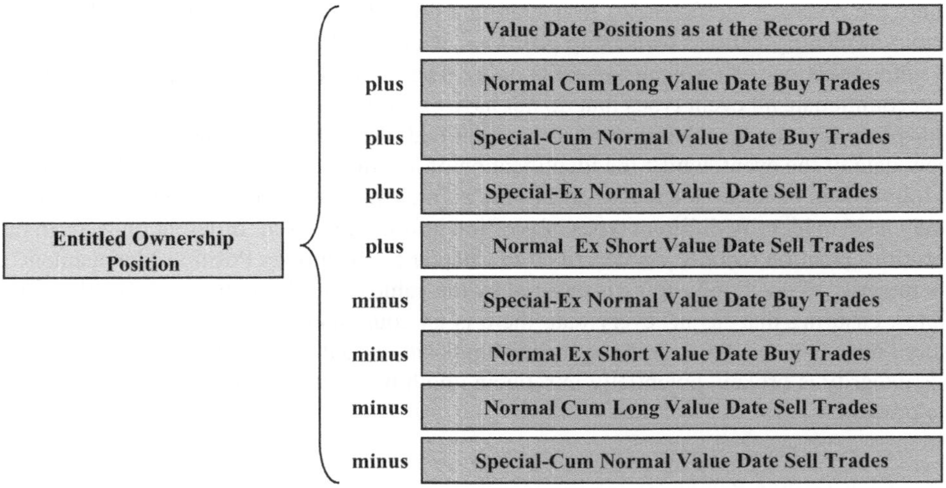

Figure 9.9 Ownership position identification.

adjust those positions for any further trading activity up to and including the record date (using the approaches described in this and the previous sections).

The application of the rule can be seen in Figure 9.10, which uses a representative selection of trade scenarios based upon an example event lifecycle for Alliance and Leicester plc.

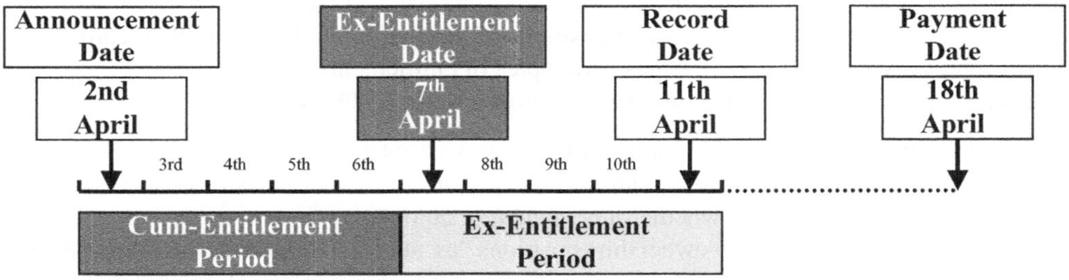

Figure 9.10 Typical benefit event timeline.

Assume that at the time of the extract of entitled ownership positions on 6th April, Trading Book 'A' has a long position of 19,000 shares as a result of trading prior to the entitlement date of the event, and therefore the value date of this position is on or prior to the record date of 11th April. This position consists of the following trades:

- 6,000 Buy Trade, Normal Cum, Normal Value Date, and
- 15,000 Buy Trade, Normal Cum, Normal Value Date, and
- 1,000 Buy Trade, Special-Ex, Normal Value Date, and
- 3,000 Sell Trade, Special-Ex, Normal Value Date.

Calculating the entitled ownership position using the earlier rule (see Figure 9.11) results in an entitled position for Trading Book 'A' of +21,000.

	Value Date Positions as at the Record Date	19,000
plus	Normal Cum Long Value Date Buy Trades	0
plus	Special-Cum Normal Value Date Buy Trades	0
plus	Special-Ex Normal Value Date Sell Trades	3,000
plus	Normal Ex Short Value Date Sell Trades	0
minus	Special-Ex Normal Value Date Buy Trades	1,000
minus	Normal Ex Short Value Date Buy Trades	0
minus	Normal Cum Long Value Date Sell Trades	0
minus	Special-Cum Normal Value Date Sell Trades	0

Figure 9.11 Ownership position calculation.

Both of the special-ex trades have a value date on or prior to the record date of 11th April, and therefore these trades are included in the 11th April value date positions, as extracted from the STO's securities position records. Nonetheless as these trades were executed on a special-ex basis the entitled ownership position required adjustment:

- the special-ex sale trade needs to be added, as Trading Book 'A' retains entitlement to this trade, and
- the special-ex buy trade needs to be deducted, as Trading Book 'A' is not entitled to this trade.

Assume that on 8th April, Trading Book 'A' purchases a further 9,000 shares, with a value date of 13th April, on a special-cum basis.

Calculating the entitled ownership position using the earlier rule (see Figure 9.12) results in an entitled position for Trading Book 'A' of +30,000.

The special-cum trade has a value date later than the record date of 11th, and therefore is not included in the 11th April value date position as extracted from the STO's securities position records. Nonetheless, as this trade was executed on a special-cum basis, the entitled ownership position requires adjustment:

- the special-cum buy trade needs to be added, as Trading Book 'A' gains entitlement to this trade.

When identifying entitled ownerships positions that meet the abovementioned rule, it is imperative for the Corporate Actions Department to record:

- the position holder's account details, and
- the quantity.

9.8.3 Identification of Settled Custodian Positions

The rule to identify settled custodian positions is relatively straightforward. The Corporate Actions Department must identify the settled custodian position in the underlying security

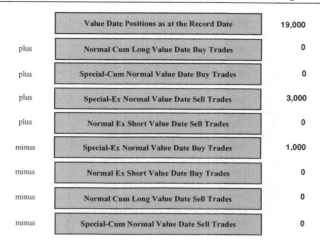

	Value Date Positions as at the Record Date	19,000
plus	Normal Cum Long Value Date Buy Trades	0
plus	Special-Cum Normal Value Date Buy Trades	9,000
plus	Special-Ex Normal Value Date Sell Trades	3,000
plus	Normal Ex Short Value Date Sell Trades	0
minus	Special-Ex Normal Value Date Buy Trades	1,000
minus	Normal Ex Short Value Date Buy Trades	0
minus	Normal Cum Long Value Date Sell Trades	0
minus	Special-Cum Normal Value Date Sell Trades	0

Figure 9.12 Ownership position calculation including special trading.

of the event as at the record date of the event. This is because it is against this position that the custodian will calculate the resultant entitlement due to (i.e. to be collected by) the STO. (Additional procedures to subsequently reconcile this position with the custodian are described later in this chapter).

For each settled custodian position the Corporate Actions Department will need to record:

- the account details (including the custodian), and
- the quantity.

9.8.4 Identification of Potential Claims

As stated previously, the Corporate Actions Department must identify those trades that may result in *claims* in favour of and against the STO, ensuring that the two are distinct.

Applying the business principles can be achieved by adoption of the following rules:

- Potential claims in favour of the STO will include trades that meet the following conditions:
  - unsettled buy normal cum trades as at the record date of the event;
  - unsettled buy special-cum trades as at the record date of the event;
  - settled sale normal ex trades as at the record date of the event;
  - settled sale special-ex trades as at the record date of the event.
- Potential claims against the STO will include trades that meet the following conditions:
  - unsettled sale normal cum trades as at the record date of the event;
  - unsettled sale special-cum trades as at the record date of the event;
  - settled buy normal ex trades as at the record date of the event;
  - settled buy special-ex trades as at the record date of the event.

These rules can be applied equally to those events with or without an *entitlement period.* Where the event does not have an entitlement period (i.e. an entitlement date) then by definition, all trades prior to and including the record date are traded on a *cum* basis.

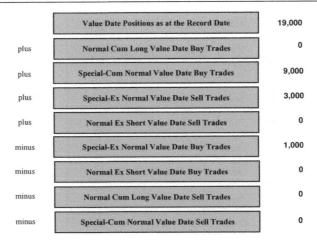

When identifying *unsettled trades* that meet the abovementioned conditions it is imperative for the Corporate Actions Department to record details of the trade, including:

- the type of trade and its operation (i.e. buy or sell);
- trade conditions, i.e. special-ex or special-cum;
- the unsettled quantity of the trade (as this may differ from the original trade quantity, if partial settlement has taken place);
- the trade *counterparty*;
- the trade date;
- the value date; and
- the unique trade identifier (trade reference).

9.9 BALANCING OF POSITIONS AND UNSETTLED TRADES

The balancing of entitled positions, including unsettled trades, is a step performed internally by the STO, designed to ensure

- the integrity of the information extracted from the STO's position keeping and trading records, and
- the correct application of the event's entitlement conditions (i.e. entitlement date and record date rules).

As described in Chapter 5 ('Securities Position Management'), the double entry nature of securities position management should at all times ensure that ownership positions are equal and opposite in sign to the location (including *settled custodian positions* and unsettled purchases and sales).

Nonetheless, as illustrated in the previous section, the identification of entitled positions including unsettled trades for the purposes of the corporate action is not simply a matter of taking a view of the securities position records on the record date of the event, as adjustments may be required to take account of special trading and settlement; the risks of errors in this procedure are all too evident.

In addition, within some STOs certain aspects of its books & records may be maintained discretely from others, for example, within securities lending systems as opposed to within the normal settlement systems. In such situations it is recommended that balancing of the position and unsettled trade information derived from each system, be performed together with balancing of the consolidated positions and unsettled trade information.

The entire procedure may be manual in the first instance, introducing the risk of human error; equally the trade information held within the position management system may be incorrect. It is important for the Corporate Actions Department to remain in control of its own operation, and therefore undertake independent balancing of the information once extracted from the position management records.

Balancing of the position and trade information can be achieved by the application of the equation, shown in Table 9.16, which ensures that the total of ownership positions equals the location sum.

Table 9.16

Ownership			=	Location				
Sum of Trading Book Positions	+	Sum of Custody Client Positions	=	Sum of Settled Positions (Custodian or Issuer)	+	Sum of Claims in Favour of STO	–	Sum of Claims against STO

Note: in some organizations, custody positions may be held entirely separately from trading book positions, and therefore balancing of positions will occur separately.

The application of the balancing equation can be seen in Figure 9.13, which uses a representative selection of trade and settlement scenarios, based upon an example event lifecycle for Singapore Airlines shares.

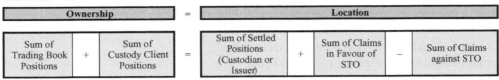

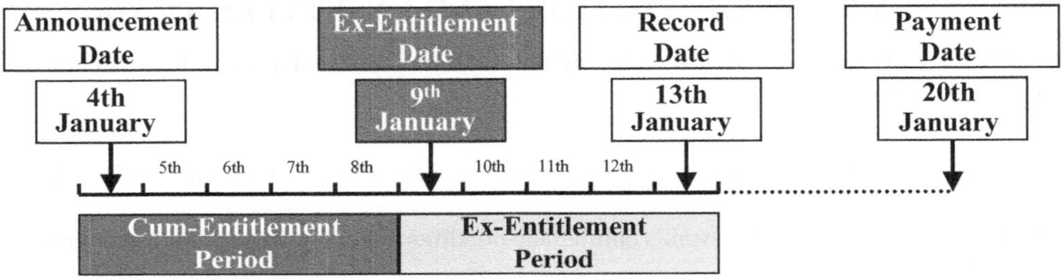

Figure 9.13 Typical benefit event timeline.

The initial extract from the STO's position records taken on 7th January is as shown in Table 9.17, with the purchase of 7,000 Singapore Airlines shares being on a normal cum basis (and value date on or prior to the record date).

Table 9.17

Singapore Airlines Shares (projected as at 13th January)			
Ownership		Location	
Trading Book 'A'	+10,000	–3,000	Custodian M, Singapore
		–7,000	Counterparty 'Y'
	+10,000	–10,000	

Using the entitlement rules previously described, the Corporate Actions Department will identify the following entitled ownership positions and location components against which the terms of the event will be applied:

- 10,000 Trading Book 'A' (ownership position);
- 3,000 Custodian M, Singapore (settled custodian position);
- 7,000 Counterparty 'Y' (claim 'in favour' of STO).

Applying the balancing equation proves that the entitled ownership position equals the location components, as shown in Table 9.18.

Table 9.18

Ownership			=	Location				
Sum of Trading Book Positions	+	Sum of Custody Client Positions	=	Sum of Settled Positions (Custodian or Issuer)	+	Sum of Claims in Favour of STO	–	Sum of Claims against STO
10,000	+	0	=	3,000	+	7,000	–	0

On 8th January, the following trade and settlement activity takes place:

- Trading Book 'B' purchases 15,000 shares on a trade basis of 'special-ex', with value date of 13th January (i.e. on record date) from counterparty 'X';
- Trading Book 'A' purchases 6,000 shares on a trade basis of 'normal cum', with value date of 13th January (i.e. on record date) from counterparty 'Y'; and
- Settle the purchase of 7,000 shares (with Counterparty 'Y') on a trade basis of 'normal cum'.

Accordingly the STO's position records will appear as shown in Table 9.19.

Table 9.19

Singapore Airlines Shares (projected as at 13th January)			
Ownership		**Location**	
Trading Book 'A'	+16,000	–10,000	Custodian M, Singapore
Trading Book 'B'	+15,000	–15,000	Counterparty 'X'
		–6,000	Counterparty 'Y'
	+31,000	–31,000	

Using the entitlement rules previously described, the Corporate Actions Department will identify the following entitled ownership positions and location components against which the terms of the event will be applied:

- 16,000 Trading Book 'A' (ownership position);
- 10,000 Custodian M, Singapore (settled custodian position);
- 6,000 Counterparty 'Y' (claim 'in favour' of STO).

With regard to the purchase of 15,000 shares, note that Trading Book 'B' is not entitled because the purchase from Counterparty 'X' was executed on a 'special-ex' basis (despite being traded prior to the entitlement date and having a value date on or prior to the record date).

Applying the balancing equation proves that the entitled ownership position equals the location components, as shown in Table 9.20.

Table 9.20

Ownership			=	Location				
Sum of Trading Book Positions	+	Sum of Custody Client Positions	=	Sum of Settled Positions (Custodian or Issuer)	+	Sum of Open Receipts	–	Sum of Open Deliveries
16,000	+	0	=	10,000	+	6,000	–	0

During the period 9th January to 13th January inclusive, the STO settles the following trades:

- Purchase 15,000 shares from Counterparty 'X' on a trade basis of 'special-ex'; and
- Purchase 6,000 shares from Counterparty 'Y' on a trade basis of 'normal cum'.

Accordingly, on 13th January the STO's position records will appear as shown in Table 9.21.

Table 9.21

Singapore Airlines Shares (as at 13th January)			
Ownership		Location	
Trading Book 'A'	+16,000	–31,000	Custodian M, Singapore
Trading Book 'B'	+15,000		
	+31,000	–31,000	

Using the entitlement rules previously described, the Corporate Actions Department will identify the following entitled ownership positions and location components against which the terms of the event will be applied:

- 16,000 Trading Book 'A' (ownership position);
- 31,000 Custodian M, Singapore (settled custodian position);
- 15,000 Counterparty 'Y' (claim 'against' the STO).

Note that as Trading Book 'B' is not entitled (because the purchase from Counterparty 'X' was executed on a 'special-ex' basis), because the trade was settled on or prior to the record date, the STO will receive entitlement from the custodian, and must return this entitlement to the selling counterparty, in this case counterparty 'Y'.

Applying the balancing equation proves that the entitled ownership positions equal the location components, as shown in Table 9.22.

Table 9.22

Ownership			=	Location				
Sum of Trading Book Positions	+	Sum of Custody Client Positions	=	Sum of Settled Positions (Custodian or Issuer)	+	Sum of Open Receipts	–	Sum of Open Deliveries
16,000	+	0	=	31,000	+	0	–	15,000

Imbalances could occur for a number of reasons, for example:

- incorrect identification of special trades;
- errors in the source of the trade and settlement information itself, (i.e. the STO's position management records);
- incorrect application of the entitlement and record dates across multiple trading systems.

In all cases, the investigation and correction of any imbalance must be treated with urgency. Correction may be required at the source of the information (outside of the Corporate Actions Department), in which case the Corporate Actions Department will need to have in place procedures to ensure that the necessary corrective action is undertaken by the appropriate department, and that when completed the Corporate Actions Department is advised in order to re-calculate the entitled positions and unsettled trades, before proceeding.

9.10 RECONCILIATION OF POSITIONS AND UNSETTLED TRADES

The process of *reconciliation* is designed to ensure that those positions held in the internal securities position records equate to those records of the external party/parties and to the front office. Whilst reconciliation is a normal function of trading and settlement operations, it is also critical within the Corporate Actions Department to ensure that the positions and unsettled trades (against which the Corporate Actions Department will calculate *resultant entitlements*) reconcile to those identified by external parties and the front office.

Typically, it is accepted that reconciliation of settled custodian positions to the custodian's records will occur, but there are also opportunities to reconcile both ownership positions and unsettled trades (which will result in claims on behalf of or against the STO). The importance and timeliness of such reconciliations cannot be overstated. The identification of any errors as soon as possible on or after the record date of the event will avoid both incorrect calculations of resultant entitlements, and potentially incorrect disbursement of resultant entitlements later in the lifecycle of the event.

9.10.1 Reconciliation of Ownership Positions

The reconciliation of entitled ownership positions is often an informal process within the Corporate Actions Department. It is common for the Corporate Actions Department to rely upon notifications from other parties and departments, if a discrepancy exists. This may occur in two ways:

- The front office (traders responsible for a *trading book* position) may have independently determined the position against which it expects to receive entitlement. Upon receipt of the notification of entitled position from the Corporate Actions Department, the front office may advise the Corporate Actions Department of any discrepancy.
- *Custody clients* may have independently calculated the expected entitlement. Upon receipt of the notification of final entitlement from the Corporate Actions Department they may advise the STO of any discrepancy.

Despite such discrepancies being identified outside of the Corporate Actions Department, the responsibility for investigation and rectification of such discrepancies lies with the Corporate Actions Department. The potential lack of formalized procedures does not absolve the Corporate Actions Department of its responsibility.

It is strongly recommended that the Corporate Actions Department take advantage of these reconciliations, in order to gain greater control in the calculation of resultant entitlements.

As with the identification of any other discrepancy, immediate investigation and corrective action is required. Should the error have occurred within the STO's records, the entitled positions and unsettled trades to which the event terms are to be applied will require re-calculation to take account of any corrections, and new advices sent to the affected position holders.

9.10.2 Reconciliation of Settled Custodian Positions

The most common of external reconciliations to take place within the Corporate Actions Department is that of internally held *settled custodian positions* to custodian's records, as at the *record date*. Reconciliation to the custodian is vital as it is the custodian's record date quantity that will form the basis for calculation and collection of resultant entitlement by the STO.

Typically, the custodian will instigate reconciliation by the issuance of a communication to the STO that states its record date position in the underlying security for the event in question. This type of communication is now issued electronically in the majority of cases, and the record date information is most often included within the custodian's advice of the event terms to the STO. At the time of writing, the *S.W.I.F.T.* MT564 message supports the communication of event terms and record date positions. Irrespective of how this information is communicated, the STO would expect a communication from its custodian(s) for every position held, at an individual account level (where relevant). The STO's Corporate Action Department should track which communications have been received and which are outstanding from the custodian, and any outstanding record date communications should be followed up in a timely fashion.

Upon receipt of the notification of the record date position from the custodian, the STO will attempt to match this against settled custodian position(s) that it has already identified for the event. Successful matching will require that not only the quantity of the record date position reconciles to that advised by the custodian, but also that the account details of the holding are accurate.

Any discrepancies in the information received from the custodian to that held by the STO will require immediate investigation and corrective action. Discrepancies may occur, for example, due to errors in the STO's record keeping, where settlements may not have been correctly updated, or as a result of delays in the timing of settlement updates.

It is important to remember that the settled custodian position is only part of the overall picture, and that therefore if it is incorrect, then an equal and opposite position, possibly an unsettled trade, is also incorrect.

Once any errors are identified and corrected with the STO's position keeping, then the positions and unsettled trades to which the event terms are to be applied will require re-calculation to take account of such corrections.

9.10.3 Reconciliation of Unsettled Trades

As previously described, unsettled trades will result in the generation of *claims* either in favour of the STO or against the STO, i.e. *resultant entitlements* that will require collection from *counterparties* or disbursement to counterparties respectively. Therefore the reconciliation of unsettled trades with the external counterparties is just as vital as the reconciliation of settled custodian positions and ownership positions to the Corporate Actions Department.

The procedures relating to this step will differ from market to market. In some cases, CSDs and ICSDs will advise participants of any unsettled trades with other participants, as at the *record date* of the event.

A less formal approach to this reconciliation is as a result of the issue and receipt of claim advices (refer to Chapter 10, 'Communication of Event Information') between the STO and the counterparty of the unsettled trade. The checking of such claim advices by the recipient will identify whether the parties agree the details of the unsettled trade and that a claim for the resultant entitlement will be made.

Errors identified through the *reconciliation* process may occur as a result of either party to the trade having failed to update trading and settlement activity accurately in their records.

Again the identification of any discrepancy requires immediate investigation and corrective action. Should the error have occurred within the STO's records, then the entitled positions and unsettled trades to which the event terms are to be applied will require recalculation.

9.11 SUMMARY

It is clear that the STO must identify entitled positions including unsettled trades against which to apply the terms of the event. Without a doubt though, the need to balance and reconcile this information in a timely fashion is a significant milestone in the early lifecycle of the corporate action.

Summing up, this information is:

- Ownership positions, comprising:
  - trading book positions; and
  - custody client positions.
- Location components, comprising:
  - settled custodian positions;
  - unsettled trades resulting in claims in favour of the STO;
  - unsettled trades resulting in claims against the STO.

The basic principle regarding balancing and reconciliation is: the longer this information remains unchecked the greater the risk to the STO of incorrect calculation of resultant entitlements, potentially resulting in incorrect deliveries and receipts of entitlements upon the payment or distribution date of the event, and significant financial losses to the STO.

Despite the reliance upon position and trade information maintained by other areas of the STO's operation, the Corporate Actions Department must ensure that it is in control of its own operation, and that procedures are in place between it and other operational areas for the urgent investigation and correction of errors.

ENDNOTE: within this chapter, certain figures, tables and text have been reproduced with permission from *Securities Operations: A Guide to Trade and Position Management*, ISBN 0-471-49758-4, author Michael Simmons, publisher John Wiley & Sons, Ltd.

10

Communication of Event Information

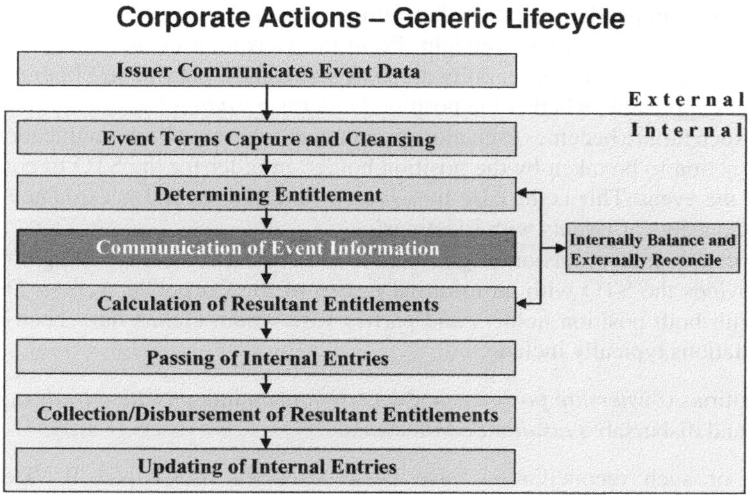

10.1 INTRODUCTION

Throughout the life of any given event, the STO will issue a variety of communications both to the *position holders*, and to any parties with whom it has identified *claims*. The purpose of these communications is initially to inform the position holder of the event, and subsequently to advise the position holder of changes to its securities and cash positions as a result of the event.

In addition, the STO may choose to communicate information to other interested parties for whom positions are not held. This could include, for example, traders (within the STO) and investment analysts.

The types of communications issued throughout the life of an event will normally differ according to

- the category (or sometimes specific type) of the event, and
- the conventions within the market to which the event applies (regulatory requirements may apply).

In addition, the specific preferences of the party to whom the communication is issued and the STO's service level agreement (*SLA*) with that party will be taken into account; that is, what specific communications are applicable and are required by the position holder.

The purpose of this chapter is to describe the various types of communications that are typically applicable to events, their characteristics, methods of communication, and the importance of *static data* in the issuance of communications. Additionally, the increasingly common practice of communicating event terms with other interested parties (i.e. non-position holders) and its benefits will be introduced.

10.2 THE STO'S RISK

From the perspective of providing a high quality service to its clients, the STO's failure to inform holders of an impending event or of resulting changes to the position holder's securities and/or cash positions is a serious oversight. From the viewpoint of the position holder, the STO will have failed in fulfilling its obligations as stated in its service level agreement with the STO. This is applicable whether the position holder is a *trading book* or a *custody client*.

The risk of such failure becomes even more pronounced where such communications require a response or action to be taken by the position holder, in order for the STO to complete the processing of the event. This is the case for events with elections and is explained further in Chapter 16, 'Concepts of Events with Elections'.

As well as the obvious provision of good service to position holders, issuing communications also provides the STO with an informal means of the Corporate Actions Department reconciling with both position holders and parties with whom claims have been identified. Such reconciliations typically include:

- entitled positions (*ownership positions* and *location*, including *unsettled trades*), and
- collectible and disbursable *resultant entitlements*.

The benefits of such reconciliation have been described in Chapter 9, 'Determining Entitlement'.

10.3 COMMUNICATING WITH POSITION HOLDERS

As indicated previously, a variety of communications to position holders may occur. Depending upon the category (or sometimes specific type) of event the position holder may receive one or multiple communications from the STO during the life of the event. In this way corporate actions communications differ from trading communications, where for the latter typically a single confirmation of the trade will be generated upon the execution of the trade.

For the purposes of this chapter each variety of communication will be known as a 'type', with each type representing a unique combination of characteristics.

10.3.1 Characteristics of Communication Types

The characteristics of each type of communication reflect the reasons for the communication, the type of position against which the communication is being issued and the timing and frequency of the communication within the lifecycle of the event. The combination of these characteristics will in turn dictate the content of the communication. The definitions of such characteristics are as follows (and are illustrated in the definition of communication types in Section 10.3.2):

- **Reasons for Communicating**
  Communications may be purely of an informative nature, for example communication of the *event terms*, or may require a response from the recipient as is the case for those events where the position holders are required to indicate an action to the STO, such as elections (refer

to Chapter 16, 'Concepts of Events with Elections' for more detail). Different information will be communicated to the position holder at different times throughout the lifecycle, for example communication of event terms, and communication of resultant entitlement.

- **Types of Position**
  The different types of positions against which the communication is being generated may give rise to different types of communications. For example, the types of communications issued to position holders will generally differ to those against unsettled trades. In both cases communication of resultant entitlement is required, but in the case of an unsettled trade this communication constitutes a claim.
- **Timing of Communication**
  The timing of each communication is intrinsically tied to the reasons for the communication and the type of position against which it is generated. For example, the communication of event terms would typically be generated early in the event lifecycle when entitled positions (including unsettled trades) are initially identified, whilst the communication of the resultant entitlement will occur towards the end of the lifecycle once positions and resultant entitlement calculations are finalized.
- **Frequency of Communication**
  Some types of communications may be issued only once during the life of the event, whilst others may be issued on multiple occasions. Typically, those that are issued on multiple occasions are those that require an action from the party to whom the communication is issued, and when notification of that action has not been received by the STO. For example, where the STO is claiming a resultant entitlement against a *counterparty*, the STO will issue a claim notice. If delivery of the claimed resultant entitlement is outstanding, the STO may regularly re-issue the *claim* notice until such time as delivery is received.

10.3.2 Generic Communication Types

Analysis of the generic event lifecycle enables the assembly of a generic set of communication types that, in turn, may be applied to any event.

The following list represents a typical set of generic communication types:

- **Event Terms Announcement**
  Typically this communication will be sent early in the event lifecycle once the event terms are captured and the position holder is identified as having a position in the *underlying security* of the event. This would be expected to be prior to the *entitlement date* or *record date* of the event (whichever is applicable).

  The communication is unlikely to contain any specific information regarding the quantity of the position holder's holding or any resultant entitlement calculation, as its purpose is purely to communicate the terms of the event.
- **Preliminary Entitlement Notice**
  The Preliminary Entitlement Notice would be issued on the entitlement date of the event, and will therefore only apply to those events for which the entitlement date is applicable and resultant entitlement exists. The notice would be issued to position holders only and not to parties with whom an unsettled trade has been identified.

  The purpose of this notice is to inform the position holder of the projected resultant entitlement that it may expect based upon its holding as at the entitlement date of the event. This is because it is at this time that the value of the underlying holding will change, as a result of the benefit (refer to Chapter 9, 'Determining Entitlement', where the impact of the entitlement date on the price of the underlying security is explained). Receipt of this information on the entitlement date will allow the position holder to account for the change in the value of its underlying position.

- **Final Entitlement Notice**
  The Final Entitlement Notice is issued to position holders only (and not to parties with whom an unsettled trade has been identified), in order to inform the holder of the final resultant entitlement (i.e. impact on its securities and/or cash position). The notice is not applicable to those events that do not generate entitlements, i.e. issuer notices.
  This notice is normally issued upon the event's close of record date or payment date −1 (according to market practice), once all *cum* trading (including special trading) has ceased, entitled positions are finalized and resultant entitlements have been calculated and reconciled (refer to Chapter 11, 'Calculation of Resultant Entitlements'). Note that some organizations may defer the issue of this notice until settlement of final entitlement occurs.
- **Preliminary Claim Notice**
  The Preliminary Claim Notice may be issued to parties with whom an anticipated outstanding receipt against an unsettled trade has been identified. It would be issued in order to alert the counterparty to the underlying unsettled trade, and the fact that in the event of settlement failing to be effected on or prior to the record date, a claim will be made.
- **Final Claim Notice**
  The Final Claim Notice will again be issued to parties with whom an outstanding receipt against an unsettled trade has been identified, in order to claim formally the cash or securities due to the STO. The notice will be issued upon the close of the record date where the unsettled trade has remained outstanding as at the record date, and notifies the counterparty that the resultant entitlement is due. This notice may be issued repeatedly to the party of the claim whilst receipt of the claim remains outstanding.

Whilst the above list provides a generic set of communication types, it is important to note nonetheless that the specific communication types that the STO issues will depend upon the service levels agreed with its various clients (and position holders), together with its assessment of the requirements for the market to which the event applies. Examples of such variations are:

- The Event Terms Announcement may not be issued to those responsible for the management of the STO's *trading book* positions, as this information may be received by them through other means, i.e. market information mechanisms provided outside of the Corporate Actions Department.
- The Preliminary Entitlement Notice may only be issued against those positions for which the STO performs the function of position valuation, in order to justify changes in valuation as at the entitlement date of the event.
- Notification of Claims, either preliminary or final, may not be required in some markets where the CSD/ICSD automatically generates and compensates *claims* between counterparties against outstanding cum settlements (refer to Chapter 13, 'Collection/Disbursement of Resultant Entitlements').

The difference in the timing of the issue of the generic set of communication types is illustrated via a typical mandatory event timeline as shown in Figure 10.1 (inclusive of an ex entitlement period).

Additionally, Table 10.1 provides an 'at-a-glance' comparison between the characteristics of the generic set of communication types described above.

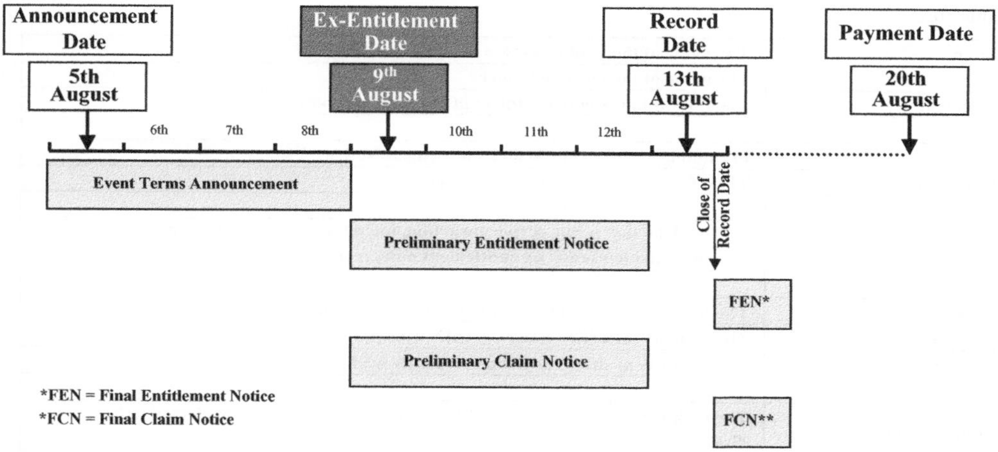

Figure 10.1 Typical mandatory (benefit) event timeline.

Table 10.1

Communication Type	Purpose?	Against Positions?	Against Unsettled Trades?	Prior to Entitlement Date?	On Entitlement Date?	Upon Close Of Record Date (or PD −1)?
Event Terms Announcement	Inform Event Terms	Yes	No	Yes	No	No
Preliminary Entitlement Notice	Inform Projected Resultant Entitlement	Yes	No	No	Yes	No
Final Entitlement Notice	Inform Final Resultant Entitlement	Yes	No	No	No	Yes
Preliminary Claim Notice	Alert of Potential Claim	No	Yes	No	Yes	No
Final Claim Notice	Notify of Claim	No	Yes	No	No	Yes

The following two tables describe the typical content relating to two of the above-mentioned communication types: Table 10.2 describes the typical content of a Preliminary Entitlement Notice and Table 10.3 describes the typical content of a Final Claim Notice.

10.3.3 Communication Features

A number of features will apply to the issuance of the communications.

- **Transmission Methods**
  The transmission method refers to the manner in which the communication is issued. In the modern era, communications are regularly required to be issued via a variety of media, with the STO being required to support any or all of the following:
  - fax (facsimile)
  - telex
  - *S.W.I.F.T.* (The S.W.I.F.T network supports specific corporate action message types to enable the communication of a variety of event information)
  - e-Mail
  - paper

Table 10.2

From	**The name of the issuing STO**
To	**The name of the position holder**
Attention	**The relevant person/department at the position holder**
Subject	**Preliminary Corporate Action Entitlement Notice**
Our Reference	**The STO's corporate action reference**
Event Description	**A brief depiction of the corporate action, including the event type and (for example) dividend rate, ex entitlement date, record date, payment date**
Underlying Security	**The full description of the security pertaining to the event**
Security Reference	**The security identifier code, e.g. ISIN, Cusip, Quick**
Current Holding	**The quantity of shares or bonds currently held**
Projected Entitlement	**The cash value or the quantity of the specific security that is projected to be disbursed or collected**
Settlement Details	**The date and method by which the cash and/or securities will be disbursed or collected**
Sign-off by the STO	**Full name and location of STO**
Transmission Time	**A clear statement of the date and time of transmission**

Table 10.3

From	**The name of the issuing STO**
To	**The name of the counterparty**
Attention	**The relevant person/department at the counterparty**
Subject	**Final Corporate Action Claim Notice**
Our Reference	**The STO's corporate action claim reference**
Event Description	**A brief depiction of the corporate action, including the event type and (for example) dividend rate, ex entitlement date, record date, payment date**
	Trade Details
Underlying Security	**The full description of the security pertaining to the event**
Security Reference	**The security identifier code, e.g. ISIN, Cusip, Quick**
Operation	**We buy/sell (from the STO's perspective)**
Quantity	**The full trade quantity**
Price	**The price at which the trade was executed**
Trade Conditions	**The specifically executed trade conditions (if applicable)**
Trade Date	**The date of trade execution**
Value date	**The intended date of settlement**
Settlement date	**The date of actual settlement**
Net Settlement Value	**The full cash value of the trade**
	Claim Details
Claim Quantity	**The full or partial trade quantity on which the claim is based**
Entitlement Claimed	**The value of cash or securities being claimed**
Settlement Details	**The STO's nostro or depot to which the claimed cash or securities are required to be credited**
Sign-off by the STO	**Full name and location of STO**
Transmission Time	**A clear statement of the date and time of transmission**

- **Communication Language**
  An STO may be required to support the issuance of communications in languages other than the native language of the STO's location.
- **Keeping internal records of outgoing communication (particularly on elective events)**
  In order to maintain a full audit trail of corporate action event information sent to clients, the STO is highly likely to record the generation time and content of communications (preferably as part of the individual event record). This is of particular importance when handling events with elections, where direct access to what was issued, and when it was issued, is essential when election deadlines are approaching.

10.3.4 Preferences of the Position Holder

The actual communications issued will depend upon the preferences of the position holder. The position holder would typically be able to select from those types of communications potentially to be generated by the STO, for a given event category/type. It would also be able to choose from the various transmission methods and communication languages supported by the STO.

Using the example types of communications listed earlier in this chapter, whilst the STO may offer to issue (against an entitled position) the Event Terms Announcement, the Preliminary Entitlement Notice and the Final Entitlement Notice, an individual position holder may decide that it requires to receive only the Event Terms Announcement and the Final Entitlement Notice, and therefore the STO does not need to issue a Preliminary Entitlement Notice to that position holder.

Such preferences are recorded against the static data record of the party (refer to Chapter 4, 'Static Data'), and will also include preferences for the method of communicating with the position holder.

A typical range of information recorded against a position holder's static data (indicating its preferences for the communication of corporate action details) would include:

- **Types of Communication Required**
  Of those communication types supported for various categories of events, the STO may allow the position holder to establish a set of preferences indicating that it requires all or any of those types available. There may be some communication types nonetheless that the STO will always issue, for example a Final Entitlement Notice, therefore not giving the position holder a choice. Depending upon the level of service that the STO wishes to offer, it could even allow such preferences to be very specific, and be set up by individual event types.
  Ensuring that the position holder receives only the required communications will reduce unnecessary production of communications and is a sign of good client service.
- **Name and Address Details for Communications**
  It is necessary to record the name and address (or addresses) to which any communication is to be issued. It should not be assumed that this would be the same name and address that the party may use, for example, for trade confirmations or other correspondence. *Institutional clients*, for example, will often have separate departments to administer corporate actions (similar to the STO itself) and therefore a specific address would apply. Similarly, individual clients may have corporate action communications sent to their financial advisor.

An individual party's requirements may in addition specify different names and addresses for:
- different categories of corporate actions, for example, making a distinction between *income* events and non-income events, and
- different markets.

- **Transmission Method**
  Whilst the STO may be able to support a number of transmission methods, the position holder will typically have a preference. The method preferred by the position holder will be recorded against the static data of the position holder.
  It is necessary to be aware of the relevant link of the transmission method to the name and address details held for communications. For example, if the party's preference is for communication via e-mail, the name and address details will need to include an e-mail address, as a postal address would not be appropriate.
  The static data records of the STO potentially need to record many transmission methods for the position holder, particularly where communications could be generated to a range of names and addresses (as described in the previous point).
- **Number of Copies**
  As indicated previously, one of the characteristics of communication to the position holder may be the need to issue multiple copies of the communication, either to a single name and address or to multiple names and addresses.
- **Communication Language**
  Where the STO is required to support the issue of communications in multiple languages, each position holder's preferred language will be recorded within its static data records.
  As discussed in Chapter 4, 'Static Data', the maintenance of static data supporting the various stages of the corporate action lifecycle is critical. None is more critical than the position holder's preferences for communications. Bearing this in mind, the STO will need to find a balance between offering the position holder great variety and complexity in the preferences it will support, and ensuring that the service required by the position holder is actually provided.

10.4 COMMUNICATING WITH INTERESTED PARTIES

As stated earlier in this chapter, the communication of event terms is not necessarily confined only to those parties for whom a position is held (in the security to which the event applies).

Those parties that hold no position may be able to make good use of such event information. Increasingly, with the introduction of more sophisticated 'event terms' cleansing tools and communication facilities, the additional opportunity exists to notify other internal parties of an event, thereby maximizing the use of the data and providing added value to the organization.

These opportunities include:

- Information to trading and research departments in order to identify trading opportunities and to formulate strategies.
- Input to pricing models of both the underlying security, together with associated derivative products.
- Communications to static data management departments, to notify of new securities and changes to existing securities.

Normally, only event announcement details are communicated to interested parties, as none of the further event lifecycle processing will be applicable (since positions are not held).

By investigating opportunities to communicate information to non-position holders, the Corporate Actions Department may be able to add to its repertoire of services to the organization as a whole, and may even be able to recoup part of the costs of event terms capture and cleansing from other departments that become eventual recipients of such information.

10.5 SUMMARY

The issuance of corporate action communications serves a number of purposes:

- the servicing of clients, ensuring that position holders are fully informed of all events and changes to their securities and cash positions;
- the trigger for informal reconciliation of entitled positions and resultant entitlements;
- the trigger for informal reconciliation of claims; and
- the dissemination of event information to a wider audience than position holders.

Corporate Action communications should be issued in a timely and accurate fashion according to the lifecycle of the event, and be able to support amendments and cancellations where required to reflect changes in event information.

The efficiency of this operation will be largely dependent upon the accuracy of static data held and the level of automation within the STO's environment.

ENDNOTE: within this chapter, certain figures, tables and text have been reproduced with permission from *Securities Operations: A Guide to Trade and Position Management*, ISBN 0-471-49758-4, author Michael Simmons, publisher John Wiley & Sons, Ltd.

11

Calculation of Resultant Entitlements

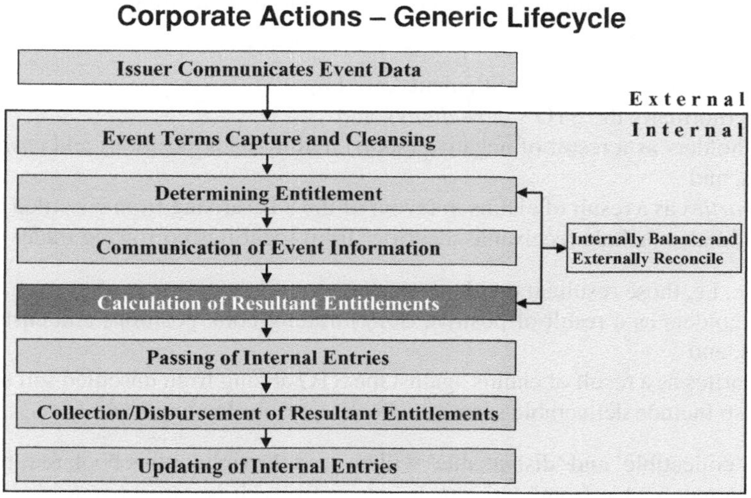

11.1 INTRODUCTION

In the purest sense, the term 'entitlement' refers to the securities and/or cash to which a *position holder* is entitled, in this case as a result of the corporate action; therefore the term could be considered to apply only to those amounts pertaining to position holders, and not to *locations*.

For example, a long book position

- has *entitlement* to a dividend, where the word 'entitlement' here refers to the securities and/or cash due to the *trading book* as a result of its *ownership position*, whereas
- the securities and/or cash due from (say) the *custodian* represent only the collection of the amount owed to the owner.

However, in a practical sense those administering the event (the Corporate Actions Department) will usually refer to all securities and/or cash amounts resulting from applying the terms of the event as '*resultant entitlements*', including ownership, locations and *claims*. Throughout this book all of these amounts will be collectively referred to as 'resultant entitlements'.

At the appropriate time in the lifecycle of an event, the calculation of the final resultant entitlement of securities and/or cash due to position holders and expected from the location and claims, is effected. For mandatory events, this typically occurs once the entitled positions (including *unsettled trades*) are finalized, balanced and reconciled at the close of the *record date*. It is important to note that the STO may calculate projected resultant entitlements earlier than this time, for instance on the *entitlement date*, in order to pass *entitlement date entries* (refer to Chapter 12, 'Passing of Internal Entries'). Note that the timing of the calculation of resultant entitlements may differ where the event includes elections (refer to Chapter 16, 'Concepts of Events with Elections').

The calculation of resultant entitlements requires the STO to apply the terms of the event that set the conditions for the resultant entitlement calculation, e.g. rates and ratios, and fractions rules, to the entitled positions, including unsettled trades (refer to Chapter 9, 'Determining Entitlement' for a full explanation of the various scenarios that will result in the calculation of collectible and disbursable entitlements). The results of these calculations will be the generation of resultant entitlements:

- Collectible, i.e. those resultant entitlements owed by:
  - locations (normally the STO's *custodians*), and
  - position holders as a result of negative (short) trading book positions and *custody client* positions, and
  - *counterparties* as a result of claims in favour of the STO arising from unsettled buy trades (this would also include receivable securities from securities borrowing trades).
- Disbursable, i.e. those resultant entitlements due to:
  - position holders as a result of positive (long) trading book positions and custody client positions, and
  - counterparties as a result of claims against the STO arising from unsettled sell trades (this would also include deliverable securities from securities lending trades).

The terms 'collectible' and 'disbursable' will be used throughout this book to refer to those resultant entitlements 'due from' and 'due to' respectively. It is imperative to understand the 'direction', i.e. whether the resultant entitlement is collectible or disbursable from the STO's perspective; the direction of the resultant entitlement will directly impact all subsequent steps.

Where the terms of the event also result in the removal of the *underlying security*, the quantity relating to the removal will be included in the calculation of resultant entitlements.

This chapter describes the four steps involved in determining the calculation of resultant entitlements:

1. the calculation of collectible and disbursable resultant entitlements, i.e. the calculation of securities and/or cash values, and the different methods that apply between the two;
2. proving the integrity of resultant entitlement calculations by ensuring that the sum of the collectible resultant entitlements is equal to the sum of the disbursable entitlements;
3. reconciliation of collectible resultant entitlements from location positions with the external custodian; and
4. identifying accounts via which resultant entitlements may be collected or disbursed, in cases where that account differs from that of the underlying holding(s).

11.2 THE STO'S RISK

The calculation of resultant entitlements may, upon initial appearance, seem a simple mathematical step (the multiplication of the *rate* or *ratio* of the event against the quantity of the entitled holding or transaction). However, the significant risks of incorrect interpretation of event conditions and resultant incorrect calculations, particularly at this stage of the event lifecycle, require that great care is taken by the Corporate Actions Department.

The STO must be aware of the different treatment of rates and ratios, and different calculation methods that apply in different markets.

Incorrect calculation of resultant entitlements can create serious and direct financial exposures for the STO, as it is the results of these calculations that will be collected or disbursed.

Frequent and robust controls to ensure the checking of securities and/or cash entitlements are highly recommended, including:

- validation of calculations via the *'four-eyes' principle*;
- internal balancing of resultant entitlements to ensure that the sum of collectible entitlements equals the sum of disbursable entitlements;
- reconciliation of collectible entitlements from locations.

11.3 CALCULATION OF RESULTANT CASH ENTITLEMENTS

Generally the calculation of a resultant cash entitlement requires a single step only, i.e. the multiplication of the quantity of the entitled holding by either

- a cash rate per share (usually applicable to *equities*), or
- a percentage relevant to the *face value* (usually applicable to *bonds*)

according to the type of *underlying security* to which the event applies.

11.3.1 Cash Rates Per Share

Where the event pertains to an underlying equity security, the cash rate is typically expressed as the quantity of cash units in the par currency relative to a quantity of units in the underlying security. For example, '5 cents per share', or '150 pence per share'.

To calculate the resultant entitlement as per the announced rate, the underlying holding is divided by the quantity of units (normally 1), and then multiplied by the cash unit. Using a rate of 150 pence per share, and assuming a holding of 10,000 XXX shares:

- divide holding by 1 ($10{,}000/1 = 10{,}000$), multiply by 150 ($10{,}000 \times 150 = 1{,}500{,}000$)

which produces an entitlement of 1,500,000 pence, or GBP 15,000.00.

Most commonly, a currency rate will be announced in the lowest unit of the entitlement currency. Nonetheless, this is not always the case, and the STO needs to be mindful of the correct interpretation of the rate and the placement of the decimal point in the entitlement calculation. For example, assume a rate of GBP 150 is captured and applied to a holding of 10,000 XXX shares. This could represent either 150 pence per share, or alternatively 150 pounds per share. The first would result in an entitlement of GBP 15,000.00, whilst the second would result in an entitlement of GBP 1,500,000.00.

11.3.2 Percentage Relevant to Face Value

Where the event relates to an underlying debt (bond) security, resultant entitlement involves the multiplication of the quantity of the entitled holding (often referred to as the bond's face value) by a percentage representing either

- the interest (also known as '*coupon*') rate, or
- the redemption price (usually payable on the bond's *maturity date*, or earlier).

In the case of a fixed-rate bond, for example, the periodic payment of interest is expressed as a percentage (e.g. 6.25%) relative to the face value of the bond holding. Using an interest rate of 6.25%, and assuming a holding of EUR 1,000,000.00:

- multiply holding (EUR 1,000,000.00) by the percentage (6.25%) = EUR 62,500.00

which produces an entitlement of EUR 62,500.00.

11.4 CALCULATION OF RESULTANT SECURITIES ENTITLEMENTS

According to the event type, the resultant securities entitlement conditions may include rules that state:

- the securities *ratio*
- the treatment of *fractions*
- the calculation sequence
- the calculation of removal of the underlying securities holding
- the calculation of cash payable to the issuer

11.4.1 The Securities Ratio

The first number of the securities ratio is known as the multiplier, whilst the second number is known as the divisor.

The securities ratio may be expressed in either of two ways, according to the market and type of event to which the rate applies, which will affect the calculation of the resultant entitlement, as described below.

European and Asia Pacific Markets

In the majority of European and Asia Pacific markets, and non-benefit US events

- the first number indicates the additional quantity of the *entitlement security* to be distributed, relative to
- the second number which indicates the quantity of the *underlying security*.

For example, assuming a ratio of three for two, and an underlying holding of 10,000 XXX shares, the securities entitlement will be calculated as follows:

- divide holding by 2 ($10,000/2 = 5,000$), multiply by 3 ($5,000 \times 3 = 15,000$)

which produces an entitlement of 15,000 shares, which when added to the position holder's existing holding will result in a final holding of 25,000 ($10,000 + 15,000$) shares.

The original holding has increased by 15,000 shares, as a result of the event.

US Markets, Benefits Only

Where the event is a securities benefit in a US equity

- the first number indicates the final holding after the event, relative to
- the second number, which indicates the quantity of the original underlying security.

For example, assuming a ratio of three for two, and an underlying holding of 10,000 XXX shares, the securities entitlement will be calculated as follows:

- divide holding by 2 (10,000/2 = 5,000), multiply by 3 (5,000 × 3 = 15,000)

which produces an entitlement of 15,000 shares, which replaces the position holder's existing holding and results in a final holding of 15,000 shares.

The original holding has increased by 5,000 shares, as a result of the event.

Based on the examples above, note how the announcement using the same terms (i.e. a ratio of three for two) produces dramatically different results due to the treatment of the securities ratio within the different markets.

It is important that the STO accurately interprets how the securities ratio has been expressed in the event terms in order to avoid the incorrect calculation of resultant entitlements.

11.4.2 The Treatment of Fractions

Frequently, the calculation of resultant entitlements produces a fractional amount, over and above the whole number. For example, an announced event of one (new) share for every three (existing) shares will produce a resultant entitlement of 33.3333 shares on an original holding of 100 shares.

Where resultant entitlements are to securities (rather than cash), the terms of the event will normally also include conditions as to the treatment of fractional entitlements. This is because it is normally not possible for partial units of the entitlement security to be distributed; an exception to this norm is, for example, mutual fund unit distributions. The result of applying the fractions conditions will be to round the resultant securities entitlement to whole denominated units or tradeable *lots* (refer to Chapter 4, 'Static Data' for the description of denominated units and tradeable *lots*).

Conditions for the treatment of fractions are rarely required for resultant cash entitlements as the announced cash rate is normally in the standard decimal values of the entitlement currency, and therefore no fractions will arise.

Rounding rules of the event will dictate the conditions for the rounding of the resultant securities entitlement, where the application of the securities ratio results in a fractional unit.

For example, assume an underlying holding of 555 ABC, and a securities ratio of one new share for every four held. As a result of the entitlement calculation the holder would be entitled to 138.75 new shares. It is not possible to distribute 0.75 of a share, so this entitlement will require fractional rounding.

The most common conditions for the rounding of a fractional securities entitlement are:

1. Round up any fraction to the next whole unit.
2. Round up fractions of 0.5 and above to the next whole unit, and round down fractions less than 0.5 to the previous whole unit.
3. Round down fractions of 0.5 and below to the previous whole unit, and round up fractions more than 0.5 to the next whole unit.
4. Round down any fraction to the previous whole unit.
5. Distribute cash in lieu of securities fractions.

(Note: in cases where fractions are rounded down to the previous whole unit (points 3 and 4 above), the event terms may include the option for the position holder to purchase a fraction of a unit in order to round up its holding to the next whole unit.)

Table 11.1 illustrates the differing *resultant entitlements* that may be calculated according to the fractions conditions of the event, using a number of different event ratios based upon an underlying holding of 10,000 shares and cash for fractions terms of GBP2.00 per share. Note that within Table 11.1, each numbered column corresponds to the numbered rounding rules above.

Table 11.1

Event Ratio	Unrounded Entitlement	(1)	(2)	(3)	(4)	(5)
1 for 7	1,428.57	1,429	1,429	1,429	1,428	1,428 shares and GBP1.14
1 for 6	1,666.67	1,667	1,667	1,667	1,666	1,666 shares and GBP1.34
1 for 3	3,333.33	3,334	3,333	3,333	3,333	3,333 shares and GBP0.66

11.4.3 Securities Ratio Calculation Sequence

The calculation sequence refers to the order in which the underlying holding is multiplied and divided by the securities ratio and that *fraction* conditions are applied.

The sequence in which these steps are performed may result in differing *resultant entitlements*, and as with all other event conditions, it is important that the STO correctly interprets the event terms in order to calculate resultant entitlements accurately.

The most common calculation sequence is the following (which has also been that used in all the previous examples in this chapter).

Divide, Multiply, Round

1. Divide the underlying quantity by the second number of the ratio (divisor), then
2. Multiply the result by the first number (multiplier), then finally
3. Apply fraction rounding rule.

Using a ratio of two for three (European style), disregarding fractions, and assuming a holding of 9,995 XXX shares, the entitlement would be calculated as follows:

- Divide holding by 3 ($9{,}995/3 = 3{,}331.66$), multiply by 2 ($3{,}331.66 \times 2 = 6{,}663.32$), and round down fractions to the previous whole unit.

This produces an entitlement of 6,663 shares.

Two other sequences include the following.

Divide, Round, Multiply

1. Divide the underlying quantity by the second number of the ratio (divisor), then
2. Apply fraction rounding rule to the result, then finally
3. Multiply the result by the first number (multiplier).

Using a ratio of two for three (European style), disregarding fractions, and assuming a holding of 9,995 XXX shares, the entitlement would be calculated as follows:

- Divide holding by 3 ($9{,}995/3 = 3{,}331.66$), disregard fractions (3,331), and multiply by 2 ($3{,}331 \times 2 = 6{,}662$).

This produces an entitlement of 6,662 shares.

Multiply, Divide, Round

1. Multiply the underlying quantity by the first number (multiplier), then
2. Divide the result by the second number (divisor), then finally
3. Apply fraction rounding rule.

Using a ratio of two for three (European style), disregarding fractions, and assuming a holding of 9,995 XXX shares, the entitlement would be calculated as follows:

- Multiply holding by 2 ($9{,}995 \times 2 = 19{,}990$), divide by 3 ($19{,}990/3 = 6{,}663.33$), and round down fractions to the previous whole unit.

This produces an entitlement of 6,663 shares.

The differing results achieved by each calculation sequence can be compared within the above examples.

11.4.4 Calculation of Removal of Underlying Securities Holdings

Where the event is a *re-organization*, holdings in the *underlying security* are normally removed in full or in part as a result of the event. In this case the event terms will also include the conditions for the removal of the underlying security, and the STO will need to include this calculation in the calculation of resultant entitlements.

In the majority of cases the removal of holdings in the underlying security will be 100%, so the calculation is quite straightforward. On other occasions, the terms of the event dictate that only part of the underlying holding be removed. In such circumstances the terms will indicate the percentage of the underlying holding to be removed.

11.4.5 Calculation of Cash Payable to the Issuer

A very limited number of mandatory events, such as a mandatory *equity call*, will also include the payment of cash to the *issuer* in order for the position holder to receive its securities entitlement.

In such events, the Corporate Actions Department will calculate the quantity of new securities to be received, together with the cash payable.

The cash payable to the issuer will typically be calculated by applying the cash price (included in the event terms) to the resultant securities entitlement. This means that a dependency will exist between the two calculations, with the calculation of the securities entitlement being required to be performed prior to the calculation of the cash payment.

The topic of cash payable to the issuer is explored further within Chapter 18, 'Management of Voluntary Events', which also includes example calculations.

11.5 CALCULATION OF RESULTANT ENTITLEMENTS AGAINST OWNERSHIP POSITIONS

To date, throughout this chapter the calculation of resultant entitlements has been based simply upon the application of the event terms (e.g. ratios, rounding rules) to the quantity of the entitled holding.

In the case of position holders, the entitled holding typically reflects their entitled position as a result of accumulated *cum* trading, irrespective of whether any of those trades are actually settled and are reflected in the *settled custodian position*, or not (as described in Chapter 9, 'Determining Entitlement'). It is in fact the *location*(s) of the owners' entitled positions that reflects the quantity settled (as settled custodian position) and the quantity still to be settled (as *unsettled trades*).

We have generically referred to the resultant entitlement calculated against an unsettled trade as a '*claim*', in favour, or against, the STO. To date, no direct relationship has been drawn between the position holder (for whom the unsettled trade was originally executed) and the unsettled trade. The collection (by the STO) of a claimed resultant entitlement from a *counterparty* is simply expected to cover the disbursable obligations of the STO to its various position holders; therefore, this is not dissimilar to the collection of the resultant entitlement from the custodian.

Nonetheless, according to the type of event, whether the resultant entitlement is collected from the counterparty of an unsettled trade or from a custodian in respect of a settled custodian position will affect the way that the STO calculates the resultant entitlement against a position holder's entitled position.

Typically, when calculating the resultant entitlement against a position holder's entitled position, the STO will distinguish between

- *benefits*, and
- *re-organizations*.

11.5.1 Benefit Events

Benefit events are those events that result in an increase to the position holder's securities or cash position, without altering the *underlying security*; for example, a *bonus issue*. As such, where an *unsettled trade* exists, the securities or cash resulting from the benefit will be claimed (in addition to the settlement of the original trade), and such claims normally have no impact on the quantity or security of the original trade.

In this instance the STO will calculate the resultant entitlements due to be disbursed to position holders based upon their accumulated *cum* trading. The calculation of resultant entitlements to be collected from locations (both settled custodian and unsettled trades) will occur virtually independently. Claims collected against unsettled trades will simply cover the STO's various disbursable obligations.

11.5.2 Re-organization Events

In the case of re-organization events, unlike benefits, the effect of the event is to re-shape or re-structure the position holder's underlying securities position. Therefore, where an unsettled trade exists, the resultant entitlement will not be in addition to the original unsettled trade, but will in fact replace the traded quantity and/or security of the unsettled trade. The act of replacement of unsettled trades is known as *transformation*. The eventual settlement of transformations is described in more detail in Chapter 13, 'Collection/Disbursement of Resultant Entitlements'.

When the unsettled trade was originally transacted, the STO will have, within its position keeping records, updated the position holder's position (ownership), and at the same time passed entries indicating the open trade with the counterparty (location). (Refer to Chapter 5, 'Securities Position Management'). Both of these entries within the STO's position keeping records arise as a result of the single trade, and will adhere to the principles of *double entry book-keeping*.

When the unsettled trade is transformed as a result of a re-organization event, the traded quantity and/or security of the trade will be amended, and consequently the original trade entries to the STO's security position keeping will also be amended to reflect the new quantity and/or security of the trade. This will include, as it did on the original trade, an entry to reflect the trade in the position holder's position. It is therefore necessary for the Corporate Actions Department to avoid duplicating the effect of this in the position holder's overall position, and exclude it from any other calculations of resultant entitlements due to be disbursed to the position holder.

To do this the Corporate Actions Department will exclude the quantity of any unsettled trades from the position holder's entitled position, and therefore the resultant entitlement calculated directly against the position holder will be based upon that remaining quantity of its entitled holding that represents settled trades, which in turn is reflected within the settled custodian positions; this portion of the position holders' entitled position will be known as the settled entitled position. Any resultant entitlement due to the position holder as a result of unsettled trades will be passed to it via the transformation of the unsettled trade.

This concept is illustrated via the following example. Assume:

- A one for two *consolidation* (or *reverse split*), where ABC SGD1.00 Ordinary Shares are replaced by ABC SGD2.00 Ordinary Shares.
- Book A is long 176,000 ABC SGD1.00 Ordinary Shares of which 100,000 shares are settled.
- The further 76,000 ABC SGD1.00 Ordinary Shares, purchased on a *cum* basis from Counterparty X on behalf of Trading Book A, remain unsettled as at the *record date* of the event.
- Depot Y has a settled position of 100,000 ABC SGD1.00 Ordinary Shares.

The security positions for ABC SGD1.00 Ordinary Shares as at the record date will appear as shown in Table 11.2.

Table 11.2

ABC SGD1.00 Ordinary Shares			
Ownership			**Location**
Trading Book 'A'	+176,000	−100,000	Custodian Y, Main A/C
		−76,000	Counterparty 'X'
	+176,000	−176,000	

The resultant entitlement calculated against the unsettled trade for 76,000 ABC SGD1.00 Ordinary Shares on behalf of Trading Book A with Counterparty X, will result in the transformation of this trade to the following:

- Purchase 38,000 ABC SGD2.00 Ordinary Shares on behalf of Trading Book A from Counterparty X.

As a consequence, the trading book's position in ABC SGD1.00 Ordinary Shares will be reduced by 76,000 shares and a position of 38,000 ABC SGD2.00 Ordinary Shares will be created.

Out of the total entitlement (i.e. 176,000 shares) due to the trading book, as the resultant entitlement relating to 76,000 shares will be transformed, the Corporate Actions Department will exclude that transformed amount from entitlement calculations relating to the remaining 100,000 shares, i.e. the settled entitled position.

With respect to the trading book's total resultant entitlement in this example, the calculations shown in Table 11.3 apply.

Table 11.3

		ABC SGD1.00 Ordinary Shares		ABC SGD2.00 Ordinary Shares
Party	**Total Entitled Position**	**Settled Entitled Position**	**Unsettled Trade (to be Transformed)**	**Resultant Entitlement**
Book A	176,000	100,000		50,000
Book A – Counterparty X			76,000	38,000
				88,000

Note that the total *resultant entitlement* is 88,000 ABC SGD2.00 Ordinary Shares. By way of proving this figure, had the calculation method involved the direct division of the total entitled position by two, the result would have been identical.

11.6 BALANCING RESULTANT ENTITLEMENTS

The balancing of collectible and disbursable entitlements is an internal step, similar to the balancing of entitled positions (including unsettled trades) (refer to Chapter 9, 'Determining Entitlement'), which in this case ensures the integrity of the calculated resultant entitlements.

Balancing of resultant entitlements requires the sum of the *collectible resultant entitlements* to equal the sum of the *disbursable resultant entitlements.*

The Corporate Actions Department cannot assume that simply because the entitled positions (including unsettled trades) balance (as described in Chapter 9, 'Determining Entitlement'), that the resulting entitlements will also balance. Imbalances in the resultant entitlements may occur as a result of human error where calculations are being performed manually (either in their entirety or in part). In the majority of cases, imbalances will occur as a result of the treatment of fractions in securities events, where multiple disbursable entitlements are rounded versus only one or a few collectible entitlements.

This is best illustrated in the following simple example (see Table 11.4), where two long *ownership positions* are held versus a single *location* position. The terms of the event are a one for three *ratio*, with *fractions* being disregarded (rounded down).

It can be seen in Table 11.4 that the underlying holdings against which the resultant entitlements have been calculated are equal. Nonetheless, as a result of the rounding rule to disregard

Table 11.4

Disbursable Entitlements			Collectible Entitlements		
Party	**Underlying Holding**	**Resultant Entitlement**	**Party**	**Underlying Holding**	**Resultant Entitlement**
Book X	10,000	3,333	Depot A	30,000	10,000
Book Y	20,000	6,666			
total	**30,000**	**9,999**	*total*	**30,000**	**10,000**

fractions the sum of the disbursable entitlements is 9,999, whilst the sum of the collectible entitlements is 10,000. In this instance the STO will receive one more share than is required to cover the resultant entitlements to be disbursed. Conversely, it is possible for the STO to receive less than the total of amounts owed to position holders, where resultant entitlement is collected from multiple locations.

A number of different actions are available to the STO in order to resolve this type of imbalance, with the choice often depending upon whether the STO identifies a long or short entitlement imbalance. Where imbalance occurs as a result of the rounding rules of the event, in order to rectify the imbalance the STO could, for example, carry out one of two actions:

- **Assign Imbalance Quantity to a Fractions Account**
  In this case the STO would maintain a Fraction Account specifically for the purpose of accounting for fractions as a result of corporate action entitlements.

  Where a securities entitlement is created against the fractions account, the normal procedure is to accumulate all long positions over a period of time, and then sell the imbalances off, and/or to buy in the market any short positions where a short fall of resultant entitlement has occurred. In the case of a shortfall the STO must take swift action in buying the shortfall in order to cover its delivery obligations.

  Where a cash entitlement is created against the Fraction Account, the STO would normally write-off to P&L any debits and credits on a regular basis.

  The creation of such entitlements should always be authorized, to ensure the proper use of such an account.

  Using the previous example, an additional entitlement entry would be added against the Fractions Account in order to account for and correct the imbalance (see Table 11.5).

Table 11.5

Disbursable Entitlements			Collectible Entitlements		
Party	**Underlying Holding**	**Resultant Entitlement**	**Party**	**Underlying Holding**	**Resultant Entitlement**
Book X	10,000	3,333	Depot A	30,000	10,000
Book Y	20,000	6,666			
Fractions A/C	–	1			
total	**30,000**	**10,000**	*total*	**30,000**	**10,000**

- **Apply an Ad-hoc Adjustment to an Ownership Resultant Entitlement**
  In this case the STO could select a resultant entitlement(s) and either increase or decrease the calculated resultant entitlement in order to bring the overall entitlements into balance. It is likely that the STO would do this only to its own trading book positions, as resultant entitlements for *custody clients*, *counterparties* and *locations* must be calculated exactly

according to the terms of the event. Any such ad-hoc adjustment of resultant entitlements should always be authorized by the appropriate senior personnel.

Using the previous example, the resultant entitlement of the Trading Book X could be increased to 3,334. This would result in the total of *disbursable resultant entitlements* increasing to 10,000, which equals that of the *collectible resultant entitlements* (see Table 11.6).

Table 11.6

Disbursable Entitlements			Collectible Entitlements		
Party	**Underlying Holding**	**Resultant Entitlement**	**Party**	**Underlying Holding**	**Resultant Entitlement**
Book X	10,000	3,334	Depot A	30,000	10,000
Book Y	20,000	6,666			
total	**30,000**	**10,000**	*total*	**30,000**	**10,000**

11.7 RECONCILIATION OF RESULTANT ENTITLEMENTS

Reconciliation of resultant entitlements is designed to ensure that the *resultant entitlements* calculated by the STO equate to those calculated by external parties. The principles are again similar to those applied to the reconciliation of entitled positions (including unsettled trades) (refer to Chapter 9, 'Determining Entitlement'). Just because the entitled positions (including unsettled trades) may have been reconciled (as described in Chapter 9) provides no guarantee that resultant entitlement calculations reconcile; this step is designed to ensure that the entitlement conditions of the event have been correctly applied by all parties.

The identification of any errors in reconciliation as soon as possible will identify potential errors in the overall resultant entitlement calculation process, and avoid the incorrect posting and settlement of resultant entitlements.

Reconciliation of resultant entitlements can include:

- *Location* Resultant Entitlements
- *Ownership* Resultant Entitlements
- *Claims*

Each of these is described below.

11.7.1 Reconciliation of Location Resultant Entitlements

The most common reconciliation of resultant entitlements to external parties is that of comparing the STO's location entitlements to the custodian's.

Some custodians may issue pre-notification of the resultant entitlement due to the STO, such as is supported by the *S.W.I.F.T.* MT564 message.

The pre-notification provides the STO with the opportunity to identify and resolve any discrepancies prior to the passing of internal entries and the eventual receipt of the resultant entitlement from the custodian. The Corporate Actions Department should track where pre-notifications are expected and received. Upon receipt of the pre-notification, the STO will compare the custodian's entitlement details against its own calculations. This comparison will require not only that the quantity of the resultant entitlement reconciles, but also that the underlying account details, and the account to which the resultant entitlement will be paid, are accurate. (Note that the custodian may maintain multiple accounts on behalf of the STO).

Any inconsistencies in the information received from the custodian to that held by the STO require immediate investigation and corrective action. Where the underlying holdings do not reconcile (a discrepancy exists between the records of the STO and the custodian), it is highly unlikely that the resultant entitlements will reconcile. The reconciliation of the underlying holdings is recommended to have taken place prior to the calculation of the resultant entitlements, and any discrepancies resolved. Once the underlying holdings have been reconciled any major discrepancies are unlikely; nonetheless variation could still occur as a result of the different interpretation of the *issuer's* terms, for example, the treatment of *fractions*.

11.7.2 Reconciliation of Ownership Resultant Entitlements

Unlike the reconciliation of location resultant entitlements, the reconciliation of *resultant entitlements* against *ownership positions* is often a more informal process within the Corporate Actions Department. It is common for the Corporate Actions Department to rely on parties and departments outside of its own notifying it if a discrepancy exists in the calculated resultant entitlement. This may occur in a number of ways:

- The front office (traders responsible for a *trading book* position) may have independently calculated the expected resultant entitlement. Upon receipt of the notification of final entitlement from the Corporate Actions Department, the front office may advise the CA department of any discrepancy.
- The Reconciliation Department, in its normal course of business (of reconciliation of the front office trading book positions to those maintained within the back office), may identify a discrepancy between resultant entitlements posted from the calculations performed by the Corporate Actions Department to those calculated within the front office system (if this has been done independently).
- *Custody Clients* may have independently calculated the expected resultant entitlement. Upon receipt of the notification of final entitlement from the Corporate Actions Department they may advise the STO.

Despite such discrepancies being identified outside of the Corporate Actions Department, the responsibility for investigation and rectification of such discrepancies lies with the department itself. Failure to have formalized procedures in place does not absolve the Corporate Actions Department of its responsibility.

It is strongly recommended that the Corporate Actions Department takes advantage of these outside reconciliations, in order to gain greater control in the calculation of resultant entitlements.

11.7.3 Reconciliation of Claims

As previously described, *claims* are generated against *unsettled trades*, and include both collectible and disbursable entitlements incorporating:

- claims made by the STO on *counterparties*, and
- claims made against the STO by counterparties.

The reconciliation of claims is just as vital as that of location resultant entitlements and ownership resultant entitlements. It is similar to that of the reconciliation of unsettled trades (refer to Chapter 9 'Determining Entitlement'), in that its degree of formality will differ from market to market, and is often dictated by the service offered by the *CSD/ICSD*.

Where the CSD/ICSD automatically identifies claims, the claim detail is normally communicated to the parties of the claim, therefore allowing the STO to reconcile its own calculations. Alternatively where such a service does not exist, a more informal reconciliation may take place by way of the verification of the details contained in claim notifications issued directly by the claiming parties (refer to Chapter 10, 'Communication of Event Information').

11.8 DETERMINATION OF COLLECTIBLE AND DISBURSABLE ACCOUNTS

In parallel with the mathematical aspects of resultant entitlement calculation, and prior to the passing of any internal accounting entries to reflect *resultant entitlements* (refer to Chapter 12, 'Passing of Internal Entries'), the Corporate Actions Department must determine the accounts over which receipt and disbursement of resultant entitlements will occur. Note: the account(s) must also form part of the location resultant entitlement reconciliation criteria.

However, it is not always the case that the same account that holds the underlying entitled position will be the account to and from which the resultant entitlement is disbursed or collected. The reasons for this include:

- A securities-only depot account is held with the custodian. When cash is distributed it is credited to a separate designated nostro (bank) account.
- A securities account and a cash account are held with the custodian, but the cash account is for a specified (normally local) currency only. The cash distribution is in a currency other than that of the specified currency account, requiring distribution to a separate designated nostro account.
- A *custody client* holds a securities-only account with the STO. All cash amounts are to be paid to the client's designated bank account.

The *static data* records of the STO would be expected to hold the details of accounts to and from which resultant entitlements should be disbursed and collected, including both normal (i.e. the same as for trading and settlement) and alternative accounts. This information is typically set up against custody clients and locations only. This is because resultant entitlements against *trading books* are satisfied via internal book keeping entries only (i.e. are not actually paid away), and claims are normally settled via the settlement account of the claim *counterparty*, typically the same account over which the underlying trade would be settled.

11.9 SUMMARY

The focus of the Corporate Actions Department is to calculate disbursable and collectible entitlements accurately, and therefore the calculation of resultant entitlements is of fundamental importance. It is at this stage that the STO will bring together the event terms and the entitled positions (ownership position and location, including unsettled trades) in order to calculate resultant entitlements.

This stage is much more than simply a mathematical process within the lifecycle of the event. The calculation of resultant entitlements includes the balancing and reconciliation of those entitlements, together with the identification of disbursable and collectible accounts.

Strict controls should be in place throughout the calculation process and prior to the passing of internal entries and final receipt and disbursement of resultant entitlements. In some ways this step can be considered the ‘point of no return’ for the STO, as unless errors are identified at this time the STO could be at serious risk.

12 Passing of Internal Entries

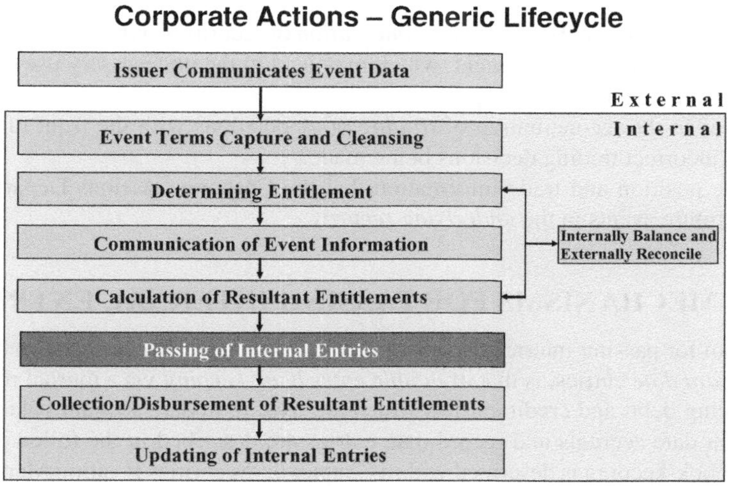

12.1 INTRODUCTION

Once resultant entitlements are calculated and reconciled, internal security and/or cash entries are passed. The entries will show any change to the *underlying security* position, and the distribution of any securities and/or cash that is expected to occur on the *distribution date* or *effective date* of the event. It is at this time that the impact of the event is reflected in the position holder's security and/or cash positions, and the differences between *benefit* events and *re-organization* events become apparent. (This difference is illustrated in the examples in Chapter 15, 'Examples of Mandatory Events').

This chapter will describe

- the various entries passed;
- their purpose;
- their impact and timing within the overall lifecycle of the event.

The chapter also illustrates the entries and results applicable to both benefit and re-organization events. Note that entries to reflect the settlement of entitlements are described in Chapter 14, 'Updating of Internal Entries'.

12.2 THE STO'S RISK

As with any other securities or cash activity, the importance of accuracy and timeliness in the passing of internal entries to reflect that activity cannot be overstated. Errors or delays in the passing of such entries means that the STO is not in full control of its securities and/or cash positions, potentially leading to incorrect business decisions.

The balancing and reconciliation of resultant entitlement calculations will enable the STO to ensure accuracy in these entries, but it is also important that the Corporate Actions Department makes sure that the entries reflecting the expected entitlements are passed in a timely manner.

Failure to pass entries in a timely manner may have repercussions within other departments within the STO, as well as that of the Corporate Actions Department. Such repercussions include:

- Discrepancies in the normal day to day *reconciliation* of securities and cash positions outside of the Corporate Actions Department, which may lead to the unnecessary use of resources to investigate and resolve.
- Discrepancies in the reconciliation of *trading book* positions with the front office, which may lead to incorrect trading decisions being made.
- Errors in the position and trade information that the Corporate Actions Department may retrieve for future events in the *underlying security*.

12.3 MECHANISMS FOR PASSING INTERNAL ENTRIES

The mechanism for passing internal entries to reflect *entitlement date* accruals (where appropriate) and *record date* entries, is that of *double entry book-keeping* via a journal representing a set of balancing debit and credit entries, which are used to update account balances. (Note that entitlement date accruals and record date entries are described in the following section. Double entry book-keeping is described within Chapter 5, 'Securities Position Management'.)

The journal (consisting of two or more balancing debit and credit entries), which the STO passes as a result of trading activity, will typically reflect the position holder and location of the securities (or cash) at a given point in the lifecycle of the trade. This is achieved because the information contained in the single trade record is sufficient to identify both the position holder and the *location*.

For example, Table 12.1 shows the position immediately after the first trade, a purchase of 2,000 Sony Corporation shares on behalf of Trading Book 'A' from Counterparty 'X', has been executed.

Table 12.1

Sony Corporation Shares (as at 15th June)			
Ownership		Location	
Trading Book 'A'	+2000	−2000	Counterparty 'X'
	+2000	−2000	

From the single trade record, the STO is able to identify both the trading book for which the purchase was executed, together with the *counterparty* from whom the securities were bought.

In this way the trade record and its corresponding journal can be said to show both sides of the trade activity, i.e. to whom the securities are owed, and from where they are to be received (or are currently located).

Entries will be passed for each collectible entitlement, the contra entry being passed to an Event Control Account (or similar), and separate entries will be passed for each disbursable entitlement with their contra entries being passed over the same Event Control Account.

Table 12.2 represents the credit of cash to the position holder (in this instance a trading book).

Table 12.2

Disbursable Entries			
Debit		**Credit**	
Event Control Account	JPY 105,000	JPY 105,000	Trading Book 'A'
	JPY 105,000	JPY 105,000	

Conversely, Table 12.3 represents the anticipated receipt of cash to the STO's bank account. Note that such concepts apply equally to corporate action events resulting in a securities impact.

Table 12.3

Collectible Entries			
Debit		**Credit**	
JPY Bank Account Projected	JPY 105,000	JPY 105,000	Event Control Account
	JPY 105,000	JPY 105,000	

Once journals have been passed for all resultant entitlements that are due to be disbursed or collected, the balance of the event control account should be zero. Should a balance remain in the event control account once all journals have been passed, this means that the journals reflecting collectible and disbursable entitlements do not balance. This could occur despite the Corporate Actions Department having already balanced the resultant entitlements (as described in Chapter 11, 'Calculation of Resultant Entitlements'), due to an error in the passing of the journal entries.

The impact of journals to the Event Control Account is summarized within Table 12.4.

Table 12.4

Event Control Account (for Sony Corporation Dividend) – JPY Account				
Entry Date	**Narrative**	**Debit**	**Credit**	**Balance**
	Opening balance			*0*
15th June	Trading Book 'A' Dividend Income	105,000		−105,000
15th June	JPY Bank Account Projected		105,000	0

Note that in order to distinguish individual events for control purposes, separate control accounts are normally used.

12.4 TYPES OF INTERNAL ENTRIES

As indicated previously, the high level reason for the passing of internal entries is to reflect the resultant entitlement as a result of the corporate action event.

Prior to settlement of resultant entitlements, two types of entries may be made by the STO (depending upon whether an entitlement date applies to the event, or not):

- Entitlement Date entries, and
- Record Date entries.

Both of these are explained within this chapter.

Two roadmap diagrams are provided within this section, for the purpose of guiding the reader through the different types of entries, their applicability and their timing to mandatory benefit events, and to mandatory re-organization events. The textual description of the types of entries follows the roadmaps.

For a mandatory event where an entitlement date is applicable, Figure 12.1 illustrates the typical entries (although exceptions exist) passed on entitlement date and record date. Note that *settlement date* entries (depicted in the 'SD' row) are detailed within Chapter 14, 'Updating of Internal Entries'.

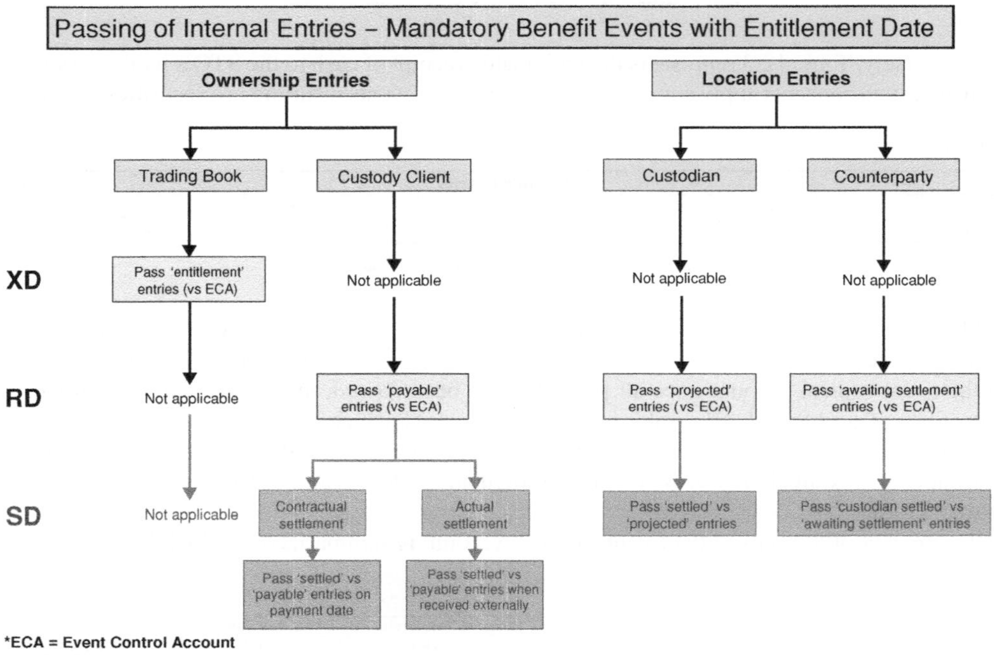

Figure 12.1 Internal entries for mandatory benefit events.

For a mandatory *re-organization* event (where an entitlement date is normally not applicable), Figure 12.2 illustrates the typical entries passed on record date. Note that settlement date entries (depicted in the 'SD' row) are detailed within Chapter 14, 'Updating of Internal Entries'.

It is important to note that *unsettled trade* entries are not applicable to *contractual settlement* custody clients, as by definition all trades for such clients settle automatically on value date and therefore no unsettled trades exist.

12.4.1 Entitlement Date Entries

Entitlement date entries are known as *Ex-Date Accrual Entries* in most markets, and are applicable to those events that have an ex period, typically *benefit* events (as described in Chapter 8, 'Event Terms Capture and Cleansing').

The purpose of these entries is to reflect the impact of *resultant entitlements* specifically on *ownership positions* at the same time as the price of the *underlying security* changes (as a result of the event). As such entries reflect the total amount of the benefit that will be received

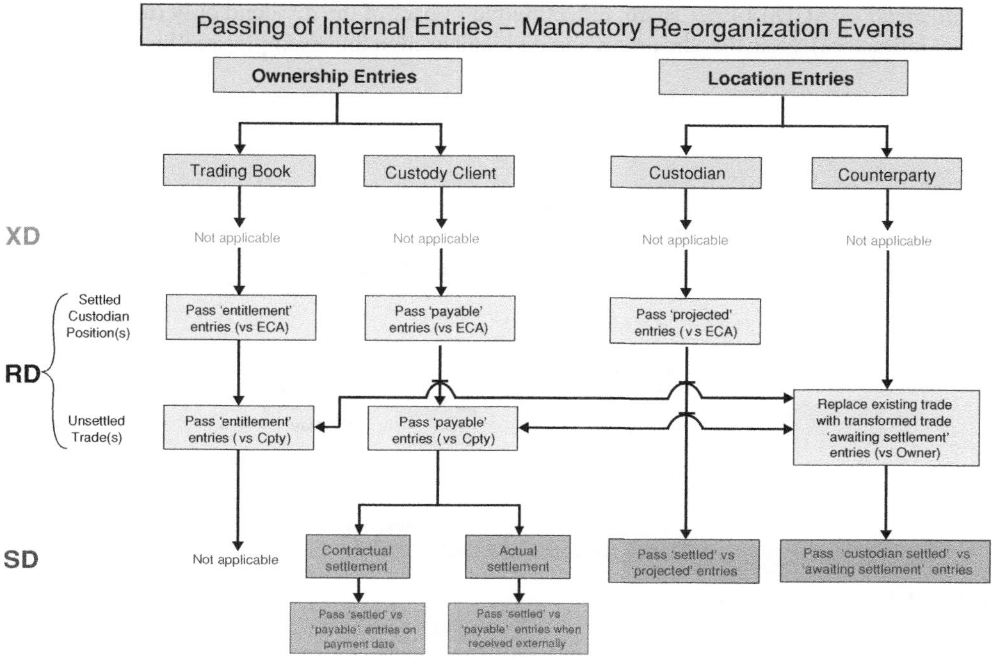

*ECA = Event Control Account

Figure 12.2 Internal entries for mandatory re-organization events.

at a later date; they are known as 'accrual entries'. (Note that entitlement date entries are not applicable to locations).

The majority of STOs will pass ex-date accrual entries against *trading book* positions, as it is standard practice to mark-to-market (explained below) such positions on a daily basis. Nonetheless the practice may be equally applicable to *custody client* positions, where the *SLA* with the client includes valuations of the client's portfolio. It is important to note that ex-date accrual entries are applicable only to position holders; accrual entries do not apply to entitlements collected from *locations* or to *claims*.

In the particular case of *re-organization* events, as the price of the underlying security normally changes on the *effective date* (equivalent to record date) ex-date accrual entries are not applicable. Therefore the record date entries will reflect the changes to securities and cash positions and their value.

As described previously in Chapter 9, 'Determining Entitlement', the market price of the underlying security will normally reflect the value of the benefit to a buyer of the security prior to the entitlement date of the event, with the market price dropping on the entitlement date to reflect that any buyers from this date forward will not be entitled to the benefit. In order to identify any theoretical ('unrealized') profit or loss, in the normal course of business the STO will perform an accounting procedure known as 'mark-to-market', whereby the current market value (based upon the current market price) of a trading book position is compared to the purchase cost (or previous mark-to-market cost) of that position.

The following example (shown in Figure 12.3 and originally used in Chapter 9) illustrates the change in the market price of QANTAS Airways ordinary shares, as a result of the declaration of a *dividend* of AUD0.14 per share, reflecting the impact of the dividend only (and no other market influences). Note that the prices and dividend used in this example are illustrative only.

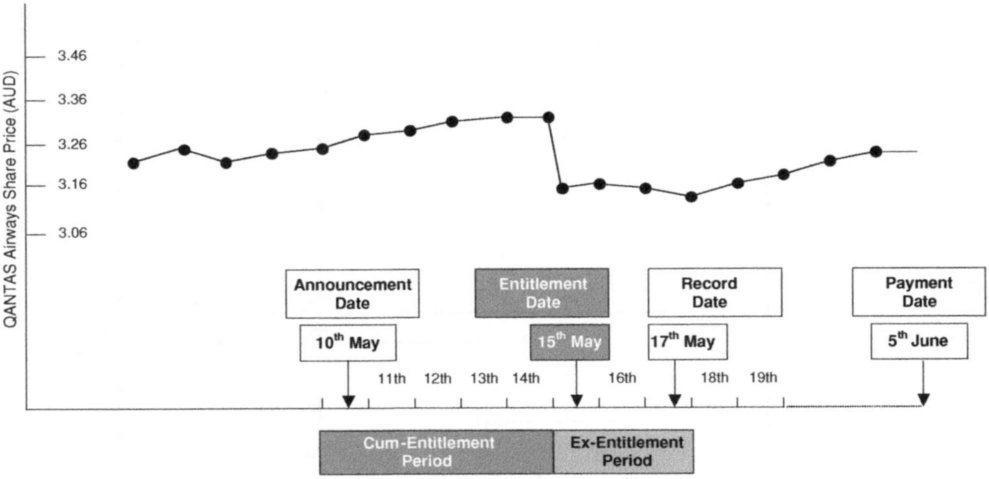

Figure 12.3 Change in market price.

As a result of the drop in the market price of the underlying security to which the benefit event applies on the entitlement date, any marking-to-market of a position in that security on or after the entitlement date would reveal a theoretical loss.

In a situation where Trading Book 'A' purchased 1,000,000 Qantas Airways shares in early May (a number of days before a dividend was announced), at a price of AUD3.20 per share, and the market price fluctuated thereafter between AUD3.20 and AUD3.30, the unrealized profit for Trading Book 'A' immediately prior to the entitlement date of a dividend would, for example, appear as shown in Table 12.5.

Table 12.5

Trading Book A – AUD Account				
Entry Date	**Narrative**	**Debit**	**Credit**	**Balance**
	Balance brought forward from 5th May			*0*
6th May	Principal value of purchase of 1m @ 3.20	3,200,000.00		+3,200,000.00
7th May	Unrealized profit on 1m @3.25	50,000.00		+3,250,000.00
8th May	Unrealized loss on 1m @3.21		40,000.00	+3,210,000.00
9th May	Unrealized profit on 1m @3.24	30,000.00		+3,240,000.00
10th May	Unrealized profit on 1m @3.25	10,000.00		+3,250,000.00
11th May	Unrealized profit on 1m @3.27	20,000.00		+3,270,000.00
12th May	Unrealized profit on 1m @3.28	10,000.00		+3,280,000.00
13th May	Unrealized profit on 1m @3.29	10,000.00		+3,290,000.00
14th May	Unrealized profit on 1m @3.30	10,000.00		+3,300,000.00

On the entitlement date (15th May), the market price of Qantas Airways shares drops to AUD3.16 reflecting the impact of the dividend. This would cause the STO to pass two entries on the entitlement date. The first of these entries represents the unrealized loss and is reflected in Table 12.6 (note that entries listed previously are in grey text).

Second, in order to reflect the true value of the trading book position, it is necessary to pass internal entries against the trading position on the entitlement date, thereby immediately compensating the trading book position for the reduction in value of the underlying security. This entry is reflected in Table 12.7.

Table 12.6

Trading Book A – AUD Account				
Entry Date	**Narrative**	**Debit**	**Credit**	**Balance**
	Balance brought forward from 5th May			*0*
6th May	Principal value of purchase of 1m @3.20	3,200,000.00		+3,200,000.00
7th May	Unrealized profit on 1m @3.25	50,000.00		+3,250,000.00
8th May	Unrealized loss on 1m @3.21		40,000.00	+3,210,000.00
9th May	Unrealized profit on 1m @3.24	30,000.00		+3,240,000.00
10th May	Unrealized profit on 1m @3.25	10,000.00		+3,250,000.00
11th May	Unrealized profit on 1m @3.27	20,000.00		+3,270,000.00
12th May	Unrealized profit on 1m @3.28	10,000.00		+3,280,000.00
13th May	Unrealized profit on 1m @3.29	10,000.00		+3,290,000.00
14th May	Unrealized profit on 1m @3.30	10,000.00		+3,300,000.00
15th May	Unrealized loss on 1m @3.16		140,000.00	+3,160,000.00

Table 12.7

Trading Book A – AUD Income Account				
Entry Date	**Narrative**	**Debit**	**Credit**	**Balance**
	Balance brought forward from 14th May			*0*
15th May	Dividend on 1m @ AUD0.14 per share		140,000.00	+140,000.00

Note that the unrealized P&L entries would be passed as a result of the daily mark-to-market procedure (not handled directly by the Corporate Actions Department), whereas the entry for the credit of the dividend would be the responsibility of the Corporate Actions Department.

Where the benefit event has resulted in:

- a cash entitlement, the ex date accruals will be immediately reflected as realized profit (as described above);
- a securities entitlement, the ex date accruals will reflect the additional securities position which will then be included in the ongoing mark-to-market process.

With regard to a benefit event that results in a securities entitlement, assume that, for example, Trading Book 'A' held a trading position of 5,000,000 Marks & Spencer shares (purchased many months previously). Entries relating to a one for four (i.e. one new share for every four currently held) *bonus issue* must be passed as at the entitlement date, to reflect the revised trading position of 6,250,000 shares.

In addition, note that it is vital for such entries to be passed not only within the STO's main books & records system, but also within the trader's trading system (where appropriate) and at the same time, in order for front office and operation's records to agree when a trading book reconciliation is attempted. This point is illustrated in Figure 12.4.

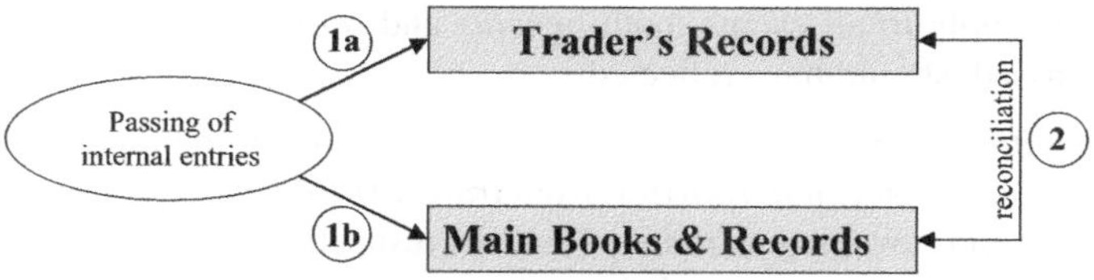

Figure 12.4 Simultaneous updating of internal records.

Step 1a: the trader's records must be updated with changes to securities positions.
Step 1b: the STO's main books & records must be updated with changes to securities positions.

Step 2: providing that steps 1a and 1b are actioned on time and at the same time, reconciliation of trading positions following a corporate action event will reveal agreement between trader's and operation's records.

Trading Between Entitlement Date and Record Date (or Payment Date −1)

As trading in the *underlying security* may continue on a *cum* basis up until the *record date* of the event, it is necessary for the Corporate Actions Department to monitor any changes in the *resultant entitlements* against trading positions, and ensure that the ex date accrual entries passed on the entitlement date are amended accordingly.

Table 12.8 depicts the owner's position as at ex date, followed by a *special cum* purchase resulting in a revised entitled position.

Table 12.8

	Trade (on a Cum basis)	Entitled Position
Securities position as at ex-date	n/a	+10,000,000
Special cum purchase on ex-date +1	+2,000,000	+12,000,000

The original ex date accrual entries (based upon a cash dividend rate of USD0.25 per share) are reflected in Table 12.9, followed by an additional entry resulting from the special-cum purchase shown in Table 12.10.

Table 12.9

Disbursable Entries			
Debit		Credit	
Event Control Account	USD 2,500,000.00	USD 2,500,000.00	Trading Book 'A'
	USD 2,500,000.00	USD 2,500,000.00	

Table 12.10

Disbursable Entries			
Debit		Credit	
Event Control Account	USD 500,000.00	USD 500,000.00	Trading Book 'A'
	USD 500,000.00	USD 500,000.00	

12.4.2 Record Date Entries

Record date entries apply to all events, both *benefits* and *re-organizations*. The result, once these entries are passed, should have reflected

- The *resultant entitlement* that is expected to be collected from the *location*; that is, from *custodians*, from *claims* on *counterparties*, from *transformed trades*. These are described as 'projected' entries and 'awaiting settlement' entries respectively.
- The resultant entitlement that is to be disbursed to position holders. These are described as 'payable' entries.

Entries such as these allow the STO to predict future securities and cash positions accurately, the business principles of which are the same as those applied to trade position keeping. (Note that these projected entries will be replaced by 'settled' entries once settlement of cash and/or securities has occurred; such entries are described within Chapter 14, 'Updating of Internal Entries'.)

The exact entries passed by the STO on the record date may vary according to whether ex-date accrual entries have already been passed, or not, and will also vary as to whether a trading book's resultant entitlement has been based upon the settled sub-position (i.e. unsettled trades that will be expected to transform).

Where ex-date accrual entries have not been passed, a journal entry will be made for every resultant entitlement that has been calculated, i.e. entitlements against *trading book* positions and custody clients (ownership positions), locations, claims (both against and in favour of the STO), and for transformed trades.

The STO will typically use a 'control account' to offset each entry. The net effect of all entries will be for the control account to have a balance of zero.

Benefit Events

In the case of benefit events, record date entries will be passed against owners (where not already passed on *entitlement date*), and against all location-types.

Table 12.11 illustrates a record date entry for cash disbursable to an owner (as entitlement date entries had not been passed previously).

Table 12.11

Disbursable Entries			
Debit		**Credit**	
Event Control Account	USD 30,000.00	USD 30,000.00	Custody Client Payable
	USD 30,000.00	USD 30,000.00	

In comparison, Table 12.12 illustrates record date entries for cash collectible from a custodian and from a counterparty (against whom the STO has issued a claim).

Table 12.12

Collectible Entries			
Debit		**Credit**	
Custodian 'X' SC a/c Projected	USD 20,000.00	USD 20,000.00	Event Control Account
Counterparty T Awaiting Settlement	USD 10,000.00	USD 10,000.00	Event Control Account
	USD 30,000.00	USD 30,000.00	

Re-organization Events

In the case of re-organization events, *record date* entries will be passed against all *position holders*, and against all *location*-types.

In contrast to benefit events, for a re-organization, where part of the position holder's *resultant entitlement* is reflected within a *transformed trade*, entries representing that entitlement will be posted between the *counterparty* of the transformed trade and the position holder, (i.e. the control account will not apply). This is because when the unsettled trade was originally transacted, the STO will have, within its position keeping records, updated the position holder's position (ownership), and at the same time passed entries indicating the open trade with the counterparty (location). (Refer to Chapter 5, 'Securities Position Management'). Both of these entries within the STO's position keeping records are as a result of the single trade, and adhere to the principles of *double entry book-keeping*.

When the unsettled trade is transformed as a result of a re-organization event, the traded quantity and/or security of the trade will be amended, and consequently the original trade entries to the STO's security position keeping will also be amended to reflect the new quantity and/or security of the trade. This will include, as per the original trade, an entry to reflect the trade in the position holder's position.

This concept is illustrated via the following example (originally detailed within Chapter 11, 'Calculation of Resultant Entitlements'). Assume:

- A one for two *consolidation* (or *reverse split*), where ABC SGD1.00 Ordinary Shares are replaced by ABC SGD2.00 Ordinary Shares.
- Trading Book A is long 176,000 ABC SGD1.00 Ordinary Shares of which 100,000 shares are settled.
- The further 76,000 ABC SGD1.00 Ordinary Shares, purchased on a *cum* basis from Counterparty X on behalf of Trading Book A, remain unsettled as at the record date of the event.
- Depot Y has a settled position of 100,000 ABC SGD1.00 Ordinary Shares.

The following three tables illustrate the record date entries relating to the introduction of the new security, ABC SGD2.00 Ordinary Shares. Table 12.13 relates to the transformed trade with the counterparty; note that equivalent entries for the original purchase cost are not required to be passed as the net settlement value will be retained.

Table 12.13

Transformed Trade Entries (ABC SGD2.00 Ordinary Shares)			
Debit		**Credit**	
Counterparty 'X' Awaiting Settlement	38,000	38,000	Trading Book 'A'
	38,000	38,000	

Table 12.14 reflects the remaining quantity of shares owned by the trading book (and which were represented by a settled custodian position as at record date).

Table 12.14

Disbursable Entries (ABC SGD2.00 Ordinary Shares)			
Debit		**Credit**	
Event Control Account	50,000	50,000	Trading Book 'A'
	50,000	50,000	

Table 12.15 represents the settled custodian position expected to be received at the custodian on the payment/distribution date.

Table 12.15

Collectible Entries (ABC SGD2.00 Ordinary Shares)			
Debit		**Credit**	
Custodian 'Y' Main a/c Projected	50,000	50,000	Event Control Account
	50,000	50,000	

Tables 12.16 to 12.18 illustrate the record date entries relating to the removal of the original security, ABC SGD1.00 Ordinary Shares. These tables are simply a mirror image of the above entries, containing the original quantities.

Table 12.16

Transformed Trade Entries (ABC SGD1.00 Ordinary Shares)			
Debit		Credit	
Trading Book 'A'	76,000	76,000	Counterparty 'X' Awaiting Settlement
	76,000	76,000	

Table 12.17

Disbursable Entries (ABC SGD1.00 Ordinary Shares)			
Debit		Credit	
Trading Book 'A'	100,000	100,000	Event Control Account
	100,000	100,000	

Table 12.18

Collectible Entries (ABC SGD1.00 Ordinary Shares)			
Debit		Credit	
Event Control Account	100,000	100,000	Custodian 'Y' Main a/c Projected
	100,000	100,000	

Where ex-date accrual entries have already been passed against position holder's *resultant entitlement*, the STO may (according to its own preferences and/or system constraints) either:

- reverse ex-date accrual entries, and pass record date entries for every resultant entitlement calculated (as described above), or
- pass location and claim entitlement entries on the record date against an offsetting entry to the event control account, i.e. not including ownership resultant entitlement entries. The aim on record date will be for the event control account to have a balance of zero.

12.5 REVIEW OF REQUIRED INTERNAL ENTRIES

As described earlier in this chapter, the conditions of a specific event plus the types of resultant entitlement will determine the required entries; these are summarized in Table 12.19.

Table 12.19

Event Types	Entry Type	Applicable to Resultant Entitlements....				
		Owners		Location		
		Trading Book	Custody Client	Claims in Favour	Claims Against	Settled Custodian
Events with an ex entitlement date	Entitlement Date (Accrual) Entries	Yes	Dependent upon SLA, but usually more rarely than trading books	No	No	No
	Record Date (Projected) Entries	Yes, if to replace entitlement date entries*	Yes, if to replace entitlement date entries*	Yes	Yes	Yes
Events without an ex entitlement date	Entitlement Date (Accrual) Entries	No	No	No	No	No
	Record Date (Projected) Entries	Yes	Yes	Yes	Yes	Yes

*Refer to Section 12.4.2 for an explanation

12.6 SUMMARY

In order for the STO to remain in full control of its assets at all times, it is vital to reflect expected resultant entitlements as a result of corporate action events, at the appropriate times.

Adoption of this practice enables close monitoring of securities and/or cash receivable from custodians and claims on counterparties, and the projection of future securities/cash balances. Failure to utilize this (or a very similar) regime is likely to result in a loss of control by the STO.

ENDNOTE: within this chapter, certain figures, tables and text have been reproduced with permission from *Securities Operations: A Guide to Trade and Position Management*, ISBN 0-471-49758-4, author Michael Simmons, publisher John Wiley & Sons, Ltd.

13
Collection/Disbursement of Resultant Entitlements

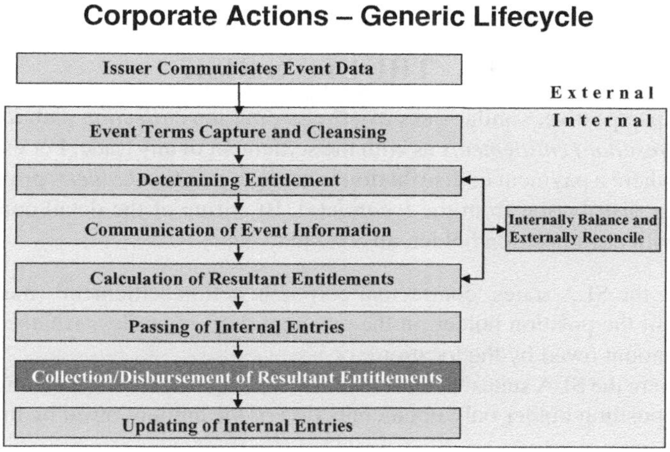

13.1 INTRODUCTION

The collection and disbursement of *resultant entitlements* represents the *settlement* of those resultant entitlements, including the collection from the *custodian* (location), collection of *claims*, disbursement of resultant entitlements against ownership positions and the disbursement of claims.

The key date for the settlement of resultant entitlements, as announced in the *event terms* (refer to Chapter 8, 'Event Terms Capture and Cleansing') is the *payment date/distribution date* or *effective date* of the event. Where an event results in the distribution of resultant entitlements or the *re-organization* of a holding, the event terms will also include a due date at which this will occur. This date may be known as the payment date or distribution date, in the case of *benefit* events, and the effective date in the case of re-organizations.

Collectible and disbursable resultant entitlements have previously been calculated in preparation for this milestone (refer to Chapter 11, 'Calculation of Resultant Entitlements') and internal entries have been passed to reflect the expected resultant entitlements (refer to Chapter 12, 'Passing of Internal Entries').

The settlement of resultant entitlements may take a number of forms, according to the prevailing settlement methods within the individual market, and the type of resultant entitlement, i.e. whether the resultant entitlement is associated with a custodian, a claim, a *trading book* or a *custody client*. Such forms are:

- for collectible resultant entitlements; electronic or physical, i.e. often electronic from the custodian, but physical where direct between the issuer and STO;

- for disbursable resultant entitlements; electronic (issuance of settlement instruction to pay-away), physical (pay-away by paper transfers or cheque), or book entry (internal credit).

The purpose of this chapter is to describe the various forms that the settlement of corporate action resultant entitlements may take. Note that whilst describing such forms, reference will be made to commonly used trade settlement terms; readers are advised that a prior understanding of such terms is recommended; refer to *Securities Operations – a Guide to Trade and Position Management* by Michael Simmons (one of the authors of this book).

13.2 THE STO'S RISK

From the STO's perspective, similar risks exist regarding the *collection* and *disbursement* of corporate action *resultant entitlements* as with the settlement of any trade. For example, risk to the STO occurs where a payment or distribution is made to *position holders*, prior to collection of the payment or distribution from the *location*(s). By virtue of the detail contained within the STO's *SLA* with each position holder, an STO may be:

- at risk – where the SLA states 'contractual corporate action settlement' (meaning that the STO must credit the position holder on the payment date, regardless whether the STO has received the amount owed by the location), or
- not at risk – where the SLA states 'actual corporate action settlement' (meaning that the STO will credit the position holder only upon collection of the amount owed by the location).

In order to maximize efficiency and minimize costs in relation to the act of settling resultant entitlements, the STO needs, prior to the due settlement date of the event, to have ensured that

- all resultant entitlement calculations are verified, balanced and reconciled (refer to Chapter 11, 'Calculation of Resultant Entitlements'), and
- all collectible and disbursable accounts have been correctly identified (refer to Chapter 11, 'Calculation of Resultant Entitlements').

In addition, the STO needs to be aware of the prevailing market conventions for the settlement of corporate action resultant entitlements as they differ from the conventions for settlement of normal trades, and the nature of its SLAs with custodians, and with its own clients.

The evolution of corporate actions market-wide practices towards an automated settlement environment has pursued a similar path to, and followed the automation of, trade settlement. Nonetheless, some corporate actions in some markets may not be automated. The varying degrees of automation that exist across market places will inevitably impact the STO's operational procedures, and the risks associated with the settlement of resultant entitlement.

In order to reduce risk, irrespective of the form that settlement may take, standard settlement procedures will be applied by the STO to reconcile the collection of expected resultant entitlements and disbursement of resultant entitlements, and to update its records accordingly (refer to Chapter 14, 'Updating of Internal Entries').

Where settlement quantities differ from that expected by the STO, urgent reconciliation is required in order to identify the nature of the discrepancy (refer to Chapter 9, 'Determining Entitlement' and Chapter 11, 'Calculation of Resultant Entitlements'), and take the appropriate corrective action.

13.3 COLLECTION OF RESULTANT ENTITLEMENTS FROM THE CUSTODIAN

In the normal course of its operations, a custodian may have previously notified the STO of the resultant entitlement amount it intends paying to the STO (refer to Chapter 11, 'Calculation of Resultant Entitlements'); the STO should have reconciled the custodian's amount with its own calculations. The notification from the custodian would typically have taken place immediately following the *record date* of the event, once all settlement processing on the record date (in the *underlying security*) has been completed.

Following on from this the STO will expect to collect the resultant entitlement on

- the *payment date/distribution date* of the event, where the event is a *benefit*, or
- the *effective date* of the event, where the event is a *re-organization*.

The actual collection of the resultant entitlement will be completely unsolicited by the STO. Unlike trade settlement, the STO is not required to issue and match settlement instructions with the delivering party. Nonetheless it is vital that the Corporate Actions Department monitors all expected collections according to their due date, and subsequently monitors overdue collections.

As stated previously, it is important that the STO has correctly identified the form that the collection from the custodian will take (i.e. how the resultant entitlement will be received), in order to monitor outstanding collections accurately. These forms are

- physical collection and
- electronic collection.

Both of these are described below. This will generally reflect the nature of the location of the underlying holding.

In some markets electronic collection of resultant entitlements is prevalent, whereas in other markets it is common to find that physical collection is the norm.

13.3.1 Physical Collection

The STO should expect physical collection (i.e. a cheque or warrant) of the resultant entitlement, when the underlying holding is held in certificated (or physical) form on the issuer's register of shareholders (i.e. not via a custodian). In this instance the location of the holding would be the *issuer*, and collection of the resultant entitlement will be directly from the issuer (or an agent acting on its behalf).

Where the event results in the distribution of new securities or cash, the STO will receive (typically via the mail) new certificates or a cheque respectively. Where the event results in the re-organization of the underlying holding, the STO will be required to return to the issuer (or to destroy) the certificates that represent the underlying holding, and will in exchange receive new certificates that represent the new holding.

Despite the increased automation in settlements processing in the majority of markets, the physical settlement of corporate action resultant entitlements is still prevalent, particularly in those markets where positions may still be held in certificated form. Needless to say, physical settlement introduces further issues to the STO in ensuring that amounts owed to the STO are received in a timely manner relative to the due date.

The STO may also, on very rare occasions, expect to collect physical payment of cash from a custodian, where its account with the custodian holds only securities positions, and the nature of the SLA with the custodian does not support the electronic payment of cash.

13.3.2 Electronic Collection

Electronic collection of resultant entitlements can be expected where the underlying position is held via a custodian or *CSD*/ICSD. The STO will be issued with an electronic message by the custodian (typically on the due date) to advise that 'good value' has been given to the resultant entitlement and that the STO's account has been adjusted to reflect the resultant entitlement (i.e. the custodian has effected the necessary book entries to reflect the resultant entitlement due).

Where the event results in the distribution of new securities or cash, the STO's account (at the custodian/CSD/ICSD) will be credited with the new securities or cash respectively. Where the event results in the re-organization of the underlying holding, the STO's account will be adjusted to reflect the removal of the *underlying security* and the crediting of the new securities.

The custodian will effect settlement either:

- to the same 'account' in which the underlying position is held – via book entry, or
- to an associated or mandated account (Refer to Chapter 11, 'Calculation of Resultant Entitlements', where determination of collectible/disbursable accounts is outlined).

The STO may also expect to collect electronic payment of cash directly from an issuer (where the underlying holding exists in physical registered form), as increasingly issuers are offering shareholders the ability to receive cash via direct credit to a designated bank account.

13.4 DISBURSEMENT OF RESULTANT ENTITLEMENTS TO POSITION HOLDERS

The actual disbursement of resultant entitlements to *position holders* may be a simple internal *book entry*, or may be paid (in the case of cash) or delivered (in the case of securities) to an external party, requiring the STO to generate *settlement instructions*.

Typically, *trading book* positions are updated via book entry only (within the STO's books & records), as the STO will maintain both the securities positions of a trading book, together with the trading book's cash P&L.

Depending upon the nature of the custody agreement, *custody client* positions may be updated via book entry or may require settlement instructions or physical delivery (via delivery of paper transfers or cheques). For example, the nature of the SLA between a custody client and the STO may be such that only securities positions (and not cash) are held in custody. In this instance, where a cash resultant entitlement is generated the STO may either credit an external bank account held in the name of the client, or (as is the norm in some markets) issue a cheque to the client.

Irrespective of whether the form of settlement is via book entry, settlement instructions or physical delivery, two methods of effecting settlement of resultant entitlements with position holders exist. The two methods essentially reflect the timing of the disbursement to the position holder, and are known as

- Contractual Settlement, and
- Actual Settlement.

Both of these are described below.

13.4.1 Contractual Settlement

The disbursement of resultant entitlements to position holders on the due date, regardless of whether the STO has received the resultant entitlement from the location, is known as *contractual settlement*. In this case the disbursement of ownership resultant entitlements has no dependency on the collection of location resultant entitlements.

Contractual settlement will be reflected within the *SLA* between the position holder and the STO, and all resultant entitlements calculated where the position holder requires contractual settlement must be identified accordingly.

Where contractual settlement is required to take place, two risks arise for the STO:

- If contractual settlement does not take place on the due date of the resultant entitlement, i.e. the STO fails to deliver or to pay on the due date, then the STO may be exposing itself to *interest claims* from the client.
- Where contractual settlement is effected on the due date, but collection of the resultant entitlement from the location has not occurred, the STO will be required to 'fund' the short-term exposure. This requires either the borrowing of cash or securities to cover the amounts owed to position holders.

Any exposure that the STO may incur can be identified via the STO's projection and actual settlement reports. The principals are the same as those applied to the settlement of trades, and the exposure could occur with respect to securities and/or cash resultant entitlements.

Table 13.1 illustrates the expected settlements of resultant entitlements in QANTAS Airways New Shares, with a distribution date of 4th April.

Table 13.1

Projected Securities Settlement Report dated 4th April, for expected settlements: Custodian A, Sydney, Custody securities account number 503345			
Resultant Entitlement Type		Disbursable Entitlements	Collectible Entitlements
Custody Client Resultant Entitlement	Custody Client 'A'	7,000	
Claim in favour of STO	Counterparty 'X'		5,000
Custodian Resultant Entitlement	Custodian 'A', Sydney		2,000
		7,000	**7,000**

Based upon the projected settlement of resultant entitlements on 4th April, the STO will expect to collect a total of 7,000 shares, and disburse a total of 7,000 shares on this date.

Assuming that disbursement to Custody Client 'A' is on a contractual basis, and that settlement of the claim in favour of the STO (from Counterparty 'X') does not occur on 4th April, the actual settlement for 4th April would appear as shown in Table 13.2.

Table 13.2

Actual Securities Settlement Report dated 4th April: Custodian A, Sydney, Custody securities account number 503345			
Resultant Entitlement Type		Disbursable Entitlements	Collectible Entitlements
Custody Client Resultant Entitlement	Custody Client 'A'	7,000	
Custodian Resultant Entitlement	Custodian 'A', Sydney		2,000
		7,000	**2,000**

The failure to settle the claim relating to 5,000 shares from Counterparty 'X' on 4th April has resulted in a shortfall of 5,000 shares to the STO. Should the STO wish to cover this shortfall (pending the actual collection from the counterparty), the STO may need to borrow securities, for which it will incur a cost.

13.4.2 Actual Settlement

The disbursement of resultant entitlements to *position holders* only after the actual collection of the resultant entitlement from the *location* is known as *actual settlement*. In this case the disbursement of ownership resultant entitlements is dependent upon the collection from the location.

Actual settlement, in a similar way as for contractual settlement, will be reflected within the SLA between the position holder and the STO, and all resultant entitlements calculated where actual settlement applies must be identified accordingly.

From the STO's perspective, actual settlement does not carry the risks that *contractual settlement* carries. Nonetheless, operational complexity may arise where a direct dependency exists between the settlement of collectible and disbursable resultant entitlements. Where only a single collectible resultant entitlement exists, then it is a very simple exercise for the STO to identify when settlement of the disbursable resultant entitlements may be effected. Unfortunately, where multiple collectible resultant entitlements exist, for which settlement may be received at different times, the STO will need to have previously identified which disbursable resultant entitlements relate to which collectible resultant entitlements. This would need to have been identified at the time that the entitled holdings and any unsettled trades were initially determined (refer to Chapter 9, 'Determining Entitlement').

Where actual settlement of resultant entitlements to position holders is to take place and the STO has been able to identify the link between collectible resultant entitlements and disbursable resultant entitlements, typically any risk of securities and/or cash exposure to the STO may be reduced.

As per the previous example, Table 13.3 illustrates the expected settlements of resultant entitlements in QANTAS Airways New Shares, with a distribution date of 4th April.

Table 13.3

Projected Securities Settlement Report dated 4th April, for expected settlements: Custodian A, Sydney, Custody securities account number 503345			
Resultant Entitlement Type		Disbursable Entitlements	Collectible Entitlements
Custody Client Resultant Entitlement	Custody Client 'A'	7,000	
Claim in favour of STO	Counterparty 'X'		5,000
Custodian Resultant Entitlement	Custodian 'A', Sydney		2,000
		7,000	**7,000**

Based upon the projected settlement of resultant entitlements on 4th April, the STO will expect to collect a total of 7,000 shares, and disburse a total of 7,000 shares on this date.

Assuming that disbursement to Custody Client 'A' is on an actual basis, and that settlement of the claim in favour of the STO (from Counterparty 'X') does not occur on 4th April, the actual settlement for 4th April would appear as shown in Table 13.4.

The failure to settle the claim relating to 5,000 shares from Counterparty 'X' on 4th April has resulted in a shortfall of 5,000 shares to the STO. The underlying trade against which the claim from Counterparty 'X' was calculated was on behalf of Custody Client 'A'. Accordingly, because settlement with Custody Client 'A' is on an actual basis, settlement of 2,000 shares only (part of the full resultant entitlement of 7,000) will occur on 4th April, reflecting the actual

Table 13.4

Actual Securities Settlement Report dated 4th April: Custodian A, Sydney, Custody securities account number 503345			
Resultant Entitlement Type		Disbursable Entitlements	Collectible Entitlements
Custody Client Resultant Entitlement	Custody Client 'A'	2,000	
Custodian Resultant Entitlement	Custodian 'A', Sydney		2,000
		2,000	**2,000**

collection of resultant entitlement from the custodian. Settlement of the balance of 5,000 shares due to Custody Client 'A' will occur upon collection of the claim from Counterparty 'X', at a later date.

13.5 SETTLEMENT OF CLAIMS

The settlement of a *claim* requires the transfer of the *resultant entitlement* due between the *counterparty* of the *unsettled trade* and the STO. Three methods exist for the settlement of claims against unsettled trades:

- Individual Settlement
- Compensation
- Transformation

Each of these is described below.

Which method applies is generally dependent upon the regulations and conventions of the given market (usually administered by the CSD/ICSD) and the type of event.

13.5.1 Individual Settlement

Individual settlement refers to those claims for which settlement will be managed directly between the STO and its counterparty, i.e. the CSD/ICSD takes no action to initiate the settlement of the claim, even though the CSD/ICSD may have notified the parties involved that there is a claimable situation.

Each claim will exist as a collectible or disbursable obligation in its own right (distinct from the underlying trade), with the delivering party being required to initiate the settlement. Where electronic settlement applies to the market, generation of settlement instructions will be required by the delivering/paying counterparty, and (if settlement instruction matching is required) also by the receiving counterparty.

According to market conventions, settlement may occur

- on the payment/distribution date of the event;
- at a date agreed with the counterparty (no earlier than the payment/distribution date of the event);
- on the same date as settlement of the original underlying unsettled trade.

It is important to be aware that actual settlement of a valid claim may take weeks or months. It is imperative that the STO has sufficient mechanisms for monitoring outstanding claims.

13.5.2 Compensation

Compensation refers to the settlement of claims automatically by the CSD/ICSD on behalf of the STO and counterparty. Typically this method is offered by CSD/ICSDs, and most commonly applies to *benefit* events where the claim requires the delivery of additional securities or cash.

Where compensation of benefits is supported, the CSD/ICSD will identify all claim situations at the close of the *record date* of the event. The CSD/ICSD is able to identify such situations based upon trade date and value date of the seller's and buyer's settlement instructions.

The CSD/ICSD may effect settlement of the claim (for example) as follows:

- in the case of a cash claim, by the adjustment of the cash value of the underlying trade by the value of the claim. Settlement of the claim will therefore be achieved within the settlement of the underlying trade.
- in the case of both securities and cash claims, by automatically settling resultant claims between sellers and buyers at the same time that settlement of the location position is effected, typically the payment/distribution date of the event.

Similar to the settlement of the location resultant entitlement from the CSD/ICSD, the STO is not required to generate a settlement instruction in order to facilitate settlement of compensated claims. The CSD/ICSD will automatically issue a compensation message, detailing which claims (identified by the underlying settlement instruction reference) are included in the compensation. Depending upon the individual CSD/ICSD, compensation may be effected via a message per claim, or a single message for the total of claims.

As the CSD/ICSD will only compensate those claims that it has identified, it is vital that the STO reconciles the incoming message with extreme care. Claims against underlying unsettled trades that were due to settle outside of the CSD/ICSD will not be compensated by the CSD/ICSD and will therefore require individual settlement.

13.5.3 Transformation

Transformation refers to the 're-shaping' of the underlying *unsettled trade* reflecting the resultant entitlement. This could include alteration of any or all of the following against the underlying unsettled trade:

- security
- quantity
- settlement value

In order to illustrate the transformation of both the security and quantity, assume an unsettled buy trade of 10,000 'XYZ' GBP1.00 shares versus settlement consideration of GBP 25,000.00, and a consolidation of one new GBP2.00 share for every two existing shares held (replacing the original security).

Against the unsettled trade a claim in favour of the STO for 5,000 'XYZ' New Ordinary GBP2.00 shares will be calculated.

As a result of transformation, both the security and quantity of the underlying trade would be updated to 5,000 'XYZ' New Ordinary GBP2.00 shares, whilst the settlement consideration will remain as GBP 25,000.00.

At a later date, the security description of 'New Ordinary' shares is changed to 'Ordinary', and as such the security description of any unsettled trades will be transformed.

Assuming that the previously transformed trade now for 5,000 'XYZ' New Ordinary GBP2.00 shares has remained unsettled, as a result of transformation the security only will be updated to 'XYZ' Ordinary GBP2.00 shares, whilst the quantity and settlement consideration will remain unchanged as 5,000 and GBP 25,000.00 respectively.

Typically this method is offered by CSDs and ICSDs, but may also be applied as a result of agreement between the claiming parties, and applies to re-organization events where the old security is replaced by a new security or quantity.

The rules of transformation will result in the replacement of either the old security and/or the traded quantity of the underlying trade. The new security or quantity will be settled against the original settlement consideration.

Under the circumstances in which the original security is replaced by more than one new security, the settlement consideration of the underlying trade will be either apportioned across each of the new security trades, or alternatively applied to a specified security only. The conventions applied in this case are generally stipulated by the appropriate CSD of the market (or ICSD) at the time of each individual event.

This is illustrated in the following examples. Assume an unsettled buy trade of 20,000 'ABC' HKD1.00 shares versus settlement consideration of HKD 50,000.00. Company 'ABC' declares a scheme of arrangement (replacing the original security) with the following resultant entitlement terms:

- one 'ABC' New HKD2.00 share for every two HKD1.00 shares held, and
- one 'ABC' Preference HKD2.00 share for every eight HKD1.00 shares held.

Against the unsettled trade the following claims in favour of the STO will be calculated:

- 10,000 'ABC' New HKD2.00 shares, and
- 2,500 'ABC' Preference HKD2.00 shares.

The two resultant entitlements replace the original unsettled trade security and quantity, in accordance with the terms of the event, nonetheless the original settlement consideration of HKD 50,000.00 remains.

The CSD/ICSD may stipulate that the New HKD2.00 shares are the primary resultant entitlement, and that the Preference HKD shares are a free distribution. Therefore, as a result of transformation the underlying trade will be replaced with the following:

- 10,000 'ABC' New HKD2.00 shares versus settlement consideration HKD 50,000.00, and
- 2,500 'ABC' Preference HKD2.00 shares, free of cost.

Alternatively the CSD/ICSD may stipulate that the settlement consideration of the underlying trade be proportionately distributed across both the resultant entitlements.

In the example below this has been effected on the basis of dividing the original settlement consideration of HKD 50,000.00 by 12,500 representing the total number of new securities to be received (i.e. 10,000 'ABC' New shares and 2,500 'ABC' Preference shares), giving a notional 'price' of HKD4.00 to be applied to each claim quantity.

Accordingly as a result of such transformation the original underlying trade will be replaced with the following:

- 10,000 'ABC' New HKD2.00 shares versus settlement consideration HKD 40,000.00, and
- 2,500 'ABC' Preference HKD2.00 shares versus settlement consideration HKD 10,000.00.

As a result of the transformation, the original value date of the underlying trade will typically be altered. This is because, as a result of the re-organization event, the underlying security is replaced by the newly issued security. The market will set the earliest value date for the new security, which will be on or after the effective date of the event.

Whether new settlement instructions are required to be issued by counterparties against the transformed underlying trade will be dependent upon the individual market's settlement conventions. The STO will need to record such rules in static data in order to ensure that settlement instructions are issued where required. Failure to issue settlement instructions where required will result in on-going settlement failure.

13.6 WRITE-OFFS

In parallel with the settlement of trades, the STO may on occasion need to *write-off* small cash amounts as a result of the settlement of corporate action resultant entitlements.

Whilst due diligence should have already been undertaken by the STO in the reconciliation of underlying positions and any *unsettled trades* with external parties, together with *resultant entitlements*, small cash differences resulting from settlement may still occur. Typically this occurs due to a small rounding error in the calculation of the resultant entitlement.

The nature of the SLA with a client may require disbursement of cash to the client in a currency other than that of the event. The STO will, in this case, be required to convert the cash to the currency of the client's choice, and in doing so small discrepancies may result in the application of the exchange rate, requiring write-off.

13.7 SUMMARY

In order to avoid the potential cost of errors and delays in the collection and disbursement of resultant entitlements, it is vitally important for the STO to be fully aware of the variety of settlement forms and methods which may apply across the expected collectible and disbursable resultant entitlements.

Furthermore, the STO should remain aware of the methods of settlement agreed with its custody clients; paying clients (on a contractual settlement basis) prior to the collection of resultant entitlement at locations is highly likely to result in funding costs for the STO.

All Corporate Actions Departments should be prepared to take account of the different treatment of

- location settlement, and
- claim settlement

according to the prevailing regulations and conventions within the appropriate markets.

14
Updating of Internal Entries

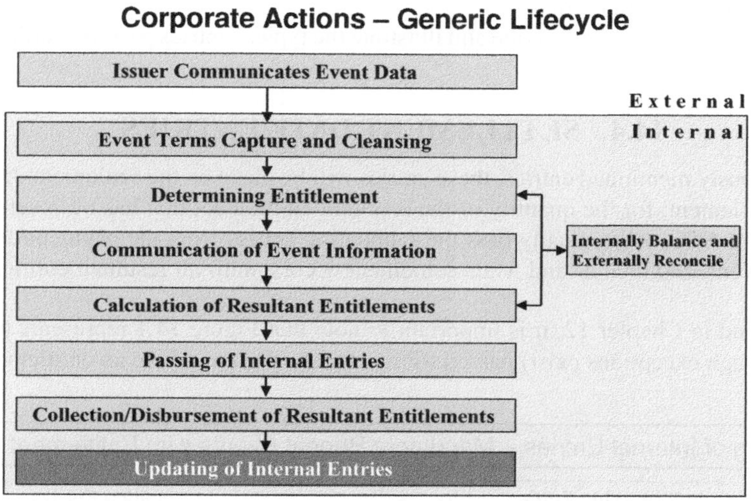

14.1 INTRODUCTION

The updating of internal entries to reflect the settlement of *resultant entitlements* effectively brings the lifecycle of the corporate action event to its closure. Such entries will occur as each resultant entitlement settles (refer to Chapter 13, 'Collection/Disbursement of Resultant Entitlements').

The STO will have previously passed *entitlement date entries* (where applicable) and *record date* entries; those entries will be updated by the *settlement date* entries to show that the expected resultant entitlements have actually been collected or disbursed.

14.2 THE STO'S RISK

The risks to the STO at this stage of the event are essentially the same as those referred to in Chapter 12, 'Passing of Internal Entries', and are reiterated below.

Failure to pass entries accurately and in a timely manner, may result in:

- discrepancies between the STO's records and that of its *custodian*,
- failure to identify available securities or cash to satisfy securities delivery and payment obligations.

14.3 MECHANISMS FOR PASSING INTERNAL ENTRIES

In parallel with the passing of *entitlement date* and record date entries, the mechanism for passing settlement date entries is that of *double entry book-keeping*. This mechanism has previously been described in Chapter 5, 'Securities Position Management' and Chapter 12, 'Passing of Internal Entries'.

As with all double entry book-keeping, a journal will be passed to reflect the settlement of a resultant entitlement, either its collection or disbursement, which consists of two or more balancing debit and credit entries.

The following section will describe and illustrate the typical entries passed in order to reflect settlement.

14.4 SETTLEMENT DATE ENTRIES

Unlike previously mentioned entries, these entries will be made on the settlement date of each resultant entitlement, for the quantity of the resultant entitlement that has been settled. For a given event the STO will typically pass these updating entries from the payment/distribution date of the event, and then as and when settlement occurs, until all resultant entitlements are settled.

As described in Chapter 12, it is important to note that Figure 14.1 represents the typical entries (although exceptions exist) passed for a mandatory event where an entitlement date is applicable;

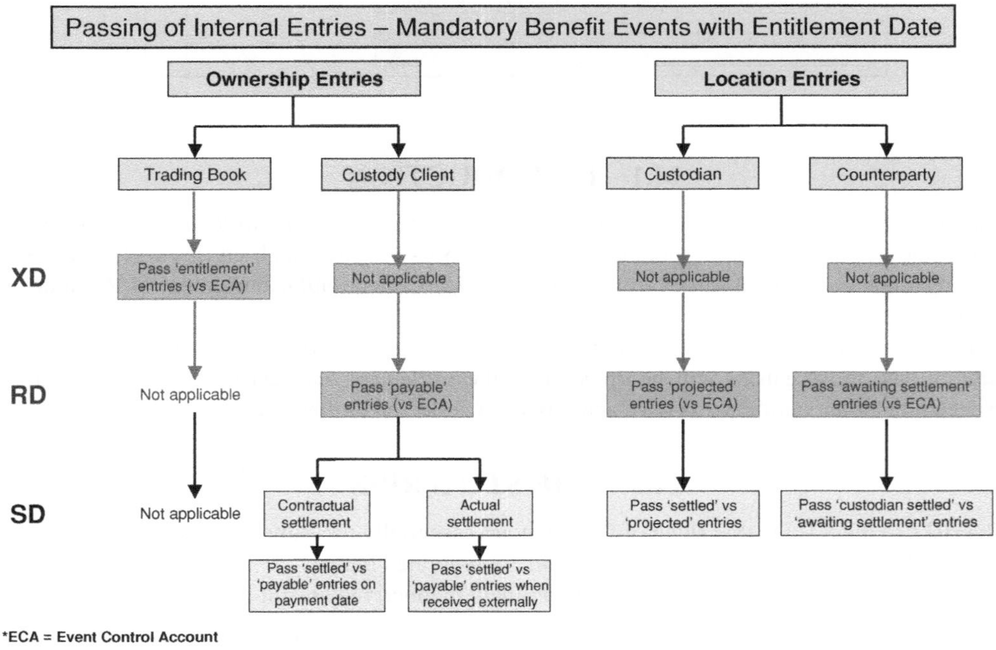

Figure 14.1 Internal entries for settlement of mandatory benefit events.

Note that entitlement date and record date entries (depicted in the 'XD' and 'RD' rows in Figure 14.1) are detailed within Chapter 12. The settlement date entries applicable to mandatory *re-organization* events are identical to those illustrated above; for this reason only one of the diagrams shown in Chapter 12 is reproduced in this chapter.

The potentially differing settlement dates of resultant entitlements generated by the event will be reflected in the overall position keeping of the entitlement security, or cash. For example, where settlement of *trading book* and *custody client* resultant entitlements is on a *contractual settlement* basis, in the absence of receipt of the *resultant entitlement* from the location, the exposure created will be reflected in the STO's securities and cash positions.

In order to illustrate a variety of circumstances by which corporate action events can be settled, three examples are provided. The event should be assumed to have an *ex entitlement date*, with

- entries having been passed on the ex entitlement date for
  - trading books,
- 'projected' entries having been passed on the record date for
  - custody clients
  - amounts due from *custodians*
  - amounts due from *counterparties*

Note that in the following tables entries passed previously are referred to as 'XD' for entries passed on ex entitlement date, and 'RD' for entries passed on record date.

It should be assumed that the STO has previously issued *claims* to counterparties for cash or securities due; the custodian would advise the STO when the claimed amount had been received and credited to the STO's account. As mentioned within Section 13.5 (Settlement of Claims), it is not unusual for claims on counterparties to take a considerable length of time to settle.

14.4.1 'Contractual' Settlement of Custody Client On Payment Date

Table 14.1 reveals that the owner has not been credited on the ex entitlement date, as in accordance with the *SLA* between the STO and the client, income and corporate action events are to be credited to the owner on payment date of the event, regardless of whether the STO has received the associated credit at the custodian.

Table 14.1

Entries Passed Previously to Owner	Entries Passed Previously to Location	Entries Due to be Passed to Owner	Entries Due to be Passed to Location
Custody Client 'J' Payable (on RD)	–	On payment date (Contractual Settlement)	–
–	Custodian 'X' SC a/c Projected (on RD)	–	Upon credit at custodian on or after payment date

Consequently, the owner is credited on payment date via the entry shown in Table 14.2.

Table 14.2

Disbursable Entries			
Debit		Credit	
Custody Client 'J' Payable	2,000	2,000	Custody Client 'J' Settled
	2,000	2,000	

When the custodian confirms that the funds have been credited (whether on or after payment date), the entry shown in Table 14.3 must be passed.

Table 14.3

Collectible Entries			
Debit		**Credit**	
Custodian 'X' SC a/c Settled	2,000	2,000	Custodian 'X' SC a/c Projected
	2,000	2,000	

Any delay in the receipt from the custodian will cause the STO to have an exposure, potentially requiring borrowing of securities or cash.

14.4.2 Settlement of Custodian Position on Payment Date

As the trading book has been credited on the ex entitlement date, upon advice of settlement from the custodian only the required entries will be passed to reflect the credit of amounts due as at the appropriate date. Tables 14.4 and 14.5 represent such entries.

Table 14.4

Entries Passed Previously to Owner	Entries Passed Previously to Location	Entries Due to be Passed to Owner	Entries Due to be Passed to Location
Trading Book 'A' (on XD)	–	None	–
–	Custodian 'X' Main a/c Projected (on RD)	–	Upon credit at custodian on payment date
–	Counterparty 'S' Awaiting Receipt (on RD)	–	Upon credit at custodian on or after payment date

Table 14.5

Collectible Entries			
Debit		**Credit**	
Custodian 'X' Main a/c Settled	10,000	10,000	Custodian 'X' Main a/c Projected
Custodian 'X' Main a/c Settled	7,500	7,500	Counterparty 'S' Awaiting Receipt
	17,500	17,500	

14.4.3 'Actual' Settlement of Custody Client as a Result of Custodian Settlement (incl. late claim settlement)

Table 14.6 reveals that the owner has not been credited on ex entitlement date, as in accordance with the SLA between the STO and the client, income and corporate action events are to be credited to the owner only upon receipt of the associated amount at the custodian. In this example, it should be assumed that a total of 5,000 shares are due to the owner, with claims outstanding against Counterparty 'U' (2,000 shares) and Counterparty 'V' (3,000 shares).

Consequently, the owner is only credited once the STO has received an advice of credit from the custodian. Initially, on payment date the custodian advises the STO that 2,000 shares have

Table 14.6

Entries Passed Previously to Owner	Entries Passed Previously to Location	Entries Due to be Passed to Owner	Entries Due to be Passed to Location
Custody Client 'K' Payable (on RD)	–	Upon receipt from custodian (Actual Settlement)	–
–	Counterparty 'U' Awaiting Receipt (on RD)	–	Upon credit at custodian on or after payment date
–	Counterparty 'V' Awaiting Receipt (on RD)	–	Upon credit at custodian on or after payment date

been credited, at which point the entry in Table 14.7 is passed (leaving 3,000 shares not yet credited to the owner).

Table 14.7

Disbursable Entries			
Debit		Credit	
Custody Client 'K' Payable	2,000	2,000	Custody Client 'K' Settled
	2,000	2,000	

In order to reflect the credit at the custodian, the entry shown in Table 14.8 must be passed.

Table 14.8

Collectible Entries			
Debit		Credit	
Custodian 'P' SC a/c Settled	2,000	2,000	Counterparty 'U' Awaiting Receipt
	2,000	2,000	

Five days after payment date, the custodian advises the STO that the remaining 3,000 shares have been credited, at which point the entry in Table 14.9 is passed.

Table 14.9

Disbursable Entries			
Debit		Credit	
Custody Client 'K' Payable	3,000	3,000	Custody Client 'K' Settled
	3,000	3,000	

In order to reflect the credit at the custodian, the entry shown in Table 14.10 must be passed.

Table 14.10

Collectible Entries			
Debit		Credit	
Custodian 'P' SC a/c Settled	3,000	3,000	Counterparty 'V' Awaiting Receipt
	3,000	3,000	

With regard to the amounts due to custody clients, the passing of the 'Settled' entries satisfies the final credit due to the client (whether on a *contractual settlement* or *actual settlement* basis). Also, the passing of the 'Payable' entries results in the clearance to zero of the anticipated cash amount due to the clients. Note that the same principles apply to cash due from custody clients, and to securities due to/from such clients.

With regard to the amounts due from custodians, the passing of the 'Settled' entry creates an exact mirror image of the credit of cash at the custodian, thereby keeping internal records in-line with the custodian's records, and in turn avoiding a reconciliation issue. Also, the passing of the 'Projected' entry results in the clearance to zero of the anticipated cash amount due from the custodian. Note that the same principles apply to cash due to custodians, and to securities due to/from custodians.

With regard to the amounts due from counterparties (following the issuance of claims), the passing of the 'Settled' entries creates an exact mirror image of the credit of cash at the custodian, thereby keeping internal records in-line with the custodian's records, and in turn avoiding a reconciliation issue. Also, the passing of the 'Awaiting Receipt' entries results in the clearance to zero of the anticipated cash amount due from the counterparties. Note that the same principles apply to cash due to counterparties, and to securities due to/from counterparties.

14.5 SETTLEMENT OF CLAIMS AND TRANSFORMATIONS

In the preceding chapters, the differing treatments of

- the calculation of resultant entitlements,
- the passing of internal entries, and
- the collection/disbursement of resultant entitlements

between claims arising against benefit events, and transformations that occur against re-organization events, have been described.

With respect to the updating of internal entries to reflect the actual settlement of either a claim or a transformed trade, the same method applies. In both cases the STO will pass entries to reflect the closure of the 'awaiting' counterparty settlement entry, and update the settled custodian position to reflect the receipt or delivery of securities and/or cash.

14.6 SUMMARY

The updating of settlement date entries within internal books & records is an essential component of the STO remaining in control of its business.

The accurate and timely updating of settlement date entries will allow the STO to reconcile securities and cash (represented within internal books & records) successfully, with the equivalent held at custodians and nostros.

Failure to do so will simply contribute to the number of discrepancies between such records, requiring the STO to expend more resources on the investigation of discrepancies, and potentially adversely affecting the STO's business decisions (as those decisions may be based upon inaccurate books & records).

15

Examples of Mandatory Events

15.1 INTRODUCTION

The objective of this chapter is to provide the reader with example corporate actions that illustrate the different styles of mandatory events, and the associated management of their lifecycle components from beginning to end, in chronological sequence.

Within the chapter, three examples will be used:

- a *bonus issue*
- a *share split*
- a bond *redemption*

Each of these examples will illustrate specific features of the generic lifecycle as detailed in Chapters 6–14 and is designed to illustrate the major operational components of such events, in the context of their operational sequence.

15.2 BONUS ISSUE

15.2.1 Purpose of Example

This example is designed to illustrate:

- the addition of a new security alongside the *underlying security*;
- existing *trading book* and *custody client positions* plus trading on a *special-cum* basis;
- the existence of an ex period, and the passing of ex date internal entries;
- claiming from a *counterparty*;
- settlement (for a custody client) on a '*contractual settlement*' basis.

15.2.2 Event Terms

The *issuer*, Rolls-Royce plc, announces on 12th March the details of a bonus issue (the distribution of additional shares free of cost to position holders, in proportion to their existing holding) as shown in Table 15.1.

This information would therefore appear, in a timeline sense, as shown in Figure 15.1.

15.2.3 Determining Entitlement

Having been advised (by a *data vendor*) of the event, the STO records the details of the event within its corporate actions system.

The Corporate Actions Department then retrieves the positions shown in Table 15.2 from the STO's main *books & records*.

Table 15.1

Event Conditions and Information	
Component	**Example**
Underlying security	Rolls Royce, GBP1.00 Ordinary Shares
Event description	Bonus Issue
Event dates	
Announcement Date	12th March
Entitlement Date	17th March
Record Date	21st March
Payment Date	28th March
Entitlement security and/or currency	Rolls Royce, GBP1.00 New Ordinary Shares
Ratios and rates	Two new ordinary shares for every five existing ordinary shares*
Treatment of fractions	Round down any fraction to the previous whole unit
Exchange rates	Not applicable
Options available	Not applicable
Additional event conditions and information	Bonus shares do not rank for the next dividend on ordinary shares

**The ratio is based on the Europe and Asia Pacific calculation method; see Chapter 8*

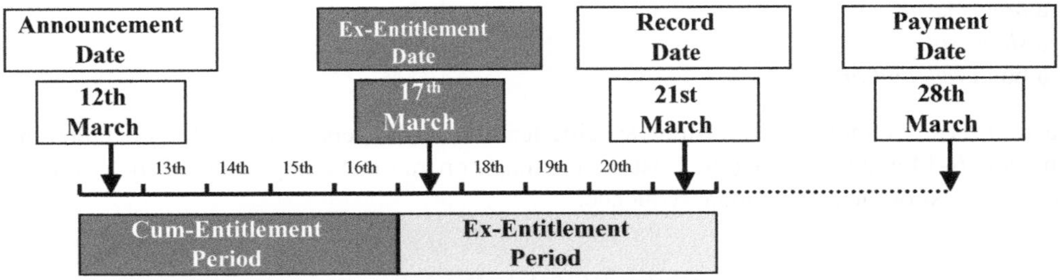

Figure 15.1 Bonus issue example: timeline

Table 15.2

Rolls Royce GBP1.00 Ordinary Shares			
Ownership			**Location**
Trading Book 'A'	+10,000	−32,071	Custodian K, Main A/C
Trading Book 'B'	+22,071		
Custody Client L	+5,800	−5,800	Custodian Z, Custody A/C 1 – treaty
	+37,871	−37,871	

This information reveals that the STO has

- two trading book positions (in total 32,071 shares), which have fully *settled custodian positions*;
- a single custody client position (+5,800), which currently has a fully settled custodian position; and
- a total of *ownership positions* that is equal to the *location* sum.

The Corporate Actions Department must also make itself aware as to whether all the component parts of this information have been reconciled (by the area within the STO that is responsible for reconciliation). If the answer is that it is fully reconciled, the Corporate Actions Department's work in relation to this event will be based upon accurate information; if it is not fully reconciled, there is an immediate risk that basic entitlement calculations will be inaccurate, thereby increasing the likelihood of poor service to clients and monetary loss to the STO.

Note that these positions are retrieved as at this date, knowing that further trades may be executed that will affect entitlement, and that further settlements may occur up to and including *record date*.

Then, on 19th March (value date 22nd March), Trading Book 'A' buys 2,559 shares from Counterparty X, on a *special-cum* basis.

The Corporate Actions Department performs a recalculation as at close-of-business on record date (21st March) to reveal the position shown in Table 15.3 from the perspective of this particular corporate action event.

Table 15.3

Rolls Royce GBP1.00 Ordinary Shares			
Ownership			**Location**
Trading Book 'A'	+12,559	−32,071	Custodian K, Main A/C
Trading Book 'B'	+ 22,071	−2,559	Counterparty 'X'
Custody Client L	+5,800	−5,800	Custodian Z, Custody A/C 1 – treaty
	+40,430	−40,430	

This final position for the event can be summarized as shown in Table 15.4.

Table 15.4

Ownership			=	**Location**				
Sum of Trading Book Positions	+	Sum of Custody Client Positions	=	Sum of Settled Positions (Custodian or Issuer)	+	Sum of Open Receipts	−	Sum of Open Deliveries
34,630	+	5,800	=	37,871	+	2,559	−	0

15.2.4 Communication of Event Information (Event Terms Announcement)

In order to advise the position holder of the impending event, on 14th March the Corporate Actions Department issues an Event Terms Announcement to each of the position holders, transmitted by fax, as shown in Table 15.5.

Table 15.5

From	***The name of the issuing STO***
To	**Custody Client 'L'**
Attention	**Corporate Actions Department**
Subject	**Corporate Action Event Terms Announcement**
Our Reference	**RR Bonus**
Event Description	**Rolls Royce, GBP1.00 Ordinary Shares – 2:5 Bonus Issue** **Eligible holders of the ordinary shares will receive two New Ordinary Shares for every five Ordinary Shares held. Fractions to be rounded down to the previous whole unit.**
Entitlement Date	**17th March**
Record Date	**21st March**
Payment Date	**28th March**
Event Conditions	**Bonus shares do not rank for the next dividend on ordinary shares**
Sign-off by the STO	***Full name and location of STO***
Transmission Time	**Transmitted at 10:47 on 14th March**

15.2.5 Calculation of Resultant Entitlements

On 22nd March, the Corporate Actions Department attempts a calculation and balancing of *resultant entitlements* (based on the '2 for 5' event), at both *collectible* and *disbursable* levels. This reveals the information shown in Table 15.6 (having rounded down fractions to the previous whole unit (see Table 15.1 that illustrates the event terms)), showing balancing totals between collectible and disbursable resultant entitlements.

Table 15.6

Disbursable Entitlements			Collectible Entitlements		
Party	**Underlying Holding**	**Resultant Entitlement**	**Party**	**Underlying Holding**	**Resultant Entitlement**
Trading Book 'A'	12,559	5,023	Custodian K Main	32,071	12,828
Trading Book 'B'	22,071	8,828	Counterparty 'X'	2,559	1,023
Custody Client L	5,800	2,320	Custodian Z Cust	5,800	2,320
total	**40,430**	**16,171**	*total*	**40,430**	**16,171**

It is important to note that this particular bonus issue results in the issue of New Ordinary Shares in addition to the continued existence of the original Ordinary Shares. Following payment of the next dividend on the Ordinary Shares, holdings in the New Ordinary Shares will rank *pari-passu* with the original Ordinary Shares, at which point they will merge with the Ordinary Shares, and the New Ordinary Shares will cease to exist. At the appropriate future date, the Corporate Actions Department must ensure that any holdings in the New Ordinary Shares are removed, and holdings in the Ordinary Shares are increased accordingly.

15.2.6 Entitlement Date Entries

Owing to the nature of this particular event (a bonus issue), the price of the original Ordinary Shares will fall as a result of issuing the new shares (i.e. the New Ordinary Shares), on the ex entitlement date 17th March. The fall in the share price will be reflected within the trader's *P&L*, following the daily mark-to-market process.

Consequently, the bonus shares become a holding of a new security for each of the entitled owners; they will have a market value and therefore a market price. From an ownership perspective, the date at which the New Ordinary Shares acquire a market value is the ex entitlement date, therefore the following entries must be passed to the STO's main books & records on that date (17th March) (see Table 15.7).

Table 15.7

Disbursable Entries (Rolls Royce GBP1.00 New Ordinary Shares)			
Debit		**Credit**	
Event Control Account	4,000	4,000	Trading Book 'A'
Event Control Account	8,828	8,828	Trading Book 'B'
	12,828	12,828	

Furthermore, equivalent entries must be passed within the trader's records to their trading book positions, at the same time (in order to avoid trading book position reconciliation issues).

As Trading Book 'A' purchased further shares (during the ex entitlement period) on a special-cum basis, the additional entries in Table 15.8 must be passed when the final position is known (on or after record date).

Table 15.8

Disbursable Entries (Rolls Royce GBP1.00 New Ordinary Shares)			
Debit		Credit	
Event Control Account	1,023	1,023	Trading Book 'A'
	1,023	1,023	

The entries contained within Table 15.8, plus the entries passed on the ex entitlement date, reflect the total entitlement due to the trading books.

15.2.7 Record Date Entries

It is at this date that the final resultant entitlements are known, and the Corporate Actions Department is in a position to pass internal entries to reflect the resultant entitlement it expects (based upon the STO's records)

- to be disbursed to *custody clients* (Table 15.9), and
- to be collected from *custodians* and from *counterparties* (Table 15.10).

Table 15.9

Disbursable Entries (Rolls Royce GBP1.00 New Ordinary Shares)			
Debit		Credit	
Event Control Account	2,320	2,320	Custody Client 'L' Payable
	2,320	2,320	

Table 15.10

Collectible Entries (Rolls Royce GBP1.00 New Ordinary Shares)			
Debit		Credit	
Custodian 'K' Main a/c Projected	12,828	12,828	Event Control Account
Counterparty 'X' Awaiting Receipt	1,023	1,023	Event Control Account
Custodian 'Z' Custody a/c Projected	2,320	2,320	Event Control Account
	16,171	16,171	

These entries will result in a zero balance within the Event Control Account, whilst at the same time creating a set of 'receivable' entries, against the respective locations. (When the necessary deliveries of the new shares have been made by each of the locations, the 'receivable' entries will be 'settled' and will no longer be regarded as open.)

15.2.8 Communication of Event Information (Final Claim Notice)

As Trading Book 'A's purchase of 2,559 shares (on trade date 19th March) on a *special-cum* basis could not possibly be received by the STO prior to close-of-business on the record date, the Corporate Actions Department must issue a *claim* to the *counterparty*.

The claim requests the counterparty to deliver 1,023 New Ordinary Shares to the STO's main account at the *custodian*. At this point, there can be no guarantee that the 1,023 shares will be delivered to the STO's custodian account on the payment date of the event; it is not unusual to experience a delay in the 'settlement' of claims.

The Corporate Actions Department creates a Final Claim Notice which is issued to Counterparty 'X', transmitted by telex, as shown in Table 15.11.

Table 15.11

From	***The name of the issuing STO***
To	**Counterparty 'X'**
Attention	**Corporate Actions Department**
Subject	**Final Corporate Action Claim Notice**
Our Reference	**RR Bonus 04**
Event Description	**Rolls Royce plc; 2:5 Bonus Issue, ex entitlement date 17th March, record date 21st March, payment date 28th March.**
	Trade Details
Underlying Security	**Rolls Royce GBP1.00 Ordinary Shares**
Security Reference	**ISIN GB1234567893**
Operation	**We Buy**
Quantity	**2,559 shares**
Price	**GBP1.02 per share**
Trade Conditions	**Special-Cum Dividend**
Trade Date	**19th March**
Value Date	**22nd March**
Settlement Date	**Not Yet Delivered**
Net Settlement Value	**GBP2610.18**
	Claim Details
Claim Quantity	**2,559 shares**
Entitlement Claimed	**1,023 Rolls Royce GBP1.00 New Ordinary Shares (ISIN GB4442228881)**
Settlement Details	**Please deliver claimed quantity to our Main account no. 12345, with Custodian K, on the payment date**
Sign-off by the STO	***Full name and location of STO***
Transmission Time	**Transmitted at 08:10 on 22nd March**

15.2.9 Settlement Details

On the payment date of the event (28th March), the Corporate Actions Department is due to credit the *custody client*, as the *SLA* between the STO and client states that corporate actions will be settled on a *contractual settlement* basis.

It is also due to receive the following securities externally:

- 12,828 New Ordinary Shares to be credited to the STO's main securities account at the custodian;
- 2,320 New Ordinary Shares to be credited to the STO's safe-custody securities account at the custodian; plus
- 1,023 New Ordinary Shares to be received from Counterparty 'X' (following the issuance of the claim by the STO immediately after record date), and credited to the STO's main securities account at the custodian.

On 28th March, the custodians advise the STO that 12,828 and 2,320 New Ordinary Shares have been credited to the STO's respective accounts.

This leaves the 1,023 New Ordinary Shares due from Counterparty 'X' as the only outstanding amount as at close of the payment date. Internally, the Corporate Actions Department continually monitors the outstanding claim, and pursues Counterparty 'X' on 4th April, by telephone.

On 6th April, the custodian reports to the STO that the 1,023 New Ordinary Shares have been credited to the STO's main account, and as a result there are now no collectible amounts outstanding for this particular event.

15.2.10 Settlement Date Entries

At the start of day on the payment date of the event, the Corporate Actions Department passes the entries shown in Table 15.12 in order to fulfil its (contractual settlement) obligation to the custody client.

Table 15.12

Collectible Entries (Rolls Royce GBP1.00 New Ordinary Shares)			
Debit		Credit	
Custody Client 'L' Payable	2,320	2,320	Custody Client 'L' Settled
	2,320	2,320	

Immediately upon receipt of the date and details of settlement from the custodians, within its books & records, the Corporate Actions Department passes the entries shown in Table 15.13 on payment date (28th March) and the entries shown in Table 15.14 on 6th April.

Table 15.13

Collectible Entries (Rolls Royce GBP1.00 New Ordinary Shares)			
Debit		Credit	
Custodian 'K' Main a/c Settled	12,828	12,828	Custodian 'K' Main a/c Projected
Custodian 'Z' Custody a/c Settled	2,320	2,320	Custodian 'Z' Custody a/c Projected
	15,148	15,148	

Table 15.14

Collectible Entries (Rolls Royce GBP1.00 New Ordinary Shares)			
Debit		Credit	
Custodian 'K' Main a/c Settled	1,023	1,023	Counterparty 'X' Awaiting Receipt
	1,023	1,023	

Passing of the settlement date entries brings the management and processing of the event to a successful conclusion.

Note that despite the fact that the custody client was credited on the payment date of the event, in this case the STO had no overnight exposure as the related securities were credited to the STO's custodian account on the same date. However, had there been a delay in the credit of securities at the custodian, the STO would have been exposed until such time that the securities were credited at the custodian.

15.3 SHARE SPLIT

15.3.1 Purpose of Example

This example is designed to illustrate:

- the replacement of the *underlying security* with a new security;
- no ex period, and therefore a single effective date, which will also act as the *record date* (for this reason no ex date internal entries are required);
- the new security trading on a *deferred delivery* basis and therefore the distribution (settlement date) of the new security being after the effective date; and
- *transformation* of *unsettled trades*.

15.3.2 Event Terms

The *issuer*, Xerox Corporation, announces on 2nd November the details of a share split (the increase in an issuer's number of issued shares proportional to a reduction in the capital (par) value of each existing share) as shown in Table 15.15.

Table 15.15

Event Conditions and Information	
Component	**Example**
Underlying security	Xerox Corporation, USD1.00 Common Stock
Event description	Share Split
Event dates	
Announcement Date	2nd November
Entitlement Date	Not applicable
Record Date	18th November
Effective Date	19th November
Payment Date	25th November
Entitlement security and/or currency	Xerox Corporation, USD0.50 Common Stock
Ratios and rates	Two new USD0.50 shares replacing every one existing USD1.00 share*
Treatment of fractions	Not applicable
Exchange rates	Not applicable
Options available	Not applicable
Additional event conditions and information	New securities trade on a deferred delivery basis until 25th November

**The ratio is based on the US calculation method; see Chapter 8*

This information would therefore appear, in a timeline sense, as shown in Figure 15.2.

Figure 15.2 Share split example: timeline.

15.3.3 Determining Entitlement

Having obtained the detail of the event from its *custodian*, the STO records the details of the event within its corporate actions system.

Then, no later than record date, the Corporate Actions Department retrieves the positions shown in Table 15.16 from the STO's main books & records.

Table 15.16

Xerox Corporation USD1.00 Common Stock			
Ownership			**Location**
Trading Book 'C'	+17,600	−2,500	Custodian T, Main A/C
		−6,100	Counterparty 'F'
		−9,000	Counterparty 'G'
	+17,600	−17,600	

This information reveals that the STO has:

- a single *trading book* position (in total 17,600 shares), which has a partially *settled custodian position* of 2500 shares, and two outstanding purchases due from *counterparties*; and
- a total of *ownership positions* that is equal to the *location* sum.

This final position for the event can be summarized as shown in Table 15.17.

Table 15.17

Ownership			=	**Location**				
Sum of Trading Book Positions	+	Sum of Custody Client Positions	=	Sum of Settled Positions (Custodian or Issuer)	+	Sum of Open Receipts	−	Sum of Open Deliveries
17,600	+	0	=	2,500	+	15,100	−	0

15.3.4 Communication of Event Information (Event Terms Announcement)

In order to make the position holder aware of the recently announced event, on 6th November the STO issues an Event Terms Announcement (refer to Chapter 10 'Communication of Event Information') to the position holder.

Note that this communication intentionally does not include details of the position holder's current holding, as there is a possibility of the holding changing prior to the record date.

15.3.5 Calculation of Resultant Entitlements

On record date +1, the Corporate Actions Department attempts a final calculation and balancing of resultant entitlements (based on the '2 for 1' event), at both collectible and disbursable levels. This reveals the information shown in Table 15.18.

Table 15.18

Disbursable Entitlements			**Collectible Entitlements**		
Party	**Underlying Holding**	**Resultant Entitlement**	**Party**	**Underlying Holding**	**Resultant Entitlement**
Trading Book 'C'	17,600	35,200	Custodian T Main	2,500	5,000
			Counterparty 'F'	6,100	12,200
			Counterparty 'G'	9,000	18,000
total	**17,600**	**35,200**	*total*	**17,600**	**35,200**

This table shows balancing totals between *collectible* and *disbursable* resultant entitlements. Note that the 2:1 ratio means that all holdings will simply double, consequently there can be no *fractions* for this particular event.

It is important to note that share splits result in the issue of a new security in replacement of the original security.

15.3.6 Entitlement Date Entries

Owing to the nature of this particular event (a share split), an ex entitlement date is not applicable; instead, all entries will be made as at the *record date* in relation to positions and *unsettled trades*.

15.3.7 Record Date Entries

On the record date, entries are passed to reflect

- the *collection* and *disbursement* of the new security, and
- the removal of all positions and trades in the original security.

First, with regard to the new security, entries are passed to reflect the *transformation* of the two unsettled trades as at record date (see Table 15.19).

Table 15.19

Transformed Trade Entries (Xerox Corporation, USD0.50 Common Stock)			
Debit		Credit	
Counterparty F Awaiting Settlement	12,200	12,200	Trading Book 'C'
Counterparty G Awaiting Settlement	18,000	18,000	Trading Book 'C'
	30,200	30,200	

Second, entries are passed to reflect the remaining quantity of shares owned by the trading book (and which are represented by a *settled custodian position* as at record date) (see Table 15.20).

Table 15.20

Disbursable Entries (Xerox Corporation, USD0.50 Common Stock)			
Debit		Credit	
Event Control Account	5,000	5,000	Trading Book 'C'
	5,000	5,000	

Finally, entries are passed to reflect the settled custodian position expected to be received at the custodian upon settlement (see Table 15.21).

Table 15.21

Collectible Entries (Xerox Corporation, USD0.50 Common Stock)			
Debit		Credit	
Custodian T Main a/c Projected	5,000	5,000	Event Control Account
	5,000	5,000	

Tables 15.22 to 15.24 illustrate the record date entries relating to the removal of the original security. These tables are simply a mirror image of the above entries, containing the original quantities.

Table 15.22

Transformed Trade Entries (Xerox Corporation, USD1.00 Common Stock)			
Debit		Credit	
Trading Book 'C'	6,100	6,100	Counterparty 'F' Awaiting Settlement
Trading Book 'C'	9,000	9,000	Counterparty 'G' Awaiting Settlement
	15,100	15,100	

Table 15.23

Disbursable Entries (Xerox Corporation, USD1.00 Common Stock)			
Debit		Credit	
Trading Book 'C'	2,500	2,500	Event Control Account
	2,500	2,500	

Table 15.24

Collectible Entries (Xerox Corporation, USD1.00 Common Stock)			
Debit		Credit	
Event Control Account	2,500	2,500	Custodian T Main a/c Projected
	2,500	2,500	

Passing such entries should, with effect from the record date, accurately represent the revised holdings; all positions and unsettled trades (in both the new and the original securities) should be proven to be accurate via the normal *reconciliation* process. This includes the original security, now with zero balances.

It is important to note that in some markets, rather than pass 'remove and replace' entries as outlined above, it is common practice to adopt an 'adjust' approach:

- amend the title of the security (within the STO's static data repository) from the old *par value* to the new par value, and
- pass entries representing the difference between the position (and unsettled trade) quantities and the old and the new security.

15.3.8 Settlement Details

The *effective date* of this event is 19th November; however the event terms state that the securities resulting from this event will not be available for delivery until the payment date of 25th November.

On 25th November, the custodian advises the STO that 5,000 USD0.50 Common Stock has been credited to the STO's respective account, and that 2,500 USD1.00 Common Stock has been debited.

On 29th November, the custodian advises the STO that the transformed trade with Counterparty 'G' has settled, consequently 18,000 USD0.50 Common Stock has been credited to the STO's respective account on that date.

On 3rd December, the custodian advises the STO that the outstanding transformed trade with Counterparty 'F' has settled, and therefore 12,200 USD0.50 Common Stock has been credited to the STO's respective account on that date.

15.3.9 Settlement Date Entries

Immediately upon receipt of the date and details of settlement from the custodian, the Corporate Actions Department passes the following entries within its books & records. Table 15.25 shows the entries passed on 25th November to reflect the credit of the new security.

Table 15.25

Collectible Entries (Xerox Corporation, USD0.50 Common Stock)			
Debit		Credit	
Custodian 'T' Main a/c Settled	5,000	5,000	Custodian T Main a/c Projected
	5,000	5,000	

Table 15.26 shows the entries passed on 25th November to reflect the removal of the original security.

Table 15.26

Collectible Entries (Xerox Corporation, USD1.00 Common Stock)			
Debit		Credit	
Custodian T Main a/c Projected	2,500	2,500	Custodian T Main a/c Settled
	2,500	2,500	

Table 15.27 shows the entries passed on 29th November to reflect settlement of one of the transformed trades.

Table 15.27

Collectible Entries (Xerox Corporation, USD0.50 Common Stock)			
Debit		Credit	
Custodian 'T' Main a/c Settled	18,000	18,000	Counterparty 'G' Awaiting Settlement
	18,000	18,000	

Finally, Table 15.28 shows the entries passed on 3rd December to reflect settlement of the remaining transformed trade.

Table 15.28

Collectible Entries (Xerox Corporation, USD0.50 Common Stock)			
Debit		Credit	
Custodian 'T' Main a/c Settled	12,200	12,200	Counterparty 'F' Awaiting Settlement
	12,200	12,200	

Passing of the settlement date entries brings the management and processing of the event to a successful conclusion.

15.4 BOND MATURITY

15.4.1 Purpose of Example

This example is designed to illustrate:

- the maturity of a *bond*, and therefore
  - the removal of the bond security and positions, and
  - distribution of cash principal
- no ex period and therefore a single *maturity date*
- settlement (for a *custody client*) on an *actual settlement* basis.

15.4.2 Event Terms

Within the prospectus that was published at the time of issue launch 20 years earlier, the *issuer*, International Bank for Reconstruction and Development (World Bank), stated that in the year of maturity, the capital sum borrowed regarding its issue of

- International Bank for Reconstruction and Development, 6.75% USD Bonds 15th August 2012

would be repaid to investors at the price of par (100% of the bond's *face value*), on 15th August 2012 (see Table 15.29).

Table 15.29

Event Conditions and Information	
Component	**Example**
Underlying security	International Bank for Reconstruction and Development, 6.75% USD Bonds 15th August 2012
Event description	Bond Redemption
Event dates	
Announcement Date	At time of issue launch
Entitlement Date	Not applicable
Effective/Record Date	14th August 2012
Payment Date	15th August 2012
Entitlement security and/or currency	USD
Ratios and rates	Price of 100% of the bond's face value
Treatment of fractions	Not applicable
Exchange rates	Not applicable
Options available	Not applicable
Additional event conditions and information	Not applicable

This information would therefore appear, in a timeline sense, as shown in Figure 15.3.

15.4.3 Determining Entitlement

Having identified the event from the STO's own repository of securities *static data*, the STO records the details of the event within its corporate actions system.

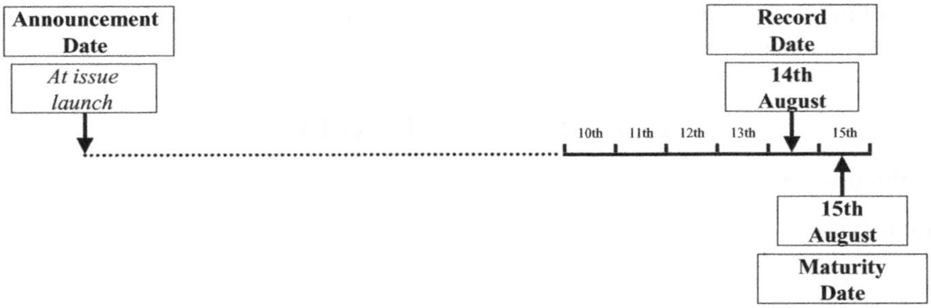

Figure 15.3 Bond maturity example: timeline

Then, on *record date*, the Corporate Actions Department retrieves the positions shown in Table 15.30 from the STO's main *books & records*.

Table 15.30

International Bank for Reconstruction and Development, 6.75% USD Bonds 15th August 2012			
Ownership		Location	
Custody Client 'M'	+6,500,000.00	−6,500,000.00	Custodian E, Custody A/C
	+6,500,000.00	−6,500,000.00	

This information reveals that the STO has:

- a single *custody client* position (in total USD 6,500,000.00), which has a fully *settled custodian position* of USD 6,500,000.00;
- a total of *ownership positions* that is equal to the *location* sum.

This final position for the event can be summarized as shown in Table 15.31.

Table 15.31

Ownership			=	Location				
Sum of Trading Book Positions	+	Sum of Custody Client Positions	=	Sum of Settled Positions (Custodian or Issuer)	+	Sum of Open Receipts	−	Sum of Open Deliveries
0	+	6,500,000	=	6,500,000	+	0	−	0

15.4.4 Communication of Event Information (Event Terms Announcement)

In order to advise the position holder of the impending event, on 25th July (approximately three weeks prior to the redemption date), the Corporate Actions Department issues a Preliminary Entitlement Notice to the position holder, transmitted by fax. (Please refer to Section 15.2.4 earlier in this chapter for an example of an Event Terms Announcement.)

15.4.5 Calculation of Resultant Entitlements

At the close of business on the record date (14th August), the Corporate Actions Department attempts a final calculation and balancing of *resultant entitlements* (based on the redemption price of 100%), at both *collectible* and *disbursable* levels. This reveals the information shown in Table 15.32.

Table 15.32

Disbursable Entitlements			Collectible Entitlements		
Party	**Underlying Holding**	**Resultant Entitlement**	**Party**	**Underlying Holding**	**Resultant Entitlement**
Custody Client 'M'	6,500,000.00	6,500,000.00	Custodian E, Cust	6,500,000.00	6,500,000.00
total	6,500,000.00	6,500,000.00	*total*	6,500,000.00	6,500,000.00

This table shows balancing totals between collectible and disbursable resultant entitlements (in this case a cash amount of USD 6,500,000.00).

It is important to note that final bond redemptions result in the security ceasing to exist.

15.4.6 Entitlement Date Entries

Owing to the nature of this particular event (a final bond redemption), an ex entitlement date is not applicable; instead, all entries will be made in relation to positions and *unsettled trades* as at the *record date*.

15.4.7 Record Date Entries

On record date, entries are passed to reflect the expected reduction (to zero) of all holdings and unsettled trades in the *underlying security* (as shown in Tables 15.33 and 15.34).

Table 15.33

Disbursable Entries (International Bank for Reconstruction and Development, 6.75% USD Bonds 15th August 2012)			
Debit		**Credit**	
Custody Client 'M' Payable	6,500,000.00	6,500,000.00	Event Control Account
	6,500,000.00	6,500,000.00	

Table 15.34

Collectible Entries (International Bank for Reconstruction and Development, 6.75% USD Bonds 15th August 2012)			
Debit		**Credit**	
Event Control Account	6,500,000.00	6,500,000.00	Custodian E, Custody A/C Projected
	6,500,000.00	6,500,000.00	

Additionally, entries are passed in order to reflect the expected receipt of the maturity proceeds from the custodian, and the credit of the same to the position holder (Tables 15.35 and 15.36).

Table 15.35

Disbursable Entries (USD)			
Debit		**Credit**	
Event Control Account	6,500,000.00	6,500,000.00	Custody Client 'M' Payable
	6,500,000.00	6,500,000.00	

Table 15.36

Collectible Entries (USD)			
Debit		**Credit**	
Custodian E, Custody A/C Projected	6,500,000.00	6,500,000.00	Event Control Account
	6,500,000.00	6,500,000.00	

Passing such entries should, with effect from the record date, accurately represent the revised holdings (now zero) and the payment of maturity proceeds; all positions and unsettled trades (in the original security) should be proven to be accurate via the normal reconciliation process.

15.4.8 Settlement Details

On the payment date of the event (15th August), the

- quantity of securities are due to be debited from, and the
- redemption proceeds are due to be credited to

the STO's safe-custody account at the *custodian*.

On 15th August, the custodian advises the STO that it has debited the securities from, and credited the required cash to, the STO's appropriate account.

The agreement between the STO and the *custody client* states that corporate actions are to be settled on an *actual settlement* basis, therefore related entries must be passed to the custody client only after having received the appropriate notification from the custodian.

15.4.9 Settlement Date Entries

Immediately upon receipt of the date and details of *settlement* from the custodian, within its books & records, the Corporate Actions Department passes the entries shown in Table 15.37 for the removal of the securities at the custodian, and the entries shown in Table 15.38 for the credit of cash at the custodian.

Table 15.37

Collectible Entries (International Bank for Reconstruction and Development, 67.5% USD Bonds 15th August 2012)			
Debit		**Credit**	
Custodian E, Custody A/C Projected	6,500,000.00	6,500,000.00	Custodian E, Custody A/C Settled
	6,500,000.00	6,500,000.00	

Table 15.38

Collectible Entries (USD)			
Debit		Credit	
Custodian E, Custody A/C Settled	6,500,000.00	6,500,000.00	Custodian E, Custody A/C Projected
	6,500,000.00	6,500,000.00	

As the arrangement with the custody client is for actual settlement of corporate actions, the entries shown in Tables 15.39 and 15.40 are passed following the above mentioned advice from the custodian.

Table 15.39

Disbursable Entries (International Bank for Reconstruction and Development, 6.75% USD Bonds 15th August 2012)			
Debit		Credit	
Custody Client 'M' Settled	6,500,000.00	6,500,000.00	Custody Client 'M' Payable
	6,500,000.00	6,500,000.00	

Table 15.40

Disbursable Entries (USD)			
Debit		Credit	
Custody Client 'M' Payable	6,500,000.00	6,500,000.00	Custody Client 'M' Settled
	6,500,000.00	6,500,000.00	

Passing of the settlement date entries brings the management and processing of the event to a successful conclusion.

Note that as the custody client was not credited until the appropriate funds had been credited to the STO's custodian account, the STO had no exposure.

Part III

Events with Elections

16

Concepts of Events with Elections

To this point the generic lifecycle of a corporate action has been outlined. The generic lifecycle can be applied to the majority of corporate action events, including those that fall into the mandatory group, as is illustrated in the examples in the previous chapter, and the majority of income events (with the exception of the additional element to calculate income tax liabilities, described in Chapter 24, 'Concepts and Management of Taxation').

This chapter and the following two focus specifically on those events with elections, both mandatory with options events and voluntary events; such events utilize the components of the generic lifecycle, and in addition introduce the concepts that are peculiar to events with elections.

16.1 INTRODUCTION

By contrast to *mandatory events*, events with elections offer the position holder a choice as to how it participates in the event, or indeed if it participates at all. Two forms of such events exist:

- Mandatory with Options Events, where the position holder will be given two or more alternatives as to the form of *resultant entitlement* it wishes to receive, but it must choose one (or more), for example an optional *scheme of arrangement*.
- Voluntary Events, where the position holder will be given the choice as to whether it wishes to participate in the event or not, for example the *conversion* of a *convertible bond*.

Elections may apply to both *re-organization* events and to *benefit* events. The alternatives available to the position holder are normally known as 'options'.

In making its choice the position holder may wish to apply that choice to all or only part of its entitled position.

For example, Trading Book X may have an entitled position of 100,000 AAA shares, and for a given mandatory with options event may have the choice as to whether to receive new securities in company Q, or to receive cash. The alternatives available to Trading Book X, would be as follows:

- elect to receive new securities Q in respect of its entire underlying holding of 100,000 AAA shares;
- elect to receive cash in respect of its entire underlying holding of 100,000 AAA shares; or
- elect to receive securities in Q in respect of a specified quantity (i.e. part) of its underlying holding in AAA shares, and cash in respect of the remainder of its holding.

In the case of a Voluntary event, the position holder would have the additional option to take no action and therefore not to participate in the event at all, for all or for part of its holding.

A position holder may opt to take-up the option on only part of its holding in order to 'hedge its bets' or to pursue an investment strategy and receive a mixture of securities and/or cash as a result of the event, thereby reducing its exposure to a single choice.

The actual choice made by the position holder is known as an 'election decision' (and 'election decisions' where more than one alternative is chosen). Each election decision must represent:

- the quantity of the underlying entitled position to which it applies, and
- the specific option that is elected in respect of that quantity.

The lifecycle of events with elections differs specifically from the generic lifecycle of mandatory events in that additional steps are required to manage and apply the position holder's *election decisions*. The management of mandatory with options events and voluntary events are described in Chapters 17 and 18 respectively.

16.2 THE STO'S RISK

Despite the relatively high volumes of mandatory events, they are rarely considered to be of the highest risk to the STO as all resultant entitlements are calculated on the same basis, using the same event terms, and are applicable to all position holders.

Events with elections, encompassing both the mandatory with options event and voluntary event groups, require the STO to obtain election decisions from the position holder and to pass those election decisions onto the *location* of the holding. Subsequent calculation of the resultant entitlements will be made according to those election decisions.

The management of events with elections entails the STO, within the stipulated deadlines of the event:

- communicating the alternatives available to the position holder in a timely and accurate manner;
- tracking the receipt of the position holder's election decisions, and ensuring the outstanding election decisions are pursued prior to the *event deadline*;
- communicating, in an accurate and timely manner election decisions to locations (normally the STO's *custodian*) in order to protect the election decisions of the STO's position holders.

The above process introduces steps in the corporate actions lifecycles of each of these categories of events that do not occur in a mandatory event, and failure to manage these steps adequately could result in severe financial penalties to the STO. For example, if the STO communicates the incorrect election decision to the location, the STO will be unable to fulfil the election decision made by the position holder, and will normally be forced to recompense the position holder at a cost to the STO. In addition, the extent of any potential losses as a result may be difficult to predict due to the variety of options that the event terms may offer.

16.3 IMPACT OF EVENTS WITH ELECTIONS

Chapter 1 ('Basic Corporate Action Concepts') describes the generic impact of events from the perspectives of the *issuer*, the *position holder*, and the market as reflected in changes to the price of the *underlying security* to the event.

This type of impact of events is just as applicable to events with *elections*, albeit more elaborate and less predictable, as a result of the alternatives offered by the issuer to position holders.

16.3.1 Impact from the Issuer's Perspective

From the issuer's perspective, the impact of any corporate action event is identified in the changes to the issuer's *balance sheet*, i.e. its issued capital, debts and cash reserves as a result of the event. Where an event involves election decisions on the part of the position holder, the issuer is unable to identify accurately the final impact until after the close of the event when all position holders' election decisions are applied to the balance sheet. In this way both *mandatory with options events* and *voluntary events* differ from the *mandatory event*, where the issuer will always know the exact impact to its balance sheet at the time of announcing the event.

The issuer will normally take advice as to which options to offer position holders, with a view to the current market conditions, and must be in a position to cover all options that could be elected within the terms of the event, i.e. have sufficient security and cash reserves in the event that position holders elect them. For example, if an issuer offered position holders a choice between securities or cash in a mandatory with options event, the issuer would require sufficient *issued capital* to ensure that it could cover a scenario where all position holders elected securities, and conversely would require sufficient cash reserves to cover a scenario where all position holders elected cash. Note that on some occasions the issuer may set limits as to the election decisions it will accept for one or more of the options offered.

From the issuer's perspective, the negative aspect to this is that at the end of the event it may find in its balance sheet either too much residual capital (un-issued), or cash reserves, as a result of either option not having been elected.

Where an event is voluntary, the issuer may find that position holders do not wish to participate in the event, thereby not achieving the desired impact to its balance sheet at all. For example, where the event is the exchange of issued debt for issued capital, as is the case with a bond *conversion*, the issuer would hope for an increase in issued capital and a decrease in issued debt in its balance sheet. If position holders do not elect to convert their debt securities to equity securities, then the issuer would achieve neither of these aims.

16.3.2 Impact from the Position Holder's Perspective

As with mandatory events, the impact of an event with elections to a position holder is measured in terms of its impact on their securities and/or cash positions.

Unlike the mandatory events described to date, where an event includes options (including the options to not participate at all, as is the case in a voluntary event) the position holder may exercise control over the impact of the event on its securities and/or cash positions within the scope of the options offered by the *issuer*. Indeed, where the event is voluntary, the position holder may choose not to participate at all, thereby having no impact on its positions.

This difference to the position holder (where the event includes options) is of fundamental importance, as the choice between options available to the position holder becomes an investment decision, similar to those made when trading. Those responsible for the trading books of the STO would typically undertake analysis as to which option(s) best suits its trading strategy, whilst a *custody client* may seek the advice of its financial advisor or salesperson.

16.3.3 Impact on the Price of the Underlying Security

As with the impact on the issuer and the position holder, the impact of an event with elections on the price of the underlying security is essentially the same as that generically described in Chapter 1, but remains less predictable.

Where the event is mandatory with options (i.e. where the position holder will be given two or more alternatives, as to the form of entitlement it wishes to receive, but must choose one or more), each alternative will effectively have the same value and therefore the impact to the price of the *underlying security* may be predicted.

Where the event is voluntary, the impact on the price of the underlying security is more speculative as it is tied to the choice of position holders to participate in the event or not, and in this way is similar to the market forces of supply and demand affecting the price of securities.

16.4 EVENTS WITH ELECTIONS LIFECYCLE

The stipulation of election decision deadlines, and the subsequent management of elections introduce additional operational milestones in the lifecycle of an event with elections, over and above those applicable to the generic (mandatory) lifecycle.

From the time when entitlement to the event is first determined and event terms are communicated to position holders, the Corporate Actions Department will, in addition to the generic lifecycle, collate the receipt of *election decisions* from position holders and issue election decisions to the location of those positions. These steps will continue until the appropriate deadline. This period is known as the *election period*.

In addition, throughout the election period the Corporate Actions Department will identify those positions for which election decisions have not been received, and issue reminders to the position holders where appropriate.

The mechanisms for the management of elections as they apply to mandatory with options events and voluntary events are described in Chapters 17 and 18 respectively. The diagram representing the overall logical flow of elements with respect to events with elections (see Figure 16.1) appears at the beginning of the relevant chapter.

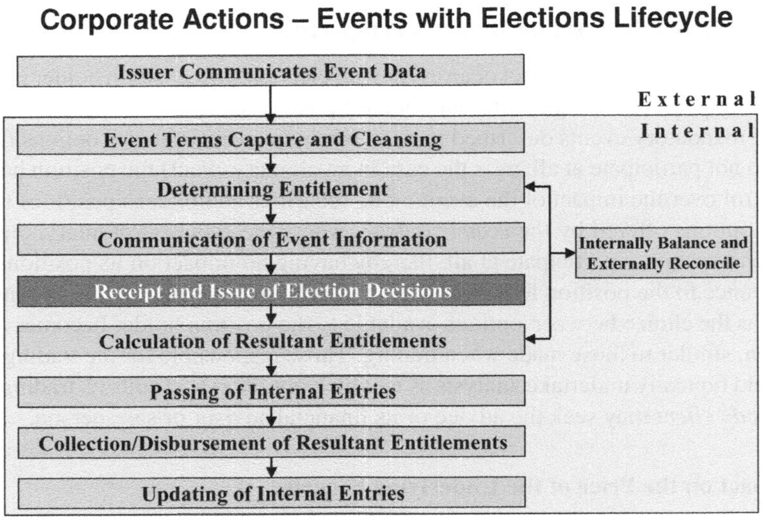

Figure 16.1 Events with elections lifecycle.

16.5 SUMMARY

Owing to the requirement to manage election decisions, events with elections introduce an additional and critical component to the lifecycle of both mandatory with options events and voluntary events.

It is of utmost importance that the Corporate Actions Department accurately identifies these events, and that operational processes employed take account of this additional operational step.

In addition, in order to identify clearly whether participation in the event is mandatory or voluntary, it is necessary to distinguish accurately between the two categories of events with elections:

- mandatory with options events, and
- voluntary events.

The method of managing these two categories of events differs, and is explored in detail in the following two chapters.

Significant losses can be incurred by the STO where events are incorrectly identified and elections are dealt with incorrectly or not in a timely manner.

17
Management of Mandatory with Options Events

17.1 INTRODUCTION

As described in the previous chapter, a mandatory with options event is one where participation in the event by the *position holder* is mandatory; however the position holder will be given two or more alternatives as to the form of *resultant entitlement* it may receive.

Upon announcement by the *issuer*, mandatory with options event terms must be captured accurately by the STO (in parallel with mandatory event terms). At the appropriate moment, the STO should communicate event terms to the position holders with a clearly stated deadline by which the STO is to be advised of the position holder's *election decision*.

Election decisions apply to both resultant entitlements due to be *disbursed* and resultant entitlements due to be *collected*. The Corporate Actions Department must capture election decisions for which it manages positions, including the STO's own *trading book* positions and *custody client* positions, together with those *counterparties* to whom it owes outstanding deliveries. Once captured, the Corporate Actions Department will use this information in order to determine which election decisions it must issue in turn to its *locations*, including any counterparties from whom the STO is owed outstanding receipts of securities.

The accurate and timely application of election decisions to both entitled positions and location components is critical to the STO avoiding losses as a result of error and delay.

Figure 17.1 illustrates the overall logical flow of elements with respect to mandatory with options events.

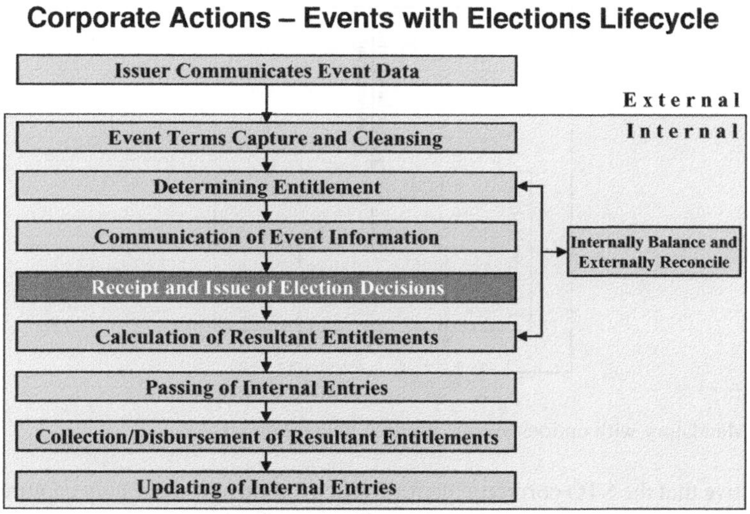

Figure 17.1 Events with elections lifecycle.

17.2 MANDATORY WITH OPTIONS EVENT TERMS

A mandatory with options event will include event terms and conditions additional to those of a mandatory event. These include:

- options available to position holders, and
- deadline(s) for lodging election decisions.

Each of these is described below.

17.2.1 Options Available

The event terms of a mandatory with options event will include the details of each of the options available to the position holder. Typically, this will include a description of that option, together with the specific conditions pertaining to calculation of the *resultant entitlement* for that option.

For example, the event terms may offer the position holder the choice between electing a) securities, or b) cash, as its resultant entitlement. The conditions for

- option A (securities) will include details of the *entitlement security*, a security *ratio*, and conditions for the treatment of *fractions*, while
- option B (cash) will include details of the entitlement currency, and a cash *rate*, and (possibly) an exchange rate.

The event terms may also indicate which of the available options may be considered a 'default' choice to the position holder. That is to say that in the case of no *election decision* being made, the *issuer* will automatically allocate an option to the position holder in order to calculate the resultant entitlement. This is common where events are optional and participation in the event is mandatory. This is represented in Figure 17.2.

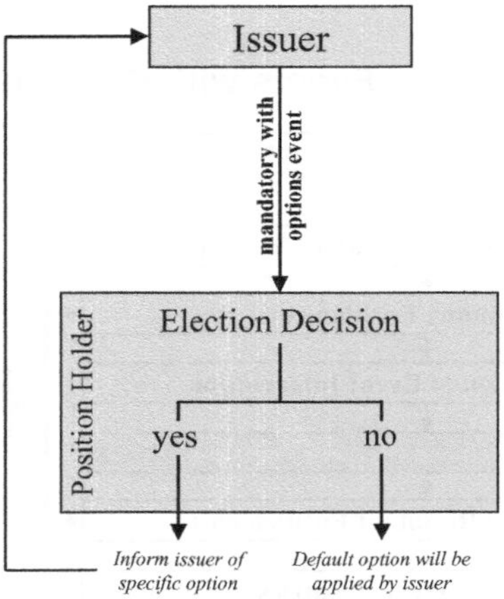

Figure 17.2 Mandatory with options events; position holder options.

It is imperative that the STO correctly identifies each option and accurately captures the conditions applying to each option, including the indication of a *default option* where applicable.

Failure to identify correctly the options available could result in incorrect communications to position holders, incorrect calculation of resultant entitlements, and the inevitable risk of the STO incurring losses.

17.2.2 Election Decision Deadlines

Mandatory with options events include a number of deadlines for both the receipt and issue of election decisions. The Corporate Actions Department must ensure that these deadlines are accurately recorded with the event terms, and monitored throughout the event lifecycle. From the STO's perspective, these deadlines can be classified as external or internal.

External deadlines refers to those time limits for the issue of election decisions to parties external to the STO, i.e. the location of positions, whether that be the *issuer*, the STO's *custodian* or a *counterparty* against whom the STO is claiming.

- **Issuer's Deadline**
  This is the deadline by which the issuer requires to be notified of the position holders' *election decisions*, and typically indicates both a date and time. Where the STO is notifying the issuer directly of its election decisions (i.e. not via its custodian), this is the last date and time which the issuer will accept any election decisions from the STO.
- **Custodian's Deadline**
  The STO's custodian will inform the STO of a deadline (including date and time) by which it requires to receive election decisions from the STO. Typically, this date will be prior to that of the Issuer's Deadline, in order to give the custodian sufficient time to collect and process all election communications, and to then forward the appropriate election decisions itself to the *issuer*.
- **Counterparty's Deadline**
  Where *claims* are identified against *counterparties* (as a result of *unsettled trades* owed to the STO), the STO will need to inform the counterparty against whom it is claiming of its election decision. Typically, this will be a date agreed between the counterparty and the STO. This date will potentially differ for each counterparty with whom the STO has a claim, and therefore the STO will need to ensure that this date is agreed and accurately recorded against each claim.

Communication of election decisions to external parties later than the appropriate deadline(s) may result in the STO not receiving the *resultant entitlement* relating to the election decisions made by its position holders.

Internal deadlines refer to those deadlines that the STO will set internally for the receipt of election decisions from its position holders (including *trading books* and *custody clients*), together with deadlines to be applied to election decisions due from counterparties claiming against the STO (as a result of unsettled trades owed by the STO).

The STO may set different internal deadlines according to the type of position holder. For example, custody clients may have an earlier deadline than trading books, as trading books are managed internally and typically communication would be expected to be quicker.

These deadlines will typically precede the earliest of any external deadlines (described previously), in order to allow the STO sufficient time to receive the election decision from the position holder and convey the election decision to the location. As a matter of control, it is recommended that when setting an internal deadline, the STO also allows sufficient time to pursue those position holders who are yet to convey their election decisions.

Figure 17.3 illustrates the typical sequence of deadlines, inclusive of example dates.

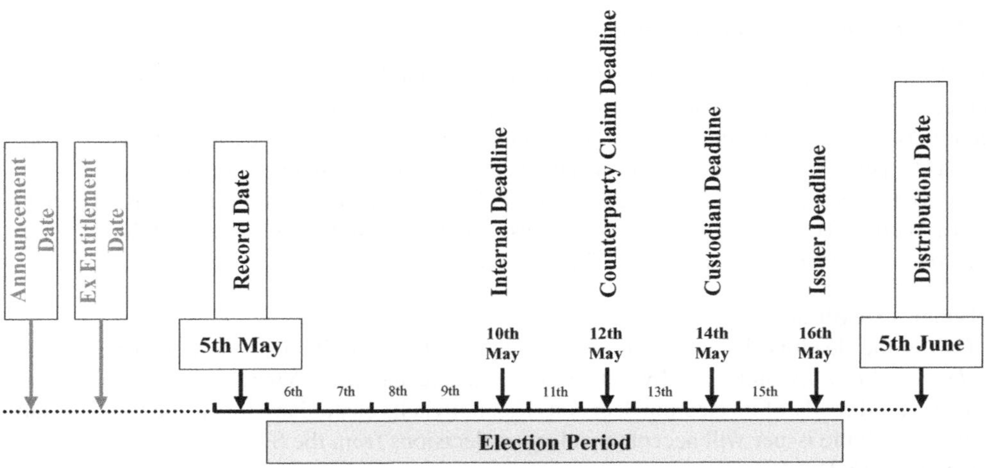

Figure 17.3 Mandatory with options events; typical sequence of deadlines.

17.3 DETERMINING ENTITLEMENT TO MANDATORY WITH OPTIONS EVENTS

The principles of *determining entitlement* to mandatory with options events do not differ to that described in Chapter 9, 'Determining Entitlement'. In parallel with the generic lifecycle, the STO must identify:

- ownership positions, comprising
  - *Trading book* positions, and
  - *Custody client* positions
- location components, comprising
  - *Settled custodian positions*
  - *Unsettled trades* resulting in claims in favour of the STO
  - Unsettled trades resulting in claims against the STO.

17.4 COMMUNICATION OF MANDATORY WITH OPTIONS EVENT INFORMATION

In Chapter 10 ('Communication of Event Information'), a generic set of communications was introduced which would typically be issued in the majority of events:

- Event Terms Announcement
- Preliminary Entitlement Notice
- Final Entitlement Notice

- Preliminary Claim Notice
- Final Claim Notice

In the majority of cases, these types of communications will also apply to mandatory with options events, nonetheless the content of the communication will differ to reflect the additional event terms, such as the options available to the position holder, and the appropriate deadlines, as described below.

- Event Terms Announcement
  The Event Terms Announcement will include, in addition to the normal event terms, the full details of each option available to the position holder, together with the applicable deadline. Typically, the STO would also state the action that it will take in the event that the position holder does not communicate its *election decision* to the STO by the deadline (refer to Section 17.2). Effectively, in the case of a mandatory with options event, the Event Terms Announcement can be considered to be a request for an election decision from the position holder.
- Preliminary Entitlement Notice
  Unlike a mandatory event, where only one *resultant entitlement* may be calculated, the resultant entitlement for a mandatory with options event will be based upon the option(s) elected by the position holder. Should the STO issue a preliminary entitlement notice for a mandatory with options event, it is the STO's choice as to whether any projected resultant entitlement will be included. For example, where a default option is applicable to the event, the STO may wish to communicate the default resultant entitlement (in the event that election decisions are not received).
- Final Entitlement Notice
  The final entitlement notice content will typically not differ from that of a mandatory event, as the resultant entitlement will be based upon the election decisions received from the position holder.
- Preliminary Claim Notice
  In parallel with mandatory events, the preliminary claim notice will alert a *counterparty* (with whom an outstanding trade exists) of a potential *claim*. Note that where the trade remains unsettled at the record date of the event, the Corporate Actions Department will be required to issue instructions to the counterparty of the claim to inform it of the STO's election decision. Such instructions are detailed in Section 17.8.
- Final Claim Notice
  The final *claim* notice will be issued subsequent to the counterparty's acceptance of any election instructions (see above) from the STO. As with mandatory events, the purpose of the final claim notice is to confirm the final details of the resultant entitlement being claimed. In the case of a mandatory with options event, this will mirror the options elected by the STO. Subsequent to the issue of the final claim notice and whilst the claim for resultant entitlement remains unsettled, the Corporate Actions Department may issue reminders to the counterparty.

In addition to the generic communications referred to above, the mandatory with options event may include the following additional types of communication to position holders:

- Request for Election Decision – Reminders
- Confirmation of Election Decision
- Over-Election Notices

- Request for Election Decision – Reminders
  Throughout the life of the mandatory with options event the Corporate Actions Department will monitor the receipt of election decisions from position holders, in accordance with the appropriate deadlines of the event. Good management practice includes the issue of reminders (at frequent intervals throughout the event) to those position holders from whom election decisions have not yet been received. Such reminders effectively contain the same information as the Event Terms Announcement, but additionally serve the purpose of urgently alerting the position holder of the approaching deadline to the event. As the deadline to the event approaches, the Corporate Actions Department may issue such reminders at increasing frequency.
- Confirmation of Election Decision
  Upon receipt of an election decision, the Corporate Actions Department may issue a notice to the position holder confirming the details of its election decision. The benefit of such a notice is to ensure that the Corporate Actions Department has correctly acted upon the position holder's decision. This is particularly beneficial where an event contains many options, and the terms of the event are quite complex.
- Over-Election Notices
  In the case of some mandatory with options events, specific options may have limits as to the election decisions that the issuer will accept. Where this is the case, it may be necessary for the Corporate Actions Department to issue a notice to the position holder indicating that the issuer's limit has been exceeded and that the position holder's election decision has been amended accordingly. The management of over-elections is expanded in Section 17.9.

17.5 RECEIPT OF ELECTION DECISIONS

Throughout the election period, the Corporate Actions Department will receive election decisions from

- position holders, and
- claiming counterparties (where claims exist against the STO).

17.5.1 Position Holder Election Decisions

Election decisions to be applied to entitled positions (held for *position holders*) may be received from a number of sources:

- Captured Election Decisions, as communicated directly by the position holder;
- Standing Election Decisions, held in *static data*;
- Default Election Decisions, normally set by the *issuer*, occasionally by the market or the STO.

Captured Election Decisions

In the majority of cases, the Corporate Actions Department will expect to receive communication of the options elected for a specific mandatory with options event from the person(s) responsible for the position, as a result of having communicated the event terms to the position holder.

In the case of a *trading book* position this would typically be the trader responsible, whilst for a *custody client* position, this could be the custody client itself, or where authority exists, the STO's salesperson responsible for the client.

Such communications may be captured electronically, or manually. Many STOs provide an online facility to enable both traders and custody clients to communicate their election decisions to the Corporate Actions Department, subsequently immediately updating the information in its records. Alternatively, where communications are received manually, it is imperative that procedures are in place to ensure accurate and timely updating of the Corporate Actions Department's records to reflect election decisions. (Note that these procedures are described more fully later in this chapter).

Standing Election Decisions

In some cases, the *static data* of a position holder may reflect its instructions with regard to its election decisions; these instructions are known as *standing elections*. Standing elections logically only apply where the combinations of options are fixed based upon the type of event, even though the specific ratios of the option are not known, i.e. the combination of options would not vary from event to event according to the issuer's announcement.

Typically standing election decisions may be held for events such as Dividend Re-investment Plans, where based upon the definition of the event, the position holder will always be given the option to elect cash or alternatively re-invest that cash into new securities. The position holder's investment strategy may be always to elect cash or alternatively always to elect *re-investment* into new securities. (Note that Dividend Re-investment Plans are described further within Section 17.10.1).

Conversely, it is unlikely that standing election decisions would be held for, say, an optional Scheme of Arrangement, where each issuer could offer any combination of securities and/or cash.

The benefit of recording standing elections in static data (where applicable) is to remove the need to receive elections from the position holder on an event-by-event basis, therefore allowing the STO to achieve STP in this instance. Any such static data must always be accurately recorded and maintained, as described in Chapter 4, with applicable dates from which such instructions become effective.

Default Election Decisions

Within the terms of the event, the issuer may indicate that one of the options available is the *default option*. This means that in the case that an election decision is not received, the default option will be applied to the position.

Default options are common in the case of mandatory with options events, where the position holder must elect at least one of the options available, i.e. it must participate in the event.

Under normal circumstances, the Corporate Actions Department will apply default election decisions to the positions it is managing where election decisions are not received from the position holder or held as standing elections, by the *election period* deadline.

Any communications of event terms to position holders should include information identifying the default option, and the STO's policy on its application in the event of outstanding election decisions.

17.5.2 Claiming Counterparty Election Decisions

Where *unsettled trades* are identified resulting in potential *claims* against the STO, the Corporate Actions Department will expect to receive from the specific *counterparty* a communication regarding the option(s) it wishes to elect with respect to its claim.

Market conventions with respect to the soliciting of this information vary greatly. Unlike procedures for position holders, where the Corporate Actions Department will actively request such election decisions, with regard to claims against the STO, in many cases the onus will be upon the claiming counterparty to initiate contact with the STO's Corporate Actions Department, to inform it of its election decisions.

The Corporate Actions Department may not actively seek *election decisions* from the claiming counterparty. If the Corporate Actions Department does not receive advice of such election decisions prior to the deadline of the event, for mandatory with options events typically the *default option* would be applied.

The process of applying election decisions to claims is known in some markets as *protection*, as the STO is endeavouring to protect the claiming counterparty for the requested *resultant entitlement*. Nonetheless, in some markets protection of the requested option is not enforced, and protection may be on a 'best endeavours' basis. This means that the STO is required only to do its best to satisfy any election decision of the claiming counterparty, and may be allowed to satisfy the claim via the delivery of one of the alternative options. Note that this is more common in the case of voluntary events; refer to Chapter 18, 'Management of Voluntary Events'.

17.6 RECORDING AND VALIDATING RECEIVED ELECTION DECISIONS

Upon receipt of *election decisions* (irrespective of the source), the Corporate Actions Department must record promptly and accurately in its records the following information:

- the specific *position holder*;
- the quantity (of the underlying entitled holding) to which the election applies;
- the specific option elected.

Additional audit trail related information would typically also include:

- the date of the election decision;
- the medium by which the election decision was conveyed;
- the source of the election decision, including the person(s) responsible for making the election decision;
- the date of recording the election decision, and by whom.

Where election decisions are received by methods other than formatted electronic message e.g. by letter, e-mail, or facsimile, it is also recommended that the Corporate Actions Department has strict procedures in place to store these communications.

The need for controls and accuracy in the recording of received election decisions cannot be overstated. Errors and delays may cause incorrect election decisions being subsequently issued to the *location*, potentially resulting in financial losses to the STO.

17.6.1 Recording Election Decision Quantities

As stated above, when receiving an *election decision* the Corporate Actions Department must record the quantity of the underlying holding to which that election decision applies. This information will allow the Corporate Actions Department to calculate accurately

- the election decisions to be issued to the location, together with
- any outstanding election decisions still to be received from the position holders.

The position holder may effectively 'split' its holding across more than one option, or may communicate election decisions at multiple times throughout the *election period* for part-quantities of its original entitled holding each time.

The example shown in Table 17.1 illustrates the scenario where the trader responsible for the *trading book* position makes multiple *election decisions* against the original underlying holding throughout the election period, and also shows the changes that occur in the Corporate Actions Department's records as a result. (Note that the specific option(s) elected are intentionally not shown).

Table 17.1

Election Decision Control				
Position Holder	Date Election Decision Received	Elected Holding Quantity	Unelected Holding Quantity	Original Underlying Holding Quantity
Trading Book 'A'	3rd July	1,000,000	3,500,000	4,500,000
	5th July	750,000	2,750,000	4,500,000
	6th July	1,500,000	1,250,000	4,500,000
	7th July	1,250,000	0	4,500,000
	total	**4,500,000**		

On some occasions the position holder may advise the Corporate Actions Department of the amount of the *resultant entitlement* that it wishes to receive, rather than the holding quantity to which it applies. When this occurs, the Corporate Actions Department will need to calculate the equivalent elected holding quantity, using the terms of the event, in order to update its records with the elected holding quantity. In doing so, care is required to take account of any fractional differences that may occur as a result of rounding, in accordance with the event terms.

For example, company X announces a Scheme of Arrangement whereby the position holder may elect to receive:

- securities; at a *ratio* of one new share for every four existing shares held, or
- cash; at a ratio of EUR 1.50 for every one existing share held, or
- any combination of securities and/or cash.

Custody Client T (who has a holding of 100,000 shares in Company X) communicates the following election decision to the STO, which is subsequently converted to the equivalent elected holding quantity based upon the terms of the offer (as stated above):

- elect a resultant securities entitlement of 20,000 new shares, and
- the balance to be elected as cash.

On the basis of the event terms of one new share for every four held, securities will be elected against a holding of 80,000 (underlying) shares, in order to receive 20,000 new shares. The balance of Custody Client T's holding, being 20,000 (underlying) shares, will receive the cash option. This will be recorded in the Corporate Actions Department's records as shown in Table 17.2.

Table 17.2

Election Decision Control					
Position Holder	Date Election Decision Received	Elected Holding Quantity	Securities	Cash	Unelected Holding Quantity
Custody Client 'T'	18th October	80,000	✓		20,000
	18th October	20,000		✓	0
		total	**80,000**	**20,000**	

17.6.2 Validating Received Election Decisions

When initially recording the elected quantity and specific option of a received *election decision*, and then throughout the election period, the Corporate Actions Department must ensure the following:

- the elected quantity does not exceed the entitled holding quantity, and
- the option elected is in fact valid for the event in question.

- **Validating the Elected Quantity**
  As a result of trading in the underlying event security throughout the *election period* (and in fact potentially up until the event's *record date* or payment date −1), it is possible for the quantity of the entitled holding to change, either increasing or reducing the quantity originally communicated to the position holder. Initially, upon receipt of the election decision, it is vital to ensure that the elected quantity does not exceed the entitled quantity, but equally this check must remain in place throughout the election period to take account of any potential changes to the entitled quantity as a result of further trading.
  Should the elected quantity exceed the entitled quantity at any time, then immediate action is required by the Corporate Actions Department, typically via contacting the position holder or person(s) responsible for the position in order to resolve the discrepancy.
- **Validating the Elected Option**
  Subsequent to the initial announcement of event terms, from time to time the available options or the terms relating to them may alter. Although this is more typical in takeover events (described in Chapter 22, 'Concepts of Takeover Events'), it could potentially occur with any event with election decisions, such as a mandatory with options event. The Corporate Actions Department must immediately identify any such changes to event terms, and identify their impact to elections already received. Typically in such cases, the Corporate Actions Department will communicate the changes to event terms to position holders and request their new instructions with regard to their election decisions.

17.7 MANAGING OVERDUE ELECTION DECISIONS

As previously described, the Corporate Actions Department will typically set an internal deadline with respect to the receipt of election decisions from position holders, with the date of this deadline being prior to those deadlines that apply to the *location* components.

By ensuring that such a deadline is prior to the location deadlines, the Corporate Actions Department should have sufficient time to receive all election decisions from position holders, and then issue the corresponding election decisions to the location.

In addition, the earlier date of the internal deadline should also provide the Corporate Actions Department with a period within which to follow up urgently any position holders for which *election decisions* have not been received.

The process of recording election decisions as and when they are received, and therefore identifying any outstanding election decisions (as illustrated in the previous section) should allow the Corporate Actions Department to monitor outstanding election decisions up to and including the internal deadline date.

As described earlier, the Corporate Actions Department will normally issue reminders against such outstanding election decisions to the position holder. Typically, the issue of such reminders would commence in the days immediately prior to the internal deadline date, rather than waiting until the last day. Depending upon the length of the period from the internal deadline date to the deadline date applicable to the location, the Corporate Actions Department may continue to issue such reminders. Nonetheless, there will come a point in time where the reminders are no longer applicable, and the Corporate Actions Department will be required to take specific action with regard to the outstanding election. For mandatory with options events, these actions are (for example):

- attempt to make verbal contact with the position holder;
- seek an internal decision from whomever is responsible for the position, e.g. head trader or custody client salesperson;
- apply *default options*, where applicable.

The above actions involve an element of risk from the Corporate Actions Department (and therefore from the STO's) perspective; included in such a risk is the Corporate Actions Department overlooking the content of the *SLA* in relation to the management of election decisions. It would be expected that such cases would be escalated to senior personnel, and would require the appropriate authorization.

For example, where election decisions have not been received from the trader responsible for a *trading book*, this may be escalated to the head trader. Alternatively, where election decisions have not been received from a *custody client*, the issue may be referred to the salesperson responsible for the client for a decision to be made.

17.8 ISSUE OF ELECTION DECISIONS

The *election decisions* received from *position holders* and claiming *counterparties* should be recorded and collated throughout the *election period* in order for the Corporate Actions Department to issue election decisions to the *location* (in order to satisfy the election decisions received).

In doing so, the Corporate Actions Department will perform the following steps:

1. Calculate each election decision to be issued.
2. Identify the location component to which the election decision will be issued.
3. Balance election decisions to be issued to those received.
4. Issue the election decision notification to the location.

In performing these steps, the Corporate Actions Department should be mindful of the deadlines applicable to the location(s), including counterparty deadlines, *custodian* deadlines and *issuer* deadlines (described in Section 17.2).

Election decisions may be issued to the location only once (immediately prior to or on the appropriate deadline) or the Corporate Actions Department may issue multiple election decisions to the location(s) throughout the election period. This will normally depend upon the length of the election period and the nature of the event.

17.8.1 Calculating Election Decisions to be Issued

As a result of having recorded the options and associated elected quantities as received from position holders and claiming counterparties (as described earlier in this chapter), the Corporate Actions Department will calculate the total quantity for each option to be elected. The following example illustrates this calculation.

Example No. 1 – Three Trading Books, One Custodian

Marks and Spencer plc (the issuer) announces a *Scheme of Arrangement* event that gives the holder the option to receive:

- Option A – cash
- Option B – securities

The STO's entitled position in Marks and Spencer shares is represented in Table 17.3 (note that in this example the entire position is held at a single custodian externally).

Table 17.3

Marks and Spencer Shares			
Ownership		**Location**	
Trading Book 'A'	+3,000,000	−23,500,000	Custodian G, London
Trading Book 'B'	+6,500,000		
Trading Book 'C'	+14,000,000		
	+23,500,000	−23,500,000	

Table 17.4 summarizes the *election decisions* advised by each position holder.

Table 17.4

Election Decision Summary					
Position Holder	Elected Holding Quantity	Option A	Option B	Unelected Holding Quantity	Original Underlying Holding Quantity
Trading Book 'A'	3,000,000	3,000,000		0	3,000,000
Trading Book 'B'	6,500,000	5,000,000	1,500,000	0	6,500,000
Trading Book 'C'	14,000,000	1,000,000	13,000,000	0	14,000,000
	total	**9,000,000**	**14,500,000**	*total*	**23,500,000**

Table 17.5 reveals the totals per option (as a result of election decisions taken by the various position holders) that will be issued by the STO to the location in the form of election decisions.

Table 17.5

Summary of Election Decisions			
Ownership			**Location**
Option A	+9,000,000	−9,000,000	Custodian G, London
Option B	+14,500,000	−14,500,000	Custodian G, London
	+23,500,000	−23,500,000	

17.8.2 Identifying the Location Component

Once the election decisions to be issued for each option have been tabulated, it is necessary to identify the *location* component to which the election decision will be issued. The Corporate Actions Department will have previously identified the location components in the underlying event security, including any *unsettled trades* (as described in Chapter 9, 'Determining Entitlement'), and it is now necessary to apply election decisions against such components.

Where a single location component exists, such as a *settled custodian position* (as illustrated in the previous example) the decision is an obvious one. Where multiple location components exist, i.e. more than one, and combinations of settled custodian positions and unsettled trades exist, it is necessary for the Corporate Actions Department to select an appropriate location to elect against, possibly with a single option being spread across more than one location.

Example No. 2 – Three Trading Books, Two Custodians

Nokia (the issuer) announces a Scheme of Arrangement event that gives the holder the option to receive:

- Option A – cash
- Option B – securities

The STO's entitled position in Nokia shares is represented in Table 17.6 (note that in this example the entire position is held between two custodians externally).

Table 17.6

Nokia Shares			
Ownership			**Location**
Trading Book 'D'	+8,000,000	−32,500,000	Custodian S, Helsinki
Trading Book 'E'	+24,500,000	−6,500,000	Custodian T, Frankfurt
Trading Book 'F'	+6,500,000		
	+39,000,000	−39,000,000	

Table 17.7 summarizes the election decisions advised by each position holder.

Table 17.7

Election Decision Summary					
Position Holder	Elected Holding Quantity	Option A	Option B	Unelected Holding Quantity	Original Underlying Holding Quantity
Trading Book 'D'	8,000,000	2,000,000	6,000,000	0	8,000,000
Trading Book 'E'	24,500,000	21,000,000	3,500,000	0	24,500,000
Trading Book 'F'	6,500,000	3,500,000	3,000,000	0	6,500,000
	total	**26,500,000**	**12,500,000**	*total*	**39,000,000**

Table 17.8 reveals the totals per option (as a result of election decisions taken by the various position holders) that will be issued by the STO to the two locations in the form of election decisions.

Table 17.8

Summary of Election Decisions			
Ownership			Location
Option A	+23,000,000	−23,000,000	Custodian S, Helsinki
Option B	+9,500,000	−9,500,000	Custodian S, Helsinki
Option A	+3,500,000	−3,500,000	Custodian T, Frankfurt
Option B	+3,000,000	−3,000,000	Custodian T, Frankfurt
	+39,000,000	−39,000,000	

The selection of a location (where multiple exist) is typically a manual exercise, nonetheless a number of guidelines can be adopted:

- Ensure that *trading book* elections (i.e. the STO's proprietary positions) are applied only to the STO's proprietary settlement accounts (held at the *custodian*).
- Ensure that *custody client* elections are applied only to the custody settlement accounts (held at the custodian).
- Where *unsettled trades* exist, attempt to identify the trading book or custody client to which the unsettled trade corresponds; then apply the position holder's election decisions to the unsettled trade accordingly. This may result in the position holders election decision being spread across both settled custodian positions and unsettled trades.

Example No. 3 – Three Trading Books, Three Custody Clients, One Custodian with Three Sub-accounts, One Unsettled Trade

HSBC (the issuer) announces a Scheme of Arrangement event that gives the holder the option to take:

- Option A – cash
- Option B – securities

The STO's entitled position in HSBC shares is represented in Table 17.9 (note that in this example the entire position for all of the owners is held in different accounts at the same custodian externally, plus securities are owed to the STO by a counterparty from which securities have been purchased). The purpose of this example is to illustrate the election decisions made across multiple location components on the basis of the election decisions received from position holders.

Table 17.9

HSBC Shares			
Ownership			Location
Trading Book 'G'	+3,000,000	−11,500,000	Custodian P, Hong Kong a/c Main
Trading Book 'H'	+6,500,000	−12,000,000	Counterparty V, Singapore
Trading Book 'J'	+14,000,000		
Custody Client 'X'	+1,000,000	−1,750,000	Custodian P, Hong Kong a/c Cust 1
Custody Client 'Y'	+750,000		
Custody Client 'Z'	+2,500,000	−2,500,000	Custodian P, Hong Kong a/c Cust 2
	+27,750,000	−27,750,000	

Table 17.10 summarizes the election decisions advised by each position holder.

Table 17.10

Election Decision Control						
Position Holder	Date Election Decision Received	Elected Holding Quantity	Option A	Option B	Unelected Holding Quantity	Original Underlying Holding Quantity
Trading Book 'G'	20th February	3,000,000	3,000,000		0	3,000,000
Trading Book 'H'	22nd February	6,500,000	5,000,000	1,500,000	0	6,500,000
Trading Book 'J'	19th February	14,000,000	1,000,000	13,000,000	0	14,000,000
Custody Client 'X'	18th February	1,000,000		1,000,000	0	1,000,000
Custody Client 'Y'	20th February	750,000	750,000		0	750,000
Custody Client 'Z'	19th February	2,500,000	1,000,000	1,500,000	0	2,500,000
		total	**10,750,000**	**17,000,000**	*total*	**27,750,000**

In order to apply ownership positions to its truly appropriate location components (as opposed to applying on a random basis), the STO will need to maintain its securities position management records at a granular level (refer to Chapter 5, 'Securities Position Management'). Such record keeping will enable the relationship to be maintained between the owner and the location; for example, Table 17.9 identifies the STO (specifically Trading Book 'J') as having 12,000,000 shares due from Counterparty V (following a purchase), as at the *record date*, and therefore the STO must advise that counterparty of the STO's *election decision* (in reality, the election decision of Trading Book 'J') in relation to that outstanding trade.

The election decision made by the owners plus those that must be issued to the locations, are summarized in Table 17.11.

Table 17.11

Summary of Election Decisions			
Ownership			Location
Option A (Trading Books)	+9,000,000	−9,000,000	Custodian P, Hong Kong a/c Main
Option A (Custody Clients)	+750,000	−750,000	Custodian P, Hong Kong a/c Cust 1
Option A (Custody Clients)	+1,000,000	−1,000,000	Custodian P, Hong Kong a/c Cust 2
Option B (Trading Books)	+2,500,000	−2,500,000	Custodian P, Hong Kong a/c Main
Option B (Trading Books)	+12,000,000	−12,000,000	Counterparty V, Singapore
Option B (Custody Clients)	+1,000,000	−1,000,000	Custodian P, Hong Kong a/c Cust 1
Option B (Custody Clients)	+1,500,000	−1,500,000	Custodian P, Hong Kong a/c Cust 2
	+27,750,000	−27,750,000	

In addition, any specific links between ownership positions and locations (as previously described in Chapter 5, 'Securities Position Management' and in Chapter 9, 'Determining Entitlement') will aid the process of applying election decisions received to the applicable associated location component.

17.8.3 Balancing Election Decisions

Once the appropriate election decisions are recorded against the location components, it is necessary to ensure that the election decisions to be issued to the location(s) balance with those received from position holders and claiming counterparties. Typically, this would be done for each option, ensuring that the election decisions received equal the election decisions to be issued.

Based upon the HSBC shares examples above, balancing of election decisions for Option A is represented as shown in Table 17.12, and Option B is represented in Table 17.13.

Table 17.12

Option A								
Ownership			=	Location				
Sum of Trading Book Positions	+	Sum of Custody Client Positions	=	Sum of Settled Positions (Custodian or Issuer)	+	Sum of Claims in Favour of STO	–	Sum of Claims against STO
9,000,000	+	1,750,000	=	10,750,000	+	0	–	0

Table 17.13

Option B								
Ownership			=	Location				
Sum of Trading Book Positions	+	Sum of Custody Client Positions	=	Sum of Settled Positions (Custodian or Issuer)	+	Sum of Claims in Favour of STO	–	Sum of Claims against STO
14,500,000	+	2,500,000	=	5,000,000	+	12,000,000	–	0

Any imbalance will require immediate investigation prior to the issue of the election decision to the location.

17.8.4 Communication of Election Decisions

Once all *election decisions* are finalized and balancing completed, the Corporate Actions Department should issue communications to each location advising its elected options and the holding quantities to which they apply, by the applicable deadline(s).

The method of transmission of election decisions is largely dependent upon the type of location (i.e. specifically whether it is the *issuer*, a *CSD/ICSD*, *custodian*, or the *counterparty* to an *unsettled trade*), together with the applicable market conventions.

- **Issuer Positions**
  Where positions are held directly (normally in physical form) with the issuer, in the majority of cases the communication of election decisions against these positions will also be a physical exercise, usually requiring the lodgement of appropriate documentation with either the issuer's registrar or the issuer itself.

  The physical process of conveying the election decision in this manner is by no means a secure method, and the Corporate Actions Department must ensure sufficient time for physical delivery of the election notice to be made prior to the issuer's deadline, and would normally obtain a receipt of such delivery.
- **CSD/ICSD Positions**
  In most cases CSDs/ICSDs will support proprietary electronic messages to accommodate the settlement of trades, corporate action entitlements, and potentially the communication of election decisions. In other cases the CSD/ICSD may accept *S.W.I.F.T.* messages, or other media, such as telex.

  The Corporate Actions Department would typically ensure that the *static data* records of the CSD/ICSD accurately reflect the required transmission method to enable election decisions to be transmitted in an *STP* fashion, where possible.

- **Custodian Positions**
  In most cases custodians will accept S.W.I.F.T messages, or other media, such as telex for the communication of election decisions, although in some cases communication via paper may still be accepted. Note that at the time of writing, custodian's websites are being considered as a medium by which election decisions can be communicated.
  As with CSDs/ICSDs, the Corporate Actions Department would typically ensure that the STO's static data records of the custodian accurately reflect the required transmission method to enable election decisions to be transmitted in an STP fashion, where possible.
- **Claims in Favour of the STO**
  Where *unsettled trades* are identified, resulting in potential *claims* in favour of the STO, the Corporate Actions Department will be required to notify the *counterparty* concerned of the STO's required *election decision.* Typically, this would be via telex, facsimile or in paper form (usually requiring physical delivery). All of these methods are less secure than the electronic messages (described for CSDs/ICSDs and custodians), and therefore it is imperative that the Corporate Actions Department takes all necessary steps to ensure that the communication is received and acknowledged by the counterparty.
  As for any election decisions being made against claims (described earlier in this chapter), *protection* of the STO's election decision is not always guaranteed. The Corporate Actions Department therefore needs to liaise with the counterparty against whom it is claiming throughout the event, to ensure that the STO's interests are being protected adequately.

The issue of an election decision communication to the location can be viewed in a similar light to the issue of a settlement instruction relating to a trade. In the same way, the Corporate Actions Department would expect to monitor the progress of the communication effectively (irrespective of transmission method), recording

- date issued
- date acknowledged by the location
- date accepted by the location

It is not sufficient to assume that once an election decision is acknowledged by the location that it is in fact accepted; the term 'accepted' is a common term that refers to the recipient having validated the election decision and that it will act upon it. The location will perform validation checks against the election decision details that are similar to those the STO performed against election decisions it received from its position holders, e.g. validation of election quantities and elected options.

Election decision notifications can be rejected by the location, in which case the Corporate Actions Department will require procedures to identify such rejections, and immediately correct any discrepancies, re-lodging the election decision prior to the location's deadline.

17.9 OVER-ELECTIONS

In the case of some mandatory with options events, the *issuer* may set a limit for the *election decisions* it will accept for a specific option based upon the elected quantity. One advantage of this to the issuer is to restrict its exposure to that option.

The conditions of any such limits would form part of the event terms, and as such should be included in any communications to position holders made by the STO.

For example, the issuer may announce a Scheme of Arrangement with the choice between electing new securities, or cash. In addition, the election of cash may be restricted to 50% of the existing issued shares. This will mean that, assuming 1,000,000 shares are currently issued, the issuer will accept only the election decision of cash against an upper limit of 500,000 shares. Any election decisions received by the issuer in excess of this will be considered as over-elections.

Where election decisions against the restricted option exceed the limit stipulated in the event terms, the issuer will reduce the elected quantity (known as 'scaling down') of all or part of the election decisions received for the specified option. This is achieved in one of two ways:

- on a pro-rata basis across all election decisions, or
- on the basis of when the election decision was received, with those election decisions received after the limit has been reached being reduced in part or in full.

The treatment of the remaining elected quantity (known as the 'over-elected' quantity) will depend upon the other options offered within the event terms. Where a default option of securities and/or cash applies, this will typically be applied to the over-elected quantity.

Continuing with the Marks and Spencer example earlier in this chapter, the election decisions of the three *trading books* resulted in the situation shown in Table 17.14.

Table 17.14

Original **Summary of Election Decisions**			
Ownership		**Location**	
Option A (cash)	+9,000,000	−9,000,000	Custodian G, London
Option B (securities)	+14,500,000	−14,500,000	Custodian G, London
	+23,500,000	−23,500,000	

Following this, the STO would have instructed Custodian G to accept Option A and Option B accordingly.

However, in this example the issuer restricts the election of cash to 50% of the existing issued shares, while election decisions for cash in total amount to 75% of *issued capital*. Therefore the issuer chooses to reduce election decisions received for cash by a third (the excess received) and apply the default option of securities to the excess (the custodian having advised the STO, following receipt of the information from the issuer). See Table 17.15.

Table 17.15

Adjusted **Summary of Election Decisions**			
Ownership		**Location**	
Option A	+6,000,000	−6,000,000	Custodian G, London
Option B	+17,500,000	−17,500,000	Custodian G, London
	+23,500,000	−23,500,000	

Upon receipt of notification of over-elections from the location, the Corporate Actions Department will need to update its records immediately of election decisions issued with the updated election decision quantities and options (where applicable). In turn, it is then necessary to apply the same rules to the original election decisions received from position holders and claiming counterparties, in order to re-balance the election decision quantities.

Continuing further with the Marks and Spencer example, in order to reflect the necessary adjustments at ownership level, the original Option A (cash) election decisions shown in Table 17.16 would require adjusting to those shown in Table 17.17.

The remaining elected holding quantity will default to Option B (securities), as shown in Table 17.18.

Table 17.16

Original Election Decision Summary					
Position Holder	Elected Holding Quantity	Option A	Option B	Unelected Holding Quantity	Original Underlying Holding Quantity
Trading Book 'A'	3,000,000	3,000,000		0	3,000,000
Trading Book 'B'	6,500,000	5,000,000	1,500,000	0	6,500,000
Trading Book 'C'	14,000,000	1,000,000	13,000,000	0	14,000,000
	total	**9,000,000**	**14,500,000**	*total*	**23,500,000**

Table 17.17

Adjusted Election Decision Summary		
Position Holder	*Original* Option A	*Revised* Option A
Trading Book 'A'	3,000,000	2,000,000
Trading Book 'B'	5,000,000	3,333,334
Trading Book 'C'	1,000,000	666,666
	9,000,000	**6,000,000**

Table 17.18

Adjusted Election Decision Summary				
Position Holder	*Original* Option A	*Revised* Option A	*Original* Option B	*Revised* Option B
Trading Book 'A'	3,000,000	2,000,000		1,000,000
Trading Book 'B'	5,000,000	3,333,334	1,500,000	3,166,666
Trading Book 'C'	1,000,000	666,666	13,000,000	13,333,334
	9,000,000	**6,000,000**	**14,500,000**	**17,500,000**

It is important to note that in managing over-elections, the STO may choose to prioritize the treatment of certain participants above others; for example to protect the interests of *custody clients* first, then *trading books*, and lastly claiming *counterparties*. Any changes to a *position holder's* or claiming counterparty's original election decisions as a result of over-elections must be communicated promptly.

Irrespective of how the over-elections are communicated, the Corporate Actions Department must at all times ensure it has control of the resultant entitlements it expects to collect and the resultant entitlement it expects to disburse.

17.10 CALCULATION OF RESULTANT ENTITLEMENTS

The calculation of *resultant entitlements* for mandatory with options events falls mainly within the same generic procedures as for mandatory events, as detailed within Chapter 11, 'Calculation of Resultant Entitlements'. This calculation occurs either

- initially (for position holders) upon receipt of its election decision, followed (for the location) upon acceptance by the location of the STO's election decision, or
- across both position holders and the location simultaneously, upon acceptance by the location of the STO's election decision.

The difference to the generic procedure for mandatory events is that the calculation is based upon the quantity of the underlying entitled holding for which the elected option applies, and not simply against the quantity of the entitled holding or location (as is the case with mandatory events). An entitlement will be calculated for each option that the position holder has elected, and in turn for each option that has been elected against the location.

Continuing again with the Marks and Spencer example, the elected option quantities that have been confirmed by the custodian are as shown in Table 17.19 which, within the STO's ownership records, will need to be reflected as shown in Table 17.20.

Table 17.19

***Confirmed* Summary of Election Decisions**			
Ownership		**Location**	
Option A	+6,000,000	−6,000,000	Custodian G, London
Option B	+17,500,000	−17,500,000	Custodian G, London
	+23,500,000	−23,500,000	

Table 17.20

***Confirmed* Election Decision Summary**		
Position Holder	***Confirmed*** Option A	***Confirmed*** Option B
Trading Book 'A'	2,000,000	1,000,000
Trading Book 'B'	3,333,334	3,166,666
Trading Book 'C'	666,666	13,333,334
	6,000,000	**17,500,000**

Where the Marks and Spencer election decisions relate to a Scheme of Arrangement of, for example,

- Option A – cash at a rate of GBP 0.95 for every one existing share held, or
- Option B – securities at a ratio of two new shares for every five existing shares held

the resultant cash (Option A) collectible entitlement will be as shown in Table 17.21.

Table 17.21

Marks and Spencer Shares – Resultant Cash (GBP) from Scheme of Arrangement			
Ownership		**Location**	
Trading Book 'A'	+1,900,000.00	−5,700,000.00	Custodian G, London
Trading Book 'B'	+3,166,667.30		
Trading Book 'C'	+633,332.70		
	+5,700,000.00	−5,700,000.00	

The resultant securities (Option B) collectible entitlement will be as in Table 17.22.

Table 17.22

Marks and Spencer Shares – Resultant Securities from Scheme of Arrangement			
Ownership		**Location**	
Trading Book 'A'	+400,000	−7,000,000	Custodian G, London
Trading Book 'B'	+1,266,667		
Trading Book 'C'	+5,333,333		
	+7,000,000	−7,000,000	

In addition, the terms of mandatory with options events may include some additional or different calculations to those detailed within Chapter 11, 'Calculation of Resultant Entitlements', and may consist of calculation of resultant securities entitlements based upon a re-investment price.

17.10.1 Calculations Based upon a Re-investment Price

As indicated in Chapter 16, 'Concepts of Events with Elections', some income events may also include options, a specific example of this being a dividend re-investment plan where the position holder is given the choice between electing cash income or securities (refer to Chapter 2 Event Description and Classification). A dividend re-investment plan includes a unique method of calculating the *resultant entitlement*.

In the case where the position holder elects to receive cash income, this will be calculated in accordance with the principles detailed in Chapter 11, 'Calculation of Resultant Entitlements', applying the cash rate (as per the event terms) to the holding quantity for which cash is elected. This calculation will determine the pre-taxed cash income entitlement. Note that the calculation of tax liabilities is detailed in Chapter 24, 'Concepts and Management of Taxation'.

Where securities are elected, the resultant entitlement will be calculated using a re-investment price per share, with the position holder re-investing its cash entitlement based upon this price. Note that although the re-investment price forms part of the event terms, it is often not available until a time closer to or following the *record date* of the event.

In calculating the resultant securities entitlement, the Corporate Actions Department must first calculate the cash income entitlement, and then divide this amount by the re-investment price.

For example, the Australian brewing company Fosters Group announces a dividend re-investment plan giving shareholders the choice of electing:

- cash income at a rate of AUD0.55 per share, or
- securities at a re-investment price of AUD2.25 per share.

Trading Book 'B' is the holder of 4,500,000 Fosters Group shares, which is represented in its entirety by a fully settled securities position at the custodian. This is represented in Table 17.23. The trading book elects to receive securities, rather than cash.

Table 17.23

Fosters Group Shares			
Ownership			Location
Trading Book 'B'	+4,500,000	−4,500,000	Custodian M, Sydney
	+4,500,000	−4,500,000	

The resultant number of shares that will be re-invested is calculated as follows:

1. Derive the cash income entitlement by multiplying the number of shares elected by the cash income rate

$$4{,}500{,}000 \text{ shares} \times \text{AUD}0.55 \text{ per share} = \text{AUD}\,2{,}475{,}000.00$$

2. Divide the cash income entitlement by the re-investment price

$$\text{AUD}\,2{,}475{,}000.00 \text{ divided by AUD}2.25 \text{ per share} = 1{,}100{,}000 \text{ shares}$$

At the appropriate time, the resultant entitlement of 1,100,000 shares must be added to the original position (providing the re-invested shares rank *pari-passu* with the original shares) to reveal the revised position shown in Table 17.24.

Entries are passed at the same time, within both trader's records and the STO's main books & records, thereby ensuring that securities positions remain in balance when attempting to reconcile.

Table 17.24

Fosters Group Shares			
Ownership			Location
Trading Book 'B'	+5,600,000	−5,600,000	Custodian M, Sydney
	+5,600,000	−5,600,000	

Note that for simplicity, the example above has not included the calculation of any tax liabilities, stamp duty or other such charges, which may be as applicable when electing re-investment to new securities as when electing cash income. For example, re-investment may occur based upon the pre-taxed or post-taxed cash income amount according to the event terms and tax regulations of the local market. The implications of this to the calculation of the securities entitlement are explored in Chapter 24, 'Concepts and Management of Taxation'.

17.11 PASSING OF INTERNAL ENTRIES

For mandatory with options events, as with mandatory events, entries will be passed by the STO to reflect

- any change to the underlying securities position, and
- the distribution of any securities and/or cash that is expected to occur on the distribution date or effective date of the event.

In the case of mandatory with options events, as with mandatory events, *entitlement date* entries and *record date* entries will be passed according to type of event.

We now describe entries relating to

- Mandatory with Options Benefit Events, and
- Mandatory with Options Re-organization Events.

17.11.1 Mandatory with Options Benefit Events

For *benefit* events that provide the owner with options, (in parallel with mandatory benefit events) prior to settlement of *resultant entitlements*, two types of entries may be passed by the STO (depending upon whether an entitlement date applies to the event, or not). These are:

- *Entitlement date* entries, and
- *Record date* entries.

Both of these are explained in this section.

Note that the following will be used as the basis for the examples in this section. Alitalia (the Italian airline company) announces a *benefit* event whereby the position holder may elect to receive:

- securities, at a *ratio* of one new share for every four existing shares held, or
- cash, at a *rate* of EUR 1.50 for every one existing share held, or
- any combination of securities and/or cash.

Trading Book 'A' (who has a holding of 100,000 shares in Alitalia) elects to receive

- a resultant securities entitlement of 20,000 new shares (equivalent to 80,000 original shares), and
- the balance to be elected as cash (equivalent to 20,000 original shares), resulting in EUR 30,000.00.

Entitlement Date Entries

As *election decisions* are typically being received from position holders for a period of time beyond the ex entitlement date, the Corporate Actions Department is unlikely to know the position holder's elected option at the time of the entitlement date when accrual entries are normally passed to reflect the resultant entitlement. Consequently, a set of initial entries are passed as at the ex entitlement date based upon the *default option*, which are subject to change once election decisions are finalized. Such changes are normally passed on record date.

Assuming that the default option is for the position holder to receive securities (rather than cash), on ex entitlement date the entries shown in Table 17.25 would be passed.

Table 17.25

Disbursable Entries (Alitalia New Ordinary Shares)			
Debit		Credit	
Event Control Account	25,000	25,000	Trading Book 'A'
	25,000	25,000	

Record Date Entries

For mandatory with options benefit events, record date entries relating to the location (i.e. *settled custodian positions* and *unsettled trades*) are required to be passed under all circumstances. In addition, under some circumstances position holder related entries are required to be passed.

Position Holder Entries

Once the Corporate Actions Department is informed by the position holder of its final *election decision*, any adjustments to the entries passed on entitlement date should be passed on record date or the issuer's deadline date (whichever is later), in order to reflect the elected option accurately. Using the example election decisions quoted above, the entries shown in Tables 17.26 to 17.28 will be passed. Table 17.26 shows the entry to reverse the Entitlement Date entry.

Table 17.26

Disbursable Entries (Alitalia New Ordinary Shares)			
Debit		Credit	
Trading Book 'A'	25,000	25,000	Event Control Account
	25,000	25,000	

Table 17.27 shows the entry to reflect the final quantity of securities elected by the position holder.

Table 17.27

Disbursable Entries (Alitalia New Ordinary Shares)			
Debit		Credit	
Event Control Account	20,000	20,000	Trading Book 'A'
	20,000	20,000	

Table 17.28 shows the entry to reflect the final amount of cash elected by the position holder.

Table 17.28

Disbursable Entries (EUR)			
Debit		Credit	
Event Control Account	30,000.00	30,000.00	Trading Book 'A'
	30,000.00	30,000.00	

Note that should the position holder's final election decision be the same as the *default option*, some STOs may choose not to reverse and replace the original entries (on the basis that the result will be identical to the original set of entries).

Location Entries

In the case of mandatory with options benefit events, a set of record date entries will be passed against the location reflecting any changes to securities and/or cash positions in line with issued election decisions. These entries will be passed on either the record date, or the issuer's deadline date (whichever is later).

Following on from the above example, Table 17.29 illustrates the record date entry for securities collectible from the appropriate custodian.

Table 17.29

Collectible Entries (Alitalia New Ordinary Shares)			
Debit		Credit	
Custodian 'X' Main a/c Projected	20,000	20,000	Event Control Account
	20,000	20,000	

The entry to reflect the amount of cash elected by the position holder (and conveyed to the custodian), is shown in Table 17.30.

Table 17.30

Collectible Entries (EUR)			
Debit		Credit	
Custodian 'X' Main a/c Projected	30,000.00	30,000.00	Event Control Account
	30,000.00	30,000.00	

Note that settlement date entries are described in Section 17.13.

17.11.2 Mandatory with Options Re-organization Events

For *re-organization* events that provide the owner with options (where an entitlement date is normally not applicable), in parallel with mandatory re-organization events, prior to settlement of *resultant entitlements* only record date entries are passed.

Such events typically require the passing of entries on record date to

- remove holdings (and any unsettled trades) in the *underlying security*;
- create holdings in the replacement security;
- represent *unsettled trades* that will be *transformed*.

Such entries are detailed in Chapter 12, 'Passing of Internal Entries' and in Chapter 15, 'Examples of Mandatory Events'.

Once the position holder has made its final election decision, record date entries may need to be reversed and replaced (as described in the Record Date Entries section earlier in this chapter).

17.12 COLLECTION AND DISBURSEMENT OF RESULTANT ENTITLEMENTS

Once the STO is certain that its election decisions (on behalf of the position holders) have been accepted by the location(s), from that point forward the *collection* and *disbursement* of resultant entitlements falls within the same procedures as for mandatory events. Such procedures are detailed within Chapter 13, 'Collection/Disbursement of Resultant Entitlements'.

17.13 UPDATING OF INTERNAL ENTRIES

The settlement of a mandatory with options event is the same in all respects as the settlement of a mandatory event. Entries passed on record date against

- custodians, in the form of 'projected' entries, and
- counterparties, in the form of 'awaiting settlement' entries

will be updated with a further set of entries against the custodian, in the form of 'settled' entries (once the custodian has advised the STO of settlement). Such entries are detailed in Chapter 14, 'Updating of Internal Entries' and in Chapter 15, 'Examples of Mandatory Events'.

17.14 SUMMARY

The management of election decisions is, for the Corporate Actions Department (and therefore for the STO), a highly risky exercise, usually required to be performed within a short time period, and with a degree of manual intervention even in a highly automated environment.

In summary, the Corporate Actions Department must

- capture mandatory with options event terms as soon as possible after announcement;
- advise position holders of their options as soon as possible, ensuring the necessary deadline for their election decision is clearly stated;
- collect, record and validate election decisions received from position holders and claiming counterparties;
- finalize overdue election decisions from position holders;
- collate election decision results, determine and issue election decisions to locations;
- monitor success of election decisions issued to locations, including over-elections.

It must always be mindful of the election decision deadlines imposed by the various locations.

Significant losses can be incurred by the STO where election decisions are dealt with incorrectly or not in a timely manner.

As deadlines approach and workload threatens to outweigh the manpower within the Corporate Actions Department, there is an increasing danger that such pressure will result in mistakes. The 'antidote' to the STO incurring such losses is for the Corporate Actions Department to work to a clearly defined timetable of actions and deadlines, with unambiguous roles and responsibilities of those involved.

18
Management of Voluntary Events

18.1 INTRODUCTION

As described in the previous chapter, a voluntary event is one where the *position holder* will be given a choice as to whether it wishes to participate in the event or not, i.e. participation is purely voluntary. Should the position holder choose to participate in the event it may, in addition, be given two or more alternatives as to the form of *resultant entitlement* it wishes to receive.

The event lifecycle of voluntary events does not differ from that of mandatory with options events. Note that for the purposes of this book, multiple stage events and takeovers are covered separately.

As with mandatory with options events, voluntary events require the management of *election decisions*, and in this respect the two categories of events are very similar.

Nonetheless the voluntary event introduces the concept of non-participation, and therefore the management of voluntary events differs in some respects to that of mandatory with options events to take account of this.

In addition, voluntary events include events that require the payment of monies to the issuer. Such payments are known as *subscriptions* and therefore require the additional step of calculating the monies due, as part of the calculation of resultant entitlements step.

Figure 18.1 illustrates the overall logical flow of elements with respect to voluntary events.

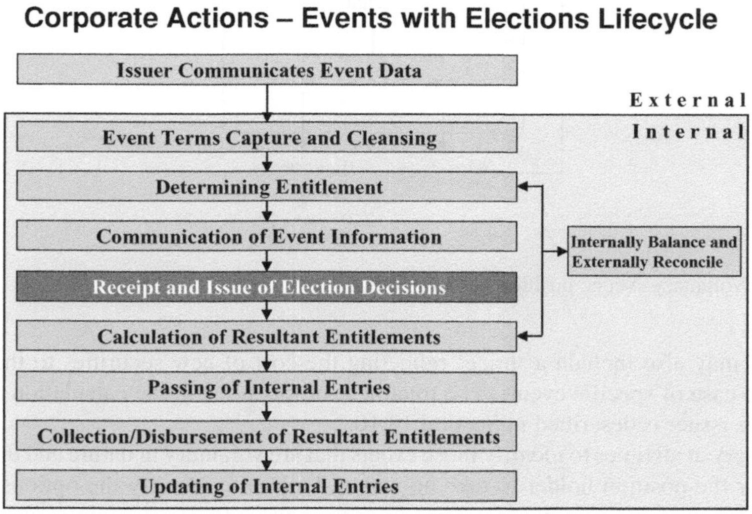

Figure 18.1 Events with elections lifecycle.

18.2 VOLUNTARY EVENT TERMS

A voluntary event includes event terms and conditions additional to those of a mandatory event. These include:

- options available to position holders;
- deadline(s) for lodging election decisions; and
- *shareholder eligibility* conditions pertaining to specific options.

Each of these is described below.

18.2.1 Options Available

Where an event is voluntary, that is, the position holder is given (in addition to any of the other options) the choice as to whether it wishes to participate in the event or not, the choice to take 'no action' can also be considered an option, and must be recorded as such by the STO against the event (thus distinguishing the event as voluntary). It can therefore be considered that the 'no action' option is the default, in that unless an election decision is made, no action will be taken and no resultant entitlement will be calculated. This is represented in Figure 18.2.

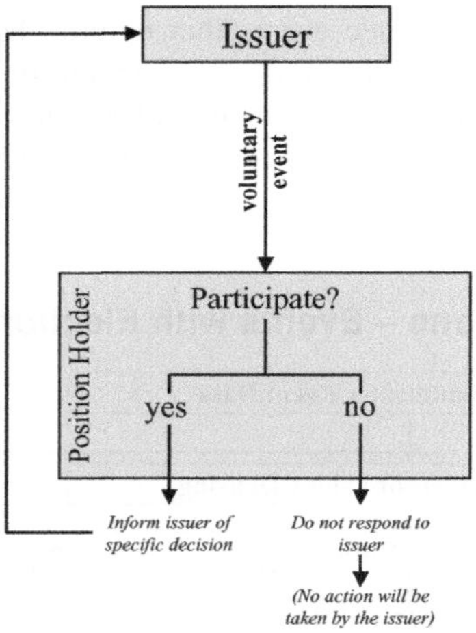

Figure 18.2 Voluntary events; position holder options.

An option may also include a 'price' reflecting the cost of new securities to the position holder, in the case of specific events. The treatment of this price in the calculation of monies payable to the issuer is described in Section 18.10.

It is necessary at all times to identify those events that are voluntary in nature and that include the ability for the position holder to take no action. Failure to identify the options available correctly could result in incorrect communications to position holders, incorrect calculation of resultant entitlements, and the inevitable risk of the STO incurring losses.

18.2.2 Election Decision Deadlines

Voluntary events include a number of deadlines, as described for mandatory with options events, for both the receipt and issue of election decisions. These include:

- external deadlines:
  - issuer's deadline
  - custodian's deadline
  - counterparty's deadline, and
- internal deadlines.

Please refer to Chapter 17, 'Management of Mandatory with Options Events'.

18.2.3 Shareholder Eligibility

As introduced in Chapter 8, 'Event Terms Capture and Cleansing', voluntary events may also include specific conditions pertaining to the position holder's eligibility to accept one or other option, or in fact participate in the event at all. Examples of this include:

- **Foreign Ownership Restrictions**
  A voluntary event may offer the position holder the option to purchase additional securities in the issuer, at a price. The option to purchase additional securities is known as a subscription. The regulations pertaining to ownership in the country of issue of the underlying security may restrict foreign ownership (as is often the case in media companies). Therefore, in this instance the option to subscribe to new shares would not be available to foreign position holders; note that this restriction is also applicable to certain mandatory with options events . The STO must record this condition and ensure that position holders are informed accordingly. Failure to do so by the STO would incur a breach of regulations.
- **Eligibility based upon Size of Holding**
  On occasions, the issuer may set conditions of eligibility based upon the size of the position holder's holding. For example, an *Odd Lot Offer* is restricted only to those position holders that have a position outside of the normal tradable lots of the *underlying security*.

18.3 DETERMINING ENTITLEMENT TO VOLUNTARY EVENTS

The principles of determining entitlement to voluntary events do not differ from those described in Chapter 9, 'Determining Entitlement'. In parallel with the generic lifecycle, the STO must identify:

- *Ownership positions*, comprising
  - *trading book* positions, and
  - *custody client* positions
- *Location* components, comprising
  - *settled custodian positions*
  - *unsettled trades* resulting in *claims* in favour of the STO
  - unsettled trades resulting in claims against the STO

The only additional aspect in determining entitlement to a voluntary event is to apply any conditions in the event terms that may restrict participation, as described in Section 18.2.3. An example of participation based upon size of holding follows.

HSBC (the issuer) announces an Odd Lot Offer; the issuer will buy at a price of HKD 11.50 per share any holdings under 100 shares (where tradable lots are 100 shares). Table 18.1 represents an STO's entire position in HSBC shares as at the record date.

Table 18.1

HSBC Shares			
Ownership		Location	
Trading Book 'A'	+16,400	−16,400	Custodian L, Hong Kong
Custody Client 'X'	+1,000	−3,378	Custodian L, Hong Kong Cust a/c
Custody Client 'Y'	+63		
Custody Client 'Z'	+2,315		
	+19,778	−19,778	

The Corporate Actions Department will immediately identify that the offer is restricted to custody client 'Y', as only that position holder has a position under 100 shares.

18.4 COMMUNICATION OF VOLUNTARY EVENT INFORMATION

In the majority of cases, the types of communications that apply to voluntary events are the same or similar to those that apply to mandatory with options events, differing only in content to include reference to the position holder's option not to participate in the event at all.

These types of communications, described in Chapter 17, include:

- Event Terms Announcement
- Preliminary Entitlement Notice
- Final Entitlement Notice
- Preliminary Claim Notice
- Final Claim Notice
- Request for Election Decision – Reminders
- Confirmation of Election Decision
- Over-Election Notices

18.5 RECEIPT OF ELECTION DECISIONS

The receipt of *election decisions* in respect of voluntary events mirrors that previously detailed for mandatory with options events.

The Corporate Actions Department will receive elections decisions from

- position holders, and
- claiming counterparties.

In the case of voluntary events, it can be considered that the choice to take no action, i.e. not to participate in the event, is the *default option*.

Under normal circumstances the Corporate Actions Department will apply default election decisions to the positions it is managing, where election decisions are not received from the position holder by the *election period* deadline. Therefore, in the specific case of a voluntary event, this means that where election decisions are not received from the position holder or claiming counterparty, the Corporate Actions Department would typically take no further action and the position holder would not participate in the event.

18.6 RECORDING AND VALIDATING RECEIVED ELECTION DECISIONS

Where a position holder elects to participate in a voluntary event, the Corporate Actions Department must record promptly and accurately in its records the same information as would be expected for any election decision, namely:

- the specific position holder;
- the quantity (of the underlying entitled holding) to which the election applies; and
- the specific option elected.

This is recorded together with additional audit trail related information, for example the date of the election decision.

In recording the quantity (of the underlying holding) to which the election applies, the Corporate Actions Department will be well placed to calculate

- the election decisions to be issued to the location, together with
- any outstanding election decisions still to be received from the position holders.

As described previously, in the case of voluntary events the position holder or claiming counterparty may elect to take no action and not participate in the event at all. Where this choice is explicitly communicated to the Corporate Actions Department, it is highly recommended that this information also be recorded, and that the elected quantity of the holding be updated accordingly. Doing so will enable the Corporate Actions Department to identify accurately whether the position holder legitimately does not wish to elect, or has simply not notified its election decision.

For example, the *convertible preference shares* in company X may be voluntarily converted during October of every year (known as the *conversion period*) to fully paid ordinary shares, until maturity of the convertible preference shares. Therefore during the conversion period the position holder may elect to

- convert its convertible preference shares to fully paid ordinary shares, or to
- take no action.

Each of the above options may be elected with respect to all or part of the position holder's holding.

Custody Client T (who has a holding of 1,000,000 convertible preference shares in Company X) communicates the following election decision to the STO:

- convert 700,000 convertible preference shares.

The Corporate Actions Department will record this as shown in Table 18.2, indicating that no election decision has been received for the balance of Custody Client T's holding, being 300,000 convertible preference shares.

Subsequently, Custody Client U (who has a holding of 800,000 convertible preference shares in Company X) communicates the following election decision to the STO:

- convert 600,000 convertible preference shares, and
- do not convert (i.e. retain) 200,000 convertible preference shares.

The Corporate Actions Department will record this as shown in Table 18.3, indicating that election decisions with respect to the total quantity of Custody Client U's holding have been

Table 18.2

Election Decision Control					
Position Holder	Date Election Decision Received	Convert (Holding Quantity)	Take No Action (Holding Quantity)	Unelected (Holding Quantity)	Original Underlying Holding Quantity
Custody Client 'T'	18th October	700,000	0	300,000	1,000,000
	total	**700,000**	**0**	**300,000**	

received, including the decision not to participate, i.e. not to convert, 200,000 convertible preference shares.

Table 18.3

Election Decision Control					
Position Holder	Date Election Decision Received	Convert (Holding Quantity)	Take No Action (Holding Quantity)	Unelected (Holding Quantity)	Original Underlying Holding Quantity
Custody Client 'T'	18th October	700,000	0	300,000	1,000,000
Custody Client 'U'	24th October	600,000	200,000	0	800,000
	total	**1,300,000**	**200,000**	**300,000**	

In explicitly recording decisions not to participate in voluntary events, the Corporate Actions Department is able to avoid any confusion between those holdings that are not to participate in the event and those for which election decisions have truly not been received.

18.7 MANAGING OVERDUE ELECTION DECISIONS

As mentioned previously, the option to take no action, i.e. not to participate in a voluntary event, is essentially the default option for that event.

Therefore once the deadline for the receipt of election decisions has passed, the Corporate Actions Department will be required to take specific action with regard to any outstanding election decisions, for example:

- attempt to make verbal contact with the position holder;
- seek an internal decision from whoever is responsible for the position, e.g. head trader or custody client salesperson;
- take no action.

The risks of financial loss to the STO as a result of incorrect actions taken at this point can be significant. Strict guidelines are recommended in order to obtain the appropriate level of authorization, and to ensure that company policies are communicated to position holders and are adhered to.

For example, the STO's policy in the case of non-receipt of election decisions for voluntary events may be to take no action with respect to the position holder's holding. Accordingly this should always be included on all communications to the position holder, and in addition a '*four eyes*' principle to outstanding election decisions is recommended.

18.8 ISSUE OF ELECTION DECISIONS

The issue of *election decisions* to the *location* with respect to voluntary events does not differ to that of mandatory with options events. Please refer to Chapter 17, 'Management of Mandatory with Options Events'.

The Corporate Actions Department will

1. Calculate each election decision to be issued.
2. Identify the location component to which the election decision will be issued.
3. Balance election decisions to be issued to those received.
4. Issue the election decision notification to the location.

It is common for voluntary events that the Corporate Actions Department performs this cycle of steps on multiple occasions throughout the election period of the event, rather than simply once towards the close of the election period. This is mainly due to the nature of voluntary events, where it is not unusual for

- new holdings issued subsequent to the event (i.e. the *resultant entitlement*) to be made available to position holders throughout the *election period* as and when election decisions are received, rather than on a single later date after the close of the election period;
- specific options to be limited (refer to Section 18.9 below).

18.9 OVER-ELECTIONS

For voluntary events, in parallel with mandatory with options events, the *issuer* may stipulate a limit to be applied to designated options with respect to the election decisions.

Where such a limit is exceeded, election decisions will be reduced either

- on a pro-rata basis across all election decisions, or
- on the basis of when the election decision was received, with those election decisions received after the limit has been reached being reduced in part or in full.

The over-elected quantity will receive, according to the terms of the voluntary event, either

- an alternative option, or
- the election decision against this quantity will be cancelled entirely. In this case this means that the position holder will not participate in the event for this quantity of its original holding.

The method of reducing election decisions based upon when they are received by the location, and the risk of position holders missing out on participating in the event, will often lead the Corporate Actions Department to issue election decisions to the location (as mentioned in the previous section) on multiple occasions throughout the election period for voluntary events. This approach ensures that the STO's position holders' election decisions are dealt with before any over-elections occur.

18.10 CALCULATION OF RESULTANT ENTITLEMENTS

In addition to the various calculation principles described to date in Chapter 11,'Calculation of Resultant Entitlements' and in Chapter 17, 'Management of Mandatory with Options Events', many voluntary events also include the calculation of cash payable to the *issuer*.

Those voluntary events that require *subscription* to new securities or *exercise* of existing securities to new securities, may include the calculation of monies payable to the issuer. Note that a very limited number of mandatory events, such as an *equity call*, will also include such a calculation.

In such events the Corporate Actions Department will calculate the quantity of new securities to be received, together with the cash payable.

The calculation of the resultant securities entitlement will be based upon the securities ratio (including fractions rules) as applied to the underlying entitled holding, as previously detailed in Chapter 11.

The monies payable to the issuer will typically be calculated by applying the cash price (included in the event terms) to the resultant securities entitlement. This means that a dependency will exist between the two calculations, with the calculation of the securities entitlement being required to be performed prior to the calculation of the cash payment.

For example, Trading Book 'A' is the holder of EUR 20,000,000.00 Acme Manufacturing, 5.25% convertible bonds, maturing 1st May 2012, which entitle the holder to convert to the underlying equity at a *ratio* of 350 shares to every EUR 1,000.00 face value of bonds, upon payment by the holder of EUR 3.00 per share. The trading position is represented in its entirety by a fully settled securities position at the custodian. This is represented in Table 18.4.

Table 18.4

Acme Manufacturing, 5.25% Convertible Bonds 1st May 2012			
Ownership			**Location**
Trading Book 'A'	+20,000,000	−20,000,000	Custodian E, Brussels
	+20,000,000	−20,000,000	

At a time of its choosing, Trading Book 'A' decides to convert its entire bond holding into the underlying equity, upon payment of EUR 21,000,000.00. The standard procedure is that once the STO has informed the relevant *custodian* of its wish to convert (normally by issuance of a specific instruction type), the STO's cash account will be debited by the custodian with the conversion cost. The STO will need to pass cash entries internally in order to reflect the cost to the trading book, the contra-entry being to the custodian *nostro account*.

In addition, and from the perspective of the securities, the conversion results in both

1. the creation of the position shown in Table 18.5 in the underlying equity;
2. the reduction to zero of the (original) position in the convertible bond (see Table 18.6).

Table 18.5

Acme Manufacturing, EUR1.00 Shares			
Ownership			**Location**
Trading Book 'A'	+7,000,000.00	−7,000,000.00	Custodian E, Brussels
	+7,000,000.00	−7,000,000.00	

Table 18.6

Acme Manufacturing, 5.25% Convertible Bonds 1st May 2012			
Ownership			**Location**
Trading Book 'A'	0	0	Custodian E, Brussels
	0	0	

Both sets of entries are passed at the same time, within both trader's records and the STO's main books & records, thereby ensuring that securities positions remain in balance when attempting to reconcile.

18.11 PASSING OF INTERNAL ENTRIES

For voluntary events, as with mandatory events and mandatory with options events, entries will be passed by the STO to reflect

- any change to the *underlying securities* position, and
- the distribution of any securities and/or cash that is expected to occur on the *distribution date* or *effective date* of the event.

In the case of voluntary events, these entries will only be passed if the position holder has chosen to participate in the event. Where the position holder does not participate in the event there will be no change to its underlying securities position, and no distribution of securities and/or cash as a result of the event.

For voluntary events (elected by the position holder), prior to settlement of *resultant entitlements* the following types of entries may be made by the STO (depending upon whether an entitlement date applies to the event or not):

- *election decision date* entries;
- *record date* entries; and
- *over-election adjustment* entries.

These entries are explained in this section. Note that *settlement date* entries are described within Chapter 14, 'Updating of Internal Entries'.

As voluntary events do not include *benefit* events, entitlement date accrual entries (as described in Chapter 12, 'Passing of Internal Entries') are not required to be passed with respect to any resultant entitlements to be disbursed to the position holders.

As with other events, the STO will pass internal entries for both position holders and locations.

18.11.1 Election Decision Date Entries

In a situation where a position holder decides (for example) to convert its holding of a *convertible bond,* in order to avoid accidentally selling the securities while in the course of being converted, the STO will usually segregate the appropriate quantity of the convertible security within its books & records, immediately upon the *election decision* being taken. It is important to note that such segregation will not remove the holding from the position holder's total holding in the security; this action merely serves to segregate it from the position that is available for sale or transfer.

Assume that British Airways convertible bonds entitle the holder to convert such bonds into the issuer's underlying equity at a *ratio* of 215 shares for every GBP 10,000 face value of bonds. Assume also that the STO holds the position shown in Table 18.7 in its books & records (prior to the election decision).

Trading Book 'D' (the position holder) elects to convert GBP 7,000,000 *face value* of bonds, which will result in 150,500 shares, upon conversion.

Table 18.7

British Airways 4.75% Convertible Bonds 15th November 2009			
Ownership		Location	
Trading Book 'D'	+12,000,000	−12,000,000	Custodian S, Main a/c
	+12,000,000	−12,000,000	

Position Holder Entries

Procedurally, immediately following the election decision, the Corporate Actions Department effects an internal transfer (from the normal trading book to the 'accepted' trading book) in order to segregate the quantity of bonds that is subject to the conversion (Table 18.8) resulting in the position shown in Table 18.9.

Table 18.8

Segregation Entries (British Airways 4.75% Convertible Bonds 15th November 2009)			
Debit		Credit	
Trading Book 'D'	7,000,000	7,000,000	Trading Book 'D' (Accepted)
	7,000,000	7,000,000	

Table 18.9

British Airways 4.75% Convertible Bonds 15th November 2009			
Ownership		Location	
Trading Book 'D'	+5,000,000	−12,000,000	Custodian S, Main a/c
Trading Book 'D' (Accepted)	+7,000,000		
	+12,000,000	−12,000,000	

Location Entries

Election decision date entries typically apply to position holders, but where the STO wishes to reflect election decisions issued to the *location* throughout the *election period*, entries will be passed that are similar to the segregation entries illustrated for the position holder.

18.11.2 Record Date Entries

As with mandatory events and mandatory with options events, the purpose of *record date* entries is to reflect

- the resultant entitlement that is expected to be collected from the *location*; that is, from *custodians*, from *claims* on *counterparties*, from *transformed* trades; and
- the resultant entitlement that is to be *disbursed* to *position holders*.

This includes the removal of *underlying securities* for which election decisions were received (from position holders) and issued (to locations).

Position Holder Entries

In order to remove the bonds in the process of conversion from the position holder, the entries shown in Table 18.10 are passed.

Table 18.10

Disbursable Entries (British Airways 4.75% Convertible Bonds 15th November 2009)			
Debit		Credit	
Trading Book 'D' (Accepted)	7,000,000	7,000,000	Event Control Account
	7,000,000	7,000,000	

In order to update the quantity of shares resulting from the conversion, the entries in Table 18.11 are passed.

Table 18.11

Disbursable Entries (British Airways GBP1.00 Ordinary Shares)			
Debit		Credit	
Event Control Account	150,500	150,500	Trading Book 'D'
	150,500	150,500	

Location Entries

In order to remove the bonds in the process of conversion from the location, the entries shown in Table 18.12 are passed.

Table 18.12

Collectible Entries (British Airways 4.75% Convertible Bonds 15th November 2009)			
Debit		Credit	
Event Control Account	7,000,000	7,000,000	Custodian S, Main a/c Projected
	7,000,000	7,000,000	

Note that the above entries assume that no election decision entries were passed previously in order to segregate the custodian position.

Table 18.13 shows the entry to reflect the pending receipt of the shares at the custodian.

Table 18.13

Collectible Entries (British Airways GBP1.00 Ordinary Shares)			
Debit		Credit	
Custodian S, Main a/c Projected	150,500	150,500	Event Control Account
	150,500	150,500	

18.11.3 Over-Election Adjustment Entries

Further to the description of over-elections (see Section 18.9), over-election adjustment entries are only required to be passed by the STO to reflect the situation where the over-election results in either

- the election decision relating to the over-elected quantity being cancelled entirely, or
- an alternative option being assigned to the position holder.

These two alternatives are described below.

Cancellation of Over-Elected Quantity

Where a portion of an election decision quantity is cancelled due to *over-election*, the STO will reverse previously passed internal entries (against both position holders and location) relating to the cancelled quantity, together with the quantities of any *resultant entitlements* (if entries have been passed prior to that time).

For example, assume that the following entries have been passed for the *trading book*, and that no resultant entitlement entries have been passed at the time the Corporate Actions Department is informed that election decisions will be reduced as a result of over-elections.

After having passed election decision date entries, the STO's security position records appeared as shown in Table 18.14.

Table 18.14

British Airways 4.75% Convertible Bonds 15th November 2009			
Ownership		**Location**	
Trading Book 'D'	+5,000,000	−12,000,000	Custodian S, Main a/c
Trading Book 'D' (Accepted)	+7,000,000		
	+12,000,000	−12,000,000	

If 40% of the election decision quantity is to be cancelled, the STO will pass the reversal entry of the above election decision date entries (Table 18.15).

Table 18.15

Segregation Entries (British Airways 4.75% Convertible Bonds 15th November 2009)			
Debit		**Credit**	
Trading Book 'D' (Accepted)	2,800,000	2,800,000	Trading Book 'D'
	2,800,000	2,800,000	

The result, as reflected in the security position records, is shown in Table 18.16.

Table 18.16

British Airways 4.75% Convertible Bonds 15th November 2009			
Ownership		**Location**	
Trading Book 'D'	+7,800,000	−12,000,000	Custodian S, Main a/c
Trading Book 'D' (Accepted)	+4,200,000		
	+12,000,000	−12,000,000	

Assignment of Alternative Option

Where over-election of an option results in the position holder being assigned an alternative option, this will impact internal entries in respect of the resultant entitlement to be collected from the location and disbursed to the position holder.

Where such entries have already been passed in respect of the originally elected option at the time the STO is notified of over-election, the STO will reverse the entries already passed and replace them with entries that reflect the resultant entitlement in the alternative option.

Where such entries have not already been passed in respect of the originally elected option at the time the STO is notified of over-election, the STO will simply pass entries reflecting the resultant entitlement using the alternative option.

18.12 COLLECTION AND DISBURSEMENT OF RESULTANT ENTITLEMENTS

Once the STO is certain that its election decisions (on behalf of the position holders) have been accepted by the location(s), from that point forward the *collection* and *disbursement* of resultant entitlements falls within the same procedures as for mandatory events. Such procedures are detailed within Chapter 13, 'Collection/Disbursement of Resultant Entitlements'.

18.13 UPDATING OF INTERNAL ENTRIES

The settlement of a voluntary event is the same in all respects as the settlement of a mandatory event, as entries passed on record date against

- custodians, in the form of 'projected' entries, and
- counterparties, in the form of 'awaiting settlement' entries

will be updated with a further set of entries against the custodian, in the form of 'settled' entries (once the custodian has advised the STO of settlement). Such entries are detailed within Chapter 14, 'Updating of Internal Entries' and within Chapter 15, 'Examples of Mandatory Events'.

18.14 SUMMARY

In parallel with other events with elections, the management of voluntary events poses the Corporate Actions Department (and therefore the STO) many challenges.

The Corporate Actions Department must ensure that it has robust procedures in place in order to manage the voluntary aspect to these events which include:

- recording of election decisions not to participate in the event;
- monitoring of outstanding elections decisions; and
- establishment of policy for the treatment of outstanding elections decisions.

In addition, procedures must be in place to ensure the timely issuance of election decisions to locations in order to protect the interests of position holders. Unlike mandatory with options events, failure to issue elections in line with the position holders wishes and by the stated deadline may result in non-participation in the event, and substantial costs to the STO.

Part IV

Multi-Stage Events

19

Concepts of Multi-Stage Events

19.1 INTRODUCTION

To date, the lifecycles of both mandatory events (via the generic lifecycle) and events with elections have been described. In each case the event lifecycles have been viewed from the perspective of a self-contained event, i.e. an individual event falls within one or the other lifecycle.

However, some events consist of two or more such lifecycles within the overall life of the event, i.e. throughout the full life of the event both the mandatory lifecycle and the events with elections lifecycle will be applicable at different times. This occurs because the terms of the event contain both mandatory and elective conditions.

The term 'multi-stage' is being used to describe such events, with each stage effectively representing the lifecycles introduced previously. Typical examples of such events include:

- Rights Issues
- Entitlement Issues
- Priority Issues
- Final Subscription and Conversion
- Dividend Re-investment Plans where rights are issued initially as an interim security, to facilitate the option to elect cash or to elect new securities

The distinction of such events being multi-staged is very much an operational one. From the *issuer's* perspective these events remain a single event, representing a single aim, for example the raising of capital. The multi-stages essentially facilitate the overall aim of the issuer.

This chapter describes the generic principles applicable to a multi-stage event, identifying operational variations to the comparatively simple lifecycle of a mandatory event or an event with elections. These principles will be detailed as they specifically apply to the life of a *Rights Issue* in Chapter 20, 'Management of a Rights Issue' and in Chapter 21, 'Example of a Rights Issue'.

In addition to the multi-stage events listed above, from an operational perspective *takeovers* may also be considered to be multi-stage. Takeovers are separately detailed in later chapters as they contain additional unique features.

19.2 THE LIFE OF A MULTI-STAGE EVENT

The combination of stages and specific sequence of stages will depend upon the type of multi-stage event. In addition, where voluntary stages exist, the actions (i.e. *election decisions*) of the *position holder* will dictate which subsequent stages (if any) are applicable to its specific holding. For example, in the case of a rights issue, although the stages described in this section are potentially applicable to the overall event life, if a specific position holder subscribes to the new rights in respect of its entire holding, then there would be no remaining un-subscribed rights to expire.

With any event with elections, the position holders' election decisions are based upon the perceived profitability of the available event options; and specifically in the case of an event requiring the payment of cash to the issuer, such as a rights issue, the decision would include considering the perceived profitability of the option to subscribe versus the cost (and availability of funds) to do so.

The possible life of a multi-stage event, the stages and dependencies within, may be illustrated via the description of a *renounceable* rights issue.

19.2.1 The Life of a Rights Issue

A rights issue is the offer of new shares (in the form of *nil paid rights*) to existing shareholders in proportion to their existing holdings, at a specified price; *subscription* by *position holders* must be made by a specified date. Once the offer is received, the shareholder may sell its nil paid rights in the market, or purchase more. Prior to the expiry of the offer, any holder of nil paid rights may convert them to the specified security, as detailed in the rights issue prospectus, upon payment of the specified price; this is known as 'exercise' or 'subscription'. Failure to subscribe the nil paid rights prior to the end of their life will result in their expiry.

A rights issue consists of four sequential, but potentially overlapping, stages, with each having dependencies upon the former:

1. distribution of nil paid rights
2. trading of nil paid rights
3. subscription of nil paid rights
4. expiry of un-subscribed nil paid rights

These stages are illustrated in the example timeline shown in Figure 19.1.

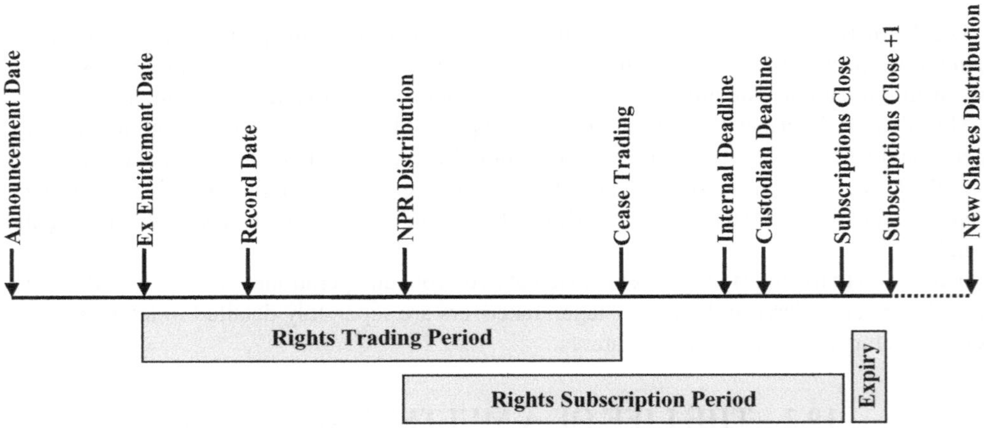

Figure 19.1 Example of rights issue stages.

Distribution of Nil Paid Rights

The initial distribution of nil paid rights to *position holders* is a mandatory benefit. Position holders in the *underlying security* of the event will be entitled to receive the free distribution of nil paid rights (i.e. securities where as yet no capital has been paid). The nil paid right can be considered an interim (or temporary) security, as it has a finite life.

The quantity of nil paid rights received by the position holder represents the quantity of new securities that the *issuer* is offering the position holder (i.e. that the position holder may subsequently purchase from the issuer).

All position holders registered on the *record date* of the event will receive this distribution based upon the stated *ratio* relative to their underlying holding (e.g. one nil paid right for every four shares currently held).

As with any other *benefit* distribution, the STO's *books & records* will be updated to reflect the nil paid rights *collected* and *disbursed* (refer to Chapter 12, 'Passing of Internal Entries', and Chapter 14, 'Updating of Internal Entries').

Despite being *nil paid*, in the case of a rights issue the nil paid right is a listed security in its own right, and as such may be traded. Once nil paid rights are distributed, the position holder may

- sell any or all of its nil paid rights entitlement;
- subscribe (i.e. convert) any or all of its nil paid rights entitlement; or
- expire (i.e. not subscribe) any or all of its nil paid rights entitlement.

All of these actions are dependent upon the position holder having received a nil paid rights entitlement in the first instance.

Trading of Nil Paid Rights

The trading of nil paid rights will typically commence upon *entitlement date* (or a specifically announced *commence trading date*), and continue until the *cease trading date* normally set by the local market. During the trading period a number of trading scenarios can occur:

- Existing nil paid right holders may sell their nil paid rights (either all or in part) thereby decreasing the holding originally received.
- Existing nil paid right holders may purchase additional nil paid rights thereby increasing the holding originally received.
- New investors may purchase and sell nil paid rights thereby creating new holdings of nil paid rights. Such investors would have no entitled holding in the original *underlying security*, and therefore would not have received a distribution of the nil paid rights on the *record date* of the event.

In the majority of cases the Corporate Actions Department will not become actively involved in the actual trading and subsequent settlement of the nil paid rights. Nonetheless, it is vital that its records are updated to reflect any changes that occur in any nil paid rights positions (including the creation of new positions), as a result of this activity.

The subscription or expiry of any nil paid rights is dependent upon the accumulated positions reflecting any initial distribution of nil paid rights, together with any trading.

Subscription of Nil Paid Rights

The subscription of nil paid rights is a voluntary stage that provides the position holder with the option to convert any or all of its nil paid rights position into new securities, upon payment of the subscription price.

This stage is based upon positions in the nil paid rights (not the original *underlying security* of the event), with the total quantity of nil paid rights that a position holder may subscribe reflecting either its original mandatory distribution, or the result of nil paid rights trading, or both.

As can be seen from the timeline in Figure 19.1, the *election period* (in this case referred to as the *rights subscription period*) commences at the nil paid rights distribution date and continues until the *issuer's deadline date* (in this case referred to as the *subscriptions close date*). During this period, additional deadlines will apply as is the case with all lifecycles for events with elections (refer to Chapter 17, 'Management of Mandatory with Options Events').

The timeline shows that the subscription period runs concurrently with, and beyond, the rights trading period. For the Corporate Actions Department this is an important concern, as it will be receiving *election decisions* from position holders (to subscribe) and issuing *election decisions* to the location(s), while the positions in the nil paid rights may be changing as a result of trading and settlement.

As stated previously, it is vital that the Corporate Actions Department receives constant updates of the changes to positions in the nil paid rights throughout this period, in order to manage the subscription stage of the event accurately.

Expiry of Un-Subscribed Nil Paid Rights

The expiry of un-subscribed nil paid rights is a mandatory event. The effect of the event is to remove all positions in the nil paid rights security that have not been subscribed to, whether that position arose as a result of the original nil paid rights distribution, or as a result of trading, or both.

This action is typically applied to all remaining un-subscribed positions immediately following the subscriptions close date.

19.2.2 Comparison of Multi-stage Events

The previous section has described the concepts relating to the stages that apply to the overall life of a rights issue. As stated a number of other events may also be considered as multi-stage events. This is most common with respect to those events that involve the voluntary subscription or conversion to a new security in exchange for an existing or *interim security*. The additional stages to the voluntary stages occur as a result of

- any initial issue of an interim security prior to the *subscription period*, and
- the *expiry* of any *un-subscribed* securities after the subscription period.

The combination of stages applicable to a selection of events (defined in Chapter 2, 'Event Description and Classification') is summarized in Table 19.1.

Table 19.1

Event Type	Stage			
	Issue of Interim Security	Trading of Interim Security	Subscription or Conversion of Interim or Underlying Security	Expiry of Interim or Underlying Security
	Mandatory		Voluntary	Mandatory
Rights Issue	Yes	Yes	Yes	Yes
Entitlement Issue	Yes	No	Yes	Yes
Priority Issue	No	No	Yes	Yes
Bond and Note Final Conversion	No	N/A	Yes	Yes

In the case of some conversion events applicable to (for example) *convertible bonds* and notes, the terms of issue of the security may permit the position holder to convert the security on multiple occasions throughout the life of the bond or note. At the end of the life of the security a final *conversion period* will be available. It is only at this time that any unconverted securities will be expired. Non-conversion throughout the life of the security up until the final conversion period will not result in expiry, and is therefore not considered a multi-stage event.

19.3 THE STO'S RISK

Throughout the descriptions of mandatory event processing and events with elections processing, many areas of potential risk to the STO have been highlighted, including:

- accuracy of *event terms*
- determination of *entitled positions* and *location* components
- communication of event terms
- calculation of *resultant entitlement*
- management of *election decisions*

All of these areas pose a risk to the STO in relation to a multi-stage event, if not managed in an accurate and timely manner.

In addition to the risks identified previously, a multi-stage event introduces additional dependencies in the processing lifecycle, which normally do not exist when only a single lifecycle applies. Where the multi-stage event consists of both a mandatory lifecycle and an events with elections lifecycle, the STO must be aware of any implications that one lifecycle may have on the other. In some cases, the stages may be managed concurrently, while in others the processing of one stage may require completion prior to the commencement of the next stage. This concept will be expanded in the following section, using a rights issue to illustrate the dependencies between stages.

19.4 IMPACT OF MULTI-STAGE EVENTS

Chapter 1, 'Basic Corporate Action Concepts', describes the generic impact of events from the perspectives of the *issuer*, the *position holder*, and the market as reflected in changes to the price of the *underlying security* to the event, while Chapter 16, 'Concepts of Events with Elections', describes that impact applicable to events with elections.

Multi-stage events reflect a combination of these impacts, usually according to the combination of stages applicable to the event, and to the stage that the event has reached in its overall life.

Predictability of any impact is no longer simply based upon whether the event is mandatory or elective in nature. Some mandatory stages can be considered to have predictable impact, whilst other mandatory stages that are dependent upon the outcome of a voluntary stage will be less predictable. As always, any voluntary stage will have a less predictable impact, as a result of the *election decisions* made by position holders.

19.4.1 Impact from the Issuer's Perspective

From the *issuer's* perspective, as with all other events the impact of any multi-stage event is identified in the changes to the issuer's *balance sheet*, i.e. its *issued capital*, debts and cash reserves.

In the case of a multi-stage event, the predictability of the overall event varies, and is highly dependent upon the nature of each stage.

Where a mandatory stage results in the distribution of new securities and/or cash to position holders, the issuer may be able to predict accurately the impact of such a distribution on its balance sheet. In some cases, such a distribution may be in an interim (or temporary) security in order to facilitate later stages, as is the case of nil paid rights. Typically, an *interim security* will have no capital value, and as such will not have any financial impact on the issuer's balance sheet.

Other mandatory stages of a multi-stage event may be less predictable for the issuer due to their dependency upon the outcome of earlier voluntary stages. This is the case where *expiry* of existing securities forms part of the overall life of the event. Typically, such an expiry would occur at the end of the event, and usually as a result of *election decisions* taken by the *position holder*. This is the case, for example, in a rights issue, where any nil paid rights that are not subscribed to at the close of the event will be expired. Accordingly, the predictability of this stage will be dependent upon the results of election decisions received from position holders.

With respect to voluntary stages, the issuer is unable to identify accurately the final impact, if any, until after the close of the event when all position holders' election decisions are applied to the balance sheet.

From the issuer's perspective, any lack of predictability with respect to multi-stage events has the same negative connotations as voluntary events.

19.4.2 Impact from the Position Holder's Perspective

As with any other event, the impact of any multi-stage event to a *position holder* is measured in terms of its impact on their securities and/or cash positions.

Unlike previously described events where the position holders' positions are typically impacted at a single point during the event, in the case of a multi-stage event, the position holders' positions may be updated with securities and/or cash on multiple occasions throughout the event, and may include:

- receipt of interim (temporary) securities;
- payment of cash to the *issuer*;
- receipt of new securities and/or cash; and
- *expiry* of securities (including interim securities).

Some of these changes may be on a mandatory basis, while others may be as a result of election decisions, and therefore based upon the investment decision of the position holder. The specific impact that could occur to position holders' securities and/or cash positions is described through this and the following chapter.

19.4.3 Impact on the Price of the Underlying Security

In parallel with the impact to the issuer and the position holder, the impact of a multi-stage event on the price of the *underlying security* is essentially the same as that generically described in Chapter 1, but remains less predictable and typically more complex as a result of the inclusion of voluntary stages within the overall life of the event.

19.5 LIFECYCLE ELEMENTS OF THE MULTI-STAGE EVENT

To date the lifecycle elements (from the perspective of the Corporate Actions Department) as they apply to generic (mandatory) events and to events with elections have been described.

All of these elements are similarly applicable to multi-stage events, with the main differences being that, as shown in Figure 19.2, a lifecycle element may occur

- only once during the overall life of the event, for example event terms capture and cleansing;
- only once as applicable to a specific stage of the event, for example receipt and issue of *election decisions*;
- at every stage throughout the life of the event, for example calculation of *resultant entitlements*.

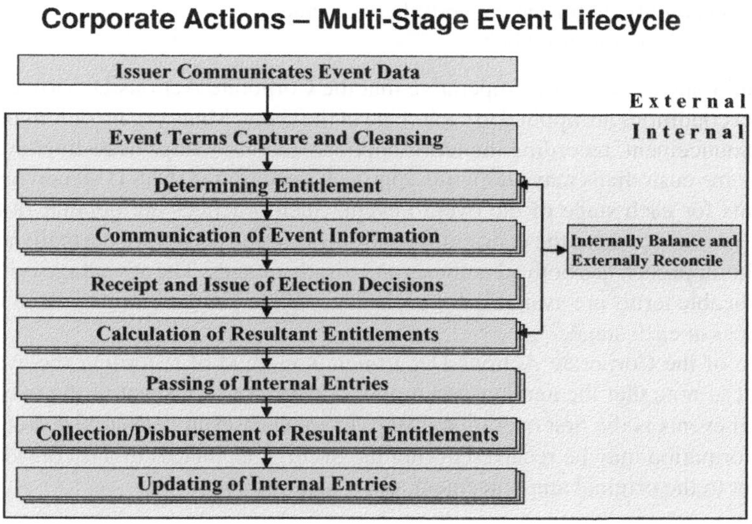

Figure 19.2 Multi-stage event lifecycle.

In addition, as previously stated in this chapter, dependencies will exist in the processing of lifecycle elements within the overall life of the event, according to the applicable stages.

The management of multi-stage events by the Corporate Actions Department must take account of

- the applicability of an element to each stage, and
- any dependencies that exist for an element to other stages within the overall life of the event.

These are now described below.

19.5.1 Multi-Stage Event Terms

As previously stated, from the *issuer's* perspective a multi-stage event is a single event, despite containing multiple stages. Accordingly, a single event announcement will be made by the issuer containing all of the information appropriate to each stage of the event, therefore including both mandatory and elective conditions. The specific conditions will reflect the combination and types of stages applicable to the event.

For example, a rights issue announcement will typically contain

- the terms of issue of the nil paid rights;
- the trading conditions for the nil paid rights;
- the *subscription* conditions for the nil paid rights;
- terms of *expiry* of *un-subscribed* nil paid rights.

The detailed breakdown of specific terms applicable to a rights issue are contained in the following chapter.

By contrast, the announcement of the final *conversion* of a *convertible bond* will typically contain

- the conversion conditions for the convertible bond, and
- terms of expiry of un-converted bonds.

With all multi-stage events it is imperative that the Corporate Actions Department ensures that the correct conditions are applied to each stage of the event. Many organizations decompose the single announcement, recording the terms applicable to each stage as distinct event terms; for example some custodians may adopt this approach, resulting in the STO receiving separate announcements for each stage of the overall event. Such practices are popular in the US in respect of rights issues, where the distribution and subscription stages are normally announced separately. This approach has both advantages and disadvantages. The advantage is in ensuring that only applicable terms are available for each stage, while the disadvantage is in the risk of dependency loss at each stage.

Irrespective of the Corporate Actions Department's method of recording the event terms, it is important to note that the announcement will occur once in respect of the overall event, and as with all events is the first operational step. In some cases updates to the event terms or additional information may be received during the event, nonetheless this is considered to be an amendment to the original announcement, not a separate event.

19.5.2 Determining Entitlement at Each Stage

Unlike mandatory events and events with elections, where entitlement is based upon a single security at a single date and based upon single conditions, multi-stage events may require entitlement to be based upon holdings in different securities at different stages of the event, and at different times in the overall event life.

The two-way interaction between the STO's securities position records and the Corporate Action Department's entitled position records throughout the life of the event is critical. It is important to note that the positions updated by the Corporate Actions Department in the initial stages of the event may well become integral to the positions extracted in later stages of the event. This dependency is illustrated as applicable to a rights issue in the following chapter.

It is imperative that the procedures practised by the Corporate Actions Department ensure that the determination of entitlements, where dependent upon earlier stages, is only performed once all securities positions are updated from those stages. In this way the timing of determining entitlement will differ to that of mandatory events and events with elections. In those cases the

Corporate Actions Department may commence determining entitlement at any time subsequent to the capture and cleansing of event terms.

In summary, the determination of entitlement for a multi-stage event will need to accommodate the

- determination of *entitlement* at each stage of the overall event;
- application of different entitlement conditions (e.g. *underlying security*, ex entitlement periods) for each stage;
- dependency on position updates performed in preceding stages.

This should be done within the principles described in Chapter 9, 'Determining Entitlement'.

19.5.3 Communication of Event Information

In Chapter 10, 'Communication of Event Information', a generic set of communications was introduced that would typically be issued in the majority of events:

- Event Terms Announcement
- Preliminary Entitlement Notice
- Final Entitlement Notice
- Preliminary Claim Notice
- Final Claim Notice

In addition to the generic communications referred to above, any stage with elections may include the following additional types of communication to position holders (as described in Chapter 17, 'Management of Mandatory with Options Events'):

- Request for Election Decision – Reminders
- Confirmation of Election Decision
- Over-Election Notices

A multi-stage event will incorporate all of these types of communications as relevant to the overall event, and any stages applicable to the event, with the content of the communication reflecting the stages of the event (where appropriate) and any additional event terms. According to the purpose of each type of communication some may be issued

- as a single communication, combining information applicable to two or more stages of the event, for example Event Terms Announcement;
- during a single stage of the event, containing information applicable only to that stage, for example Request for Election Decision – Reminders;
- repetitively at each stage of the event containing appropriate information for that stage only, for example Final Entitlement Notice.

For example, where a multi-stage event contains the following three stages:

1. issue of *interim security*
2. *subscription* of interim security, and
3. *expiry* of interim security

then the following communications (at minimum) may be expected throughout the life of the event:

1. Event Terms Announcement, communicating the conditions applicable to all three stages of the event;
2. Preliminary Entitlement Notice, communicating the projected *resultant entitlement* as a result of the issue of the interim security;
3. Final Entitlement Notice, communicating the *record date* position of the underlying security and the final resultant entitlement in the interim security;
4. Confirmation of Election Decision, confirming the position holder's *election decision* as received in respect of the subscription of interim security stage;
5. Final Entitlement Notice, communicating the resultant entitlement as a result of election decisions received from the position holder to subscribe during the subscription of interim security stage;
6. Final Entitlement Notice, communicating the expiry of any un-subscribed interim securities. Note that this final communication could be combined with the previous, to include both resultant entitlement from subscription and expiry.

It is not sufficient for the Corporate Actions Department simply to issue a set of communications for each stage of the event, based upon whether the stage is mandatory or voluntary. At all times the process should be sensitive of the event having one set of event terms, while incorporating multiple calculations for entitlement and resultant entitlement.

In summary, the communication of event terms for a multi-stage event should accommodate

- a single communication of event terms, encompassing all stages;
- the communication of entitled positions and resultant entitlements at each stage; and
- the issue of reminders to position holders, where required for voluntary stages.

19.5.4 Receipt and Issue of Election Decisions

The receipt and issue of election decisions will apply to any voluntary stage within a multi-stage event. The management of elections decisions falls within the same procedures as detailed within Chapter 17, 'Management of Mandatory with Options Events'.

19.5.5 Calculation of Resultant Entitlements

Similar to the determination of entitlement, the calculation of *resultant entitlements* will apply at each stage of a multi-stage event. At each stage the calculation of resultant entitlement will apply the calculation conditions of that stage as contained within the *event terms* to the entitled positions and location (including *unsettled trades*).

At each stage any of the following calculation components could differ:

- the *underlying security*
- the quantities of entitled holding position and *location* components
- securities *ratios* and cash *rates*.

In addition, where a stage is voluntary, the calculation of resultant entitlements will also depend upon the election decisions received and issued.

For example, where a multi-stage event contains the following three stages:

1. issue of interim security
2. subscription of interim security, and
3. expiry of interim security

the following calculations may occur at each stage:

1. resultant entitlement in interim security, based upon a security ratio (inclusive of treatment of *fractions*) as applied to the underlying security of the event;
2. resultant entitlement in new securities and calculation of cash payment to the *issuer*, as a result of election decisions (subscriptions) received in respect of entitled holdings in the interim security;
3. quantity of interim securities to be removed (expired) from positions as a result of non-subscription.

Therefore, unlike mandatory events and events with elections, multiple calculations for resultant entitlements are necessary at the appropriate milestones throughout the event. The Corporate Actions Department must have sufficient controls in place to ensure that the calculation of resultant entitlements has been performed (and appropriate securities positions updated) prior to the processing of subsequent stages of the event.

19.5.6 Passing of Internal Entries

Internal entries will be passed at each and every stage of a multi-stage event in order to reflect

- any change to the underlying securities position in that stage, and
- the distribution of any securities and/or cash that is expected to occur on the *distribution date* or *effective date* of that stage.

These entries will adopt the principles for both mandatory and voluntary events as outlined in earlier chapters.

For example, where a multi-stage event contains the following three stages:

1. issue of interim security
2. subscription of interim security, and
3. expiry of interim security

the following internal entries may occur at each stage, reflecting

1. the resultant entitlement in the interim security, based upon those applicable to a mandatory benefit event, and including accrual entries and entries reflecting the distribution of the interim security due on the distribution date;
2. the subscription to new securities, based upon those applicable to a voluntary event, and including the distribution of the newly subscribed securities on the distribution date, any cash payment to the issuer, and the removal of the interim securities which were subscribed;
3. the removal of any remaining un-subscribed interim securities.

In addition, internal entries may also need to be passed in respect of over-election adjustment entries.

As always, timely and accurate passing of internal entries is vital, and in a multi-stage event the Corporate Actions Department is highly dependent upon accurate position data in order to process each stage of the event accurately.

19.5.7 Collection/Disbursement of Resultant Entitlements

The collection and disbursement of resultant entitlements will again apply to each stage of the event. Within a multi-stage event, the STO can expect to collect and disburse

- interim securities as with a mandatory benefit;
- cash in respect of subscription monies; and
- new securities in exchange for old or interim securities, as with a mandatory re-organization event.

The procedures for the collection and disbursement of resultant entitlements throughout a multi-stage event fall within the same procedures as for mandatory events. Such procedures are detailed in Chapter 13, 'Collection/Disbursement of Resultant Entitlements'.

19.5.8 Updating of Internal Entries

The settlement of *resultant entitlements* throughout each stage of a multi-stage event is the same in all respects as the settlement of a mandatory event, as entries that are passed on *record date* against

- *custodians*, in the form of 'projected' entries, and
- *counterparties*, in the form of 'awaiting settlement' entries

will be updated with a further set of entries against the custodian, in the form of 'settled' entries (once the custodian has advised the STO of settlement). Such entries are detailed in Chapter 14, 'Updating of Internal Entries' and Chapter 15, 'Examples of Mandatory Events'.

19.6 SUMMARY

The management of multi-stage events, for the Corporate Actions Department (and therefore the STO), can be a highly risky exercise, not least due to the dependencies that exist between stages, as introduced in this chapter.

As with other events, it is of critical importance that the event terms captured are applied accurately, but in addition with a multi-stage event, the Corporate Actions Department must correctly identify each stage and its implications within the overall event lifecycle.

20
Management of a Rights Issue

20.1 INTRODUCTION

The stages within a rights issue have been introduced in the previous chapter as representative of the possible combination of stages and life of a multi-stage event. In addition, Chapter 19 describes the impact of multiple stages on the more generic operational components of an event lifecycle (as they apply to mandatory events and events with elections).

The purpose of this chapter is to apply in detail those principles to the management of a rights issue (one of the most common of such events), which consists of the following sequential, but potentially overlapping stages:

1. distribution of nil paid rights
2. trading of nil paid rights
3. subscription of nil paid rights
4. expiry of un-subscribed nil paid rights

These stages are illustrated in the timeline shown in Figure 20.1 (which was also included in the previous chapter).

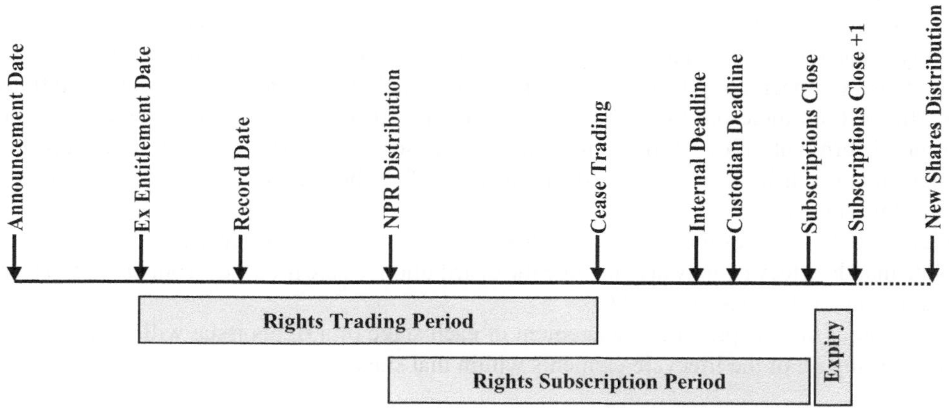

Figure 20.1 Example of rights issue stages.

Note that a detailed and chronological example of a rights issue follows in Chapter 21.

20.2 THE OPERATIONAL LIFE OF A RIGHTS ISSUE

As described in the previous chapter, not all lifecycle elements will apply at every stage of a multi-stage event. With respect to a rights issue, the lifecycle elements applicable to each stage will include:

- Announcement Date
  - capture and cleansing of *event terms*
- Nil Paid Rights Distribution
  - determine entitled holdings in the event *underlying security*
  - communicate event terms to entitled *position holders*
  - calculate *resultant entitlements* in nil paid rights
  - communicate resultant entitlements in nil paid rights (including *claim* notices)
  - update securities position records with nil paid rights
  - *collection* and *disbursement* of nil paid rights
- Nil Paid Rights Subscription
  - determine entitled holdings in nil paid rights
  - receive and issue *election decisions*
  - calculate resultant entitlements in the new security(s) and *subscription* cash
  - communicate resultant entitlements in the new security(s) (including claim notices)
  - update securities position records with new security(s) and reduce positions of nil paid rights to reflect subscriptions
  - update cash position records with subscription monies
  - collection and disbursement of new securities
- Un-Subscribed Nil Paid Rights Expiry
  - determine remaining positions in nil paid rights
  - calculate quantities of nil paid rights to be reduced
  - update securities position records to zeroize remaining nil paid rights positions

Note that although the trading of nil paid rights is illustrated as an additional stage in the previous timeline, in the majority of cases the Corporate Actions Department will not become actively involved in the actual trading and subsequent settlement of the nil paid rights. This stage does not specifically result in any operational activities within the Corporate Actions Department (and therefore this topic is not detailed in this chapter). Nonetheless, it is vital that any determination of entitlement during the subscription period accurately reflects any changes that occur in nil paid rights positions (including the creation of new positions), as a result of trading and settlement.

Figure 20.2 illustrates the possible result(s) at each stage of the lifecycle.

Note that the lifecycle may also include the distribution of sale proceeds from *un-subscribed* nil paid rights; refer to Section 20.6.4.

Throughout this chapter the management of each stage of a rights issue will be described, encompassing all of the lifecycle elements within that stage.

20.3 RIGHTS ISSUE EVENT TERMS

The announcement (by the issuer) of the event terms of a rights issue will be a single announcement, containing all of the terms and conditions applicable to each stage of the event. As such this milestone will occur at the beginning of the overall life of the event (and not at each stage). The Corporate Actions Department will expect to capture and cleanse the event terms in accordance with the principles described in Chapter 8, 'Event Terms Capture and Cleansing'.

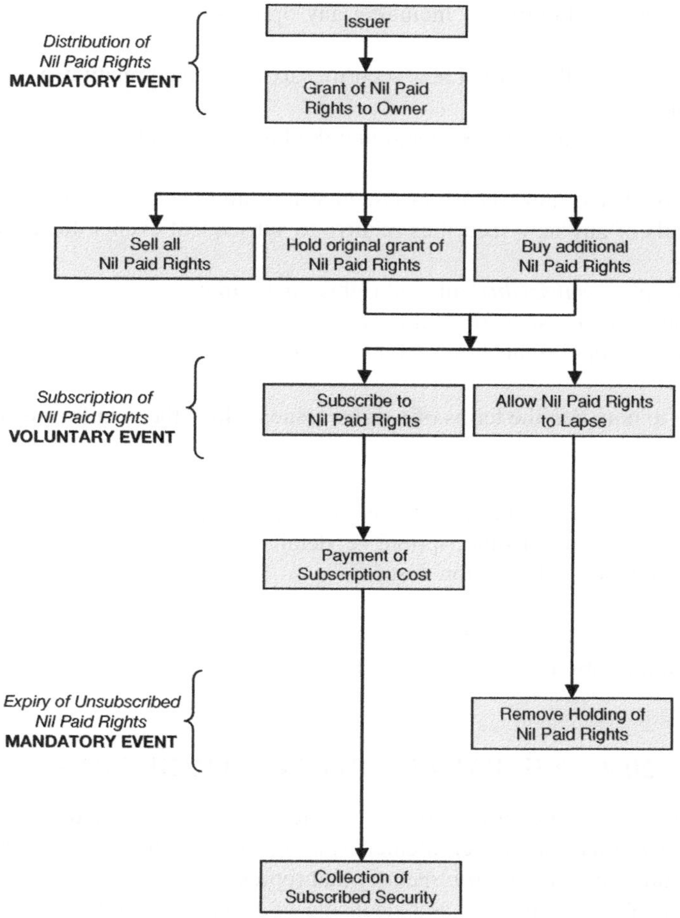

Figure 20.2 Rights issue; operational lifecycle.

A rights issue announcement will typically contain:

- The *underlying security* to which the overall event applies
- The terms of issue of the nil paid rights, including:
  - the *entitlement date*, *record date* and *distribution date*
  - the issue *ratio* of nil paid rights relative to the quantity of the entitled holding in the underlying security
- The trading conditions for the nil paid rights, including:
  - the *commence trading date* (also known as the listing date)
  - the *cease trading date* (last date of trading)
- The *subscription* conditions for the nil paid rights, including:
  - details of the new security(s) to be issued as a result of subscription
  - restrictions on position holders resident in specified countries

  - subscription price and currency, including any options for the payment of subscription cost
  - subscription ratio, i.e. the ratio of new securities to be received relative to each subscribed nil paid right
  - the subscription (election) period, including the last date to subscribe known as the *subscriptions close date*
  - the distribution date of new securities issued as a result of subscription
  - *ranking* details of any new securities relative to subsequent events, for example income distributions
- Terms of expiry of *un-subscribed* nil paid rights, including:
  - the date upon which un-subscribed nil paid rights will expire
  - sale of expired nil paid rights terms (if applicable)

It is important to note that the terms of a rights issue include the details of resultant entitlements in both

- nil paid rights, i.e. details of the security and the security ratio, and the
- new security(s) as a result of subscription, i.e. details of those securities and the applicable security ratios and their subscription cost.

The variations and application of the above event terms to their applicable stage will be expanded upon in the subsequent sections of this chapter.

20.4 NIL PAID RIGHTS DISTRIBUTION

This is a mandatory stage, the purpose of which is to distribute to entitled *position holders* of the event's *underlying security*, the entitlement (the right) to purchase new securities from the *issuer*. The nil paid right is an *interim security* that represents this entitlement.

This stage will follow the capture and cleansing of event terms and include the following generic lifecycle elements:

- determine entitled holdings
- communication of full event information
- calculation of *resultant entitlements*
- passing of internal entries
- *collection* and *disbursement* of resultant entitlements
- updating of internal entries

These elements are described below.

20.4.1 Determination of Entitled Holdings

Entitlement to the distribution of nil paid rights is based upon the holder's positions in the original underlying security of the event, using the generic entitlement rules described in Chapter 9, 'Determining Entitlement'.

The Corporate Actions Department will perform this step using the

- underlying security,
- *entitlement date*, and
- *record date*

as stated in the event terms.

As with all other events, and as detailed in Chapter 9, this step will include:

- the extraction of entitled positions and location components (including unsettled trades) from the STO's securities position records;
- the balancing of entitled positions and *location* components;
- the reconciliation of entitled positions and location components.

The rules pertaining to entitlement to this stage of the event are consistent with those applicable to the majority of *benefit* events, with both an entitlement date and record date applying to the event. Therefore this stage includes an ex entitlement period, and as such, care must be taken to account for both *special trading* and settlement between the entitlement date and record date.

20.4.2 Communication of Event Information

The first stage of the rights issue (the distribution of nil paid rights) will see the issue of the full generic set of communications as described in Chapter 10, 'Communication of Event Information', these being:

- Event Terms Announcement
- Preliminary Entitlement Notice
- Final Entitlement Notice
- Preliminary Claim Notice
- Final Claim Notice

The Event Terms Announcement will include details of all stages of the rights issue event, including trading conditions of the nil paid rights, while entitlement and claim notices (both preliminary and final) will contain information specific to the distribution of nil paid rights only.

20.4.3 Calculation of Resultant Entitlements

This calculation will not differ from the calculation of the majority of securities entitlements for mandatory events. The result will be to calculate the quantity of nil paid rights to be *collected* (from *locations*) and *disbursed* (to *position holders*).

In parallel with mandatory events, once the entitled positions (including *unsettled trades*) in the underlying security to the event are finalized, balanced and reconciled at the close of the *record date* for the distribution of nil paid rights, the calculation of resultant entitlements in the nil paid rights may be performed.

The Corporate Actions Department will perform this step using the securities *ratio*, together with the conditions dictating the treatment of *fractions* and calculation sequence as described in Chapter 11, 'Calculation of Resultant Entitlement'. These conditions will be applied to the quantity of any entitled positions (including unsettled trades) in the *underlying security*.

20.4.4 Passing of Internal Entries

Internal entries reflecting the distribution of nil paid rights are the same as those in respect of any mandatory benefit event. Accordingly, the Corporate Actions Department will pass entries that reflect the distribution of the nil paid rights that is expected to occur on the distribution date. These are

- *entitlement date* entries, and
- *record date* entries.

Both of these are explained in Chapter 12, 'Passing of Internal Entries'.

20.4.5 Collection and Disbursement of Resultant Entitlements

The nil paid rights security exists as

- an *interim security* representing the position holders right to *subscribe* to new securities from the *issuer*, and
- a tradeable security in its own right.

As with all other securities distributed as a result of a corporate action, the *resultant entitlements* will be collected from the *location* and *disbursed* to the *position holders*, representing the settlement of those resultant entitlements. The existence of the nil paid rights as an interim security does not negate this step. The event terms will include the distribution date of the resultant nil paid rights.

As with any other corporate actions resultant entitlement, the settlement of the nil paid rights entitlement may take a number of forms, according to the prevailing methods within the individual market, and whether the resultant entitlement is to be collected or disbursed.

Collectible Resultant Entitlements

The Corporate Actions Department will expect to settle all resultant entitlements for nil paid rights that are to be collected as a result of this stage.

Collection of nil paid rights may be effected electronically or physically. Where electronic, the collection of the nil paid rights entitlement will mirror that of any other security resultant entitlement. Where physical, this would typically be where settlement of the resultant entitlement is collected directly from the issuer (as a result of a registered physical underlying holding). The physical entitlement is supported by an Entitlement and Acceptance form, which details the *record date* position of the registered holder, and its resultant entitlement in nil paid rights. This form facilitates the transfer of nil paid rights between parties (in principle similar to a share certificate), as well as any subsequent subscription of these rights to new shares.

Disbursable Resultant Entitlements

Whether the resultant entitlement of nil paid rights is to be settled will largely depend upon to whom it is owed, i.e.:

- *trading book*
- *custody client*
- claiming *counterparty*

As with all other resultant security entitlements, typically trading book positions are updated via book entry only (within the STO's *books & records*).

In the case of custody clients, it is unlikely that the nil paid rights entitlement of these position holders will require to be transferred from the STO to a third party; this is because the subsequent management of the nil paid rights position, including any trading, subscription and expiry is likely to remain with the STO. Nonetheless it is important to be aware that in some exceptional cases a custody client may utilize the services of more than one STO. In this case, it may instruct the Corporate Actions Department to transfer its nil paid rights entitlement to another STO. This transfer may be electronic (via the issuance of settlement instructions) or physical (via paper transfers). Once such a transfer has been effected any further management of this entitlement (including trading and settlement, subscription and expiry) is the responsibility of the receiving party.

Where the resultant entitlement of nil paid rights is owed to a claiming counterparty, transfer may be electronic or physical. Ideally, the settlement of any *claims* is recommended as early as possible once resultant entitlements are collected. Once the nil paid rights entitlement is transferred to the claiming counterparty, any subsequent management of trading and settlement, subscriptions and expiry will become its responsibility, and not that of the STO.

In the case of nil paid rights, it is highly unlikely that any securities borrowing market exists, unlike other securities. For this reason where transfer to another party of nil paid rights is required (as described above), this may only take place on an *actual settlement* (rather than on a *contractual settlement*) basis.

20.4.6 Updating of Internal Entries

The settlement of resultant entitlements in nil paid rights will be as per a mandatory benefit event. Security positions will be updated with a further set of entries against the custodian, in the form of 'settled' entries (once the custodian has advised the STO of settlement). Such entries are detailed within Chapter 14, 'Updating of Internal Entries' and Chapter 15, 'Examples of Mandatory Events'.

20.5 NIL PAID RIGHTS SUBSCRIPTION

This is a voluntary stage, the purpose of which is to manage the process of subscribing (following the position holder's positive election decision) and the subsequent distribution of the new securities.

This stage commences at the nil paid rights distribution date continuing until the *subscription close date*, and includes the following elective lifecycle elements:

- determine entitled holdings
- communication of event information
- receive and issue election decisions
- calculate resultant entitlements
- passing of internal entries
- collection and disbursement of resultant entitlements
- updating of internal entries

These elements are described below.

As illustrated in the timeline diagram shown in Figure 20.1, this stage will occur concurrently with the nil paid rights trading period. At all times throughout this stage, when performing the above steps, it is imperative that the Corporate Actions Department takes account of the impact of any trading and settlement in the nil paid rights. Throughout this section, reference will be made to where this impact occurs.

20.5.1 Determine Entitled Holdings

Entitlement to subscribe to nil paid rights is based upon the holder's position in the nil paid rights, reflecting any original entitlement distribution, together with trading (and settlement) of nil paid rights, as at the *subscriptions close date* of the event.

The Corporate Actions Department will perform this step using the

- nil paid rights security, and
- subscriptions close date

as stated in the *event terms*.

During the voluntary stage of the rights issue, the subscriptions close date of the event effectively becomes the *record date* for the purposes of identification of entitled positions and location (including *unsettled trades*). The Corporate Actions Department will identify all ownership positions and location up to and including the subscriptions close date.

As with all other events, this step will include:

- the extraction of entitled positions and location components (including unsettled trades) from the STO's securities position records;
- the balancing of entitled positions and location components;
- the reconciliation of entitled positions and location components.

This process is as detailed in Chapter 9, 'Determining Entitlement'.

This step will typically commence immediately following the passing of internal entries to reflect resultant entitlements in nil paid rights (approximately record date +1), and will utilize the principles of projected positions as described in Chapter 9, taking account of subsequent trading and settlement activity in the nil paid rights up until the subscriptions close date.

As a result of trading in nil paid rights, the following may occur:

- Existing nil paid rights holders may sell their nil paid rights (either all or in part) thereby decreasing the holding originally received.
- Existing nil paid rights holders may purchase additional nil paid rights thereby increasing the holding originally received.
- New investors may purchase and sell nil paid rights thereby creating new holdings of nil paid rights. Such investors would have no entitled holding in the original *underlying security*, and therefore would not have received a distribution of the nil paid rights on the record date of the event.

As such, it is possible that the positions originally created by the distribution of nil paid rights, will not bear a great deal of similarity to those subsequently extracted from the STO's securities position records for the purposes of subscription processing.

Note that in some cases the subscription of nil paid rights may be restricted to position holders according to their residency as described in Chapter 18, ('Management of Voluntary Events'). In this case foreign position holders will still be entitled to receive the nil paid rights distributions, but will only be able to trade or expire the nil paid rights. Their position would be included in the extraction of nil paid rights security positions, but the action to subscribe will not be available to them.

20.5.2 Communication of Event Information

This stage of the rights issue (the subscription stage) involves the issue of communications similar to those described within Chapter 17, ('Management of Mandatory with Options Events'), these being:

- Preliminary Entitlement Notice
- Final Entitlement Notice
- Preliminary Claim Notice
- Final Claim Notice
- Request for Election Decision – Reminders
- Confirmation of Election Decision

Unlike other events with elections, it is unlikely that over-election of specific options will occur in a rights issue, and therefore this communication type is not included in the above list.

The above communications will contain information specific to the subscription of nil paid rights only. For example, the Final Entitlement Notice will contain the details of the final *resultant entitlement* to new securities as a result of *subscription*.

The above list does not include the Event Terms Announcement communications that have featured against both mandatory events and events with elections. This is because this communication is issued to position holders in the *underlying security* at the commencement of the event (during the distribution of nil paid rights stage).

It may be necessary nonetheless to communicate subscription terms to those holders of nil paid rights who acquired their position via trading, and not the previous distribution stage, as they will not have received the full event terms announcement. In this case the Corporate Actions Department may issue an abridged version of the Event Terms Announcement, or utilize the Request for Election Decision – Reminder.

20.5.3 Receive and Issue Election Decisions

During this voluntary stage of the rights issue, the management of election decisions falls within the same procedures as for all voluntary events. Such procedures are detailed within Chapter 17, 'Management of Mandatory with Options Events'.

The procedures will include the requirement for the Corporate Actions Department to

- record and validate received *election decisions* from position holders, and claiming *counterparties*;
- monitor and follow up *overdue elections*;
- calculate and issue election decisions to location(s), including counterparties against whom the STO is claiming;
- monitor the status of all election decisions issued to *location*(s), including counterparties.

The subscription terms of the rights issue may allow the position holder to elect from more than one option with respect to the new security(s) to be received and the associated subscription cost. For example, the terms may allow the position holder to subscribe to new fully paid securities or partly paid securities. The subscription cost of each option will be proportional to the *par value* of the new security. It is necessary therefore to record the option required, and not simply that the position holder wishes to subscribe; note that this should be treated as a refinement to those actions stated within Chapter 17, 'Management of Mandatory with Options Events'.

As stated previously, in some cases the subscription of nil paid rights may be restricted to position holders according to their residency as described in Chapter 18, 'Management of Voluntary Events'. In this case, foreign position holders will still be entitled to receive the nil paid rights distributions, but the action to subscribe will not be available to them. The only alternatives will be to sell their nil paid rights entitlement or to allow them to expire.

20.5.4 Calculate Resultant Entitlements

Once the STO is certain that its election decisions (on behalf of the position holders) have been accepted by the location(s), the final calculation of resultant entitlements subsequent to subscription of nil paid rights falls within the same procedures as for other events with elections, as detailed within Chapter 11, 'Calculation of Resultant Entitlements'.

The Corporate Actions Department will perform this step using the

- details of the new security(s) to be issued as a result of *subscription*;
- subscription price and currency, including any options for the payment of subscription cost;
- subscription *ratio*, i.e. the ratio of new securities to be received relative to each subscribed nil paid right.

These items are as stated in the event terms.

As a result of election decisions to subscribe, this step will calculate the quantity of

- any reduction in the nil paid rights holdings;
- *resultant entitlement* in new securities;
- cash (subscription cost) to be paid.

In practice, payment is effected at the same time as issuing election decisions, and consequently it will be necessary for the calculation of subscription costs (to be paid to the *issuer*) to be calculated at the time of issuing the election decision.

Reduction of Nil Paid Rights Holding

The reduction in the nil paid rights holding will reflect the quantity relating to the election decision.

Resultant Entitlement to New Security(s)

According to the terms of the event, subscription may result in the distribution of one or more new security(s) for each available option. Typically subscription will result in the issue of a primary security, with possible additional secondary securities.

The calculation of the resultant entitlement in the primary security is normally as a result of applying the subscription ratio to the elected quantity of each option, and as such does not fundamentally differ to that approach described in Chapter 17, 'Management of Mandatory with Options Events'.

The calculation of any secondary entitlement securities will typically be as a result of a further securities ratio, as applied to either the

- elected quantity of each option (as per the primary security entitlement), or
- the resultant entitlement in the primary security.

Subscription Cost

As stated previously, the event terms may support a choice of subscription options with the subscription cost typically differing according to the option elected.

The monies payable to the issuer will typically be calculated by applying the subscription price (according to the elected option) to the resultant securities entitlement. This means that a dependency will exist between the two calculations, with the calculation of the securities entitlement being required to be performed prior to the calculation of the cash payment.

In the majority of cases the calculation of subscription costs will be based upon the primary security entitlement only (as described in the previous section). Typically the issue of secondary securities is on a free-of-cost basis as a result of subscription to the primary security.

20.5.5 Passing of Internal Entries

Internal entries reflecting the subscription to new shares are the same as those in respect of any other voluntary event. Accordingly, the Corporate Actions Department will pass entries that reflect

1. the distribution of the newly subscribed shares
2. the payment of subscription monies
3. the removal of nil paid rights that have been subscribed

Such entries are

- election decision date entries
- record date entries
- over-election adjustment entries (if applicable)

These are explained in Chapter 18, 'Management of Voluntary Events'.

20.5.6 Collection and Disbursement of Resultant Entitlements

The event terms will include the distribution date for all securities issued as a result of subscriptions. This will be a date at any time after the subscriptions close date.

As with any securities distributed as a result of a corporate action, the *resultant entitlements* will be *collected* from the *location* and disbursed to the *position holders*, representing the *settlement* of those entitlements. The collection and disbursement of resultant entitlements falls within the same procedures as for other events. Such procedures are detailed within Chapter 13, 'Collection/Disbursement of Resultant Entitlements'.

20.5.7 Updating of Internal Entries

Securities positions will be updated with a further set of entries against the *custodian*, in the form of 'settled' entries (once the custodian has advised the STO of settlement). Such entries are detailed within Chapter 14 'Updating of Internal Entries'.

20.6 UN-SUBSCRIBED NIL PAID RIGHTS EXPIRY

This is a mandatory stage, the purpose of which is to expire (also known as 'lapse') any unsubscribed nil paid rights subsequent to the subscription stage.

As detailed previously, the nil paid rights security is an interim security representing the position holder's right to subscribe to new securities. Accordingly once subscription ceases, the nil paid rights cease to exist as a security. Effectively this stage exists to remove any remaining positions in the nil paid rights.

This stage typically occurs immediately following the closure of the *subscription period*, i.e. following the *subscriptions close date*, and includes at minimum the following mandatory lifecycle elements:

- determine entitled holdings
- calculate resultant entitlements
- passing of internal entries

Each of these is described below. The STO may in addition issue communications to the position holder effectively confirming the quantity of nil paid rights expired. In the case of a simple expiry, the steps reflecting collection and distribution of resultant entitlements and updating of internal entries do not apply, as no actual securities or cash are being distributed as a result of the stage.

20.6.1 Determine Entitled Holdings

Entitlement to this stage is based upon the holder's remaining position in the nil paid rights. This step will commence following the passing of internal entries to reflect reductions in nil paid rights positions as a result of subscription.

20.6.2 Calculate Resultant Entitlements

The calculation of resultant entitlements will simply calculate the quantity of nil paid rights to be removed. In all cases this will be 100% of the entitled holding (i.e. the un-subscribed nil paid rights).

20.6.3 Passing of Internal Entries

To reflect the expiry of the unsubscribed nil paid rights, the Corporate Actions Department will simply pass entries to remove any remaining positions in respect of position holders and locations. These entries are illustrated in Chapter 21, 'Example of a Rights Issue'.

20.6.4 Distribution of Sale Proceeds from Un-Subscribed Nil Paid Rights

In some cases un-subscribed nil paid rights will be purchased from the *issuer* by an underwriter or third party (who will subsequently subscribe to the new securities outside of the normal terms of the issue). In this case the issuer may distribute cash to the *position holders* of un-subscribed nil paid rights, representing a portion of these sale proceeds.

This cash distribution will occur on a mandatory basis and potentially at some time subsequent to the close of the nil paid rights subscription, and will be initiated by either an additional event announcement or amendment to the original event announcement, informing position holders that cash will be distributed in exchange for their un-subscribed nil paid rights.

Under these circumstances, the lifecycle will mirror that of any mandatory event where cash is exchanged for the underlying holding, and unlike the simple expiry detailed above will include the capture and cleansing of the additional event terms (i.e. details of the cash proceeds), and the collection and distribution of cash proceeds.

It is common for many Corporate Actions Departments to treat expiries including the distribution of cash proceeds as independent events to the actual rights issue.

20.7 SUMMARY

In parallel with other multi-stage events, the management of a rights issue poses the Corporate Actions Department (and therefore the STO) with many challenges.

The Corporate Actions Department (and the STO in general) must ensure that it has robust procedures in place in order to manage the multiple stages of such events, with specific emphasis on the accurate and timely recording of internal entries throughout the event, to reflect changes in nil paid rights positions as a result of

- initial distribution of nil paid rights;
- trading of nil paid rights;
- subscription.

In addition, as with voluntary events, procedures must be in place to ensure the timely issuance of subscription decisions to locations in order to protect the interests of position holders. Unlike mandatory with options events, failure to issue subscription decisions in-line with the position holders wishes and by the stated deadline may result in non-participation in the event, and substantial costs to the STO.

21

Example of a Rights Issue

As the nature of rights issues incorporates a number of stages, this entire chapter is dedicated to illustrating this event type by way of a continuous example.

21.1 INTRODUCTION

The objective of this chapter is to provide the reader with an example rights issue that is designed to illustrate the different facets of a multi-stage event, and the associated management of its lifecycle components from beginning to end, in chronological sequence.

21.2 EVENT TERMS

The *issuer*, Nokia, announces on 11th August the details of a rights issue (the offer to the existing shareholders to purchase additional shares in proportion to their existing shareholding) (see Table 21.1).

Table 21.1

Event Conditions and Information	
Component	**Example**
Underlying security	Nokia EUR1.00 Shares
Event description	Rights Issue (Renounceable)
Nil Paid Rights Issue Ratio	One Nil Paid Right for every four existing EUR1.00 shares*
Subscription Price and Currency	Subscription Price of EUR14.50 per Share
Entitlement security and/or currency	Nokia Nil Paid Rights
Subscription Ratio	One Nokia Share for every one Subscribed Nil Paid Right
New Shares Ranking Details	The new shares issued as a result of subscription will rank *pari-passu* in all respects with the existing shares
Announcement Date	11 August
Nil Paid Rights Distribution	
Nil Paid Rights Entitlement Date	16 August
Nil Paid Rights Record Date	20 August
Nil Paid Rights Distribution Date	26 August
Nil Paid Rights Trading Period	
Nil Paid Rights Commence Trading Date	16 August
Nil Paid Rights Cease Trading Date	2 September
Nil Paid Rights Subscription Period	
Opening Date for Subscriptions	26 August
Closing Date for Subscriptions	9 September
Nil Paid Rights Expiry	
Unsubscribed Nil Paid Rights Expiry Date	10 September
New Shares Availability	
Distribution Date of New Shares	17 September
Restrictions	None Applicable
Treatment of fractions	Disregard
Exchange rates	Not applicable
Options available	Not applicable

**The ratio is based on the Europe and Asia Pacific calculation method; see Chapter 8.*

In addition to the dates listed in the table, the STO's *custodian* issues a communication to the STO stating that its deadline for the receipt of *subscription* decisions is 7th September (two days prior to the *issuer's deadline*). Consequently, the STO's Corporate Actions Department decides that its deadline for the receipt of subscription decisions from its position holders is one day earlier, on 6th September.

Figure 21.1 is a pictorial representation of the timetable for this particular event.

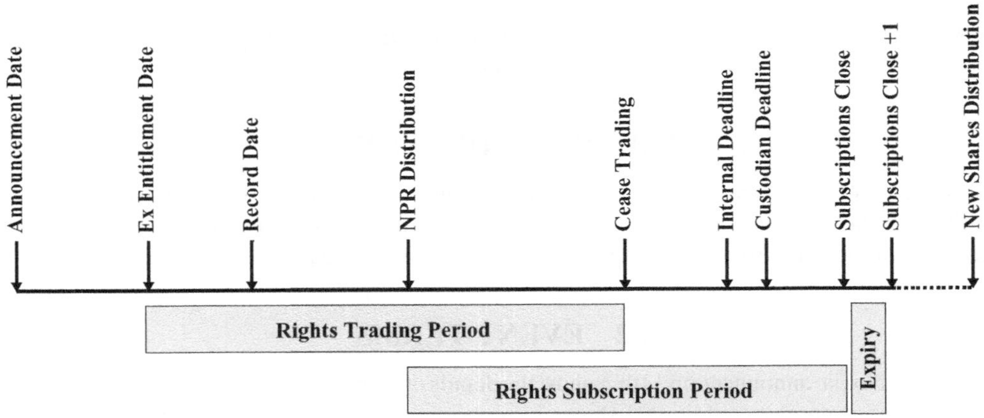

Figure 21.1 Rights issue example; timeline.

21.3 NIL PAID RIGHTS DISTRIBUTION

This section outlines the steps performed by the STO throughout this stage.

21.3.1 Determining Entitlement in the Event Underlying Security

Having obtained the details of the event from a *data vendor*, the STO records the details of the event within its corporate actions system.

In order to determine entitled holdings in the event's *underlying security*, the Corporate Actions Department (on 16th August, the *ex entitlement date*), retrieves the positions shown in Table 21.2 from the STO's main *books and records*.

Table 21.2

Nokia EUR1.00 Shares			
Ownership			Location
Trading Book 'D'	+800,000	−800,000	Counterparty G, Zurich
Custody Client 'G'	+100,000	−100,000	Custodian V, Custody A/C
	+900,000	−900,000	

This information reveals

- that the STO has a single *trading book* position (800,000 shares), which is fully outstanding with the *counterparty*;
- that the STO has a single *custody client* position (100,000 shares), which has a fully *settled custodian position*;
- that the total of *ownership positions* is equal to the *location* sum.

21.3.2 Communication of Event Information

In order to advise the position holders of the announced event, on 16th August (following the determination of entitled positions), the Corporate Actions Department issues an Event Terms Announcement to the custody client, transmitted by telex.

Note that the communication (see Table 21.3) contains no specific information regarding the quantity of the position holder's holding or any *resultant entitlement* calculation, as its purpose is purely to communicate the *event terms*.

Table 21.3

From	***The name of the issuing STO***
To	**Custody Client 'G'**
Attention	**Corporate Actions Department**
Subject	**Event Terms Announcement Notice**
Our Reference	**Nokia Rights August**
Event Description	**Nokia EUR1.00 Shares; Offer of 1:4 Nil Paid Renounceable Rights at a price of EUR14.50 per share to shareholders registered on 20th August, quoted ex-entitlement on 16th August**
Rights Trading Commences	**16th August**
Rights Trading Ceases	**2nd September**
Issuer's Subscriptions Close	**9th September**
Underlying Security	**Nokia EUR1.00 Shares**
Security Reference	**ISIN 9876543218**
Additional Information	**Please note that this notice will be followed shortly by a Final Entitlement Notice that will specify your holding in Nil Paid Rights, the cost of subscription, and the deadline by which we require your subscription decision.**
Sign-off by the STO	***Full name and location of STO***
Transmission Time	***Transmitted at 09:14 on 16th August***

For the trading book position, a similar communication is issued by internal e-mail to the appropriate trader responsible for the book.

21.3.3 Calculation of Resultant Entitlement in Nil Paid Rights

On 21st August (the day following *record date*), the Corporate Actions Department attempts a calculation and balancing of resultant entitlements (based on the '1 for 4' event), at both *collectible* and *disbursable* levels. Table 21.4 shows the results of these calculations, including the balancing totals between collectible and disbursable resultant entitlements in the nil paid rights.

21.3.4 Communication of Resultant Entitlement in Nil Paid Rights

On 21st August, following calculation of resultant entitlement, the Corporate Actions Department issues a Final Entitlement Notice to the custody client and to the trading book. Note that

Table 21.4

Disbursable Entitlements			Collectible Entitlements		
Party	**Underlying Holding**	**Resultant Entitlement**	**Party**	**Underlying Holding**	**Resultant Entitlement**
Trading Book 'D'	800,000	200,000	Counterp'ty G Zch	800,000	200,000
Custody Client G	100,000	25,000	Custodian V Cust	100,000	25,000
total	**900,000**	**225,000**	*total*	**900,000**	**225,000**

this is a further communication following the issuance of an Event Terms Announcement on 16th August, and also serves as a request to position holders for their *subscription decision*. The communication to the custody client is illustrated in Table 21.5.

Table 21.5

From	***The name of the issuing STO***
To	**Custody Client 'G'**
Attention	**Corporate Actions Department**
Subject	**Final Entitlement Notice**
Our Reference	**Nokia Rights August**
Event Description	**Nokia EUR1.00 Shares; Offer of 1:4 Nil Paid Renounceable Rights at a price of EUR14.50 per share to shareholders registered on 20th August, quoted ex-entitlement on 16th August**
Underlying Security	**Nokia EUR1.00 Shares**
Security Reference	**ISIN 9876543218**
Current Holding	**100,000 shares**
Decision Deadline	**Please advise us no later than 6th September whether you wish to accept the offer for all, some or none of the entitled quantity.**
Entitlement	**25,000 Nokia Nil Paid Rights**
Subscription Cost	**EUR 362,500.00**
Rights Trading Commences	**16th August**
Rights Trading Ceases	**2nd September**
Settlement Details	**Providing you wish to accept all or some of the entitled quantity, we will require the appropriate payment amount to our account number 200553 at Bank XXX, Frankfurt, on the deadline date of 6th September**
Sign-off by the STO	***Full name and location of STO***
Transmission Time	**Transmitted at 11:14 on 21st August**

Furthermore, the Corporate Actions Department issues a Final Claim Notice to Counterparty G, Zurich; the claim requests the counterparty to deliver 200,000 nil paid rights to the STO's main account at Custodian V. At this point, there can be no guarantee that the nil paid rights will be delivered to the STO's custodian account prior to the *subscriptions close date*; should delivery fail by that date, the STO will need to communicate the position holder's subscription decision to the counterparty so that the position holder's (and the STO's) interests will be protected.

21.3.5 Passing of Internal Entries re Nil Paid Rights

As the distribution of nil paid rights is a mandatory event, following the calculation of resultant entitlements the Corporate Actions Department is in a position to pass internal entries to reflect the resultant nil paid rights entitlements it expects (based upon the STO's records)

- to be disbursed to position holders (Table 21.6);
- to be collected from custodians and from counterparties (Table 21.7).

Table 21.6

Disbursable Entries (Nokia Nil Paid Rights)			
Debit		Credit	
Event Control Account	200,000	200,000	Trading Book 'D'
Event Control Account	25,000	25,000	Custody Client 'G'
	225,000	225,000	

Table 21.7

Collectible Entries (Nokia Nil Paid Rights)			
Debit		Credit	
Counterparty G, Zurich Awaiting Receipt	200,000	200,000	Event Control Account
Custodian V Custody a/c Projected	25,000	25,000	Event Control Account
	225,000	225,000	

21.3.6 Collection and Disbursement of Resultant Entitlements in Nil Paid Rights

On the nil paid rights *distribution date* (26th August), the Corporate Actions Department is due to receive the following securities externally:

- 200,000 nil paid rights to be received from Counterparty G (following the issuance of the *claim* by the STO), and credited to the STO's main securities account at the custodian, and
- 25,000 nil paid rights to be credited to the STO's safe-custody securities account at the custodian.

At close-of-business on 26th August, the custodian advises the STO that 200,000 and 25,000 nil paid rights have been credited to the STO's respective accounts. Immediately upon receipt of the date and details of settlement from the custodians, within its *books and records*, the Corporate Actions Department passes the entries shown in Table 21.8.

Table 21.8

Collectible Entries (Nokia Nil Paid Rights)			
Debit		Credit	
Custodian V Main a/c Settled	200,000	200,000	Counterparty G, Zurich Awaiting Receipt
Custodian V Custody a/c Settled	25,000	25,000	Custodian V Custody a/c Projected
	225,000	225,000	

Following settlement of the nil paid rights, the STO's overall position, as reflected in its books and records, is as shown in Table 21.9.

Table 21.9

Nokia Nil Paid Rights			
Ownership			**Location**
Trading Book 'D'	+200,000	−200,000	Custodian V, Main A/C
Custody Client 'G'	+25,000	−25,000	Custodian V, Custody A/C
	+225,000	−225,000	

It is important to note that this position is subject to change during the nil paid rights trading period that follows.

21.4 NIL PAID RIGHTS TRADING

For this particular event, the rights trading period commenced on 16th August and ceased on 2nd September. During that period, two trades in nil paid rights were executed:

- Custody Client 'G' sold 5,000 nil paid rights, part of an original entitlement of 25,000 nil paid rights (which settles prior to the close of the rights trading period).
- Trading Book 'E' purchased 100,000 nil paid rights from Counterparty H, Paris (which remains unsettled at the close of the rights trading period).

Note that Trading Book 'D', originally entitled to 200,000 nil paid rights, retains all 200,000 nil paid rights.

Following closure of the rights trading period, the STO's overall position, as reflected in its books and records, is as shown in Table 21.10. These positions are the result of both the nil paid rights distribution, and trading activity.

Table 21.10

Nokia Nil Paid Rights			
Ownership			**Location**
Trading Book 'D'	+200,000	−200,000	Custodian V, Main A/C
Trading Book 'E'	+100,000	−100,000	Counterparty H, Paris
Custody Client 'G'	+20,000	−20,000	Custodian V, Custody A/C
	+320,000	−320,000	

Note that trading in the nil paid rights has been carried-out by the traders, and the settlement of trades in nil paid rights has been carried-out by the settlement staff. Both activities have been undertaken entirely independently of the Corporate Actions Department; however, it is essential that the Corporate Actions Department remains aware of any nil paid rights trading and settlement activity, as the resultant positions will be inherited by the Corporate Actions Department.

21.5 NIL PAID RIGHTS SUBSCRIPTION

As illustrated in Figure 21.1, this stage will occur concurrently with the nil paid rights trading period. At all times throughout this stage it is imperative that the Corporate Actions Department takes account of the impact of any trading and settlement in the nil paid rights.

21.5.1 Determining Entitlement in Nil Paid Rights

The Corporate Actions Department must ascertain the final entitled holdings (i.e. relevant position holders and their relevant holding quantities) in the nil paid rights, in order to assess the related subscription decisions. The final entitled holdings position is that which is stated in Section 21.4.

Entitlement to subscribe to nil paid rights is based upon the holder's position in the nil paid rights, reflecting any original entitlement distribution, together with trading (and settlement) of nil paid rights, as at the *subscriptions close date* of the event.

21.5.2 Receiving and Issuing Subscription Decisions

Custodian V has advised the STO that its deadline for receiving subscription decisions is 7th September; this is the *issuer's deadline* minus two days. The STO's deadline for receiving subscription decisions from *position holders* is 6th September.

On 3rd September, three days prior to the *internal deadline date*, the Corporate Actions Department runs its report of nil paid rights position holders and holdings, revealing the positions shown in Table 21.11.

Table 21.11

Nokia Nil Paid Rights			
Ownership			**Location**
Trading Book 'D'	+200,000	−200,000	Custodian V, Main A/C
Trading Book 'E'	+100,000	−100,000	Counterparty H, Paris
Custody Client 'G'	+20,000	−20,000	Custodian V, Custody A/C
	+320,000	−320,000	

Those position holders that held Nokia shares and who received nil paid rights through the nil paid rights distribution process (see Section 21.3), have been made aware of the STO's deadline for subscription decisions through the content of the Final Entitlement Notice.

With regard to the purchase by Trading Book 'E' of 100,000 nil paid rights, the *trade confirmation* issued by the STO contained the subscription details, inclusive of the STO's subscription deadline.

As at close-of-business on 5th September (the STO's deadline minus one day), the Corporate Actions Department had been advised (in writing) of subscription decisions for both trading books, but at this time no decision had been received from the custody client. The Corporate Actions Department's records had been updated to reflect the subscription decisions received to date, as shown in Table 21.12.

Table 21.12

Subscription Decision Control (as at close-of-business on 5th September)					
Position Holder	Date Subs Decision Received	Elected Holding Quantity	Subscription Decision	Unelected Holding Quantity	Original Underlying Holding Quantity
Trading Book 'D'	5th September	150,000	Subscribe	50,000	200,000
	5th September	50,000	Do not subscribe	0	200,000
Trading Book 'E'	4th September	100,000	Subscribe	0	100,000
Custody Client 'G'	–	–	**No decision received**	20,000	20,000

Despite issuing written reminders and attempts to contact the *custody client* by telephone, no response was received by midday on 6th September (the STO's deadline). Within the STO, the Corporate Actions Department contacted the relevant salesman who made a decision (on behalf of the client) to subscribe, as the subscription price showed a reasonable discount to the market price of the original shares. A further communication was now necessary in order to advise the client of this decision. This resulted in the final subscription decisions shown in Table 21.13.

Table 21.13

Subscription Decision Control – Final (as at close-of-business on 6th September)					
Position Holder	Date Subs Decision Received	Elected Holding Quantity	Subscription Decision	Unelected Holding Quantity	Original Underlying Holding Quantity
Trading Book 'D'	5th September	150,000	Subscribe	50,000	200,000
	5th September	50,000	Do not subscribe	0	200,000
Trading Book 'E'	4th September	100,000	Subscribe	0	100,000
Custody Client 'G'	6th September	20,000	Subscribe	0	20,000

From a positive subscription decision perspective, the overall picture is as shown in Table 21.14.

Table 21.14

Summary of Positive Subscription Decisions			
Ownership		Location	
Trading Book 'D'	+150,000	−150,000	Custodian V, Main A/C
Trading Book 'E'	+100,000	−100,000	Counterparty H, Paris
Custody Client 'G'	+20,000	−20,000	Custodian V, Custody A/C
	+270,000	−270,000	

In order to formally advise Custodian V of the STO's subscription decisions, on 7th September (Custodian V's deadline), the Corporate Actions Department issues a S.W.I.F.T. MT565 message to the custodian, instructing the custodian to subscribe to

- 150,000 nil paid rights within the STO's main account at a cost of EUR 2,175,000.00, and
- 20,000 nil paid rights within the STO's custody account at a cost of EUR 290,000.00.

The costs are to be debited to the STO's account with the custodian.

With regard to the purchase of nil paid rights (by Trading Book 'E') during the nil paid rights trading period, as at this date Counterparty H, Paris has not yet delivered the securities. Consequently, the Corporate Actions Department issues a communication to the counterparty, requesting the counterparty to subscribe to

- 100,000 nil paid rights at a cost of EUR 1,450,000.00

with the cost paid (on the same date) to the counterparty's EUR account of its choosing.

21.5.3 Passing of Subscription Decision Date Entries

Following each decision to subscribe, in order to avoid accidentally selling the securities while in the course of subscription, the STO will usually segregate the appropriate quantity of the nil paid rights security within its *books and records*, immediately upon the subscription decision being taken. It is important to note that such segregation will not remove the holding from the *position holder's* total holding in the nil paid rights; this action merely serves to segregate it from each position holder's total nil paid rights position.

The entries shown in Table 21.15 are passed to achieve this.

Table 21.15

Segregation Entries (Nokia Nil Paid Rights)			
Debit		Credit	
Trading Book 'D'	150,000	150,000	Trading Book 'D' Accepted
Trading Book 'E'	100,000	100,000	Trading Book 'E' Accepted
Custody Client 'G'	20,000	20,000	Custody Client 'G' Accepted
	270,000	270,000	

Note that subscription decision date entries typically apply to position holders (as illustrated above), but where the STO wishes to reflect subscription decisions issued to the *location* throughout the *subscription period*, entries will be passed that are similar to the segregation entries illustrated for the position holder.

Following the passing of all subscription decision date entries, the total position in the nil paid rights within the STO's books and records is as shown in Table 21.16.

Table 21.16

Nokia Nil Paid Rights			
Ownership			Location
Trading Book 'D' Accepted	+150,000	−200,000	Custodian V, Main A/C
Trading Book 'D'	+50,000		
Trading Book 'E' Accepted	+100,000	−100,000	Counterparty H, Paris
Custody Client 'G' Accepted	+20,000	−20,000	Custodian V, Custody A/C
	+320,000	−320,000	

21.5.4 Calculation of Resultant Entitlement in the New Security(s) and Subscription Cash

Following the final subscription decisions, Table 21.17 reveals the cash subscription costs due from position holders, as well as the corresponding subscription costs payable to the custodian and the counterparty.

Table 21.17

Ownership			Location		
Owner	**Subscription Quantity**	**Subscription Cost (EUR14.50 p.s.)**	**Location**	**Subscription Quantity**	**Subscription Cost (EUR14.50 p.s.)**
Trading Book 'D'	150,000	EUR2,175,000.00	Custodian V Main a/c	150,000	EUR2,175,000.00
Trading Book 'E'	100,000	EUR1,450,000.00	Counterparty H, Paris	100,000	EUR1,450,000.00
Custody Client 'G'	20,000	EUR290,000.00	Custodian V Cust a/c	20,000	EUR290,000.00

With regard to resultant entitlement to the securities, each subscribed nil paid right entitles the holder to receive one new Nokia share.

21.5.5 Communication of Resultant Entitlement in the New Security

On the day following subscriptions close (10th September), the Corporate Actions Department issues a Final Entitlement Notice to the *custody client* and to the *trading book*. Note that this is a further communication following the issuance of a Final Entitlement Notice (relating to the nil paid rights) on 21st August. The communication to the custody client is illustrated below in Table 21.18; note that the 'Details' section of this communication is very specific to the custody client, as in this particular case the STO took the decision to subscribe on the client's behalf, and this communication reflects that fact.

Table 21.18

From	***The name of the issuing STO***
To	**Custody Client 'G'**
Attention	**Corporate Actions Department**
Subject	**Final Entitlement Notice**
Our Reference	**Nokia Rights August**
Event Description	**Nokia EUR1.00 Shares; Offer of 1:4 Nil Paid Renounceable Rights at a price of EUR14.50 per share to shareholders registered on 20th August, quoted ex-entitlement on 16th August**
Underlying Security	**Nokia Nil Paid Rights**
Security Reference	**ISIN 4567891236**
Current Holding	**20,000 Nokia Nil Paid Rights**
Details	**Following our decision (on your behalf) to subscribe to your full entitled holding of Nil Paid Rights, you are the owner of the following securities:**
Entitlement	**20,000 Nokia EUR1.00 Shares**
Subscription Cost	**EUR 290,000.00**
Settlement Details	**As we have paid the subscription cost on your behalf, kindly remit EUR 290,000.00 to our account number 200553 at Bank XXX, Frankfurt, without delay.**
Sign-off by the STO	***Full name and location of STO***
Transmission Time	**Transmitted at 08:22 on 10th September**

21.5.6 Passing of Internal Entries to Reflect Subscriptions

Securities Positions in the New Security

The Corporate Actions Department must now pass entries to reflect the subscription to the new security. Note that the shares resulting from this rights issue rank *pari-passu* with the original Nokia shares.

In order to reflect the acquisition of the shares by the position holders, the entries shown in Table 21.19 are passed.

Table 21.19

Disbursable Entries (Nokia EUR1.00 Shares)			
Debit		Credit	
Event Control Account	150,000	150,000	Trading Book 'D'
Event Control Account	20,000	20,000	Custody Client 'G'
	170,000	170,000	

In order to reflect the shares due from the custodian and the counterparty, the entries shown in Table 21.20 are passed.

As the purchase of 100,000 nil paid rights was unsettled as at the *subscriptions close date* (9th September), the entries shown in Table 21.21 represent the *transformation* of that trade

Table 21.20

Collectible Entries (Nokia EUR1.00 Shares)			
Debit		**Credit**	
Custodian V, Main A/C Projected	150,000	150,000	Event Control Account
Custodian V, Custody A/C Projected	20,000	20,000	Event Control Account
	170,000	170,000	

(in conjunction with the subscription cost entries and the removal of the nil paid rights entries below).

Table 21.21

Transformed Trade Entries (Nokia EUR1.00 Shares)			
Debit		**Credit**	
Counterparty H, Paris Awaiting Settlement	100,000	100,000	Trading Book 'E'
	100,000	100,000	

Subscription Costs Relating to the New Security

In addition to passing entries for the subscribed securities, the Corporate Actions Department (as at the close of the *subscription period*) now needs to pass entries to reflect the subscription costs paid.

In order to reflect the subscription costs paid by the position holders, the entries shown in Table 21.22 are passed.

Table 21.22

Disbursable Entries (EUR)			
Debit		**Credit**	
Trading Book 'D'	2,175,000.00	2,175,000.00	Event Control Account
Custody Client 'G'	290,000.00	290,000.00	Event Control Account
	2,465,000.00	2,465,000.00	

In order to reflect the subscription costs paid to the *custodian* and the *counterparty*, the entries shown in Table 21.23 are passed.

Table 21.23

Collectible Entries (EUR)			
Debit		**Credit**	
Event Control Account	2,175,000.00	2,175,000.00	Custodian V, Main A/C
Event Control Account	290,000.00	290,000.00	Custodian V, Custody A/C
	2,465,000.00	2,465,000.00	

As the purchase of 100,000 nil paid rights was unsettled as at the *subscriptions close date* (9th September), the entries shown in Table 21.24 represent the *transformation* of that trade.

In order to derive the full cash value owed to the counterparty, the subscription cost of EUR 1,450,000.00 will be added to the original purchase cost.

Table 21.24

Transformed Trade Entries (EUR)			
Debit		**Credit**	
Trading Book 'E'	1,450,000.00	1,450,000.00	Counterparty H, Paris Awaiting Settlement
	1,450,000.00	1,450,000.00	

Securities Positions in the Nil Paid Rights

For the *position holders*, in order to reflect the replacement of the nil paid rights with the new security, the entries shown in Table 21.25 are passed.

Table 21.25

Disbursable Entries (Nokia Nil Paid Rights)			
Debit		**Credit**	
Trading Book 'D' (Accepted)	150,000	150,000	Event Control Account
Custody Client 'G' (Accepted)	20,000	20,000	Event Control Account
	170,000	170,000	

As the purchase of 100,000 nil paid rights was unsettled as at the subscriptions close date (9th September), the entries shown in Table 21.26 represent the transformation of that trade.

Table 21.26

Transformed Trade Entries (Nokia Nil Paid Rights)			
Debit		**Credit**	
Trading Book 'E' (Accepted)	100,000	100,000	Counterparty H, Paris Awaiting Settlement
	100,000	100,000	

21.5.7 Collection and Disbursement of New Securities

Upon settlement of the outstanding deliveries of the Nokia shares (including the transformed trade), the custodian issues an advice of settlement (on 17th September) to the STO, and the entries shown in Table 21.27 are passed.

Table 21.27

Collectible Entries (Nokia EUR1.00 Shares)			
Debit		**Credit**	
Custodian V, Main A/C Settled	150,000	150,000	Custodian V, Main A/C Projected
Custodian V, Main A/C Settled	100,000	100,000	Counterparty H, Paris Awaiting Settlement
Custodian V, Custody A/C Settled	20,000	20,000	Custodian V, Custody A/C Projected
	270,000	270,000	

21.6 UNSUBSCRIBED NIL PAID RIGHTS EXPIRY

Also, on the close of the *subscription period*, the Corporate Actions Department must zeroize any records of nil paid rights holdings for which the *position holder* has chosen not to subscribe.

21.6.1 Determining Remaining (Unsubscribed) Positions in Nil Paid Rights

Following the subscription decisions by the position holders, Table 21.28 represents the remaining (unsubscribed) position in the nil paid rights.

Table 21.28

Nokia Nil Paid Rights			
Ownership			Location
Trading Book 'D'	+50,000	−50,000	Custodian V, Main A/C
	+50,000	−50,000	

21.6.2 Calculation of Nil Paid Rights to be Reduced

All (i.e. 100%) of the nil paid rights represented in Table 21.28 must be reduced.

21.6.3 Passing of Internal Entries to Zeroize Remaining Nil Paid Rights Positions

In order to reflect the expiry of the unsubscribed nil paid rights from the perspective of the position holders, the entries shown in Table 21.29 are passed.

Table 21.29

Disbursable Entries (Nokia Nil Paid Rights)			
Debit		Credit	
Trading Book 'D'	50,000	50,000	Event Control Account
	50,000	50,000	

Similarly, in order to reflect the fact that the nil paid rights have expired from the perspective of the *custodian*, the entries shown in Table 21.30 are passed.

Table 21.30

Collectible Entries (Nokia Nil Paid Rights)			
Debit		Credit	
Event Control Account	50,000	50,000	Custodian V Main a/c
	50,000	50,000	

Passing of these entries zeroizes the STO's records of nil paid rights.

21.7 FINAL SECURITIES POSITIONS

Following completion of the management of the event, the total securities position in Nokia Shares, as recorded within the STO's books and records is as shown in Table 21.31.

Table 21.31

Nokia EUR1.00 Shares			
Ownership			Location
Trading Book 'D'	+950,000	−1,050,000	Custodian V, Main A/C
Trading Book 'E'	+100,000		
Custody Client 'G'	+120,000	−120,000	Custodian V, Custody A/C
	+1,170,000	−1,170,000	

Tables 21.32 to 21.34 show a summation of how the final securities positions were derived, for each of the position holders.

Table 21.32

Trading Book 'D'		
	Nokia Nil Paid Rights	**Nokia EUR1.00 Shares**
Pre-Rights Issue Trading Position	n/a	+800,000
Entitlement to Nil Paid Rights	+200,000	
Purchases of Nil Paid Rights	nil	
Sales of Nil Paid Rights	nil	
Nil Paid Rights Allowed to Lapse	+50,000	
Nil Paid Rights Subscribed	+150,000	
Result of Subscription to New Shares	n/a	+150,000
Post-Rights Issue Trading Position		**+950,000**

Table 21.33

Trading Book 'E'		
	Nokia Nil Paid Rights	**Nokia EUR1.00 Shares**
Pre-Rights Issue Trading Position	n/a	nil
Entitlement to Nil Paid Rights	nil	
Purchases of Nil Paid Rights	+100,000	
Sales of Nil Paid Rights	nil	
Nil Paid Rights Allowed to Lapse	nil	
Nil Paid Rights Subscribed	+100,000	
Result of Subscription to New Shares	n/a	+100,000
Post-Rights Issue Trading Position		**+100,000**

Table 21.34

Custody Client 'G'		
	Nokia Nil Paid Rights	**Nokia EUR1.00 Shares**
Pre-Rights Issue Trading Position	n/a	+100,000
Entitlement to Nil Paid Rights	+25,000	
Purchases of Nil Paid Rights	nil	
Sales of Nil Paid Rights	−5,000	
Nil Paid Rights Allowed to Lapse	nil	
Nil Paid Rights Subscribed	+20,000	
Result of Subscription to New Shares	n/a	+20,000
Post-Rights Issue Trading Position		**+120,000**

These tables highlight the variety of options that can be taken in a rights issue, and the degree of care required in the management of such events.

22

Concepts of Takeover Events

In recent chapters, multi-stage lifecycles have been introduced and described, where the overall life of an event comprises a combination of both mandatory and elective lifecycles.

Within the definition of its lifecycle, a takeover is one such event. Nonetheless the takeover is being singled out here because of its additional unique features. This chapter will identify those unique features and describe the additional operational milestones beyond those previously introduced in mandatory and elective lifecycles, which the Corporate Actions Department will need to accommodate in order to control and manage such events properly.

22.1 INTRODUCTION

The term takeover is used to describe a change in *controlling interest* of a company, achieved via the accumulation of *issued capital* in that company by the person(s) or organization launching the takeover.

The person(s) or organization launching the takeover is known as the *offeror*, as it is making an offer for the issued capital of the *target company*. The target company is known as the *offeree*.

As stated in Chapter 2, 'Event Description and Classification', the reasons for takeovers can generally be categorized from the economical viewpoint to the offeror, as a desire to:

- control competition in the same market (although legislation is often in place to guard against monopolies developing);
- control either supplier or distribution networks in the same market;
- extend or diversify product range or market.

A takeover could combine any or all of these desires.

The offeror will accumulate issued capital via the purchase of securities from the position holders of the target company. In consideration of this purchase the position holders may receive either securities offered by the offeror, or cash, or a combination of both.

Note that in accordance with the descriptions previously provided in Chapter 2, takeovers are distinguished from mergers (a similar event type) in that in a takeover the offeror bids for control of the offeree, whilst in a merger both companies combine (and cease to exist) to form a new company.

In all markets, takeovers and the trading of securities under takeover is closely monitored and regulated, by market authorities. This is for a number of reasons, including:

- restriction of monopolies, ensuring that competition is maintained within the market place;
- restriction of overseas control of local enterprise.

In the majority of circumstances the offeror will need to seek approval from the appropriate regulatory authority prior to launching a takeover bid for the offeree. Typically this is done once the offeror has accumulated a stipulated percentage of the offeree's issued capital (although the regulatory authority will no doubt have been monitoring any accumulation up until this point). At this time the offeror must make known to the market place its intentions, i.e. whether it intends to launch a formal bid or not, and seek regulatory approval for such a bid.

The terms of any takeover bid are contained within an *offer document* (similar to a prospectus) issued by the offeror. The offer document contains details of the offeror's intentions, the precise terms and features of the event. The range of features that may be applicable to a takeover event, and of which the Corporate Actions Department must be aware, include:

- the percentage of the offeree that the offeror wishes to acquire;
- the period for which the offer is initially valid;
- any special conditions pertaining to the offer.

From the offeree's perspective the takeover bid may be either welcome (friendly) or unwelcome (hostile). Typically, the directors of the offeree will issue a document (or statement) to the market place and to its position holders stating whether it views the offer as friendly or hostile, and making a recommendation to its position holders regarding what action they should take with respect to the acceptance of the offer.

As previously stated, the overall life of a takeover represents multiple lifecycle stages. In its initial stage the acceptance of a takeover is purely voluntary on the part of the position holder (irrespective of any recommendations from the directors of the offeree). In the closing stages of some takeovers, where the offeror acquires sufficient shares as to result in the offeree no longer being able to be listed, acceptance of the offer by any remaining position holders (known as *dissenting shareholders*) may become mandatory; this is known as *compulsory acquisition*. The various aspects and management of these stages will be described throughout this and the following chapter.

22.2 THE STO'S RISK

Particular emphasis is being given to the complexity of takeover events, beyond many of the events illustrated to date within this book. The reason for this is to highlight the implications to the STO in terms of any financial risk as a result of incorrect handling and management of such events.

A takeover possesses all the fundamental characteristics of other event types, that is:

- capture of *event terms*
- determination of entitled positions and *location* components
- communication of event terms
- calculation of *resultant entitlement*
- management of *election decisions*

It is imperative, however, that the Corporate Actions Department must furthermore and at all times be aware of the additional features and milestones pertaining to a takeover, the possibility that changes to event terms can occur, and the potential risks associated with them.

22.3 FEATURES OF TAKEOVERS

It has previously been stated that *takeover* events introduce features that may be applicable to the takeover beyond those described as pertaining to mandatory events, events with elections and indeed other multi-stage events. The purpose of this section is predominantly to describe the features specific to a takeover that influence its subsequent management by the Corporate Actions Department:

- market and off-market offers
- partial and full offers
- competing offers
- offer consideration
- conditional and unconditional status

These are now described below. Many of these features directly impact the resultant entitlement terms, duration and voluntary or mandatory nature of the offer.

22.3.1 Market and Off-Market Offers

Once approval is obtained from the appropriate regulatory authority, a takeover may be executed in either of two ways by the offeror:

- market offer, or
- off-market offer

Market Offer

A market offer means that the *offeror* will pursue the acquisition of listed securities in the *offeree* via normal purchases in the stock market.

The offeror will publicly announce its intentions, an offer price (this method is only applicable where cash consideration is being offered for the acquisition), and appoint a 'broker' to 'stand in the market' on its behalf. Essentially the offeror places an 'order' with its broker to purchase securities in the offeree at a set price for a set period of time (as with other offers the offeror may choose to increase this price during the period of the offer).

Acceptance of the offer is achieved by *position holders* placing an order to sell at the specified price with their representative (STO or broker).

The result of matching the sell orders of position holders with the buy order of the offeror, is the execution of a trade. Transference of the position holder's position to the offeror will occur upon *settlement* of the trade.

One disadvantage of this method, to the position holder, is that in the execution of a trade it will incur normal trading costs, such as brokerage or commission and stamp duty, in accordance with local market conventions.

Within some organizations, the Corporate Actions Department may not become involved in the management of this type of takeover, as it becomes absorbed in the normal trading and settlement operations of the STO. At most the Corporate Actions Department may simply notify position holders of the existence of the offer, and after that take no further action.

Off-Market Offer

In contrast to a market offer, an off-market offer occurs when the acquisition of securities in the offeree by the offeror occurs outside of the normal market trading mechanism, as a result of direct agreement and transference of positions between the position holder and the offeror.

In this instance the offeror (or its agent) will directly contact all position holders in the offeree, advising them of the terms of the offer via the offer document. Acceptance of the offer is achieved by the position holder communicating its desire to accept the offer to the offeror (or its agent). Such acceptance will trigger the transference of the position holder's position to the offeror. (The full lifecycle of this process is described in Chapter 23, 'Management of Takeover Events').

In the majority of cases the costs of such transference (e.g. stamp duty) are borne by the offeror.

The management of off-market takeovers traditionally will fall to the Corporate Actions Department of the STO. It will be this department's responsibility to

- capture the terms of the offer;
- determine entitlement;
- communicate *event terms*;
- manage the receipt and issue of offer acceptances (*election decisions*);
- calculate *resultant entitlements*;
- ensure that throughout the lifecycle the STO's position keeping records are updated to record acceptances of the offer, any changes in the 'state' of the offer, and the final *collection* and *disbursement* of offer consideration.

22.3.2 Partial and Full Offers

As stated in the introduction to this chapter, the desire of the offeror in making a takeover offer is to acquire *issued capital* in the *offeree*. This desire may simply be to acquire sufficient capital to exercise a *controlling interest* in the offeree, or may be for the total of issued capital in the offeree. These are known as partial and full offers respectively.

Whether an offer is partial or full will directly impact the management of the event from the Corporate Actions Department's perspective, specifically in the following areas:

- offer period
- over-acceptances
- compulsory acquisition

Offer Period

As with all other events with elections, the event will have an *election period*, in this case representing the *offer period*. In some cases, where the offer is partial, the offeror may be allowed to shorten the offer period, once the desired capital has been acquired, i.e. *election decisions* have been received that satisfy the quantity of securities the offeror wishes to acquire.

Equally the offer could close early in a full offer, where full acceptances are received by the offeror prior to the original offer close date.

The Corporate Actions Department will need to monitor the progress of such events, being aware that the offer could close earlier than the intended date, in order to ensure that the interests of its position holders are protected.

Over-Acceptances

Additionally where an event is partial and election decisions exceed the offeror's required quantity of securities, the offeror will return any *over-elections*. This process has been described previously with respect to events with elections in Chapter 17, 'Management of Mandatory with Options Events', and will be expanded upon with respect to takeovers in Chapter 23, 'Management of Takeover Events'. In addition the offer period may be shortened in some circumstances to prevent further acceptances, as indicated above.

Compulsory Acquisition

Where an offer is for the full *issued capital* of the *offeree*, then at a point approaching full acceptances, the *offeror* will be allowed to acquire compulsorily any remaining positions from *position holders* (that have not already accepted the offer). This point normally occurs when the quantity of any outstanding acceptances is less than the minimum percentage that allows a company to be listed. For example, market regulations may stipulate that a minimum of 5% of a company's issued capital must be publicly held. Once acceptances are received in excess of 95%, then less than 5% of the issued capital will remain publicly held (outside of the offeror). Consequently the offeree will be delisted, and the remaining securities held by minority position holders will be compulsorily acquired. The Corporate Actions Department must be aware of this change to the offer, specifically because now the terms of the offer must be applied to any remaining positions on a mandatory basis.

22.3.3 Competing Offers

On occasions, a company may become a takeover target to more than one offeror at the same time. From the position holder's perspective, this means that it has to choose from more than one set of offer terms, and make its decision. From the Corporate Actions Department's perspective this means that it has more than one event to manage against the same entitled positions.

Managing the competing offers entirely independently of each other is not recommended. The Corporate Actions Department must ensure that, for example:

- position holders are accurately informed of all terms pertaining to both offers;
- received *election decisions* are recorded against the correct offer;
- positions are correctly updated upon acceptance of an offer, to ensure that the position is no longer available to accept any competing offer.

The existence of competing offers may result in the competing offerors continually increasing their offer consideration, and even potentially extending the offer period in order to attract acceptances from position holders and provide them with ample opportunity to accept their offer. Note that in some markets, a maximum offer period may be set by the regulatory authority.

22.3.4 Offer Consideration

The *offeror* will announce the consideration that it will make to a *position holder* in exchange for its position in the *offeree*, when initially making the offer.

At this stage, whilst the offer is purely voluntary, the position holder may be offered combinations of securities and/or cash for its position, together with the option not to accept the offer at all. The consideration offered by the offeror, may include a number of options representing various combinations of securities and/or cash, with the position holder being able to elect which option it requires in the event that it chooses to accept the offer. The terms of the offer may also include restrictions upon the *election decisions* that the offeree is willing to accept for any single option. Election decisions received in excess of the limits on any one option, would typically receive the *default option* (or basic offer consideration). In offering multiple options the offeror is making the offer more attractive to position holders, while restricting the election decisions against any one option allows the offeror to limit its exposure to any specific options.

Unlike other events, the terms of any options may alter throughout the life of the event. This would typically occur to attract more *offer acceptances* from position holders. While under offer the securities of the offeree are still tradeable, and as such have a market value. In order to attract acceptances the offeror must generally offer more than the market price. Increasing market prices, together with possible competing offers, may force the offeror to increase its offer consideration at any time throughout the offer (it is highly unlikely that the offer consideration would be reduced).

It is critical that the Corporate Actions Department monitors any changes to the options and offer consideration throughout the life of the offer, taking into account its impact on both received and outstanding election decisions, and where necessary communicating such changes to position holders.

22.3.5 Conditional and Unconditional Status

Another feature, somewhat unique to a takeover is the concept of 'success' as applied to the event. In other types of event, including voluntary events, once announced the issuer is committed to the event, even if very few *election decisions* are received (in the case of a voluntary event).

In the case of a takeover, the offeror will stipulate minimum conditions that must be met; otherwise it will not be obliged to stand by its offer to acquire the offeree. One such condition is the offeror receiving a minimum number of offer acceptances, for example the offeror may wish to acquire 100% of the offeree, but sets a minimum percentage of 51%; this means that once acceptances of at least 51% are received (and any other conditions of the offer met) the offer is deemed successful.

If the conditions of an offer are not met, the offeror will return all acceptances received to date to the position holders, and their positions in the offeree are re-instated. Effectively the offer is deemed unsuccessful and the event is cancelled.

Until the conditions of the offer are met, the offer is considered *conditional*; once the conditions have been met, the offer becomes *unconditional*.

The Corporate Actions Department must ensure that it is aware of the status of the offer at all times, recording the point at which it becomes unconditional. Up until this point, any offer acceptances received to date may be returned by the offeror, while after this point the progression of the offer is guaranteed. Note that in some markets, the position holders may be permitted to withdraw their acceptances while the offer remains conditional.

Until an offer is deemed unconditional the offeror will hold any acceptances received to date in trust (also known as escrow) for the position holders, thereby protecting their interests should the takeover not proceed to completion. Once the offer is deemed unconditional the ownership of any acceptances received will be transferred to the offeror, and offer consideration is payable.

22.4 IMPACT OF TAKEOVER EVENTS

Chapter 1, 'Basic Corporate Action Concepts', describes the generic impact of events from the perspectives of the *issuer*, the *position holder*, and the market as reflected in changes to the price of the *underlying security* to the event, while Chapter 16, 'Concepts of Events with Elections', describes that impact as applicable to events with elections.

The impact of such events is just as applicable to takeovers, together with some specific impacts that are unique to takeovers. One significant difference compared with the categories of events previously described, is that a takeover will have a direct impact not only upon the issuer (in this case known as the *offeree*) and the price of the underlying security, but also upon the person(s) or organization launching the takeover offer (known as the *offeror*) and potentially upon the price of its *issued capital*.

The impact to the following is described in the next sections:

- Offeror
- Offeree
- Position Holder
- Price of the Underlying Security
- Price of the Offeror's Issued Capital

22.4.1 Impact from the Offeror's Perspective

From the offeror's perspective, the impact of a takeover may be directly measured in terms of changes to its balance sheet, i.e. its issued capital, debts and cash reserves, as a result of the successful acquisition of issued capital in the offeree.

The offeror will expect to pay cash and/or distribute securities in exchange for the acquisition of capital in the offeree. The impact of a takeover offer to the offeror may therefore be measured in terms of the cost of the acquisition, together with any future gains to the offeror as a result of such an acquisition.

The impact of the cost of any acquisition of issued capital to the offeror, as with all events with elections that are voluntary in nature, is difficult to predict accurately. Besides the cost being based upon the acceptances received from position holders, the offeror may also find themselves increasing the consideration being offered for acquisition throughout the offer period, in order to make the offer more attractive to position holders. The final cost of the acquisition will not be known until all *offer acceptances* from position holders are received, and the offer closed.

The impact of the potential gains of such an acquisition will depend in part upon whether the offer is intended to acquire all or part of the issued capital of the offeree, and again the extent to which position holders in the offeree accept the offer. In acquiring all of the issued capital, the offeror will effectively acquire the assets, liabilities and goodwill of the offeree; while in acquiring part it will expect to acquire a *controlling interest* in the offeree, thereby influencing its future profitability and reaping the rewards of such control.

22.4.2 Impact from the Offeree's Perspective

The impact of a takeover offer from the offeree's perspective will depend specifically on whether the takeover offer is successful or not and whether the offer is made for the acquisition of all or part of the issued capital in the offeree. Again, as with all other events with elections where position holder participation is of a voluntary nature, the final impact of the event is impossible to predict accurately, and this is also true of takeovers.

The success of any takeover offer will result in the transference of ownership and its control of the acquired securities to the offeror. Such transference would typically be for a significant portion or all of the issued capital of the offeree (in accordance with the acceptances received from position holders).

If the offer is for only part of the issued capital, where successful the offeror may acquire sufficient issued capital to exercise influence and control over the future direction and day to day operations of the offeree, the impact being to reduce the control of the existing directors (and shareholders).

Alternatively if the offer is for all of the issued capital, where successful the offeree would cease to exist as a listed company, and essentially be absorbed into the offeror's organization, possibly as a subsidiary or division of the offeror.

22.4.3 Impact from the Position Holder's Perspective

As with all other events, the impact of a takeover on a position holder is measured in terms of the final impact on its securities and/or cash positions.

With respect to a takeover, during its voluntary stage, the position holder may exercise control over the impact to its securities and/or cash positions within the scope of the options offered by the offeror, including the choice not to accept the offer at all (thereby not participating in the event). In the event that the offeror acquires sufficient shares as to result in the offeree no longer being able to be listed, then any minority position holders will have their position compulsorily acquired. This stage is mandatory, and as such the position holder is not able to exercise control over the impact to its securities and/or cash positions.

In accepting a takeover offer the position holder is making an investment decision to dispose of all or part of its security holding in the offeree, in exchange for the securities and/or cash offered by the offeror. Such a decision is even more significant than the investment decisions made in previously discussed events with elections, as it potentially involves the re-direction of the position holder's investment from one issuer (the offeree) to another (the offeror). In making such a decision the position holder is essentially taking a view on the future profitability of both the offeree and the offeror.

22.4.4 Impact on the Price of the Underlying Security

As with many other events, the price of the *underlying security* (in this case the issued capital of the offeree) will typically increase to reflect the value to the position holder as a result of the event. In the case of a takeover, this increase would be expected to reflect the value of the consideration being offered by the offeror to shareholders for their acceptance of the offer and subsequent transference of their holdings to the offeror.

As previously stated, this consideration may be in the form of securities in the offeror or cash, or combinations of both. Irrespective of the form the consideration takes, the market price of the underlying security would be expected to increase to reflect this value. Despite this, and because initially takeovers are voluntary, the exact change in value of the underlying security is less predictable than for mandatory events.

Throughout the life of the takeover offer, the offeror may increase the value of the consideration being offered to position holders in the offeree with a view to making the offer more attractive. This does not typically occur in other event types where the terms of the event are fixed throughout the life of the event. Any such change in the offer consideration throughout the life of the offer would again be expected to be reflected in the market price of the underlying security. The result could be continual increases between the price the offeror is willing to pay to acquire securities in the offeree, and the price the offeree's securities are trading at in the open market place. In effect the offeror is in competition with the open market in terms of the price investors are willing to pay for the securities.

In addition, the offeror may come under direct competition from other person(s) or organizations who wish to launch a takeover offer for the offeree. It is not uncommon for rival bids to occur, and a bidding 'war' to ensue. The winner of such a bidding war would typically be the offeror who makes the most attractive (albeit highest) bid. The market price of the underlying security would reflect such a situation, continually increasing to reflect the value of the available offers.

This activity and its influence on the market price of a security under takeover offer can seem daunting, nonetheless an appreciation of it is vital to those making decisions as to whether to accept the (or any competing) takeover offers.

22.4.5 Impact on the Price of the Offeror's Security

As a result of launching a takeover offer, the price of issued securities in the *offeror* will also be impacted. Such an impact reflects the market's expectations for the value of the offeror as a result of a successful takeover. A successful takeover would result in the offeror acquiring the assets, liabilities and goodwill of the *offeree* at a cost. If the market place believes that this is advantageous to the offeror, resulting in future increased profitability and returns on investments, thereby making it a more attractive investment, the market price of the securities issued by the offeror would normally increase to reflect this expectation. Conversely if the market place perceives that profitability and returns on investment will not increase as a result of a successful takeover, the market price of securities issued by the offeror may well decrease.

The price of the offeror's security may also be impacted by the continuing success or lack of success of the takeover offer throughout its life. If the market place detects that position holders in the offeree are not accepting the offer, then it may take a negative view of the value of the offeror, this being reflected in the price of its issued securities.

Any changes in the market price of the offeror's securities will undoubtedly have an impact upon the perceived value of any offer consideration that includes such securities, therefore influencing the decisions made by shareholders in the offeree to accept such an offer, or not.

It is obvious that significant links exist between the value of any offer consideration, the price of the underlying security and the price of the offeror's securities. Changes in one may set in motion a chain of events which results in changes to the other securities.

22.5 TAKEOVER EVENT LIFECYCLE

The possible multiple stages (i.e. voluntary and mandatory) of a takeover event have been introduced earlier in this chapter, together with descriptions of features that will directly impact the lifecycle of the event. These are illustrated by the timeline shown in Figure 22.1.

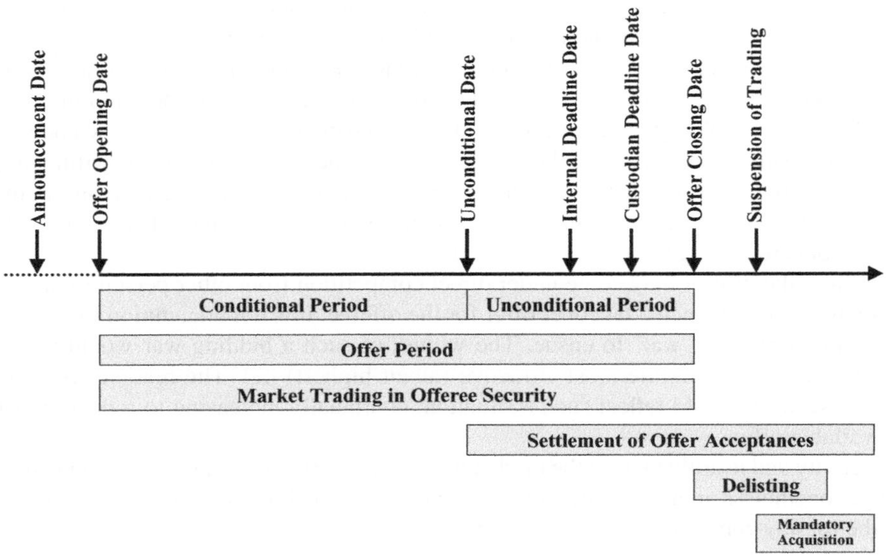

Figure 22.1 Takeover event lifecycle.

22.6 SUMMARY

As introduced in this chapter, takeover events, although having a lifecycle that is multi-stage in nature, further incorporate specific characteristics that do not apply to other types of events. Such characteristics include:

- the event is initiated by a third party (the offeror) and not the issuer of the underlying securities;
- a competing takeover event may be initiated by a further offeror;
- specific conditions are attached to the offer, which may result in the offer being withdrawn if they are not met.

These characteristics make the management of takeovers risky and sometimes manually intensive for the STO. It is difficult to automate fully the conditions of a takeover and particularly difficult where competing offers exist. Robust procedures must exist within the Corporate Actions Department together with a strong understanding of the characteristics of takeovers and the ability to apply those to a given event, if the risks are to be mitigated.

23

Management of Takeover Events

23.1 TAKEOVER EVENT TERMS

The terms and conditions of the offer are contained within the *offer document* as issued by the *offeror*. The principles of capturing and cleansing the terms of takeover events are fundamentally the same as those applied to any other type of event, as described in Chapter 8, 'Event Terms Capture and Cleansing', including those attributes specific to events with elections (refer to Chapter 17, 'Management of Mandatory with Options Events'), for example, the options available to position holders, and deadlines applicable to *election decisions*.

As described in Chapter 22, 'Concepts of Takeover Events', additional features exist with respect to takeover events that will directly impact the information to be captured and managed as *event terms*. It is necessary for the Corporate Actions Department to capture, verify, record and manage any changes to these terms as they occur during its lifecycle. Such additional features of the event terms (including those that may change during the life of the event) include:

- percentage to be acquired
- *offer period*
- *offer consideration*
- *conditional/unconditional* status of the offer
- *compulsory acquisition* terms

These are now described below.

23.1.1 Percentage to be Acquired

The offeror will state within the offer document the percentage of *issued capital* in the *offeree* that it wishes to acquire. In some cases the offeror may state both a minimum percentage and a maximum percentage, with typically the minimum percentage being one of the conditions for the success of the offer, i.e. if the minimum percentage is not successfully acquired, the offer will be withdrawn.

For instance, in the case of a full takeover, the offeror may state that it wishes to acquire 100% of the issued capital of the offeree, but that the offer is conditional upon 75% being acquired. This means that although the desire of the offeror is a full takeover of the offeree, it will be happy with a lesser percentage (which in this example would still gain them *controlling interest* in the offeree).

A further example illustrates where the offeror's intention is to acquire part of the issued capital of the offeree. Under these circumstances the offeror may state that it wishes to acquire 51% of the offeree, and no more. In this case the offer is conditional upon 51% of issued capital being accepted, but it also means that should the offeror receive acceptances in excess of this figure, over-acceptances will be declined (the treatment of over-acceptances is detailed later in this chapter).

The percentage to be acquired may be stated in a number of ways, usually depending upon whether the offer is intended as a partial or full takeover:

- Full Takeover
  - 100% only
  - 100% maximum, with a lesser minimum
- Partial Takeover
  - single percentage
  - minimum percentage, with a greater maximum

This information will typically be included in the content of position holder communications, as it is critical in the decision making process of the position holder. Equally, these percentages will directly impact the conditional/unconditional status of the offer, whether over-acceptances may require treatment, and in the case of a full takeover, whether it is likely that compulsory acquisition will occur.

23.1.2 Offer Period

Upon initial announcement of a takeover offer, the offeror will announce an

- *offer open date*, and an
- *offer close date*.

These two dates define the *offer period*, representing the period of time for which the issuer will accept *offer acceptances*, and apply specifically to the voluntary stage of the offer.

The offer open date is the earliest date from which the offeror will accept notification of offer acceptances. The offer close date serves the same purpose as the issuer deadline date in any event with elections, and is the last date that the offeror will accept notification of acceptance of the offer from a position holder. Associated deadlines, such as internal deadlines, *counterparty* deadlines and *custodian* deadlines will also apply to the event, as described in Chapter 17, 'Management of Mandatory with Options Events'.

Nonetheless, as introduced in the previous chapter, circumstances may occur that prompt the offeror to extend the offer close date for the offer. Typically this would occur where insufficient acceptances have been received from position holders; by extending the offer, the offeror is allowing position holders more time to consider and accept the offer. The offer period may also be extended where a competing offer is announced, as the original offer will typically adopt the timescale of the competing offer.

Alternatively, the offer could close earlier than initially announced, based upon the percentage of acceptances received by the offeror.

The Corporate Actions Department must have procedures in place to capture and record any changes in the offer close date throughout the offer, and the subsequent extensions in the offer period. Such changes will in turn have a domino effect upon the lifecycle of the event, including:

- re-assessment of internal, counterparty, and custodian deadlines;
- communication of the new offer close date and any associated deadline(s) to position holders;
- determination of entitled positions up to and including the new offer close date.

23.1.3 Offer Consideration

As with any other voluntary event, the *offer terms* will include details of the option(s) available to *position holders*, stating the offer consideration conditions for each option, whether it be based upon the distributions of securities, cash or combinations of both. This is in addition to the option to take no action, and not accept the offer (during its voluntary stage).

During the voluntary stage of the offer, the position holder (having made a positive *election decision*) may be offered either

- one or more alternatives as to the offer consideration it may receive, or alternatively
- no choice, where only one form of offer consideration exists.

Irrespective of the alternatives available during the voluntary stage, it is likely that in the case where the takeover proceeds to compulsory acquisition only a single form of offer consideration will apply. It is necessary that the Corporate Actions Department accurately identifies the exact offer consideration terms as they apply to each stage of the event.

In addition, as introduced in the previous chapter, the offeror may place limits upon the election decisions it will accept pertaining to any one specific option. Election decisions received in excess of the limits on any one option would typically receive the default option (or basic offer consideration). As a consequence, throughout the offer, the offeror may announce that one or more of the previously announced options are no longer available.

Unlike the majority of other events, the *ratio* and *rate* applied to the distribution of securities and cash respectively in consideration for acceptance of a takeover, may increase throughout the offer period. This normally occurs as the offeror's response to the increasing market price for the offeree's issued capital or competing offers (both of which are described in the previous chapter). Such increases in the offer consideration may occur at any time throughout the life of the offer, and may apply to all acceptances received to date together with any acceptances received once the change is announced, or may simply apply to only those acceptances received once the change is announced. It is critical that the Corporate Actions Department, in identifying such a change, also accurately identifies the date from which any such change is to apply.

It is imperative that the Corporate Actions Department ensures that the procedures employed to record the terms of a takeover offer are sufficiently robust to take account of all such changes in the offer consideration, throughout its life. Such changes will impact

- communications to positions holders, informing of the updated offer terms, and
- calculation of *resultant entitlements*.

23.1.4 Conditional/Unconditional Status of the Offer

The concept of *conditional* and *unconditional* status as it applies to a takeover offer has been described in the previous chapter. The Corporate Actions Department's event records must accurately reflect the conditional/unconditional status of an offer at any time, and in addition record the exact date upon which an offer becomes unconditional (where applicable).

The status of a takeover offer will directly impact

- The state of any *offer acceptances* received; while conditional, the beneficial ownership of the accepted securities still legally resides with the position holder, but once an offer becomes unconditional ownership transfers to the offeror. The STO's securities position records will need to reflect this.
- The expected distribution date of offer consideration; typically offer consideration is not payable until an offer is deemed wholly unconditional. At this time, offer consideration can be expected to be received for all acceptances to date (typically within a time period specified by the regulator of the market), and thereafter upon the issue of any further acceptances to the offeror.

23.1.5 Compulsory Acquisition

Compulsory acquisition constitutes the second stage of a takeover event, and is applicable to full takeovers where the total of minority positions in the offeree drops under the regulatory listing requirements as a result of offer acceptances received to date. This could occur prior to the original offer close date, or may not be known until following this date. It is not guaranteed that compulsory acquisition will occur at all.

The announcement of compulsory acquisition will include conditions pertaining to the offer consideration payable to the minority position holders, together with the *effective date* of the acquisition.

These conditions are in effect an addendum to the original offer terms. It would be easy for the Corporate Actions Department to view the compulsory acquisition stage of the takeover as a separate event, nonetheless as with any other multi-stage event, processing dependencies will exist between the voluntary stage and the mandatory compulsory acquisition stage, not least of these being the determination of entitlement at this stage. It is imperative that the Corporate Actions Department is mindful of these dependencies to ensure that the correct positions and *resultant entitlements* are calculated for compulsory acquisition.

23.2 DETERMINING ENTITLEMENT TO TAKEOVER EVENTS

The principles of determining entitlement to takeover events do not differ from those described in Chapter 9, 'Determining Entitlement'. In parallel with the generic lifecycle, the STO must identify

- *Ownership positions*, comprising
  - *Trading book* positions
  - *Custody client* positions
- *Location* components, comprising
  - *Settled custodian positions*
  - *Unsettled trades* resulting in *claims* in favour of the STO
  - Unsettled trades resulting in claims against the STO

As with all other multi-stage events, this exercise must be performed for each stage of the event; the voluntary stage, and the mandatory stage for compulsory acquisition (where it applies), with respect to holdings in the *underlying security* of the event.

During the voluntary stage of the takeover the offer close date of the event effectively becomes the *record date* for the purposes of identification of entitled positions and location (including unsettled trades). The Corporate Actions Department must identify all ownership positions and location up to and including the offer close date. This step will typically commence prior to the offer open date, and utilize the principles of projected positions, taking account of subsequent trading and settlement activity as described in Chapter 9, 'Determining Entitlement'.

As described in the previous section, the offer close date may be extended throughout the life of the takeover event. In cases where this occurs, the determination of entitled positions and location(s), must be updated to take account of this extension. Failure to do so would result in the (incorrect) omission of trading and settlement activity between the original close date and the new close date.

Where compulsory acquisition of minority positions is applicable (as described above), entitlement will be based upon the *effective date* of this acquisition to any remaining positions and location components in the STO's securities records. It is critical for this reason that all voluntary acceptances of the offer have been accurately updated in the STO's securities position records.

23.3 COMMUNICATION OF EVENT INFORMATION

A takeover event, as with any other multi-stage event (as described in Chapter 19, 'Concepts of Multi-Stage Events') will incorporate a combination of those communication types that are typically applicable to mandatory and voluntary events. Such communications will occur as relevant to the overall events, and at individual stages of the event. These communications may include:

- Event Terms Announcement
- Preliminary Entitlement Notice
- Final Entitlement Notice
- Preliminary Claim Notice
- Final Claim Notice
- Request for Election Decision – Reminders
- Confirmation of Election Decision
- Over-Election Notices

In addition to the above, a takeover event will require communications that update the *position holder* with specific changes to the event throughout its lifecycle (should they occur). Such changes may include:

- changes to offer consideration;
- update of takeover status, for example the offer becoming *unconditional*, or *compulsory acquisition*;
- notice of a competing offer.

Where a position holder elects to accept the takeover offer, the Corporate Actions Department could expect to issue the following communications (at minimum) throughout the lifecycle of the event:

1. Event Terms Announcement, communicating the *event terms*, conditions applicable and requesting *election decisions* from the position holder;
2. Confirmation of Election Decision, confirming the position holder's election decision received to accept the takeover offer;
3. Update of Takeover Status to unconditional, advising the position holder that the offer is now deemed successful;
4. Final Entitlement Notice, communicating the resultant entitlement as a result of election decisions received from the position holder to accept the takeover offer.

Alternatively, where a position holder has not elected on all or part of its holding, the Corporate Actions Department could expect to issue the following communications:

1. Event Terms Announcement, communicating the event terms, conditions applicable and requesting election decisions from the position holder;
2. Update of Takeover Status to unconditional, advising the position holder that the offer is now deemed successful;

3. Request for Election Decision – Reminders;
4. Update of Takeover Status to compulsory acquisition, advising the position holder that the offer is now mandatory;
5. Final Entitlement Notice, communicating the resultant entitlement as a result of mandatory acceptance of the offer in respect of the position holder's position.

The specific content and combination of communications issued will vary according to the stage of the takeover, and its status. As such, the processes employed by the Corporate Actions Department must be sensitive to the changing nature of the takeover event.

23.4 MANAGEMENT OF ELECTION DECISIONS

During the voluntary stage of the takeover event the management of *election decisions* falls within the same procedures as for all other voluntary events. Such procedures are detailed within Chapter 17, 'Management of Mandatory with Options Events'.

The procedures will include the requirement for the Corporate Actions Department to

- record and validate received *election decisions* from *position holders*, and claiming *counterparties*;
- monitor and follow up overdue election decisions;
- calculate and issue election decisions to *location*(s), including counterparties against whom the STO is claiming;
- monitor the status of all election decisions issued to location(s), including counterparties.

All of these functions, during the voluntary offer period, must be performed mindful of the potentially changing terms of the offer, specifically changes in the offer close date, offer consideration and the conditional/unconditional status of the offer (as detailed earlier in this chapter).

Failure to take account of such changes may result in errors, including:

- the non-issue of election decisions to location(s) prior to the appropriate deadline date;
- acceptance of incorrect offer consideration;
- incorrect updating of the STO's securities positions as a result of acceptances (dependent upon the conditional/unconditional status of the event).

From an operational perspective it is recommended that the Corporate Actions Department processes all election decisions received, as and when they are received, immediately issuing equivalent election decisions to the appropriate location. This approach particularly accommodates those instances where the offer period and/or offer consideration may be changed during the offer period, and ensures that the interests of the STO's positions are protected. Delay in the issuance of election decisions to the location(s) may result in the offer consideration elected by the position holder being no longer available, or the offer being closed earlier than expected. In this way the practical management of election decisions with regards to a takeover may differ to other events with elections (where the deadline and terms are fixed), allowing the Corporate Actions Department potentially to accumulate all election decisions received throughout the election period, and issue election decisions to the location(s) at a single point in time towards the end of the election period.

23.5 MANAGING UNSUCCESSFUL TAKEOVERS

The feature of 'success' as it applies to takeover events has been described in Chapter 22, 'Concepts of Takeover Events'. In summary, a takeover is successful when it meets the conditions set out in the offer document (e.g. minimum acceptances), and consequently becomes *unconditional*. Once unconditional the offer is guaranteed, conversely while the offer is *conditional* it may be withdrawn by the *offeror* at any time.

The offeror may withdraw the offer, despite having received acceptances, and in doing so will announce the withdrawal and decline all acceptances received to date. In the case of an offer being withdrawn the Corporate Actions Department must

- update its *event terms* records to show the event as 'withdrawn', and the applicable date;
- communicate the withdrawal to all positions holders, both those from whom *election decisions* have been received, and those from whom election decisions were still outstanding, at the time of withdrawal;
- ensure that the STO's securities position records are correctly updated to reflect that securities for which election decisions had previously been received are now again available for trading, i.e. they are no longer committed to the takeover.

In summary the Corporate Actions Department must act to reverse all actions taken, and inform position holders accordingly.

23.6 OVER-ACCEPTANCES

Over-acceptances with respect to takeovers may arise as a result of either or both of two scenarios, these being *offer acceptances* in excess of

- a specific option, and/or
- the required percentage of *issued capital* in the *offeree* (in the case of a partial offer)

being received by the *offeror*.

In both cases the offeror will announce the specific conditions with respect to its treatment of such over-acceptances, as described below.

23.6.1 Over-Acceptance of a Specific Option

The management of over-acceptances of a specific option is only applicable in takeover events where multiple options for the offer consideration are offered, and the terms of the offer include limits upon the election decisions that the offeror is willing to accept for any single option. In this instance the offer terms will also include details of the *default option* (or basic offer consideration).

Where acceptances exceed any limits set by the offeror for a specified option, normal practice is to apply the default option in its place. This practice may apply to all or part of an election decision, and may be effected on a pro-rata or 'first-come, first-served' basis (as detailed in Chapter 17, 'Management of Mandatory with Options Events'). The acceptance will not be declined, unlike practices that may be applicable in other voluntary events.

Any such treatment of election decisions previously issued will be communicated to the STO by the offeror (or its agent). Upon receipt of such information, the Corporate Actions

Department must update its records to

- reflect the change in option against the issued election decision to which it applies;
- update the elected option against the appropriate received election decision;
- inform position holders of any changes to their election decisions as a result of such changes;
- inform outstanding position holders of the future unavailability of the options (if applicable).

23.6.2 Over-Acceptance of a Partial Offer

As described in the previous chapter, in some takeovers the offeror's desire may be to gain *controlling interest* in the *offeree* only, and as such it may offer to acquire less than the total *issued capital* of the offeree. The offer terms will specify the percentage of issued capital that the offeror wishes to acquire, together with the conditions with respect to the treatment of any acceptances received in excess of this percentage. Two alternatives exist as to the treatment of *over-acceptances* in this instance, these being the decline of the over-acceptance on a pro-rata or first-in basis.

Pro-Rata

Where a pro-rata treatment of over-acceptances is applied, the offeror will typically keep the offer open until the originally announced closing date, accepting all offer acceptances received, and then applying the pro-rata ratio to all acceptances once the offer has closed. The excess quantity of each acceptance will be declined accordingly.

For example, company X announces a partial takeover offer for 51% of company Y, indicating that any over-acceptances will be reduced on a pro-rata basis at the close of the offer.

Custody Client T (who has a holding of 100,000 shares in Company Y) communicates its *election decision* to the STO to accept the offer with respect to its entire holding. Upon receipt of the election decision from Custody Client T, the Corporate Actions Department will

- pass internal entries to reflect that Custody Client T has accepted the offer, and
- communicate the election decision to the *location* to accept the offer in respect of 100,000 shares.

The effect of the Corporate Actions Department passing internal entries reflecting the position holder's acceptance of the offer, is to reduce the position holder's trading position by 100,000 shares to nil, and create an 'accepted' position of 100,000 shares. These entries are as previously described in Chapter 18, 'Management of Voluntary Events', and are referred to again later in this chapter.

At the close of the offer acceptance period, company X announces that it has received offer acceptances in respect of 70% of company Y. This represents an acceptances excess of 19% of issued capital (being the difference between the 70% of issued capital received and the 51% of issued capital required). Accordingly, company X announces that all *offer acceptances* will be reduced by 27.142%, being the excess received (19%) expressed as a percentage of the acceptances actually received (70%).

Upon receipt of this announcement, the Corporate Actions Department will apply this adjustment to all election decisions in its records. With respect to Custody Client T, its acceptance will be reduced as follows:

1. Derive the acceptance quantity to be reduced by multiplying the number of shares 'accepted' by the adjustment percentage:

$$100{,}000 \text{ shares} \times 27.142\% = 27{,}142 \text{ shares}$$

2. Derive the adjusted acceptance quantity by subtracting the acceptance quantity to be reduced from the original acceptance quantity:

$$100{,}000 \text{ shares} - 27{,}142 \text{ shares} = 72{,}858 \text{ shares}$$

Consequently, the final acceptance quantity in respect of which Custody Client T will receive resultant entitlement is 72,858 shares. The 27,142 shares (by which its original acceptance was reduced on a pro-rata basis) will be reverted to their trading position and Custody Client T will retain ownership of these shares. The internal entries passed to reflect this adjustment are referred to later in this chapter.

First-In

Where a first-in treatment of over-acceptances is applied, the *offeror* will effectively close the offer and refuse the receipt of any further acceptances once the maximum acquisition percentage is reached. Any election decisions issued after this point will be rejected. The final offer acceptance received by the offeror may also be reduced in order to keep acceptances within the maximum percentage. In this case the STO will be advised of such an adjustment to the elected quantity.

Any such treatment of over-elections with respect to a partial offer will be communicated to the STO by the offeror (or its agent) at the point in time when they are applied. Upon receipt of such information, the Corporate Actions Department must update its records as appropriate to

- reflect the early closure of the event (if applicable), communicating the same to all position holders;
- update the election quantities against the issued election decision to which it applies;
- inform position holders of any changes to their election quantities as a result of such changes.

23.7 CALCULATION OF RESULTANT ENTITLEMENTS

The calculation of *resultant entitlement* is required for both the voluntary stage, together with any mandatory *compulsory acquisition* stage.

23.7.1 Voluntary Stage

During the voluntary stage of the takeover, the Corporate Actions Department would not typically calculate any entitlements as a result of acceptance of the offer until the offer is deemed *unconditional* (and therefore guaranteed to proceed) and the treatment of any *over-elections* pertaining to specified options or a partial offer are finalized.

Once these milestones are passed, the Corporate Actions Department should proceed in calculating the changes that will occur to the position holder's securities and/or cash positions, together with its *location*(s) positions, as a result of the offer. The calculations fall within the same basic generic procedures as detailed within Chapter 11, 'Calculation of Resultant Entitlements', while being applicable to the elected quantity as per events with elections detailed within Chapter 17, 'Management of Mandatory with Options Events'.

Acceptance of the offer will result in the removal of the quantity of the *underlying security* position in the offeree to which the election decision applied, in exchange for the elected security and/or cash option offered by the offeror.

At the same time the Corporate Actions Department will determine the expected settlement date of the offer consideration. The offeror will normally include the rules for this within the terms of the offer document. The offer consideration is unlikely to be paid by the offeror until after the offer has become unconditional, as until this time the offer could be withdrawn should its conditions not be met.

The rules for the distribution of offer consideration include

- a single date following the offer close date, or
- a date calculated following the unconditional date or *election decision* date, whichever is the later.

Where a single date following the offer close date is stipulated, the offeror will distribute all offer considerations on a single date once the offer is closed, irrespective of when the offer became unconditional or election decisions were received.

Where the *distribution date* is based upon the unconditional date and the election decision date, the offeror will, initially on a single date, distribute all offer considerations in respect of election decisions received up until the unconditional date; thereafter offer considerations will be distributed as and when further election decisions are received, until the close of the offer. This is illustrated in the timeline shown in Figure 23.1.

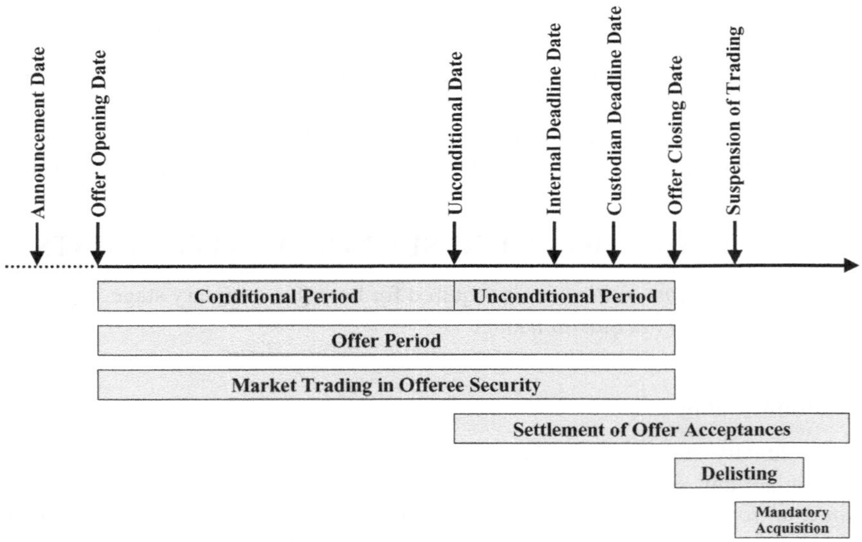

Figure 23.1 Takeover event lifecycle.

Assume that the takeover is announced as *unconditional* on 15th September, whilst the Offer Closing Date is the 10th October. The offer terms previously announced advised that offer consideration (*resultant entitlements*) will be distributed to accepting position holders within five days of offer acceptance, or the event becoming wholly unconditional, whichever is the later.

As at 15th September (when the offer becomes unconditional), the Corporate Actions Department's records indicate the status shown in Table 23.1 with respect to election decisions received and outstanding.

Table 23.1

Election Decision Control				
Position Holder	Date Election Decision Received	Accept (Holding Quantity)	Unelected (Holding Quantity)	Original Underlying Holding Quantity
Trading Book 'A'	12th September	200,000		200,000
Trading Book 'B'	13th September	700,000	300,000	1,000,000
Custody Client 'T'	18th September	400,000		400,000
	total	**1,300,000**	**300,000**	

Based upon the event being announced as unconditional, the Corporate Actions Department will calculate resultant entitlement with an expected settlement date of 20th September, being five days after the unconditional date, in respect of the following offer acceptances:

- Trading Book 'A'; 200,000 shares
- Trading Book 'B'; 700,000 shares
- Custody Client 'T'; 400,000 shares

On 22nd September, after the offer has become unconditional, Trading Book 'B' elects to accept the offer in respect of its remaining position of 300,000 shares. The Corporate Actions Department will update its records to reflect the receipt of this *election decision* and its date (Table 23.2).

Table 23.2

Election Decision Control				
Position Holder	Date Election Decision Received	Accept (Holding Quantity)	Unelected (Holding Quantity)	Original Underlying Holding Quantity
Trading Book 'A'	12th September	200,000		200,000
Trading Book 'B'	13th September	700,000		1,000,000
	22nd September	300,000		
Custody Client 'T'	18th September	400,000		400,000
	total	**1,600,000**	–	

The Corporate Actions Department will calculate resultant entitlement in respect of the final acceptance of 300,000 shares on behalf of Trading Book 'B' with an expected settlement date of 27th September, being five days after the acceptance date.

23.7.2 Mandatory Compulsory Acquisition Stage

Where *compulsory acquisition* of minority positions (*dissenting shareholdings*) occurs this will be, as previously stated, on a mandatory basis.

Once compulsory acquisition is announced the specific terms of this stage will be applied to any remaining positions in the *offeree* in the STO's securities position records. The *resultant entitlements* will remove the underlying position and distribute either securities and/or cash as stated by the *offeror*.

The terms of compulsory acquisition will also include an *effective date*, which will serve as the expected value date of the resultant entitlements.

23.8 PASSING OF INTERNAL ENTRIES

As with all other events, entries will be passed by the STO to reflect

- any change to the *underlying securities* position, and
- the distribution of any securities and/or cash that is expected to occur on the *distribution date* or *effective date* of the event.

Accordingly, the Corporate Actions Department will pass entries that reflect

1. the distribution of the offer consideration in the form of securities and/or cash, and
2. the removal of underlying securities in respect of which the offer has been accepted.

The specific nature of these entries will depend upon whether the takeover is still in the voluntary stage or has progressed to *compulsory acquisition*.

23.8.1 Voluntary Stage

Entries will only be passed during the voluntary stage if the position holder has elected to accept the takeover offer. Such entries are

- Election Decision Date entries
- Unconditional Date entries
- Withdrawal of offer entries (if applicable)
- Over-election adjustment entries (if applicable)

Election Decision Date Entries

These entries will result in the segregation of securities in respect of which the position holder has accepted the takeover offer, as described in Chapter 18, 'Management of Voluntary Events', and will apply to position holders and (depending upon market convention) to *location* positions.

Also, some CSDs/ICSDs commonly set-up an *escrow account* for each option, and transfer securities into this account as election decisions are received from the STO.

Unconditional Date Entries

These entries are passed at the time that the takeover event is deemed as unconditional and guaranteed to proceed. In nature, these entries equate to those passed on the *record date* with respect to voluntary events.

At this time the Corporate Actions Department will pass entries that reflect

- the resultant entitlement that is expected to be collected from the *location*; that is, from *custodians*, from *claims* on *counterparties*, from *transformed trades*, and
- the *resultant entitlement* that is to be *disbursed* to *position holders*.

These entries include the removal of *underlying securities* (from segregated positions) for which election decisions were received (from position holders) and issued (to locations).

Withdrawal of Offer Entries

On those occasions where an offer is deemed unsuccessful and subsequently withdrawn, the Corporate Actions Department will pass internal entries that re-instate the securities positions of those position holders that have previously elected to accept the offer relating to their trading position. Effectively, these entries will reverse the election decision date entries.

Over-Election Adjustment Entries

Where more than one option is offered or the offer is partial and *over-elections* occur, the Corporate Actions Department will be required to pass internal entries to adjust the over-election as described in Chapter 18, 'Management of Voluntary Events'.

23.8.2 Compulsory Acquisition Stage

If the takeover offer proceeds to *compulsory acquisition*, and where positions still exist for which the STO's position holders have not accepted the offer, upon announcement of compulsory acquisition the Corporate Actions Department will pass entries to reflect

- the resultant entitlement that is expected to be collected from the location; that is, from custodians, from claims on counterparties, from transformed trades, and
- the resultant entitlement that is to be disbursed to position holders.

These entries include the removal of underlying securities that have been compulsorily acquired.

23.9 COLLECTION AND DISBURSEMENT OF RESULTANT ENTITLEMENTS

Once election decisions are accepted by the *offeror*, the offer is deemed unconditional, over-acceptances are treated (where applicable) and resultant entitlements calculated (including the expected value date), the actual collection and disbursement of entitlements falls within the same general procedures as with other events. Such procedures are detailed within Chapter 13, 'Collection/Disbursement of Resultant Entitlements'.

The Corporate Actions Department must remain aware that, in some cases, such settlements may occur over a period of time, according to the value dates calculated (as described in previous sections).

The impact is that the Corporate Actions Department may be collecting entitlements throughout the distribution period, and will subsequently need to identify which disbursable resultant entitlements to settle in turn.

23.10 UPDATING OF INTERNAL ENTRIES

Securities and/or cash positions reflecting the *resultant entitlement* (offer consideration) will be updated with a further set of entries against the *custodian*, in the form of 'settled' entries (once the custodian has advised the STO of settlement). Such entries are detailed within Chapter 14, 'Updating of Internal Entries'. Note that (as previously described in this chapter) settlement may occur progressively over a period of time, once the event is declared *unconditional*, and that updating of internal entries subsequent to settlement is critical in order to monitor any outstanding resultant entitlements.

23.11 SUMMARY

The management of takeovers poses the Corporate Actions Department (and therefore the STO) with significant challenges.

As described in the previous chapter, the Corporate Actions Department (and the STO in general) must ensure that it has robust procedures in place in order to manage

- the multiple stages of such events, with specific emphasis on the accurate and timely recording of internal entries throughout the event, to reflect changes in the underlying security as a result of offer acceptances;
- changes to the event terms and status throughout the lifecycle of the event, which may require immediate action by the Corporate Actions Department or communication to the position holder;
- possible competing offers.

Consequently, timely and accurate processing of event announcements and updating of securities positions are of utmost importance in the management and processing of such events.

Part V
Taxation

24

Concepts and Management of Taxation

24.1 INTRODUCTION

Taxation refers to a levy imposed upon individuals, partnerships or corporations by countries for the support of the state. Taxation levies may be based upon the value of earnings, property, or goods and services.

Taxation based upon the value of earnings specifically relates to the earning of

- income (known as 'income tax'), or
- profits (known as 'capital gains tax').

The majority of individuals in employment are familiar with the payment of income tax on income received from their employer, and income received from investments, for example interest earned on cash held in bank accounts. Capital gains tax applies to the profits earned from the buying and subsequent selling of assets (which were held for investment purposes).

The basic principles and differences between income tax and capital gains tax with respect to investments can be illustrated as they apply to property that is owned purely for the purposes of investment. The weekly rent received from renting the property is classed as income and is liable to income tax. Should the property be sold at a later time, then any profit from that sale (i.e. sale proceeds less the original purchase cost) is classed as a gain (or return) on the original investment (known as capital) and is liable to capital gains tax. In some countries, if the subsequent sale of the property results in a loss, then the property owner may be permitted to use this loss to reduce its overall tax liabilities (from other profits and income).

These principles are also applicable to investments in securities markets, and as such apply to changes in position holders' securities and/or cash positions, as a result of both trading and corporate action events. This chapter specifically describes the concepts of taxation as applicable to corporate action events and the impact on the STO's management of those events and their securities and/or cash positions.

Note that the precise regulations applicable to the calculation and collection of any tax liability will differ from country to country, and it is not the authors' intention to detail specific tax legislation for any individual country. However, in order to help convey concepts, representative examples will be utilized within this chapter and the following chapter (Chapter 25,'Management of Income Tax').

24.2 TAXABLE AND NON-TAXABLE EVENTS

The *event terms* will clearly state whether an event is taxable or non-taxable with respect to its immediate impact on the *position holders'* securities and/or cash positions (i.e. the *resultant entitlement*).

24.2.1 Taxable Events

Designating an event as taxable means the position holder will incur a change in its securities and/or cash position as a direct result of the event, which may immediately generate either income or a capital gain.

This may be as a result of

- the distribution of income in the form of either *dividends* or *coupons*;
- the exchange of old securities for cash, for example the maturity of bonds;
- the exchange of old securities for a combination of new securities and cash, which combines the market value of the new securities and the face value of the cash, for example, a *takeover* or *merger*;
- the exchange of old securities for new securities, where the new securities are distributed to position holders on the basis of the market value of those securities; for example, a takeover or merger, where the *offeror* distributes shares that have their own market value in exchange for securities in the *offeree*.

Note that in designating an event as taxable, no presumption as to the profit a position holder may make (if any) is being made. In fact the original cost of the position holder's position in the *underlying security* may be more than the value of any new securities and/or cash, resulting in a loss as a result of the corporate action event.

24.2.2 Non-Taxable Events

Non-taxable events are those events where the change in the position holder's securities and/or cash position as a direct result of the corporate action does not immediately generate *income* or a *capital gain* for the *position holder*. This may include

- the exchange of old securities for new securities, where the original cost of the old securities is also transferred to the new securities, for example a *share split*, and
- the free distribution of securities (i.e. at no cost to the position holder), for example a *bonus issue*.

Note that although an event itself may be considered non-taxable, this does not remove any capital gains tax liability from the position holder upon the eventual disposal of the securities received as a result of the corporate action event in the normal course of securities trading.

24.3 INTRODUCTION TO CAPITAL GAINS TAX AND INCOME TAX

The type of tax applicable to a taxable corporate action will be based upon the specific type of event, according to whether the resultant entitlement of securities and/or cash is classed as capital gain or income. As well as stating that an event is taxable or non-taxable, the terms of an event will clearly state whether securities and/or cash (to be disbursed to the position holders) are drawn from the *issuer's* capital reserves, or represent distribution in the form of income as a result of company profits, or interest on debt.

24.3.1 Capital Gains Tax

As stated previously, capital gains tax is applicable to any profit earned as a result of investment. Specific taxation regulations and accounting conventions apply to the calculation of capital gains tax (from country to country); however, in principle, any tax liability is not normally incurred until such time as any profit is realized by the position holder.

Two scenarios may result in a capital gain, these being

- the disposal of securities in exchange for new securities and/or cash, or
- the receipt of cash from the *capital reserves* of the *issuer* with no exchange of the *underlying securities*.

Where such capital gain may be realized immediately as a direct result of the event, the event is considered taxable.

With respect to non-taxable events, any gain that will be liable to capital gains tax will not be realized until the disposal (i.e. sale via normal trading) of the securities received as a result of the corporate action event.

Any potential liability to capital gains tax will not directly impact the calculation of *resultant entitlements* (as described in earlier chapters). Within the organizational structure of the STO, it is rare for the Corporate Actions Department to become directly involved in the calculation of profits and any subsequent capital gains tax liabilities; this would normally be the responsibility of the Financial Control (or similar) department. (Note that as calculation of capital gains tax is not normally managed within the Corporate Actions Department, this topic will not be elaborated beyond this chapter).

Nonetheless this does not alleviate the Corporate Actions Department of all responsibility, as it is the source of information pertaining to any changes in securities and/cash positions as a result of a corporate actions event. It is imperative that all changes to the STO's securities and/or cash positions are effected on a timely and accurate basis, and that events are identified correctly as taxable or non-taxable.

In addition, where the event results in the distribution of new securities, either in exchange for existing securities, or as a pure *benefit* in addition to the position holder's existing position, the cost of those securities (as described above) must be correctly referenced in any securities distribution journals, thus allowing the correct calculation of gain irrespective of whether it be immediate or upon later disposal of the securities.

The cost of the new securities may be calculated according to one of the following four methods, dependent upon the type of event and the event taxability announced by the issuer. Securities may be

- Distributed in exchange for existing securities, with a value as designated by the issuer or the current market value; e.g. a *takeover*. Note that this would be designated as a taxable event.
- Distributed in exchange for existing securities, with a value equal to the purchase cost of original securities; e.g. a *share split*. Note that this would be designated as a non-taxable event with any potential gain being incurred at a later date upon the sale of the new securities.
- Distributed as a free benefit and therefore the cost is zero; e.g. a *bonus issue*. Note that this would be a non-taxable event with any potential gain being incurred at a later date upon the sale of the new securities, and normally any subsequent sale proceeds will de deemed 100% profit.

- Purchased from the issuer by way of *subscription* and therefore the cost of the new securities will be equivalent to the subscription monies paid; e.g. subscription in a *rights issue*. Note that this would be designated as a non-taxable event with any potential gain being incurred at a later date upon the sale of the new securities.

24.3.2 Income Tax

Income tax is applicable to those *resultant entitlements*, whether in the form of cash or securities, which represent the distribution of company profits as *dividend* on equity, or interest (*coupon*) on debt, to position holders. The type of income distribution (i.e. whether dividend or interest) is an important distinction as this may subsequently impact the rate of income tax applicable.

Specific taxation regulations will apply in respect of the calculation and collection of income tax from country to country; however, in the majority of circumstances income tax liabilities exist in both the country where the income is earned and the country where the position holder permanently resides. For example, a resident of the United Kingdom may receive income as a result of a dividend on a German equity. The profits being distributed to the position holder have effectively been earned in Germany and are liable for German income tax. In addition, the position holder is liable to pay income tax in the United Kingdom on the dividend as it is a permanent resident of that country. Of course where the country where the income is earned and the country where the position holder permanently resides are the same, the position holder is liable for only one instance of income tax.

In some instances the issuer may reduce the tax liability of the position holder by effectively pre-paying the tax liability, and making the income distribution at a lower rate. This is applicable to dividend payments on equities, and the event terms will indicate whether the dividend rate is pre-taxed or not. In some markets (for example, Australia), a dividend that has had the tax pre-paid is known as *franked*, while a dividend that has not had tax pre-paid is known as *unfranked*. In addition, the event terms may indicate that the dividend is partly franked, meaning that tax has been pre-paid upon a portion of the dividend only.

Note that payments of overseas income tax, as referred to in the earlier example, together with the pre-payment of any tax by the issuer may allow the position holder to reduce its tax liability in its country of residence. This is explored more fully in the next chapter.

Unlike *capital gains tax*, the calculation of income tax liabilities will directly impact the calculation of *resultant entitlements* for income events. This is because in the majority of cases the resultant income entitlement is reduced by any income tax payable. To date, references to income events have always been made on the basis of calculating resultant entitlements, without the impact of tax. Throughout the following chapter, the additional calculations to take account of the income tax liability, and the calculation of the resultant income entitlement incorporating tax liabilities, will be detailed. This will include the principles of identifying the applicable tax rates to be applied to an individual position holder.

The responsibility for the calculation of tax on income events lies, in the majority of cases, with the Corporate Actions Department. This is due to the impact of income tax amounts on the calculation of the resultant entitlement. In addition, the Corporate Actions Department may also be responsible for the actual payment of tax liabilities to the appropriate tax authorities.

24.4 THE STO'S RISK

The collection and payment of tax on investments, whether capital gains tax or income tax, is a legal requirement. Incorrect calculations and non-payment by appropriate deadlines can result in the STO incurring serious and costly fines.

As stated previously the specific regulations surrounding the calculation and collection of income tax will differ from country to country. In accommodating the variety of regulations, it has been historically difficult to apply high levels of automation and STP to this aspect of the Corporate Actions Department's responsibilities, and accordingly the calculation, collection and management of income tax amounts are notoriously manual.

In addition, due to the variety of regulations, the calculation and collection of income tax requires specialist knowledge, and in most cases a dedicated team within the Corporate Actions Department will be responsible for the management of income events and associated tax calculations.

To avoid the risk of losses and fines, the STO should ensure that all automatic and manual procedures are correctly monitored and validated. The procedures within the Corporate Actions Department must include the identification of income, and taxable and non-taxable capital events; additionally the maintenance of current tax regulations and rates is critical.

24.5 SUMMARY

The principles of taxation of income and capital gains are as applicable to securities as they are to other forms of investment.

Those that administer investments owned by others are confronted with a challenging (and historically manually intensive) task in the accurate and timely management of taxes on such investments.

25

Management of Income Tax

25.1 INTRODUCTION

This chapter describes the calculation and collection of income tax liabilities, and how they impact the calculation of resultant income entitlements by the Corporate Actions Department.

To date the calculation of *resultant entitlements* with respect to *income* events has been illustrated by simply multiplying the entitled holding quantity by the *dividend* (cash) rate or *coupon* rate; or in the case of Dividend Re-investment Plans (*DRPs*), applying the re-investment terms to calculate a securities income entitlement.

It is now necessary to extend these calculations in order to take account of the tax liabilities of the position holder, incorporating these amounts into the final resultant entitlement to be collected from the *location* and disbursed to the position holder.

Income tax liabilities withheld at source (i.e. by the *issuer* on behalf of its country's tax authority) are commonly known as *withholding tax*. Within this book, the following terms will be used:

- tax deducted overseas (from the perspective of the STO) will be referred to as *Foreign Withholding Tax*, whereas
- tax deducted in the position holder's country of residence will be referred to as *Position Holder's Domestic Income Tax* (which may or may not be withheld at source, according to domestic legislation).

The calculation of a resultant income entitlement will normally include calculation of

- Gross Income, representing the resultant entitlement prior to the calculation and deduction of any tax amounts;
- Foreign Withholding Tax, representing tax deducted by the issuer or *custodian* and payable to the issuer's national tax authority;
- Net Income (after deduction of foreign withholding tax), representing the amount typically receivable by the STO from the custodian, following deduction at source of the Foreign Withholding Tax;
- Position Holder's Domestic Income Tax, representing those tax amounts deducted by the STO and payable to a tax authority in the country of residence of the position holder;
- Net Income, representing the final resultant entitlement to be disbursed by the STO to position holders once all applicable tax amounts have been deducted from the gross income.

In order to guide the reader through this chapter, the information in Table 25.1 will be repeated at the beginning of each relevant section; the table contains definitions of each calculation component, and a simple calculation example.

The previous chapter described how all income distributions are potentially liable for income tax, and these principles will apply to those distributed in the form of both cash and securities; nonetheless the specific conventions for applying income tax amounts to an entitlement will differ according to whether the entitlement is distributed as cash or securities. These differences

Table 25.1

Chapter section	Definition of calculation component	Calculation example
Gross Income	Result of multiplying entitled holding by the dividend rate or coupon rate	EUR15,000.00
Foreign Withholding Tax (FWT)	Tax deducted by issuer or custodian (and payable to issuer's national tax authority)	–EUR2,250.00 (15% of gross income)
Net Income (after FWT)	The amount remaining after deduction of Foreign Withholding Tax, and paid to STO by custodian	EUR12,750.00
Position Holder's Domestic Income Tax (PHDIT)	Tax deducted by the STO (and payable to holder's national tax authority)	–EUR750.00 (5% of gross income)
Net Income (after FWT and PHDIT)	The amount payable to the position holder after deduction of Foreign Withholding Tax and Position Holder's Domestic Income Tax	EUR 12,000.00

will be described throughout this chapter. Note that the example tax rates used in this chapter and their treatment within stated countries are entirely fictitious, are used for illustrative purposes only and are not intended to reflect actual tax rates or their treatment.

25.2 GROSS INCOME

The calculation of gross income (Table 25.2) is the first step in the calculation of net income or final *resultant entitlement*; the majority of tax amount calculations are based upon the gross entitlement. The gross income is relevant to income calculations for both *position holders* and the *location*.

Table 25.2

Chapter section	Definition of calculation component	Calculation example
Gross Income	Result of multiplying entitled holding by the dividend rate or coupon rate	EUR15,000.00
Foreign Withholding Tax (FWT)	Tax deducted by issuer or custodian (and payable to issuer's national tax authority)	–EUR2,250.00 (15% of gross income)
Net Income (after FWT)	The amount remaining after deduction of Foreign Withholding Tax, and paid to STO by custodian	EUR12,750.00
Position Holder's Domestic Income Tax (PHDIT)	Tax deducted by the STO (and payable to holder's national tax authority)	–EUR750.00 (5% of gross income)
Net Income (after FWT and PHDIT)	The amount payable to the position holder after deduction of Foreign Withholding Tax and Position Holder's Domestic Income Tax	EUR 12,000.00

The gross income is normally calculated by multiplying the entitled holding quantity by the cash rate, *coupon* rate or securities *ratio* of the income event. This calculation is consistent with those described in Chapter 11, 'Calculation of Resultant Entitlements'. (Note that the variations required for *DRP* are described in Chapter 17, 'Management of Mandatory with Options Events').

For example, using a cash dividend rate of 150 cents per share, and assuming an entitled holding of 10,000 XXX shares:

$$\text{divide holding by } 1 (10{,}000/1 = 10{,}000), \text{ multiply by } 150 (10{,}000 \times 150 = 1{,}500{,}000)$$

which produces gross income of 1,500,000 cents, or EUR15,000.00.

25.3 FOREIGN WITHOLDING TAX

Foreign withholding tax (Table 25.3) is income tax deducted from the gross income by the *issuer* or the *custodian* and payable to the issuer's national tax authority. Foreign withholding tax is relevant to income calculations for both position holders and the location.

Table 25.3

Chapter section	Definition of calculation component	Calculation example
Gross Income	Result of multiplying entitled holding by the dividend rate or coupon rate	EUR15,000.00
Foreign Withholding Tax (FWT)	Tax deducted by issuer or custodian (and payable to issuer's national tax authority)	–EUR2,250.00 (15% of gross income)
Net Income (after FWT)	The amount remaining after deduction of Foreign Withholding Tax, and paid to STO by custodian	EUR12,750.00
Position Holder's Domestic Income Tax (PHDIT)	Tax deducted by the STO (and payable to holder's national tax authority)	–EUR750.00 (5% of gross income)
Net Income (after FWT and PHDIT)	The amount payable to the position holder after deduction of Foreign Withholding Tax and Position Holder's Domestic Income Tax	EUR 12,000.00

For example, assume that the gross dividend illustrated above is paid on a German equity and held by a position holder who is a permanent resident of the United Kingdom. In this instance, German income tax would be withheld by the issuer or custodian and paid to the German tax authority.

Foreign income tax is withheld prior to payment because as the position holder is not resident in the country that is the source of the income, the position holder will not be declaring the income in that country. As such, in order for the issuer's national tax authority to guarantee the collection of the income tax that it is due, income tax must be deducted (withheld) prior to payment of the income to the position holder.

Foreign withholding tax is calculated by multiplying the gross income by the applicable tax rate. For example, using a gross income amount of EUR15,000.00 and foreign withholding tax rate of 15%:

$$\text{multiply gross income by} 15\% \ (15{,}000.00 \times 15/100)$$

which produces a foreign *withholding tax* amount of EUR2,250.00.

It is important to note that the deduction of foreign withholding tax does not free the position holder from any tax liabilities within its own country of residence, i.e. to its domestic tax authority. Therefore the incurrence of tax liabilities in two countries may serve to discourage some position holders from investment overseas. Consequently many countries band together to agree lower foreign withholding tax rates for foreign position holders in order to encourage mutual overseas investment between their respective investors.

One of two types of foreign withholding tax rates may apply to individual foreign position holders, and the applicable type will depend specifically upon the position holder's country of residence and the issuer's country. The two types are

- Treaty Rates, where a treaty (known as a *double taxation agreement*) is signed to agree that income earned from investment between the two countries will be taxed at a reduced rate (compared with the higher non-treaty rate – see below), or
- Non-treaty Rates, where no such treaty exists between the two countries and income earned will be taxed at the higher rate.

Irrespective of the existence of a treaty or not, the actual foreign withholding tax rate applicable is dictated by the tax authority of the issuer's country.

25.4 NET INCOME AFTER DEDUCTION OF FOREIGN WITHHOLDING TAX

When foreign income is collected by the Corporate Actions Department from the *location*, the foreign withholding tax will have already been deducted, and therefore the amount received by the STO will be the remaining net income amount. Net income after deduction of foreign withholding tax is relevant to income calculations for the location (Table 25.4). (Note that net income calculations for the position holder are described later in this chapter).

Table 25.4

Chapter section	Definition of calculation component	Calculation example
Gross Income	Result of multiplying entitled holding by the dividend rate or coupon rate	EUR15,000.00
Foreign Withholding Tax (FWT)	Tax deducted by issuer or custodian (and payable to issuer's national tax authority)	–EUR2,250.00 (15% of gross income)
Net Income (after FWT)	**The amount remaining after deduction of Foreign Withholding Tax, and paid to STO by custodian**	**EUR12,750.00**
Position Holder's Domestic Income Tax (PHDIT)	Tax deducted by the STO (and payable to holder's national tax authority)	–EUR750.00 (5% of gross income)
Net Income (after FWT and PHDIT)	The amount payable to the position holder after deduction of Foreign Withholding Tax and Position Holder's Domestic Income Tax	EUR 12,000.00

Assuming that the STO is aware of an income event and has calculated entitlement due in advance of the payment (or distribution) date, the Corporate Actions Department would be expecting to receive the appropriate credit at its custodian account(s), on the due date. The amounts due must take into account the residency status of the position holders (whether *trading books* or *custody clients*) and consequently whether *treaty* rates are applicable or not.

Net income after deduction of foreign withholding tax is calculated by deducting the foreign withholding tax from the gross income. For example, using a gross income amount of EUR 15,000.00 and foreign withholding tax rate of 15%:

deduct foreign withholding tax from gross income (EUR 15,000.00 – EUR 2,250.00)

which produces a net income after deduction of foreign withholding tax amount of EUR 12,750.00.

Conventions to manage foreign withholding tax deducted at the location versus that applicable to position holders are explored later in this chapter.

25.5 POSITION HOLDER'S DOMESTIC INCOME TAX

Position holder's domestic income tax (Table 25.5) is tax deducted by the STO from income due to position holders (on an investment in an overseas security (i.e. foreign income) and payable to the position holder's domestic tax authority. Furthermore, such tax is applicable to an investment in a security issued within the country of residence of the position holder (i.e. domestic income). Position holder's domestic income tax is relevant to income calculations for position holders only (and not to the location).

Table 25.5

Chapter section	Definition of calculation component	Calculation example
Gross Income	Result of multiplying entitled holding by the dividend rate or coupon rate	EUR15,000.00
Foreign Withholding Tax (FWT)	Tax deducted by issuer or custodian (and payable to issuer's national tax authority)	–EUR2,250.00 (15% of gross income)
Net Income (after FWT)	The amount remaining after deduction of Foreign Withholding Tax, and paid to STO by custodian	EUR12,750.00
Position Holder's Domestic Income Tax (PHDIT)	Tax deducted by the STO (and payable to holder's national tax authority)	–EUR750.00 (5% of gross income)
Net Income (after FWT and PHDIT)	The amount payable to the position holder after deduction of Foreign Withholding Tax and Position Holder's Domestic Income Tax	EUR 12,000.00

25.5.1 Applicability of Position Holder's Domestic Income Tax

At this stage, it is essential to note that the STO may be required to deduct position holder's domestic income tax from those clients that are resident within the STO's country of residence according to the tax legislation of that country.

In a situation where the STO holds securities in *safe custody* for a number of clients, some of those clients may be resident within the STO's country of residence (the STO therefore being obliged to deduct position holder's domestic income tax from income due to such clients). For example, if the STO is based in the UK, the STO may be required to deduct position holder's domestic income tax from UK resident position holders. An exception occurs where the position holder is exempt from such tax (as is the case for registered charities).

Conversely, some of the STO's clients may be resident overseas, and therefore not subject to tax within the STO's country of residence; under these circumstances, the STO must pass-on the income to clients resident overseas after having had only foreign withholding tax deducted. An exception to this rule occurs where the position holder is resident overseas but fails to complete non-residency declaration documents, in which case the STO may be obliged to deduct tax. Overseas resident position holders are typically required to declare income to their own national tax authority; this is normally the responsibility of the position holder (and not the STO).

The text in Section 25.5.2 is written from the perspective of the STO needing to deduct position holder's domestic income tax from applicable position holders only.

25.5.2 Calculation of Position Holder's Domestic Income Tax

As with all other income received, for example salary, rental returns on investment property, and interest on savings, income earned from investment in securities must be declared to the position holder's national tax authority and is liable for domestic taxation. (Throughout this chapter this is being described as domestic tax, as it represents the tax payable to the country of residence of the position holder).

The domestic tax is calculated on the gross income amount irrespective of any other tax amounts already paid either as foreign *withholding tax* or pre-paid tax paid by the *issuer* (described later in this chapter).

Using the example in the previous section under foreign withholding tax, assume that under normal circumstances the UK resident will be liable for UK income tax at a rate of 20% on the gross income earned (in this case EUR 15,000.00).

The domestic tax is calculated by multiplying the gross income by the applicable tax rate, in this case 20%:

$$\text{multiply gross income by } 20\% \ (15{,}000.00 \times 20/100)$$

which produces a domestic tax amount of EUR 3,000.00. (Note that domestic tax deducted in a currency other than the natural currency of the position holder's national tax authority will require the STO to effect a foreign exchange transaction to raise the appropriate currency; in the example quoted, the appropriate currency is GBP).

It is important to note that the position holder may, according to domestic income tax regulations, be able to reduce its domestic tax liability where

- foreign withholding tax has been applied (see section below);
- domestic tax has been pre-paid by the issuer (described later in this chapter).

Note that where the STO has deducted position holder's domestic income tax prior to passing-on the income to the position holder, the STO will need to

- hold the deducted tax in an appropriate account, and
- remit the tax to the STO's national tax authority at the required time.

These topics are explored in more detail later in this chapter.

25.5.3 Offsetting Foreign Withholding Tax

The deduction of foreign *withholding tax* at source does not exempt the position holder from any domestic income tax liability within its own country of residence.

Under some circumstances, the position holder may be required to pay domestic income tax completely over and above any foreign withholding tax amount already deducted. However, under other arrangements (particularly where a *treaty* is involved between the *issuer's* country and the *position holder's* country), the foreign withholding tax deducted may be used (by the position holder's domestic tax authority) to reduce (via offsetting) the position holder's domestic tax liability.

It is the responsibility of the STO to remain aware of current offsetting arrangements and to deduct the correct tax amounts accordingly.

When two countries enter into a *double taxation agreement*, the overall aim is that investors in both countries will not pay an amount of tax greater than the full domestic income tax rate payable within the investor's country. In order to achieve this, the tax authorities within the investor's country may declare that withholding tax deducted at source is offsettable against the domestic income tax due. The Corporate Actions Department must be aware as to whether this is applicable within its country of residence.

Consequently, following on from the example in the previous section, where German income tax of EUR 2,250.00 (at a rate of 15%) has previously been deducted from the United Kingdom position holder's gross income of EUR 15,000.00, if this amount is offsettable against its United Kingdom domestic tax liability of EUR 3,000.00, the calculation would appear as follows:

deduct foreign withholding tax from domestic tax (EUR 3,000.00 – EUR 2,250.00)

which produces a final domestic tax amount of EUR 750.00 (which will be converted to the domestic currency, in this case GBP, as described previously).

Consequently, the final domestic tax liability in the example is effectively 5% of the gross income, as represented by the difference between the domestic tax rate (20%) and the foreign withholding tax rate (15%).

The extent to which foreign withholding tax may be offset against domestic tax liabilities will differ from country to country. As such it is not simply a matter of always reducing the domestic tax liability by the amount of the foreign withholding tax. The Corporate Actions Department will need to identify the amount of foreign withholding tax (or the equivalent rate) that may be offset. Many organizations hold the rate (5% in the above example) that may be offset as an additional item of data in their tax rate records in order to perform this calculation automatically.

The effect of regulations allowing the offsetting of foreign withholding tax against domestic tax liabilities is to reduce the position holder's overall tax liability, and encourage further foreign investment.

Note that where the STO has deducted position holder's domestic income tax prior to passing-on the income to the position holder, the STO will need to

- hold the deducted tax in an appropriate account, and
- remit the tax to the STO's national tax authority at the required time.

These topics are explored in more detail later in this chapter.

25.6 NET INCOME AFTER DEDUCTION OF FOREIGN WITHHOLDING TAX AND POSITION HOLDER'S DOMESTIC INCOME TAX

Once the gross income, foreign tax amounts and domestic tax amounts (if applicable) are calculated the net income to be disbursed (to position holders) can be calculated (Table 25.6). Net income after deduction of foreign withholding tax and position holder's domestic income tax is relevant to income calculations for position holders only (and not to the location).

Table 25.6

Chapter section	Definition of calculation component	Calculation example
Gross Income	Result of multiplying entitled holding by the dividend rate or coupon rate	EUR15,000.00
Foreign Withholding Tax (FWT)	Tax deducted by issuer or custodian (and payable to issuer's national tax authority)	–EUR2,250.00 (15% of gross income)
Net Income (after FWT)	The amount remaining after deduction of Foreign Withholding Tax, and paid to STO by custodian	EUR12,750.00
Position Holder's Domestic Income Tax (PHDIT)	Tax deducted by the STO (and payable to holder's national tax authority)	–EUR750.00 (5% of gross income)
Net Income (after FWT and PHDIT)	**The amount payable to the position holder after deduction of Foreign Withholding Tax and Position Holder's Domestic Income Tax**	**EUR 12,000.00**

25.6.1 Position Holders Resident Within the STO's Country of Residence

From the STO's perspective, for those position holders that are resident within the STO's country of residence, the net income to be credited to such position holders will normally, in the case of foreign income, be the result of the deduction of

- foreign *withholding tax*, and
- position holder's domestic income tax (which may have been offset by the foreign withholding tax).

The (fictitious) example income event quoted throughout this chapter reflects a specific circumstance where

- the STO is resident in the UK;
- the STO holds securities on behalf of a *custody client* that is also resident in the UK;
- the issuer is resident in Germany;
- the UK has a *double taxation agreement* with Germany (and therefore withholding tax is charged at the *treaty* rate);
- withholding tax is offsettable against UK income tax payable by the position holder.

The summarized view of all the components relating to the above mentioned example is shown in Table 25.7.

Table 25.7

	EUR
Gross dividend	15,000.00
Deduct withholding tax at 15% (treaty rate)	−2,250.00
Net income after withholding tax	12,750.00
Deduct PHDIT at 5% (WT offsettable)	−750.00
Net income after all taxes	**12,000.00**

Conversely, had the foreign withholding tax not been offsettable against UK income tax (but in all other respects the circumstances are as described above), the summarized view of all the components would be as shown in Table 25.8.

Table 25.8

	EUR
Gross dividend	15,000.00
Deduct withholding tax at 15% (treaty rate)	−2,250.00
Net income after withholding tax	12,750.00
Deduct PHDIT at 20% (WT not offsettable)	−3,000.00
Net income after all taxes	**9,750.00**

For those position holders that are resident within the STO's country of residence, the net income to be credited to such position holders will normally, in the case of domestic income, be the result of the deduction of position holder's domestic income tax.
In a specific circumstance where, for example

- the STO is resident in the UK;
- the STO holds securities on behalf of a custody client that is also resident in the UK;
- the issuer is resident in the UK; and
- UK income tax is payable by the position holder.

The summarized view of all the components relating to the above mentioned example is shown in Table 25.9.

Table 25.9

	GBP
Gross dividend	15,000.00
Deduct PHDIT at 20%	–3,000.00
Net income after all taxes	**12,000.00**

25.6.2 Position Holders Resident Outside the STO's Country of Residence

From the STO's perspective, for those position holders that are resident outside the STO's country of residence, the net income to be credited to such position holders will normally be the result of the deduction of only foreign *withholding tax*.

In an example where the following circumstances apply (and due to these circumstances the deduction of UK income tax is not applicable), the summarized view of the applicable components is as shown in Table 25.10.

- the STO is resident in the UK;
- the STO holds securities on behalf of a custody client that is resident in Mexico;
- the issuer is resident in Germany;
- Mexico has no double taxation agreement with Germany (and therefore withholding tax is charged at the *non-treaty* rate).

Table 25.10

	EUR
Gross dividend	15,000.00
Deduct withholding tax at 20% (non-treaty rate)	–3,000.00
Net income after withholding tax	**12,000.00**

The above applies equally to the situation where the issuer's country of residence is the same as the STOs. For example:

- the STO is resident in the UK;
- the STO holds securities on behalf of a custody client that is resident in Mexico;
- the issuer is resident in the UK;
- Mexico has no double taxation agreement with the UK (and therefore withholding tax is charged at the non-treaty rate).

After the STO has credited the position holder with the net income, it is the responsibility of the position holder to declare the receipt of such income to its national tax authority (who may or may not state that the withholding tax is offsettable against the position holder's domestic income tax liability).

25.6.3 Calculation of Position Holder's Net Income

Typically, the Corporate Actions Department will maintain sets of rules that dictate how to arrive at the final net income to be disbursed to the position holder and whether to incorporate any of the tax (foreign withholding and/or domestic income tax) in that calculation.

This is because irrespective whether foreign withholding tax or domestic income tax has been calculated prior to this point, either of those tax amounts may not actually be deducted in order to derive the final net income amount. In some cases, where tax has been calculated but not actually deducted, this would simply be notified to the position holder as information for them to advise the tax authorities independently via the position holder's own tax returns.

The above mentioned rules include

- the type of position holder, i.e. *trading book* or *custody client*;
- domestic tax legislation in the country in which the STO operates;
- whether the income is being distributed in the form of cash or securities.

The method of final net income calculation will be a collaboration of these rules.

Type of Position Holder

In the case of trading books, while foreign withholding tax may have been withheld and in addition the STO will be required to pay domestic income tax on income earned, the net income actually credited to the P&L of the trading book may not take these tax amounts into account. It is a matter of company (STO) policy and accounting preferences as to whether these amounts of tax are accounted for separately or accounted for within the net credit to the trading book's P&L. The Corporate Actions Department will need to be aware of the requirements (which may differ between different trading books) in order to ensure that the resultant net entitlement credited to the trading book's P&L is correct.

In the case of custody clients, foreign withholding tax (where applicable) will be included as a deduction in the calculation of the net entitlement (as illustrated earlier in this chapter). The inclusion of any domestic income tax in the calculation of the custody client's net income will depend upon the domestic tax legislation in the country where the STO operates, as described below.

Domestic Tax Legislation in the Country where the STO Operates

As stated previously in this chapter, the deduction of domestic income tax from those clients resident within the STO's country of residence may be required according to the tax legislation of that country.

Accordingly in these cases the Corporate Actions Department must not only calculate, but also deduct this amount prior to any disbursement of income, and this will therefore be included in the calculation of the net income.

It is important to note that in a situation where the STO is not obliged to act as collector of taxes (due to domestic tax legislation), as a service to custody clients the STO may calculate domestic income tax on behalf of the position holder, even where the STO does not actually deduct that income tax, so that the client is aware of the domestic tax amount that it is required to pay to its own tax authority.

Cash Versus Security Income Entitlements

Whether the income is distributed in the form of cash or securities will greatly impact whether income tax is deducted prior to disbursement of the entitlement to the position holder.

Where the resultant entitlement is distributed as cash income, any or all of the tax amounts previously described could be applicable in the calculation of the net income (in consideration of the other factors described above).

Where the income is distributed in the form of securities, the way in which tax amounts are treated will largely depend upon the basis of the security entitlement calculation in the first instance. This would be via either a securities *ratio* or a *re-investment* price; see below.

Securities Ratio

Where the resultant income entitlement is in the form of securities, for which the calculation has been based purely upon a securities ratio and no equivalent income value is known, it will not be possible for the Corporate Actions Department to calculate income tax (or therefore, to incorporate such taxes into the calculation of the *resultant entitlement*). In such cases any applicable taxes will typically be calculated by the financial control department of the STO based upon subsequent research as to the tax implications of the event.

Re-Investment Price

Where a nominal cash value is attributed to the resultant securities entitlement, it is possible to calculate applicable tax amounts. The resultant security entitlement may be calculated based upon the

- *gross income* cash equivalent, excluding tax liabilities, or
- *net income* cash equivalent, including tax liabilities according to the previously described conventions.

Whether re-investment is based upon the gross income cash equivalent or the net income cash equivalent is normally dependent upon the domestic market regulations, and the specific event. Even where the re-investment is based upon the gross income cash equivalent, the Corporate Actions Department will normally calculate the tax amounts, and report the tax information to the position holder.

Whether income is re-invested on a gross or net basis will impact the resultant quantity of securities to be disbursed to the position holder, as illustrated below.

For example, the Australian brewing company Fosters announces a dividend re-investment plan giving shareholders the choice of electing

- cash income at a rate of AUD0.55 per share, or
- securities at a re-investment price of AUD2.25 per share.

Custody Client 'T' is the holder of 4,500,000 Fosters Group shares, which is represented in its entirety by a fully *settled custodian position*. This is represented in the Table 25.11.

Table 25.11

Fosters Group Shares			
Ownership			Location
Custody Client 'T'	+4,500,000	−4,500,000	Custodian M, Sydney
	+4,500,000	−4,500,000	

The custody client elects to receive securities, rather than cash.

Where the terms of the event stipulate that the dividend will be re-invested on a gross basis, the resultant number of shares that will be reinvested is calculated as follows:

1. Derive the gross cash income entitlement by multiplying the number of shares elected by the cash income rate:

$$4{,}500{,}000 \text{ shares} \times \text{AUD}0.55 \text{ per share} = \text{AUD } 2{,}475{,}000.00$$

2. Calculate position holder's domestic income tax at 20% on the gross income (on the basis that the custody client is resident in the same country as the issuer and the STO):

$$\text{AUD } 2{,}475{,}000.00 \times 20\% = \text{AUD } 495{,}000.00$$

3. Divide the gross cash income entitlement by the re-investment price:

$$\text{AUD } 2{,}475{,}000.00 \text{ divided by AUD}2.25 \text{ per share} = 1{,}100{,}000 \text{ shares.}$$

In this case the position holder will receive 1,100,000 shares as a result of re-investment. The position holder will also have a domestic income tax amount owing of AUD 495,000.00, which will either be collected separately by the STO, or charged by the tax authority via the position holder's end of year tax return.

Alternatively, where the terms of the event stipulate that the dividend will be re-invested on a net basis the resultant number of shares that will be reinvested is calculated as follows:

1. Derive the gross cash income entitlement by multiplying the number of shares elected by the cash income rate:

$$4{,}500{,}000 \text{ shares} \times \text{AUD}0.55 \text{ per share} = \text{AUD } 2{,}475{,}000.00$$

2. Calculate position holder's domestic income tax at 20% on the gross income (on the basis that the custody client is resident in the same country as the issuer and the STO):

$$\text{AUD } 2{,}475{,}000.00 \times 20\% = \text{AUD } 495{,}000.00$$

3. Calculate the net cash income entitlement by deducting the position holder's domestic income tax from the gross cash income:

$$\text{AUD } 2{,}475{,}000.00 - \text{AUD } 495{,}000.00 = \text{AUD } 1{,}980{,}000.00$$

4. Divide the net cash income entitlement by the re-investment price:

$$\text{AUD } 1{,}980{,}000.00 \text{ divided by AUD}2.25 \text{ per share} = 880{,}000 \text{ shares.}$$

In this case the position holder will receive 880,000 shares as a result of re-investment. This is less than received when re-investment was on a gross basis, but the position holder's same domestic income tax amount of AUD 495,000 has already been paid. As such the position holder would expect to have no further tax liability with respect to this income event.

25.7 DETERMINING TAX RATES FOR POSITION HOLDERS

To date, the types of tax that may be applicable to a position holder's resultant income entitlement have been described, including their treatment in the calculation of the net income entitlement to be collected and disbursed.

In the calculation of each of such taxes, it is first necessary to identify the applicable tax rate. This needs to be done for each resultant entitlement to be calculated. The decision points that determine

- the applicable tax type, and
- the rate of tax to be deducted

are illustrated in Figure 25.1.

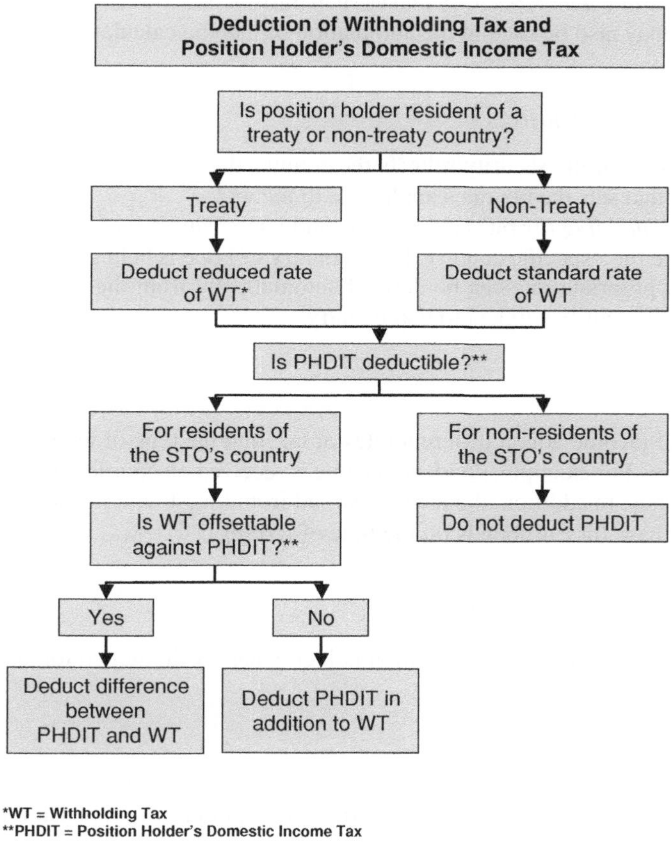

Figure 25.1 Tax decision points.

25.7.1 Position Holder and Security Tax Attributes

Given the various considerations described to date within this chapter, in order to derive the correct net income to be distributed to position holders, it is essential that accurate calculations of foreign withholding tax and domestic income tax take place. To achieve this, it is critical that the Corporate Actions Department identifies the correct tax rate(s) to be applied to each position holder.

The determination of the applicable type of tax and tax rate will normally depend upon a combination of the following position holder and security attributes:

- country of issue of the security;
- type of security;
- position holder's country of residence;
- tax status of the position holder.

These are described below. Note that in each case, holding the following information within the STO's central *static data* repository makes such information available to all within the STO that need it, and may also be used in the automation of income calculations.

Country of Issue of the Security

The country of issue of the security reflects the country that is the source of the income and the tax authority that sets the tax rates applicable to income.

The current *withholding tax* rates (both *treaty* and *non-treaty*) are typically recorded by the STO as applicable for a specific country. If the country of issue is held as part of the securities static data, the appropriate rate can be derived automatically from the single set of rates for that country for all securities linked to that country.

Type of Security

Different types of income attract different rates of tax, and the type of income earned reflects the type of security. For example, *dividend* income is received on equities, and *coupon* interest is received on bonds. In addition, the income earned from investment in some securities is tax exempt, as is the case for Eurobonds (at the time of writing).

Position Holder's Country of Residence

This is the country within which the position holder is legally domiciled for tax purposes.

Tax Status of the Position Holder

Different types of position holder are likely to attract different rates of income tax. For example, an individual may attract a different tax rate from a corporation or a pension fund, whereas charities are likely to be subject to zero-rate income tax.

In most cases, the designation of a tax status relating to a position holder is supported by the submission of official documentation with the tax authority or collector of tax, for example, a 'W8BEN', which is a US Tax form certifying the position holder's status as a non-resident of the US. Often, such documentation is required to be re-submitted periodically.

In order to calculate the tax liabilities of a specific position holder accurately, the STO would ideally record the tax status that the position holder has established with each country's tax authority. This approach requires detailed research and maintenance of the position holder's static data. A simpler alternative adopted by many STOs is to apply a single status such as individual, corporation, etc. to the position holder. This less detailed approach satisfies the correct calculation of tax liabilities in the majority of cases and is far easier to maintain.

25.7.2 Maintaining Tax Rate Information

In addition to the above attributes relating to position holders and securities, the STO will need to maintain records of the applicable tax rates for each combination of those attributes. For example, to support tax calculations on income for which Japan is the source country, it is necessary to record the tax rates applicable (and their effective date) to each type of security, within which will be recorded the tax rates for domestic and foreign position holders (according to country of residence), for each position holder tax status.

Figure 25.2 illustrates fictitious example withholding tax rates for equities and bonds by country of issuer, and the tax rates (based on treaty status) for investors resident in different countries.

Example Withholding Tax at Treaty and Non-Treaty Rates

		Country of Residence of Investor			
Country of Issuer	**Issue Type**	**Canada**	**Japan**	**UK**	**USA**
Country A	Equity	15%	20%	15%	20%
	Bond	10%	20%	10%	20%
Country B	Equity	15%	15%	10%	10%
	Bond	20%	20%	20%	20%
Country C	Equity	30%	30%	30%	30%
	Bond	30%	30%	30%	30%

Key: Double-taxation agreement (treaty) | No double-taxation agreement (non-treaty)

Figure 25.2 Example withholding tax rates.

The maintenance of such tax information is complex and requires a great deal of ongoing research and care to maintain accurately. Errors in these records will result in the incorrect calculation of tax liabilities of the STO itself, and its clients, which could result in financial loss and/or fines from tax authorities.

25.8 ENSURING CORRECT WITHHOLDING TAX IS DEDUCTED BY THE LOCATION

Where STOs hold securities for *custody clients* (as well as its own *proprietary* positions), it is essential that the correct rate of foreign *withholding tax* is deducted at source for all of its *position holders*. By ensuring that this is the case, the STO will receive the appropriate income amount from its *custodians*, and in turn credit the various position holders with the appropriate income amount. Failure in this regard may result in the STO crediting its position holders with the incorrect income amount, or incurring a loss (due to the difference between income received and paid).

The method by which STOs typically ensure that the correct rate of withholding tax is deducted at source, is by the STO maintaining a number of 'accounts' at the location, with each 'account' reflecting the collective tax situation of like position holders.

Under normal circumstances, in addition to the 'main' account (within which the STO's proprietary positions are held and over which the STO's purchases and sales will be settled), the STO will usually maintain the following safe custody accounts:

- one *treaty* custody account, representing the holdings of all custody clients who reside in countries for which a treaty is held with the *issuer's* country of residence, and
- one *non-treaty* custody account, representing the holdings of all custody clients who reside in countries for which a treaty is not held with the issuer's country of residence.

As indicated earlier, proof of residency will be required in order for a treaty rate to be applied to a custody client.

In maintaining separate accounts that reflect the tax situation of the position holders, it is essential that the STO ensures settlement of all trades is effected via the correct account. This requires that all securities purchased by custody clients must be delivered into and held within the appropriate safe custody account, and that all securities sold by custody clients must be delivered from the appropriate safe custody account. Failure to adhere to this procedure will result in mismatches between (incorrect) tax deducted by the location and the (correct) tax to be deducted by the STO from position holders.

Adherence to this procedure means that when income falls due, the correct amount of foreign withholding tax is deducted, for example:

- 15% (reduced rate) tax deducted from holdings within the treaty account, and
- 20% (standard rate) tax deducted from holdings within the non-treaty account.

The STO will in turn pass-on this to the position holders (after deduction of position holder's domestic income tax, where appropriate).

Figure 25.3 illustrates example internal records of the country of residence of various position holders, and the respective accounts at the custodian within which the clients' securities are held, according to treaty status.

25.9 THE STO AS COLLECTOR OF TAXES

As stated earlier in this chapter, in some countries the STO may be authorized (and in some cases obliged) to collect domestic income tax applicable to domestic residents, prior to the disbursement of the income payment.

For custody clients located overseas, the STO will ask such clients to complete a non-residency declaration form; should the client sign this declaration, the STO will not deduct domestic income tax on payment of income. Conversely, should the client fail to sign the form (for whatever reason), the STO may well be obliged by its tax authority to deduct domestic tax (as has been the case in the UK).

Where domestic tax is to be deducted, the Corporate Actions Department will calculate the domestic income tax liability taking into account the impact of any foreign *withholding tax* where appropriate, and deduct the domestic income tax from the payment to be disbursed to the position holder.

Ensuring Correct Withholding Tax is Deducted

STO's Safe Custody Books and Records
Sony Corp Shares

Safe Custody Clients	Country of Residence	Treaty Holdings	Non-Treaty Holdings
Client A	Hong Kong	5m	
Client B	Canada		6m
Client C	Sweden	14m	
Client D	New Zealand	1m	
Client E	France		4m
	totals	20m	10m

STO's Custodian
Sony Corp Shares

Treaty Account	Non-Treaty Account
20m	10m

Figure 25.3 Ensuring correct deduction of withholding tax.

Where domestic tax has been deducted, the STO will subsequently

- hold the domestic tax deducted within an internal account entitled 'Domestic Income Tax Payable' (or similar), pending payment to the tax authority;
- remit the tax deducted to the tax authority by the deadline stated by the tax authority, as part of a periodic tax return;
- provide each position holder with an income tax certificate (or statement) as proof to the tax authorities that the position holder has paid tax on the income earned.

25.10 TAX RECLAIMS AND TAX REBATES

Under some circumstances, the processing of an income event can result in the position holder paying an amount of tax, some or all of which is either

- reclaimable from the relevant tax authority, or
- rebateable against the position holder's annual tax liability.

25.10.1 Tax Reclaims

The process of recovering tax (whether foreign *withholding tax* or domestic income tax) by or on behalf of the position holder, from tax authorities to whom the tax has been paid, is known as tax reclaims.

Tax reclaim situations arise where the position holder has been overcharged tax due to (for example) the following:

- Foreign withholding tax was originally charged at a *non-treaty* rate, but the position holder is subsequently able to prove that it is resident in a *treaty* country.

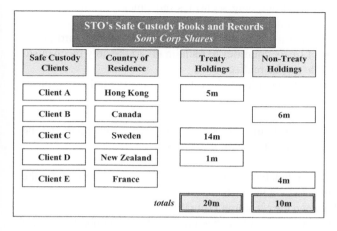

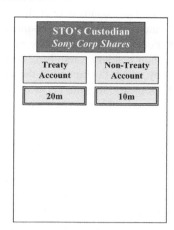

- Foreign withholding tax was originally charged at a non-treaty rate where the holder is known to be resident in a treaty country; this can occur where the STO has failed to operate adequate controls over the incoming and outgoing securities movements within its treaty and non-treaty sub-accounts at the custodian.
- Foreign withholding tax was charged at a single rate to all position holders regardless of their residency, requiring residents of treaty countries to reclaim tax as the only mechanism by which the benefit of the treaty rate can be realized.
- Domestic income tax was charged to the position holder, but the position holder is subsequently able to prove it is non-resident.

The cash amount that is reclaimable is normally 100% of the amount overcharged, and the calculation of an individual tax reclaim falls into one of two types:

- an explicit reclaim rate (if this is a predictable reclaim scenario such as occurs where the benefit of the treaty can only be realized via the reclaim of tax), or
- the calculation of the difference between the net amount actually received (where an incorrect rate is used) versus the net amount which would have been received (based upon the correct rate).

Reclaims are made direct to the tax authority to which the tax was originally paid, and requires the completion (by the claimant or its agent) of the tax authority's specific tax reclaim documentation, which may include declarations and proof as to the position holder's residency and status. The tax reclaim process is notoriously manually intensive and time consuming, whichever countries are involved.

The successful reclaim of tax from a tax authority can take an inordinate length of time, as long as months or even years in some cases. For this reason, whether for a *trading book* or *custody client*, many STOs will have a minimum value threshold, under which they choose not to initiate a reclaim, as the time and effort involved can outweigh the reclaimed tax amount eventually received. An STO therefore may choose to reimburse a position holder (whether trading book or safe custody client), without reclaiming the tax from the tax authority; under these circumstances the STO will *write-off* the relevant reclaim amount.

Where the amount of the reclaim exceeds the write-off threshold the STO will initiate the reclaim either direct with the tax authorities or via the STO's custodian. Many custodians provide a tax reclaim service to their participants, although others may not.

Where a reclaim is required on behalf of a trading book, the STO (via the Corporate Actions Department) will initiate the reclaim.

Alternatively, where a reclaim is required for a custody client, whether the STO initiates the claim on the custody client's behalf or not will depend upon the service level agreement between them. Many STOs are not eager to offer a tax reclaim service because of the typical time and effort involved in reaching resolution of a reclaim. Clearly, the STO will want to avoid paying a custody client the tax reclaim until the reclaim is received from the tax authority. From the STO's perspective, the preference is for the client to effect the reclaim itself, but under these circumstances the STO will usually provide the client with the necessary information to effect a successful reclaim. However, should the STO's error be the cause of over-taxation of a custody client, the STO is highly likely to manage the reclaim itself.

As reclaims from the tax authority are very likely to be settled later than the *resultant entitlement*, the STO must be prepared to monitor outstanding reclaims until settlement occurs.

25.10.2 Rebateable Tax

As introduced in the previous chapter, the *issuer* may pre-pay tax and reduce the actual income rate (i.e. cash rate per share) of the income distributed. The term 'pre-pay' refers to the issuer's decision to deduct a certain rate of tax from the dividend due, and to pay to the shareholders the resultant net dividend. An example is illustrated in Table 25.12.

Table 25.12

Gross dividend per share	0.10
Deduct domestic tax at 20%	0.02
Net rate per share declared (after domestic tax deducted)	**0.08**

It is important to note that the rate per share declared by the issuer is the net rate following deduction of domestic tax.

From the position holder's perspective, the income receivable from the issuer following the deduction of domestic tax is potentially subject to a further deduction of domestic tax, according to legislation within the position holder's country of residence. Consequently, for the sake of clarity, the net amount receivable after deduction of domestic tax by the issuer will be referred to as the 'provisional net rate'.

This is known in some markets as *franking*, and may apply to part or all of the income payment. The amount of tax pre-paid by the issuer is reflected as an allowable rebate of tax to the position holder against its own annual domestic tax liabilities (rather than on an individual dividend payment basis). This is known as a tax credit, imputed credit or franking credit (according to local terminology).

The tax credit may only in part offset the position holder's annual domestic tax liability, or alternatively it may exceed the position holder's annual domestic tax liability. In some countries, the excess tax credit may be offsettable against future income tax liabilities.

In most cases tax credits may only be used by residents of that country, i.e. the same country as that of the issuer, where the tax has been pre-paid. Foreign position holders will not gain any benefit from franking or tax credits, as they have no domestic tax liability in the country where the tax was pre-paid.

In distributing income payments to position holders where tax has been pre-paid, issuers are making their own securities more attractive for investment.

Where domestic tax is pre-paid by the issuer, the position holder must still declare the income received as if tax had not been pre-paid. In order to calculate the domestic tax liability to the position holder, it will be necessary to gross-up the income entitlement either collected or disbursed.

The difference between the grossed up income and the income actually distributed by the issuer reflects the total amount of tax pre-paid by the issuer.

It is important to note that the calculation of the grossed-up income is purely an interim calculation, to facilitate the calculation by the position holder of its annual domestic tax position, and the tax credit to which it is entitled, and in addition any position holder's domestic income tax that the STO may be required to calculate and deduct as a collector of domestic income tax. Any resultant entitlements collected or disbursed will use the gross income amount (as described earlier in this chapter). How such calculations and amounts come together in order to derive the net entitlement will be illustrated towards the end of this chapter.

The event terms will indicate the portion of income on which tax has been pre-paid, and the tax year to which it refers. Domestic tax regulations will stipulate the rate at which tax is pre-paid according to the tax year to which the income refers, as the rate of tax that the issuer may pre-pay can differ according to the tax year in which the issuer earned the profits.

Using the event terms, the Corporate Actions Department will calculate the

- grossed-up income;
- tax credit;
- position holders domestic income tax.

Grossed-Up Income

The grossed-up income is derived from taking the provisional net entitlement (calculated based upon the net dividend rate) and converting it into a pre-taxed amount, using the issuer's corporate tax rate.

For example, assume a dividend of AUD 2,000.00, where the dividend was fully franked and paid out at AUD0.20 per share, and the issuer pre-paid tax prior to distribution of the dividend at a rate of 31%.

Calculating the grossed-up income:

$$\text{divide the provisional net entitlement by } (1 - \text{pre paid tax rate}), 2{,}000.00/(1 - 31\%)$$

which produces a grossed-up income amount of AUD 2,898.55.

Tax Credit

The tax credit represents the amount of tax pre-paid by the issuer, and is derived by deducting the provisional net income from the grossed-up income

Calculating the tax credit:

$$\text{Subtract the provisional net entitlement from the grossed-up income, } 2{,}898.55 - 2{,}000.00$$

which produces a tax credit of AUD 898.55.

Position Holders Domestic Income Tax

The calculation of the amount of domestic tax payable by the position holder will be as described earlier in this section, but where tax has been pre-paid by the issuer the calculation will be based upon the grossed-up income, not the provisional net entitlement.

25.11 COMMUNICATING INCOME AND TAX DETAILS

Generically, the communication of the *resultant entitlement* to the *position holder* will advise the quantity of securities and/or cash that it is to receive as a result of the corporate action event (in addition to event terms information), as described in Chapter 10, 'Communication of Event Information'.

As with other corporate action events, the STO will communicate the resultant entitlement to the position holder, but will in addition include details of any further amounts and any tax amounts that have been deducted in order to arrive at the final net income entitlement (as described earlier in this chapter). Such amounts are

- the gross income amount;
- any foreign withholding tax deducted;

- any domestic income tax deducted;
- the final net income amount, which will reflect the resultant income entitlement to be disbursed to the position holder.

Note that where both foreign *withholding tax* and position holder's domestic income tax are deducted, the STO may also include in the communication an amount that shows the net entitlement after the deduction of foreign withholding tax and prior to the deduction of position holder's domestic income tax.

In addition to the above, depending on the applicability to the resultant income entitlement in question, the communication may also include details of

- taxes to be reclaimed;
- grossed-up income;
- tax rebates (tax credits).

The primary purpose of communicating the above details, beyond just the amount of the resultant entitlement, is to provide the position holder with the information that it is in turn required (according to tax legislation) to communicate to its tax authority at the end of the year. This is no different than an employer providing an employee with a statement of gross income earned, tax paid, and net income earned, together with any other amounts that may affect his or her end of year tax calculations.

The exact format of, and details to be included in, this communication to the position holder, will differ in each country in which the STO may operate, according to the regulations of that country's tax authority. Possibilities include any, or combinations of, the following:

- A *resultant entitlement* notice similar to that issued for any other type of event issued by the STO, but including the additional required amounts (as listed above) for each income entitlement.
- An income and tax notice (often known as a *tax voucher*) that details the gross income earned and taxes deducted for a specific income entitlement. The format and content is regulated by the tax authority and is standardized and to be used by all STOs (and other organizations) operating within that country. Therefore, this notice differs to the STO's own resultant entitlement notice. In some cases, the tax authority may even supply the physical forms for the STO to complete and provide to the position holder.
- A single statement at tax year-end of all income earned and tax deducted, the format and content of which is regulated by the tax authority. Year-end statements are common in many European countries, for example in Germany.
- A separate notice that details the tax rebate or tax credit to which the position holder is entitled, and the calculations supporting this amount. Again, typically the format and content of this type of notice will be regulated by the tax authority, and it may supply physical forms for completion.

As stated previously the STO may issue combinations of the above, according to the *SLA* with the position holder and the applicable tax regulations. For example, the STO may choose to issue its own entitlement notice that includes the tax details (as described in the first bullet point above) even though it may not meet the criteria of the tax authority. This may be because the STO's own notice provides additional account and entitlement information to the position holder such as settlement information. If such a notice does not meet the criteria of the tax authority, the STO will be required also to issue a tax authority approved notice such as a tax voucher.

It is of vital importance that communications to position holders, which are required to support the position holder's end of year tax return, comply with the regulations of the applicable tax authority in both content and format. In the majority of cases the communication will be in paper form, and may include the generation of multiple copies, in order that the position holder may pass a copy to the tax authority and retain a copy themselves. As stated above, in some cases the tax authority may provide to the STO the physical forms for completion.

Figure 25.4 is an illustrative example (it is not intended to represent an approved content and format by any tax authority) of the information that is typically required on a tax certificate produced by the STO.

Certificate number:

XYZ Investment Bank

Overseas Securities Income Tax Certificate

Name of Beneficiaries ***Date***

We hereby certify that the dividend stated below has had domestic income tax deducted by us which has been or will be paid to the domestic tax authorities. The net amount due has been credited to the beneficiary stated above.

Gross Amount	Withholding Tax deducted at source Rate: 15%	Domestic Tax deducted by us Rate: 5%	Net Amount
EUR 15,000.00	*EUR 2,250.00*	*EUR 750.00*	*EUR 12,000.00*

Entitlement	Security Description	Payment Date	Dividend Rate
10,000	*XXX Group EUR1.00 Shares*	*15th March 2010*	*EUR 1.50*

for XYZ Investment Bank

XYZ Investment Bank
Registered Office Address
Telephone Number

Authorized Signatory

Figure 25.4 Example tax certificate.

Even where an STO has not acted in the capacity of collector of a position holder's domestic income tax, in some countries the STO is required to communicate the details of income earned and tax deducted (regardless who has deducted it) for position holders that are resident in the same country as the STO, directly to that country's tax authority. This requirement is in addition to the communication of income and tax details to the position holder. Typically this communication would occur yearly or based upon a regular schedule (perhaps monthly) as specified by the tax authority. The communication would take the form of either a paper based or electronic report, the content and format of which will be stipulated by the tax authority. The purpose of the report is to cross reference and validate the information declared by position holders via their year end tax returns.

25.12 SUMMARY

The accurate and timely management of income tax are essential elements in a well-controlled Corporate Actions Department (income processing area). Understanding of the operational processes that result in the appropriate rates of tax being deducted from position holders is paramount. Such processes include:

- the holding of treaty and non-treaty securities accounts at custodians;
- awareness of the current rates of withholding tax deductible at source;
- awareness of the current rates of tax deductible domestically;
- awareness of taxes deducted but which are subject to reclaim.

Furthermore, the STO must ensure that any taxes it deducts from position holders are securely segregated, pending payment to the tax authorities.

ENDNOTE: within this chapter, certain figures, tables and text have been reproduced with permission from *Securities Operations: A Guide to Trade and Position Management*, ISBN 0-471-49758-4, author Michael Simmons, publisher John Wiley & Sons, Ltd.

Part VI

Issuer Notices

26 Concepts and Management of Issuer Notices

26.1 INTRODUCTION

Thus far the conditions, lifecycles and management of events that result in direct changes to the security and/or cash positions of the *position holder* have been described. There exists a further set of events that are, in addition to those that impact security and/or cash positions, managed by the Corporate Actions Department.

These events will be collectively described as *issuer notices*.

The primary purpose of these events is to disseminate information from the *issuer*, regarding the activities of the company and its officers, to position holders. In many cases the information will be required from a statutory perspective to be advised to the shareholders. On occasions, the purpose of issuer notices is to notify position holders of issuer meetings and in addition request the ratification of corporate decisions from position holders via the motions and resolutions of the issuer meeting. In response to the notification of a company meeting, the position holder may choose to issue a proxy vote to allow holders to vote on the issues without attending the meeting in person.

The most significant difference between issuer notices and those events described and illustrated to date throughout this book is that issuer notices do not directly impact the security and/or cash position of the position holder. As a consequence of this the lifecycle of an issuer notice event contains far fewer steps than have previously been described. Steps that relate specifically to the impact upon a security and/or cash position of a position holder such as 'calculation of resultant entitlement' and 'management of election decisions' are not required to support the lifecycle of an issuer notice event.

For the purposes of management, from the Corporate Action Department's perspective, issuer notices may fall into one of two types:

- Information Only, where information only is disseminated to position holders, requiring no response, and
- Issuer Meetings with Proxy Voting, which include the collection of proxy votes from position holders and the subsequent issue of proxy votes to the issuer (or its agent).

The management of these two types of issuer notice events is described in this chapter.

26.2 THE STO'S RISK

As a direct consequence of no resulting changes to the security and/or cash positions of positions holders, issuer notices generally pose far less of a risk of direct financial loss to the STO. The requirement to service position holders is a fairly simple one, requiring dissemination of information only; although for those events where *proxy voting* is involved, the

STO additionally must ensure accuracy in the collection and collation of proxy votes and the subsequent issue of votes to the issuer (or its agent).

Irrespective of the lack of risk of any direct financial loss, as with any other service provided by the STO to its clients, there is always the risk of damage to professional reputation when errors occur. This is also the case with the management of these events.

26.3 INFORMATION ONLY EVENTS

The most distinguishing feature of this event is that it requires a simple one way communication from the STO to its positions holders only. The lifecycle of an information only event may therefore be illustrated as shown in Figure 26.1.

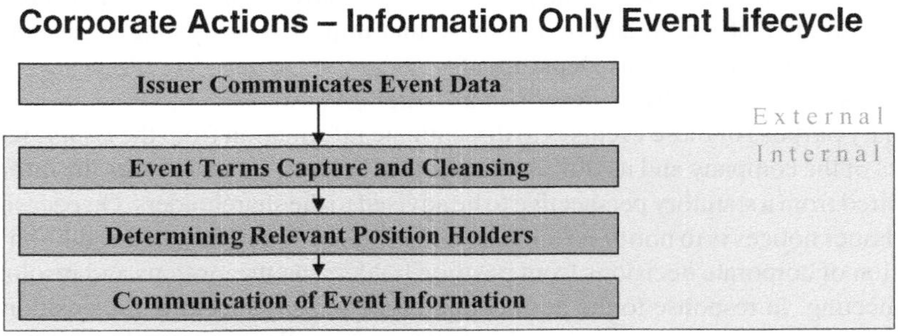

Figure 26.1 Information only event lifecycle.

26.3.1 Event Terms Capture and Cleansing

As described in Chapter 2, 'Event Description and Classification', information only events inform position holders of, for example:

- extension to the *maturity date* of a bond;
- advice of a bond in default of its *coupon* payment;
- adjustment of a bond coupon rate (this usually has previously required the approval of bond holders and is often referred to as a remarketing agreement);
- a change in the identification of a security, e.g. name change or change in *ISIN* code;
- a change in the *lot* size of a security;
- changes to the trading status of a security, e.g. suspension or delisting;
- bankruptcy or impending legal action against the issuer;
- change to the company's place of incorporation.

According to the purpose of the issuer notice, the content of the event announcement will differ. This can be illustrated via two of the above purposes.

Extension to the Maturity Date of a Bond

The event terms typically include

- the *announcement date*;
- the description of the security (in this case the bond) to which the announcement applies, including an identifier such as ISIN code;

- the reason for the announcement, in this case 'extension of maturity';
- the new maturity date.

Changes to the Trading Status of a Security – Security Active Announcement

The event terms typically include

- the announcement date;
- the description of the security to which the announcement applies, including an identifier such as ISIN code;
- the reason for the announcement, in this case to inform that the security will be re-activated;
- the re-activation date.

26.3.2 Determining Relevant Position Holders

With any corporate action event, the Corporate Actions Department must determine to which position holders the event is relevant (as described in Chapter 9, 'Determining Entitlement'). This step is equally applicable to information only events, despite the fact that the outcome will not produce any resultant entitlements of securities and/or cash to the position holder.

In the case of information only events, it is necessary for the Corporate Actions Department to determine relevant position holders in order to ensure that the issuer notice is communicated to those position holders.

Unlike other corporate action events, information only events do not contain any specific dates (such as record date) that determine the relevant position holders. Typically, the Corporate Actions Department will identify the position holders to communicate with as at the date of the event announcement.

26.3.3 Communication of Event Information

Communication to *position holders* with respect to information only events is generally very simple, as reflected in the nature of the event. The STO will issue only a single communication to the position holder in order to pass-on the information announced by the *issuer*. Communications would not occur against unsettled trades (unlike other events) as no requirement exists to claim resultant entitlements.

Typically the single communication will be issued to the position holder only, once the event terms are received and cleansed. The communication is the equivalent of the Event Terms Announcement referred to in Chapter 10, 'Communication of Event Information'. This communication will contain the text of the issuer's announcement, but will not normally make reference to the quantity of the position holder's holding, or resultant entitlement terms, as they are not applicable.

26.4 ISSUER MEETINGS WITH PROXY VOTING EVENTS

In the case of these events the issuer will advise *position holders* of an issuer meeting at which the position holder is able to vote with respect to various motions and resolutions proposed for the meeting.

Such resolutions could include the

- election of company directors;
- adoption of financial statements;
- sale of capital;
- distribution of income.

The company meeting will be either the Annual General Meeting (AGM) or an Extraordinary General Meeting (EGM).

Where a position holder is entitled to vote with respect to such motions and resolutions, but is unable to attend the company meeting, it is able to

- communicate its voting intentions prior to the meeting to the issuer or its agent, (effectively an absentee vote), or
- instruct and nominate a third party to execute its vote on its behalf.

Where the position holder nominates a third party to execute its vote on its behalf, this is known as proxy voting. The remainder of this section will describe specifically the STO's management of proxy voting on behalf of its position holders.

Where the STO is managing positions, either its own *trading book* positions or *custody client* positions, the STO may issue to the issuer (or its agent) a *proxy vote* reflecting the vote of the position holder.

Voting on motions 'for' the proposal(s) is not compulsory and is entirely at the discretion of the position holder.

The extent to which the management of proxy votes is supported will depend upon the level of service that the STO wishes to offer its positions holders, particularly custody clients. The STO may choose to disseminate the information only to its position holders, and not to manage voting.

The lifecycle of an issuer meeting with proxy voting event may be illustrated as shown in Figure 26.2.

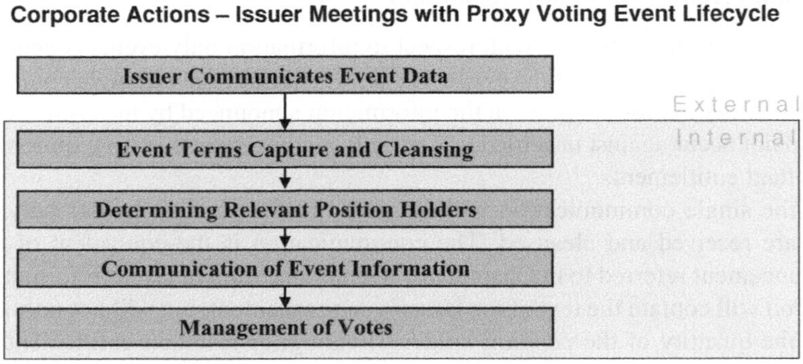

Figure 26.2 Issuer meetings with proxy voting event lifecycle.

26.4.1 Event Terms Capture and Cleansing

The significant inclusions in the event terms will be

- the *announcement date* of the event;
- the date and location of the issuer meeting;

- the type of issuer meeting, i.e. AGM or EGM;
- the full details of the motions and resolutions on which position holders may vote;
- any restrictions in the eligibility to vote;
- the deadline for proxy votes;
- the details of the issuer's agent (where applicable) for the receipt of proxy votes.

26.4.2 Determination of Relevant Position Holders

The determination of relevant position holders that are entitled to vote at issuer meetings is similar to that described in the previous section with respect to information only events, with a few notable exceptions.

The Corporate Actions Department will initially identify position holders upon the announcement date of the event. Relevant position holders will then continually be identified until the deadline for voting in order to ensure that all new position holders between the announcement date and the voting deadline are given an opportunity to vote.

In some cases the issuer may have set restrictions on voting eligibility. Such restrictions could include:

- setting a minimum position holding quantity to discourage militant position holders who purchase a single share purely in order to 'buy' a vote, and gain a voice at the company meetings, or
- restrictions upon overseas position holders, where only position holders resident in the country of the issuer are permitted to vote. This may occur where general restrictions to the extent of foreign ownership exist according to government legislation, for example as is common in media companies.

Where any restrictions exist as to the eligibility to vote, the Corporate Actions Department must ensure that these restrictions are applied within this step and that such positions are not included in the event processing.

26.4.3 Communication of Event Information

In addition to the features applicable to communications relating to information only events, where the issuer notice includes voting, and the STO is offering proxy voting to its position holders, then the communication to position holders will also include:

- the date and type of the applicable issuer meeting;
- details of motions and resolutions to be voted upon;
- deadlines for the receipt of the position holders voting decision by the STO.

Depending upon the service level offered, the STO may issue communications to the position holder to chase where voting decisions are not received, and as an acknowledgement to the position holder when voting decisions are received.

26.4.4 Management of Proxy Voting

The management of proxy voting by the STO on behalf of position holders is in some respects similar to the management of election decisions applicable to events with elections, as described in Chapter 17, 'Management of Mandatory with Options Events'.

The Corporate Actions Department must

- receive and record the proxy voting decision from position holders, and
- issue equivalent proxy voting decisions to the issuer (or its agent).

As previously described, the issuer meeting may contain a number of different resolutions that the position holder may vote 'for' or 'against'. In the recording of the proxy voting decisions from position holders, the Corporate Actions Department must ensure that it records the position holder's specific wishes accurately with respect to each resolution. In addition, it may be necessary to record the quantity of the holding to which the voting decision applies as this may be required when the proxy votes are submitted at the company meeting. As with any other instruction received from a position holder, the Corporate Actions Department will validate the information contained, in this case that the position holder is entitled to vote, and that the motions and resolutions are correct for the meeting in question.

The following example illustrates the scenario where Company X announces its AGM and the resolutions to be voted on, whereby the position holder may vote:

- Yes, in favour of all resolutions, or
- No, against all resolutions.

The STO is holding positions on behalf of three custody clients in company X, and will record the voting decisions of each client with respect to its holding as the decisions are received (Table 26.1).

Table 26.1

Proxy Vote Control				
Position Holder	Date Election Decision Received	Elected Holding Quantity	Yes	No
Custody Client 'T'	3rd July	80,000	✓	
Custody Client 'U'	5th July	50,000	✓	
Custody Client 'V'	6th July	20,000		✓
		total	**130,000**	**20,000**

Where a proxy voting decision has not been received from the position holder by the internal deadline, the STO's decision as to whether to manage overdue proxy votes will normally be a matter of policy and the *SLA* with the specific position holder. In general, this process is not seen as a priority by the STO as these events do not carry a direct risk of financial impact to either the position holder or the STO.

Once the STO's internal deadline has passed, and prior to the issuer's (or its agent's) deadline, the Corporate Actions Department will collate the voting decisions received from position holders and issue the equivalent voting decisions to the issuer (or its agent). The proxy voting decision issued will reflect each of the voting decisions made by the position holders in respect of the sum total of their holdings.

Table 26.2 reveals the totals per proxy voting option (as a result of voting decisions taken by the various position holders) that will be issued by the STO to the location in the form of proxy votes.

Table 26.2

Summary of Election Decisions			
Ownership		Location	
'Yes' option	130,000	130,000	Custodian G, London
'No' option	20,000	20,000	Custodian G, London
	150,000	150,000	

Note that in practice the proxy voting options offered to position holders may be far more extensive than those shown in Table 26.2. The position holder may, in addition to the voting options illustrated, also be permitted to vote 'for' or 'against' individual resolutions.

Even though the above does not result in changes to any security and/or cash positions, as a matter of good practice the Corporate Actions Department should also ensure that the voting decisions received from position holders are accurately reflected in the issue of voting decisions to the issuer (or its agent), in order to protect the wishes of its position holders.

26.5 SUMMARY

The lifecycle of issuer notices is significantly simpler than that of other events that result in changes to the securities and/or cash position of position holders. Nonetheless, the information pertaining to such announced events may impact position holder investment decisions, and may also require position holder ratification on some occasions.

Therefore, it is vital that the Corporate Actions Department ensures accuracy and timeliness in the communication of information to position holders as a result of such event announcements.

Part VII

Objectives and Initiatives

27

Objectives and Initiatives

The previous chapters in this book are intended to set the scene for the fundamental corporate action aspects of the securities industry. The intention of this chapter is for the reader to become aware of the objectives and initiatives currently shaping the industry's corporate action characteristics.

27.1 INTRODUCTION

As will be apparent from having read all the previous chapters, the subject of corporate actions (including income and tax processing), comprises a logical series of steps. These processes may not be considered tremendously complex or intellectually challenging, however, the Corporate Actions Department must operate in a highly structured and disciplined manner in order to process its work in a timely fashion, while minimizing the array of risks involved.

A number of steps in the process involve external parties, upon whom the STO is extremely reliant, including:

- *issuers*
- *CSDs* and *custodians*
- *data vendors*
- *S.W.I.F.T.*

Historically, each aspect of the industry has evolved (according to the circumstances at the time) to be the most expedient way forward, and unsurprisingly this has not always equated to having a common set of standards that suit all interested parties regionally or globally. Such differing standards adopted by many countries and regions leads to difficulties in communication and understanding, frequently requiring corporate action events to be handled in a piecemeal manner while being heavily reliant upon manual (rather than automated) processes and procedures.

The above mentioned situation is well recognized throughout the industry, and consequently a number of objectives are being set and initiatives are being actioned (at the time of writing) in order to rectify such deficiencies and to achieve a much higher level of *STP* within the world of corporate actions.

This chapter describes some of the specific objectives, and the initiatives designed to meet those objectives that are underway.

27.2 OBJECTIVES

Over recent years industry practitioners have focused on many areas of securities operations with a view to development and improvement. Such focus has resulted in advancements within securities markets in the areas of both trading and settlement.

At the time of writing (early in 2005), industry practitioners have set the following objectives, with respect to corporate actions:

- Harmonization of international corporate action processing standards; due to the ways in which the corporate actions market place has evolved, there remains a clear need to create a situation where areas such as communication methods, message formats and event timetables are being operated to agreed global standards. In parallel with the trade lifecycle, the coordination of global standards in the corporate actions environment will prove beneficial to all parties concerned, enabling event processing to be conducted in a predictable, timely and as risk-free a manner as possible.
- The achievement of STP, both internally within individual organizations and in the market place as a whole; meeting this objective will prove beneficial in terms of speed and efficiency of processing, as the intention is that corporate action events will be automated completely from the beginning to the end of the process. Even for those individual aspects of an event that cannot be processed on an STP basis (e.g. because the specific client's address details are missing and therefore the Event Terms Announcement cannot be issued automatically), in a highly automated environment such 'exceptions' can be identified automatically and forwarded to the desktop of the appropriate individual responsible for resolution. Operating in such a manner provides real control over the processing and management of corporate action events.
- Minimizing operational costs, relating specifically to high resource outlay incurred as a result of manually intensive operations; the average Corporate Actions Department has historically had a high number of people, and little in the way of automation. Such a situation has been inevitable as, until quite recently, corporate actions systems containing the necessary event functionality at an acceptable cost were few and far between. Therefore, with a high degree of human involvement in corporate action event processing, it is unsurprising that the costs are considered to be quite high.
- Minimizing the risk of error; in some part due to the manual nature of the work within Corporate Actions Departments, many firms (not just STOs) have suffered occasional losses, some of which have been greater than USD 100,000.00. Errors can arise in a variety of ways, and where the error results in a loss to the *position holder*, the STO may well feel obliged to reimburse the position holder (at the STO's expense). For example, losses can arise due to
  - incorrect calculation of entitlement;
  - failure to advise *custody clients* of their right to subscribe to a *rights issue*;
  - incorrect instructions to a *custodian* regarding the take-up quantity of an event with elections;
  - failure to advise clients of their right to convert a *convertible bond*;
  - incorrect calculation of *income* tax.
- Provision of top-quality service to position holders. In the highly competitive market place that is the securities industry today, STOs can win or lose clients by the quality of services offered, and the day-to-day reality of such services. Where the STO offers safe custody services to its clients, the corporate action events that inevitably fall due on custody clients' holdings provide the STO with the opportunity to maintain or even enhance its service quality. For example:
  - the STO may utilize the services of *data vendors* in order to be advised of corporate action events, and as such improve the quality of the content of communications to its clients;

– an STO may not be a *S.W.I.F.T.* subscriber historically, and may be capable of issuing communications to clients (e.g. Final Entitlement Notice) only by telex or fax, whereas the STO has an opportunity to provide timely, automated and structured messages to clients by choosing to subscribe to S.W.I.F.T.

27.3 INITIATIVES TO ACHIEVE THE STATED OBJECTIVES

Achieving any or all of the objectives stated above is very unlikely to be achieved through a single project as the scope is so vast; consequently a number of initiatives are underway or are intended to be progressed in the near future that are designed to advance matters nearer to the desired state.

Implementation of some initiatives are completely within the control of the STO and can therefore be considered as internal projects, while others require the interaction of the market at large and should be regarded as external.

27.3.1 Internal Initiatives

Any desired change to the STO's own corporate actions environment is highly likely to be managed within the boundaries of an official project, requiring a project sponsor, budgetary approval, and expertise in the fields of business, IT and project management. The project would usually be required to operate to an agreed plan, and to remain within the agreed budget and to be completed by the agreed deadlines.

In developing plans for such a project, consideration must also be given as to whether changes

- are required to existing software solutions;
- will involve external software vendors;
- are required to current operational practices only (i.e. without major software changes);
- will impact only the Corporate Actions Department;
- will involve other departments within the STO;
- may be undertaken in conjunction with the implementation of an external initiative (e.g. the upgrade of communications internally may be accomplished in conjunction with the external introduction of new messaging standards).

Several typical internal initiatives that are being undertaken within many STOs will now be described.

Automating the Corporate Actions Lifecycle

This initiative involves automation of any or all or the lifecycle steps described in this book, with a view to reductions in manual processing costs and risks associated with manual processing, together with STP where appropriate.

Certain benefits in the automation of a selection of lifecycle steps (as per the generic lifecycle diagram, see Figure 27.1, used as a roadmap for mandatory events at the beginning of Chapters 6–14) are described below.

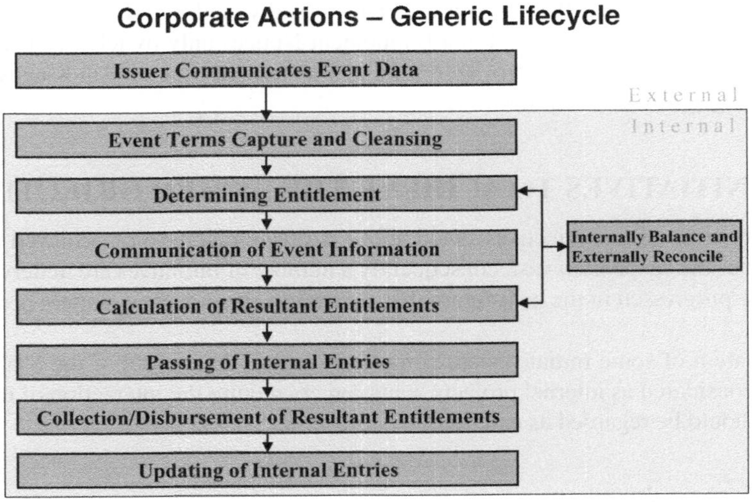

Figure 27.1 Generic (mandatory event) lifecycle.

Event Terms Capture and Cleansing

Historically and currently, the receipt of event details requires the creation of an internal record, whether in manual or automated form. In many cases, the creation of the event record would have followed manual input of event details, with the inherent risk of keying errors. Such risks can be overcome if the event details are supplied to the STO electronically.

The accuracy of event information from different sources has also been questionable historically, therefore many STOs have, in recent years, sought the services of *data vendors* to supply information that

- lists the event details received from two or more sources (where the details differ), or
- proposes 'blended' event details following the comparison of data from two or more sources.

Event data that have proven to be insufficiently reliable cause (for example) *resultant entitlements* to be calculated using erroneous dates, and subsequent cash dividend calculations to be incorrect.

As a result, the automation of the receipt of the incoming event announcement in order to improve quality and timeliness of event data is now an initiative and focus of many STOs, with the aim of ensuring that the starting point of processing is using the most accurate data available.

Determining Entitlement

An essential action within the determination of entitlement step is that of reconciliation of internally held *settled custodian positions* to *custodian's* records, as at the *record date*. This is essential as it is the custodian's record date quantity that will form the basis for calculation and collection of resultant entitlement by the STO.

A number of aspects of determining entitlement are candidates for automation. For example: automation of both the receipt of custodian's record date information and the reconciliation of that information against internal records will enable the Corporate Actions Department to focus its efforts only on non-reconciling items (rather than having to reconcile all internal custodian positions manually).

Communication of Event Information

Historically, within many STOs the communication of event information to *position holders* has involved a mixture of manual communication methods according to the limitations of the STOs systems, the available external communications media, and the preferred method of receipt by the position holder.

The initiatives that the STO would wish to put in place in this regard, relate to the

- automation of outgoing communication to position holders, and
- *election decision* response monitoring and reminder generation.

Such initiatives require the STO's own systems to be capable of merging entitlement calculations with client address information and their communication media preferences, use of standardized external communication methods, and the ability to register responses and, in the case of mandatory with options and voluntary events, to alert the user where response deadlines have been reached without having received a response from the position holder.

In an attempt to achieve automation, the STO could take a number of different approaches, such as the automation of

- a specific step that applies across all lifecycles, for example communication of event information (as described above), which gives benefit to all event types, or
- automation from the beginning to the end of a specific lifecycle (for example, mandatory events), which would also include the calculation of resultant entitlements, passing of internal entries, collection/disbursement of resultant entitlements and updating of internal entries. This approach enables the Corporate Action Department's personnel to focus on the more complex events, which legitimately require a greater degree of manual management.

The approach that best suits each STO will be that which provides the maximum benefit versus the cost of automation.

Centralized Processing

Whereas some STOs have operational responsibility only for their own business, within other STOs securities trading can be executed via multiple legal entities that are based in a number of different locations.

In some cases, the concept of 'centralized processing' or of the 'processing hub' is used, typically meaning that a regional centre is responsible for operational activities not only of business executed by its 'home' entity, but also for all (or a number of) the entities located elsewhere. Such an arrangement is illustrated in Figure 27.2.

This arrangement is typically employed for reasons of economies of scale, meaning that there is a concentration of staff within the hub that are responsible for the processing and management of operational activities of a number of entities. The reduction in operations staff in each originating entity provides the STO's group with benefits in terms of staffing costs,

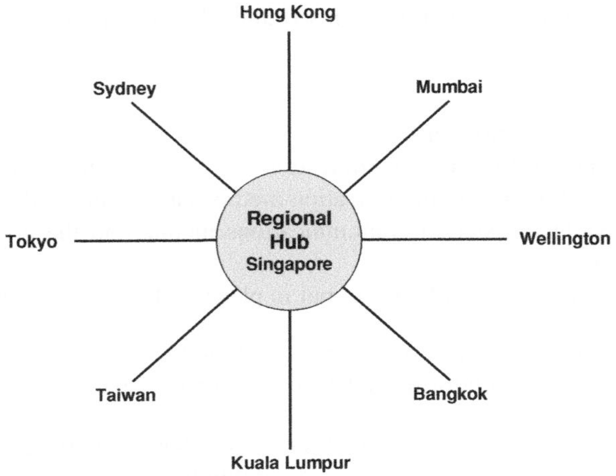

Figure 27.2 Centralized processing concept.

potentially system costs, and in concept is applicable as much to corporate actions as it is to the trade lifecycle.

Linking Books and Records

Historically, typically due to systems limitations, the STO's settlement system has been developed in a manner that creates no direct linkage between the settlement status of a trade and the *position holder* of that same trade.

This lack of system functionality has meant that (for example, in the case of a partially failing trade), there is no obvious mechanism to relate the fail to the position holder. Then, when a corporate action event falls due and the trade is still partially failing as at the *record date*, a *claim* situation (relating to the partial fail) may result in an inability to identify the position holder. This can create a risk to the STO where the position holder's account is operated on an *actual settlement* basis.

Therefore, if the STO's trading and settlement records can be maintained with a link between position holders and the location, the benefits to the STO can include the management of exposure in the settlement of *resultant entitlements* (refer to Chapter 13), and accurate management of tax liabilities between position holders and *locations* (refer to Chapter 24).

Regular Reconciliation of Books and Records

Operating accurate and reconciled *books & records* is clearly one of the fundamental doctrines in the successful and risk-minimized processing of corporate actions. Regular reconciliation of books & records positions (outside of the Corporate Actions Department), including position holders' positions, *unsettled trades* and *settled custodian positions*, is essential in order to avoid surprises when an event is to be processed against those positions. This is also a cornerstone of achieving *STP*.

The successful daily *reconciliation* of operational records of *trading book* positions, to those held in the front office, provides the Corporate Actions Department with a high degree of confidence that the positions upon which an event is based, are correct. If this basic reconciliation is not attempted at all, or is not attempted on a sufficiently frequent basis (preferably daily), the staff responsible for processing events are very likely to have to undertake that reconciliation themselves at the initiation of an event, whereas the formal responsibility should lie with the Reconciliations Department.

With regard to unsettled trades (i.e. forward value dated trades, and failed trades), the successful daily reconciliation of operational records to the outside world provides the Corporate Actions Department with a high degree of confidence that unsettled trades shown within internal books & records, as at the *record date* of an event, will mean that the *counterparties* will agree that a '*claim*' situation is applicable.

The successful daily reconciliation of operational records of settled securities positions, to those held by the STO's custodians, provides the Corporate Actions Department with a high degree of confidence that such positions, as at the record date of an event, will enable the accurate prediction of entitlements due to be credited to the STO's account(s) on payment/distribution date.

Electronic Communications

Recent technical advancements have provided STOs with the opportunity to communicate to position holders in an electronic fashion. The advantages of the electronic communication medium are a reduction in (for example):

- costs of manually intensive management of non-electronic forms of communication with position holders, such as paper, fax, and even telex, and
- delays in communications between parties, and therefore
- the risks associated with missing or delayed communications, particularly in the case of events with elections.

Note that in this context, electronic communications includes the Internet.

27.3.2 External Initiatives

Those initiatives that are undertaken by the market at large are regarded as external to the STO, and fall into two main categories:

- those that are imposed upon the market place (and therefore the STO by default), i.e. mandatory market changes, or
- those that promote changes in market practice which the STO may choose to adopt.

The following lists a number of the current external initiatives:

- Standardization of structure and format of communications between parties, e.g. issuers, custodians, STOs and clients, via S.W.I.F.T. ISO 15022 messages. The intended benefit (to all involved parties) is a two-way, single method of communication, resulting in reduced costs of supporting multiple structures and formats. Standardization of messages will also facilitate the straightforward comparison of data from multiple sources and multiple markets, as it is expected that most (if not all) parties will be communicating in the same manner.

- The introduction of the English language in addition to the primary language on all non-English communications. English will therefore become the standard language across all types of communications, even though it may not be the primary language of the STO or the client. For example, a client receiving communications in German, will also receive an English translation on that communication, as would a client receiving communications in French. Consequently, the two communications could be compared if required via the common language of English.
- Shortening of settlement cycles (and by association ex entitlement periods) across markets in order to reduce the instance of claims with respect to unsettled trades. This is expected to reduce:
  - manually intensive processes associated with the identification of *claims*, issuance of claims to counterparties, and the management of overdue settlement of claims;
  - risks associated with the non-collection of *resultant entitlements* arising from claims;
  - risks associated with the non-protection of *election decisions* in respect of unsettled trades.

  The shortening of settlement cycles (i.e. the number of days between trade date and value date) will have a beneficial effect on the management of corporate actions. In equity markets, the introduction of for example, T+1 settlement in a market where T+3 has previously been the norm, will result in shorter ex entitlement periods. This in turn should mean that there is less scope for trades to remain unsettled as at the record date of an event.
- Standardization of *record dates* and *ex dates*. At the time of writing, a corporate action event on a security that is traded in two or more markets is likely to have market-specific conventions applied to record dates and ex dates. For example, security X traded in one market may have a convention of record date being one day prior to ex date, whereas the convention in another market may be for the record date to be three days after ex date. Such market-specific conventions mean that different treatments of the same corporate action event are necessary. The standardization of date conventions would avoid the need for significantly different processes in order to manage multiple markets.

The external initiatives described above are being pursued by a number of industry working groups; these groups primarily analyse the needs of the market place, and advocate and promote changes. The working groups usually have representation from the market professional community, institutional investors, stock exchanges and market authorities, and when appropriate the regulatory authorities.

Listed below are some of these groups with their current focus:

- European Securities Forum (ESF) – focusing of specific issues such as the standardization of record date and ex date structures of events;
- Securities Market Practice Group (SMPG) – focusing mainly on the standardization of messaging (S.W.I.F.T is a key participant within this group);
- European Central Securities Depositories Association (ECSDA) – focusing on the design of solutions at an international level that are aimed at the reduction of risk and increase of efficiency within the European securities industry, including custody, settlement and corporate actions operations.

The purpose of these groups is to achieve consensus across the markets or within their membership and lobby legislators and market regulators for change.

27.4 CHALLENGES IN ACHIEVING THE STATED OBJECTIVES

In parallel with other industries and other historical changes within the securities industry, attempting to implement major programmes of change within the corporate actions arena is likely to be very costly, time consuming, and not without significant difficulties and challenges.

The following are examples of such challenges:

- The conversion of *issuer* event information, for example the translation of legal information contained within a corporate action event *prospectus*, into a single standard message.

  When a corporate action event is announced, whether at the beginning of the life of a *bond* or at any point after issuance in the case of *equity*, the issuer will publish a prospectus (or similar communication) for dissemination to the holders and/or the market place. Such documents are produced with the involvement of lawyers, in order to abide by company law and the local stock exchange (or market authority) regulations. As it is highly likely that no two countries have the same requirements in these respects, (primarily due to evolution in different markets), achieving standardization of event information and the way in which such information is presented, are major challenges.
- Agreement over communication standards with all interested parties.

  In order to achieve true standardization on a global scale, the decision makers will need to take account of the perspectives of many types of organizations, including issuers, market authorities, CSDs, ICSDs, custodians, STOs, institutional investors, regulators, tax authorities, etc. Unless the views of all such organizations are considered, the result of implemented initiatives may be that compromise is still necessary on a day-to-day basis, ultimately meaning that the objective has not in fact been reached.
- The ability to achieve agreement over priorities across multiple markets, countries, regions and types of organizations.

  For example:
  - objectives that are of highest importance in Europe may not be regarded as important within the Asia Pacific region;
  - the viewpoints of legislators and regulators in North America may differ from those in Europe;
  - co-ordination of the objectives of so many working groups, and agreeing sequencing and dependencies between the various projects, may be difficult.
- The costs of both internal and external initiatives.

  From an internal perspective, the challenge is whether a strong enough business case can be presented to management in order to secure funding for change initiatives. At any one moment in time, STOs normally have a whole range of improvements to existing processes, procedures and systems that it would ideally wish to implement immediately. The reality, however, is that a limited amount of budget is set aside for a given fiscal period, and the STO's management must decide which projects will provide the greatest benefits. It is normal practice for each initiative to have a project sponsor who creates and presents the rationale and justification (commonly known as a 'business case') to management, in the hope of gaining approval for the project. The business case for one or more corporate actions-related projects will need to be made alongside those representing initiatives from other areas of the organization. Possibly the most difficult aspect of making the corporate actions case is to state that the initiative is designed to guard against potential losses; quantifying the scale of a likely loss is extremely difficult. For example, if a loss were to be incurred, it could be on

– a relatively small position that has a single holder, or up to
– numerous large positions held by many clients

making the business case very difficult to justify. Clearly, a serious error in the second case may incur a far greater monetary (and reputational) loss than the same error relating to the first case. Conversely, if the STO has had the misfortune to have incurred in the past one or more serious losses on corporate action events, gaining budgetary approval may be relatively straightforward.

From an external perspective, the challenge is whether the market participants would be willing to make the necessary investment, and if so, on what basis. The professional market community (or other groups such as institutional investors) may decide that they will invest in order to realize their objectives, but are likely to demand that certain conditions must be met, for example in terms of meeting agreed deadlines and budgets, and achieving certain levels of functionality and performance.

Glossary of Terms

This glossary contains many of the terms mentioned within the book, and additionally contains frequently used terms not used within the book, but which may be of use to the reader. Words and phrases in *italics* within the description of terms indicate that an associated glossary item exists.

Acceptance Period The period within which the *offeror* will accept *election decisions* (to accept the *takeover* offer) from position holders in the *offeree*.

Accrual Internal accounting entries representing the accumulation of income, payment of which is due at the next income payment date.

Accrued Interest On interest-bearing bonds, the accumulated interest since the most recent *coupon payment date* and payable at the next coupon payment date.

Acquisition An attempt to purchase by one company, all or part of the *issued share capital* of another company. Also known as *takeover* or *tender*.

Actual Settlement In the context of corporate actions, the crediting of the position holder by the *STO* following collection of the amount owed at the *location*. Conversely, the debiting of the position holder by the STO following payment of the amount owed at the location.

Agency Trading Effecting the purchase or the sale of securities in the capacity of an agent, on behalf of clients.

Agent for Investors An organization that acts as an intermediary between its clients and a market participant with whom the agent trades. Agents usually do not hold securities positions on their own behalf. See *Proprietary Trading*.

AGM Annual General Meeting. A gathering of shareholders at which company proposals are made for which the shareholders are entitled to vote.

Amortized Coupon A coupon payment which also includes a *capital* portion representing the redemption or repayment of part of the capital value of the debt.

Announced Event An event declared by the issuer during the 'life' of the security resulting from decisions made by the issuer's board of directors, and potentially ratified by *shareholders*. (This differs from a predictable event where the event terms form part of the issue conditions of the security. For example *coupon payments* for *bonds*.)

Announcement In the context of corporate actions, the declaration of corporate action terms.

Announcement Date The date upon which the issuer declares to the market place the terms of an event.

Annual Yearly.

Assimilation The amalgamation of two securities with previously different characteristics, now becoming identical in all respects, e.g. ranking *pari-passu* for future dividends.

Balance Sheet The representation of a company's financial position at a specified date. The balance sheet includes assets, liabilities and owner's equity.

Bearer Security A *security* having no facility for the issuer to record the owner of the security, and where proof of ownership is physical possession of the security *certificate*; historically, mainly *bonds* rather than *equities* were issued in bearer form. See *Registered Security*.

Beneficial Owner In the context of corporate actions, the *trading book* or *custody client* on behalf of whom the STO holds a position. It is the beneficial owner who receives the benefit of the corporate action.

Benefit An amount of cash or a quantity of securities payable by an issuer to *shareholders* or *bondholders* as a reward for or return on their investment.

Benefit Events Those corporate action events that result in an increase to the *position holder's* securities or cash position, without altering the *underlying security*. For example a *bonus issue*.

Board Lot A standard trading quantity (such as 500 or 1,000 shares) for a given *security*; trading is usually conducted in multiples of the board lot. The cost of trading in board lots is typically cheaper than for trading in non-board lot quantities. See *Odd Lot*.

Bond A type of *security* that represents a loan of cash by an investor to a government, government agency, supranational organization or company, for which the investor usually receives a fixed rate of interest periodically during the term of the loan, and receives repayment of capital at maturity of the bond, usually years later.

Bondholder The owner of bonds.

Bond Conversion See *conversion*.

Bond Redemption The repayment of *capital* by the issuer to the bondholders on or before the *maturity date* of the *bond*.

Bonus Issue The grant of additional *shares* by an issuer to its *shareholders*, free of cost to the shareholders, typically at a fixed ratio of additional shares to original shares.

Book Entry A method by which *settlement* of trades is effected, whereby the exchange of *securities* and cash involves no physical movement of securities, as both the seller and buyer use the same custodian; under such circumstances, settlement results in a transfer of securities and cash between seller and buyer, within the custodian's books.

Books & Records The official record of an organization's trading activity, *securities* positions and cash positions.

Books Closing Date The date at which a company's share register is temporarily closed for the purpose of identifying, for example, the *shareholders* to whom *corporate action* benefits, such as *dividends* or *bonus issues*, will be paid. Also known as *record date*.

Broker An organization that executes trades on behalf of its clients (rather than on its own behalf), by finding buyers where clients wish to sell and finding sellers where clients wish to buy *securities*. Brokers normally charge commission to clients for providing this service.

Buy-Back The repurchase of all or part of the *issued share capital* (equity) by the issuer from shareholders at a published price.

Call See *full call* and *partial call*.

Capital In a corporate actions sense

1. The assets of a securities issuer after all liabilities have been deducted
2. The funds paid by investors to an issuer of securities.

Capital Gain Profits earned from the buying and selling of assets (which were held for investment purposes).

Capital Gains Tax The tax on profits earned from the buying and selling of assets (which were held for investment purposes).

Capital Value The face value of an *equity security*. See *par value*.

Capital Repayment A reduction in the *capital value* of an equity, thereby reducing the *position holder's* ownership in the company. The capital reduction is paid by the *issuer* to the position holder, and the original security is exchanged for securities appropriate to the new capital value, on a one for one basis. Note that capital repayments on bonds are known as *bond redemptions*.

Capital Reserves Amounts of capital retained in a company's balance sheet to be used in the future or for a special purpose.

Cash Dividend Payment The payment to *shareholders*, by an issuer, of *income* in the form of cash.

Cash for Fractions The distribution of cash to the *position holder* in lieu of the fractional amount of a securities resultant entitlement.

Cash Position A position in cash representing the accumulated trading of a position holder.

CCASS Central Clearing & Settlement System; the normal place of settlement for *equities* traded in Hong Kong.

CDS Canadian Depository for Securities; the normal place of settlement for *equities* traded in Canada.

Cease Trading Date The last day upon which a security may be traded. Typically this forms part of the event terms or the issue terms of a security. For example, this date is applicable to the trading of *nil paid rights* (in a *rights issue*).

Central Counterparty An organization that places itself between the counterparties to trades, becoming the counterparty to both seller and buyer; the resultant *settlement* obligation is between seller and central counterparty, and buyer and central counterparty.

Central Securities Depository The ultimate storage location of securities within a financial centre, in which the record of ownership is typically maintained electronically (by book-entry); settlement of trades may be effected as an additional service. A type of *custodian* organization.

Certificate Document of ownership in a *security*; certificates have historically been issued in *registered* or *bearer* form. In many financial centres today, certificates are not issued and proof of ownership is held electronically within *book-entry* systems.

Certificated A *security* where the *issuer* (or a registrar acting on the issuer's behalf) maintains a record of owners of the security, subsequently issuing a certificate to the owner as proof of ownership, rather than being represented by an electronic holding. When sold, the certificate is surrendered and cancelled, and a new certificate is issued in the buyer's name.

CHESS Clearing House Electronic Subregister System; the normal place of *settlement* for equities traded in Australia. CHESS effects settlement for its account holders on a *book-entry* basis.

Claims All situations where *resultant entitlement* of securities or cash are due to be received from or paid to counterparties (as a result of *unsettled trades* in the underlying security of the event).

Clearstream Banking Frankfurt The normal place of settlement for *equities* traded in Germany.

Clearstream International Located in Luxembourg, one of the two *International Central Securities Depositories* (ICSDs) offering custody and settlement services to its participants; the other ICSD is *Euroclear*.

Close Date The last date of an *election period*. See *issuer deadline date*.

Collectible Resultant Entitlement The *resultant entitlement* of an event that is to be collected by the STO from the location of its holdings, i.e. the *custodian*, and the counterparties to *claims*.

Collection In the context of corporate actions, 'collection' refers to the receipt of the resultant entitlement from the location.

Commence Trading Date The first day upon which a security may be traded. Typically this forms part of the event terms or the issue terms of a security. For example, this date is applicable to the trading of *nil paid rights* (in a *rights issue*).

Common Stock The standard description of *shares* issued by companies in the United States. See *Ordinary Shares*.

Company Earnings The profits of a business enterprise.

Compensation In the context of corporate actions, the settlement of *claims* automatically by the *CSD/ICSD* on behalf of the STO and its counterparty.

Compensation Date See *Depot Adjustment Date*.

Compulsorily Acquired See *Compulsory Acquisition*.

Compulsory Acquisition The mandatory possession of outstanding positions in the *offeree* by the *offeror* in a *takeover offer*.

Conditional The status of a *takeover offer* reflecting that the minimum conditions set by the *offeror* still apply. While the takeover offer remains conditional the offeror is able to withdraw the offer.

Conditional Period A phase of a *takeover* offer during which the minimum conditions set by the *offeror* must continue to be met in order for the offer to proceed.

Consolidation A decrease in an issuer's number of issued shares proportional to an increase in the *capital value* of each existing share.

Contractual Settlement The distribution to a position holder of *securities* and/or cash to reflect settlement on *payment* or *distribution date* of the *corporate action*, regardless of whether the securities and/or cash have been collected from the *location*.

Contractual Settlement Date The intended date of exchange of *securities* and cash between buyer and seller. Another term for *value date*.

Controlling Interest A level of ownership (i.e. percentage of issued capital) in a company that allows the *position holder* to exercise control over the management of that company.

The level of ownership typically exceeds that of the combined ownership of all other owners.

Conversion The exchange of one security for another security. This normally results from a conversion decision by the position holder, frequently involving convertible bonds being converted to the underlying equity in the issuer.

Conversion Period The timeframe during which a *convertible security* is eligible for conversion.

Convertible Bonds A bond that entitles the holder to convert that security into the underlying equity of the issuer, at a fixed ratio to the face value of the bond, during pre-specified periods during the life of the bond.

Convertible Preference Share A type of *preference share* that entitles the holder to convert that security into the underlying *ordinary* shares of the issuer, at a fixed ratio to the face value, during pre-specified periods during the life of the preference share.

Corporate Action Event An event in the life of a security (typically) instigated by the issuer, which affects a *position* in that security. For example a *coupon payment*, or a *bonus issue*.

Corporate Action Lifecycle The sequential steps involved in the processing of a corporate action, predominantly determined by the nature of the corporate action.

Corporate Action Data Provider An organization that supplies information to subscribers regarding the detail of *corporate actions* as and when announced, typically on an electronic basis.

Counterparty The opposing entity with which a *securities trading organization* executes a *securities* transaction.

Counterparty Deadline Date The final date stipulated by the counterparty of an unsettled trade by which it requires to receive any *election decisions* from the STO pursuant to the STO's claim for *resultant entitlement*.

Counterparty Risk The risk that the *counterparty* to a trade will fail to honour its contractual obligation to pay cash or to deliver *securities*.

Coupon On interest bearing bonds, bonds are issued with coupons attached; each coupon represents interest due on one specified *coupon payment date*. In order to receive interest on the bond, the coupon must be detached and presented to the coupon paying agent.

Coupon Paying Agent An organization appointed by an issuer to collect coupons from the bondholders, verify the validity of the coupons and make coupon payments to the bondholders on behalf of the issuer.

Coupon Payment The scheduled payment of interest in cash against the face value (i.e. the quantity, also known as nominal value) of a bond (whether it be fixed-rate bonds or floating rate notes), to the holder.

Coupon Payment Date The scheduled date of a coupon payment.

Coupon Period The timeframe between each payment of interest on a bond.

Coupon Rate The rate of interest payable by the bond *issuer* to the *bondholders*.

CREST The normal place of *settlement* for *equities* traded in the UK and Ireland; CREST effects settlement for its members on a *book-entry* basis.

CSD The abbreviated form of *central securities depository*.

Cum Latin for 'with'. From a corporate actions perspective, trades may be executed on either a 'cum' or 'ex' basis. See 'Ex'.

Cum Dividend Execution of a trade on a cum-dividend basis entitles the buyer to the *dividend* while the seller loses entitlement.

Cum Entitlement Period The timeframe prior to the *entitlement date*, during which under normal trading circumstances

- the purchaser of a trade with a trade date prior to the entitlement date will be entitled to the benefit, and
- the seller of a trade with a trade date prior to the entitlement date will lose entitlement to the benefit.

Cum Trading Under normal circumstances, trading prior to the entitlement date is known as cum trading, during which time buyers are normally entitled to participate in the event (and sellers will normally lose entitlement).

Custodian An organization that specializes in holding *securities* and cash and effecting movements of securities and cash on behalf of its account holders.

Custodian Deadline Date The final date stipulated by the custodian by which it requires to receive any *election decisions* from its account holders.

Custody The holding of *securities* (and in some cases cash) in safekeeping on behalf of the *beneficial owner* of the assets, and the provision of associated services, such as the collection of income payable to the beneficial owner. Also known as *safe custody*.

Custody Client A client on behalf of whom the STO holds securities (and in some cases cash) in *safe custody*.

Custody Client Position The net sum (by quantity) of all trades in each security per custody client.

Data Cleansing The process of comparing and cleansing data (e.g. securities or corporate actions data) received from two or more sources, in order to identify accurate information. Also known as *data scrubbing*.

Data Scrubbing The process of comparing and cleansing data (e.g. securities or corporate actions data) received from two or more sources, in order to identify accurate information. Also known as *data cleansing*.

Data Vendor An organization that supplies information to subscribers regarding the detail of *corporate actions* as and when announced, typically on an electronic basis.

Debt The issuance of *bonds* signifies that the issuer is in debt to the investors; a 'debt issue' is synonymous with the term 'bond issue'.

Default Option In the context of corporate action events with *elections*, the option that the issuer will apply to holdings where no *election decision* has been received from the position holder.

Deferred Delivery The intentional (and market-wide) postponement of securities settlement to a date later than the standard settlement cycle.

Deferred Delivery Date The earliest date that settlement can occur on a new issue of *securities*; also known as *primary value date*.

Delivery versus Payment The simultaneous, irrevocable, and risk-free exchange of *securities* and cash between seller and buyer (or their custodians). Commonly known as *DvP*.

Dematerialized *Securities* holdings that were previously represented by *certificates* of ownership, but which have been replaced by electronic holdings; settlement of subsequent sales and purchases are typically effected via *book-entry*.

Demerger See *spin-off*.

Depot An organization that holds *securities* and effects *settlement* of trades on behalf of its account holder; also known as *custodian*.

Depot Account The specific account held by a *depot* or *custodian* in which *securities* are held.

Depot Adjustment Date The date up to which a CSD/ICSD will take account of *cum trading* settled past *record date*, in determining entitlement. The CSD/ICSD will adjust the record date quantity for which entitlement will be paid, thereby avoiding the need for *claims*.

Determining Entitlement The function of applying the terms of an event to the STO's *books & records* to identify *entitled positions* and the *location* of those positions.

Disbursable Resultant Entitlement The resultant entitlement of an event which is to be disbursed by the STO to the *beneficial owners* i.e. trading books and custody clients.

Disbursement The payment or delivery of *resultant entitlement* of an event to the *beneficial owners.*

Discount In the context of corporate actions announced data, a price less than the *par value* of a security, when applied to the *subscription* of new securities.

Dissenting Shareholder A holder of equity who has not voluntarily accepted a *takeover* offer which proceeds to *compulsory acquisition*. The dissenting shareholder's position will normally be compulsorily acquired by the *offeror*.

Distribution The delivery of securities and/or payment of cash *resultant entitlements* as a consequence of a corporate action event; typically used in conjunction with *benefit* events.

Distribution Date The date upon which any securities and/or cash resultant entitlements are due to be distributed to position holders. Also known as *payment date*.

Dividend See *dividend payment.*

Dividend Payment The distribution of earnings by a company to its *shareholders*, whether in the form of cash or *securities*.

Dividend Re-investment Plan The payment to *shareholders* by an issuer, of *income* in either the form of cash or *securities*. The shareholder has the option to re-invest its cash dividend value in further securities, at a *discount* to the current market price.

Double Entry Book-keeping A basic accounting principle whereby each accounting entry is offset by a contra (debit or credit) entry.

Double Taxation Agreement An arrangement between two countries, whereby residents of one country who invest in *securities* issued by *issuers* within the other country, will have *withholding tax* deducted at a lower rate than the standard rate payable by investors. Also known as a *Treaty*.

Drawing The repayment of *capital* of selected holdings of debt by the *issuer* prior to the published *maturity date* of the *bond.*

DRP or DRiP Acronyms for *Dividend Re-investment Plan.*

DTC Depository Trust Company; the normal place of *settlement* of *equities*, corporate and municipal bonds traded in the United States. DTC effects settlement for its account holders on a *book-entry* basis.

DTC Swing Date The date upon which an individual security that is held in DTC is moved from the original security identifier to a new security identifier. This applies to *re-organization* events.

DvP Acronym for *Delivery versus Payment.*

Due Bill A document provided by one party (of a securities transaction) to its counterparty, as an undertaking to deliver securities or to pay cash resulting from a corporate action.

Early Redemption See *full call.*

Earnings Per Share The net earnings of a company expressed in terms proportional to the issued capital of the company.

Earnings Period The timeframe within which the profits of a business enterprise have been earned. Typically, the distribution of dividends (income) relates to a stated earnings period.

Effective Date The date upon which the re-organization of position holders' positions in the underlying security is due to take effect.

Elect In the context of corporate actions, to choose between the options that have been announced by the issuer with respect to the *resultant entitlement* to be received for a *mandatory with options* event or *voluntary event.*

Election(s) Events with elections enable position holders a choice as to how they participate in an event, if at all.

Election Decision The selection by positions holders of the option(s) that they require with respect to mandatory with options events and voluntary events.

Election Decision Date The date upon which an *election decision* is made by a position holder.

Election Period The timeframe within which *election decisions* can be made. The election period is defined within the event terms by an *open date* and a *close date.*

Entitled Position The cumulative trading positions of trading books and custody clients which have *entitlement* relating to certain types of corporate actions.

Entitlement The right of ownership relating to certain types of *corporate action.*

Entitlement Currency The currency that will either be distributed as a result of a *benefit*, or that will replace the underlying security in the case of a re-organization. See also *payment currency.*

Entitlement Date The key date in determining whether a buyer or seller is entitled to participate in an event; normally applicable to benefit events. Also known as Ex Date.

Entitlement Date Entries Internal accounting entries that reflect the impact of *resultant entitlements* specifically on *ownership* positions. Such entries are normally passed at the same time that the price of the *underlying security* changes (as a result of the event).

Entitlement Issue An offer by an *issuer* (that wishes to raise further capital) to the existing *shareholders* to purchase additional *shares* in proportion to its existing shareholding. The offer to purchase additional shares is not transferable or *renounceable* (unlike a *rights issue*).

Entitlement Period The timeframe prior to the *Entitlement Date* of an event within which buyers of securities will become entitled to participate in an event.

Entitlement Security The security that will either be distributed as a result of a *benefit*, or will replace the *underlying security* in the case of a *re-organization*.

Equity An alternative description for the term *shares*; an 'equity issue' is synonymous with the term 'share issue'.

Equity Call The payment of further capital (relating to an existing *partly-paid* equity issue) by the shareholders when called by the issuer.

Equity Restructure The change in quantity of shares issued and/or the *par value* of those shares.

Escrow Accounts (or Escrow Agent) Special accounts held for the purposes of segregating securities in custody for a third party until certain conditions are fulfilled. Escrow accounts are commonly used with respect to *takeover events*, where securities are held until takeover conditions are met, after which they will be transferred to the *offeror*.

Eurobond A type of *bond* that is usually sold to investors outside the country relating to the currency of issue. No *withholding tax* on income is payable by investors.

Euroclear Located in Brussels, one of the two *International Central Securities Depositories* (ICSDs) offering *safe custody* and *settlement* services to its participants; the other ICSD is *Clearstream International*.

Event See *Corporate Action Event*.

Event Control Account An internal account used to offset corporate action entries within a set of *internal entries*, for the purpose of ensuring balancing of debit and credit entries.

Event Data See *Event Terms*.

Event Dates Dates applicable to a corporate action event that are contained within the *event terms*, including dates that set the conditions for entitlement to the event, due dates for the distribution of resultant entitlements or the effective date of the event, and deadline dates where the position holder is required to communicate with the issuer.

Event Deadline The final date stipulated by the issuer in the event terms by which it requires to receive any *election decisions*. This is also the *close date* of an *election period*. Also known as *issuer's deadline date*.

Event Terms The collective conditions and information stipulated by the *issuer* pertaining to a *corporate action event*.

Event Terms Announcement The declaration by the issuer of the terms of a corporate action event. Also the initial notice that the STO may issue to position holders to inform them of the impending event.

Ex 'Without', the opposite of *cum*. From a corporate actions perspective, trades may be executed on either an 'ex' or 'cum' basis. See 'Cum'.

Ex Date The date used to determine whether seller or buyer has *entitlement* to certain types of *corporate action* on (primarily) equity *securities*.

Ex Date Accrual Entries See *entitlement date entries*.

Ex Dividend Execution of a trade on an ex dividend basis entitles the seller to the *dividend* whilst the buyer does not gain *entitlement*.

Ex Entitlement Date See *ex date*.

Ex Entitlement Period The timeframe commencing with the *entitlement date*, during which under normal trading circumstances:

- the purchaser of a trade with a trade date on or after the entitlement date will not gain entitlement to the benefit, and
- the seller of a trade with a trade date on or after the entitlement date will retain entitlement to the benefit.

Ex Trading Under normal circumstances, trading on and after the *entitlement date* is known as ex trading, during which time buyers do not normally gain entitlement to participate in the event (and sellers will retain entitlement).

Exchange Rate The 'price' at which one currency is exchanged for another.

Execution The agreement to trade between two parties, whether buying or selling, lending or borrowing, etc.

Exercise The process of converting a security to an associated (or underlying) security.

Expiry The termination of a security with a limited life, such as a *nil paid right* or *warrant*. Upon expiry the security ceases to exist and the position holder's position is removed.

Face Value See *par value*.

Failed Settlement A trade for which *settlement* has not yet occurred, where the *value date* is in the past.

Final Claim Notice A communication issued by a buyer of securities to a seller, requesting payment of cash or delivery of securities to which the buyer is entitled (relating to a corporate action). Such situations arise where purchased securities are not delivered by close of the *record date*.

Final Entitlement Notice A communication to position holders of the final *resultant entitlement* that they are owed.

Fixed-Rate Bond Debt securities that pay *coupon* on specified dates at a fixed rate of interest, and that mature on a fixed date. Also known as 'straight bonds'.

Floating Rate Note A form of *bond* that pays variable rates of interest in accordance with a specified 'benchmark' rate, as opposed to the majority of bonds that have a fixed rate of interest throughout their lives.

FoP Acronym for *Free of Payment*.

Foreign Withholding Tax Income tax deducted from the *gross income* (on equity and debt) by the *issuer* or the *custodian* and payable to the issuer's national tax authority.

'Four Eyes' Principle The practice of having work verified by another person prior to acting on the information.

Fractions Less than a whole unit of a security. Some corporate action event *ratios* may result in fractional *resultant entitlements*, to which *rounding rules* will be applied in order to round the resultant entitlement to whole units.

Free of Payment The separate (non-simultaneous) exchange of *securities* and cash between seller and buyer (or their *custodians*). Commonly referred to as *FoP*.

Friendly Takeover A *takeover* offer where the directors of the *target company* (*offeree*) recommend to its *shareholders* to accept the offer by the *offeror.* The alternative is a *Hostile Takeover*.

Front Office A collective term used to describe those who are involved with trading and market making directly or indirectly.

FRN Acronym for *Floating Rate Note*.

Full Call The repayment of the full *capital value* by the *issuer* to all bondholders prior to the published *maturity date* of a *bond.*

Fully Paid The designation with respect to issued shares that indicates that each share represents its full face value as equity in the issuer. See *equity call*.

General Ledger The monetary transaction records of an organization, which are recorded as debits and credits. Cash entries resulting from corporate actions events will update the *STO's* general ledger.

Gross Income An amount of income prior to the deduction of any tax.

Hostile Takeover A *takeover offer* where the directors of the *target company* (*offeree*) recommend to its *shareholders* not to accept the offer by the *offeror.* The alternative is a *Friendly Takeover.*

ICSD Abbreviated form of *International Central Securities Depository.*

Income Earnings from investments in securities, normally associated with *dividends* and *coupon*. Also applicable to earnings from other forms of investment, and employment.

Income Tax The tax applied to earnings from investment in securities, other forms of investment, and employment.

Indeval The normal place of *settlement* for *bonds* and *equities* traded in Mexico.

Initial Public Offering A method of bringing a new *equity issue* to the *securities* market place, whereby the general public is given the opportunity to apply for shares in the issue. A term used in the United States; the equivalent of an Offer for Sale in the UK.

Instalment Call See *equity call.*

Institutional Clients See *institutional investors.*

Institutional Investors A generic term given to end-investors that are organizations, as opposed to individuals; such investors include *fund managers*, *hedge funds*, *insurance companies* and *pension funds*.

Interest Cash payable by a cash borrower to a cash lender; in a corporate actions sense, interest (*coupon*) is payable by a bond *issuer* to the bondholders.

Interest Claims A request by a seller to the buyer for reimbursement of lost cash interest, where the seller was able to deliver securities (on or after the *value date*) but the buyer was unable to pay/settle. This equally applies to the disbursement of corporate action r*esultant entitlements,* where the *position holder* suffers loss of interest due to a delay in *disbursement* by the STO.

Interim Security A temporary security having a short and finite life, distributed in order to facilitate the final calculation of *resultant entitlements* (which are based upon the position holder's position in the interim security). A *nil paid right* is an example of an interim security.

Internal Deadline Date The final date by which the STO requires to receive *election decisions* from its *position holders.*

Internal Entries Accounting entries passed within the STO's books & records to reflect changes to the *underlying securities* position, and the distribution of any securities and/or cash that is expected to occur on the *distribution date* or *effective date* of the event.

International Central Securities Depository A *central securities depository* that holds overseas *securities* and usually facilitates *settlement* of trades in numerous currencies. Euroclear (Brussels) and Clearstream International (Luxembourg) are two recognized ICSDs.

Investor An individual or institution that has purchased and owns *securities.*

IPO Acronym for *Initial Public Offering.*

ISIN International Securities Identification Number; a uniform global standard providing unique reference numbers (ISIN numbers) for individual securities, enabling unambiguous identification of the issue being traded and delivered.

ISMA International Securities Market Association; a body (headquartered in Zurich) that makes rules and recommendations governing trading and *settlement* in the international *securities* markets, including *Eurobonds*. ISMA's members are located around the globe.

ISO The International Organization for Standardization promotes the development of consistency around the globe relating to goods and services within many industries.

ISO Currency Codes A set of internationally recognized three-digit codes representing each of the world's currencies.

Issue An individual *security.*

Issue Currency The currency of issue of an individual security, whether the denominated currency of a bond that represents the cash received by the issuer, or the par value currency of an equity issue that represents the value of ownership in the issuer.

Issued Share Capital The nominal cash value of equity issued in an issuer, calculated by multiplying the number of shares issued by the par value of the share. Note: this typically has no relevance to the market value of an issue.

Issuer The originating entity that supplies *securities* to the market place in order to raise cash; such entities include companies, sovereign entities, governments, government agencies and supranational organizations.

Issuer Deadline Date The final date stipulated by the issuer by which it requires to receive *election decisions*. This is also the *close date* of an *election period.*

Issuer Meetings with Proxy Voting An assembly organized by an issuer in order to obtain shareholder ratification of company decisions, for example the adoption of financial statements, the sale of capital, the distribution of income. In order to participate when unable to attend the meeting, the position holder may choose to issue a *proxy vote.*

Issuer Notices Events used for the dissemination of information from the issuer to position holders (for example the notification of an Annual General Meeting), which result in no change to either the securities or cash position of the position holder.

Issuer Tender Offer See *buy-back*.

JASDEC Japan Securities Depository Center; the normal place of *settlement* for *equities* traded in Japan.

Journal A set of balancing debit and credit accounting entries, which are used to update account balances.

KSD Korea Securities Depository; the normal place of *settlement* for *bonds* and *equities* traded in Korea.

Liquidation The termination of an *issuer* via the selling of its assets and the subsequent distribution of proceeds to meet outstanding liabilities and creditors claims.

Liquidation Distribution The distribution of proceeds from the *liquidation* of an *issuer* to *position holders*. See *liquidation*.

Listed Company Companies whose shares are publicly traded in the market place via a registered stock exchange.

Location The organization or site that holds securities; typically held by a custodian, but may also include unsettled trades where securities are still located with the counterparty.

Long First Coupon A term given to the first payment of interest after a *bond* has been issued, specifically where the elapsed time between issuance of the bond and the first *coupon payment date* is greater than the normal *coupon period* for that bond. See *Short First Coupon*.

Long Trading Position The positive net sum (by quantity) of all trades in a security, per individual owner.

Long Value Date A *trade date* to *value date* period that is longer than the standard *settlement cycle*.

Lot See *board lot*.

Lottery See *drawing*.

Mandatory Event A corporate action event where the position holder has no choice as to whether and how it participates in the event.

Mandatory with Options Event A corporate action event where the position holder has no choice as to whether it participates in the event, but is given a choice by the issuer as to the form that its resultant entitlement will take, i.e. securities and/or cash.

Manufactured Dividend A payment of an amount equal to an income payment made by a borrower of securities to a lender of securities, so that the lender receives the income amount that it would have received had it not lent or repoed out the security.

Mark to Market Revaluation of a *securities* position with the current market price; this is used for example, when calculating *unrealized profit and loss* and when calculating the current value of collateral.

Market An environment within which *securities* are traded, for example the US Treasury bond market and the Hong Kong equity market.

Market Price The price at which a security is currently able to be bought or sold in the market place, determined by market forces of supply and demand.

Maturity Date The intended date of repayment of borrowed cash. Specifically, the date of *capital repayment* by a bond issuer to *bondholders*.

Merger The union of two (previously distinct) companies, resulting in the combination of assets.

Multi-Stage Event A corporate action event that combines two or more stages (lifecycles) in its overall life. From the *issuer's* perspective each of these events are a single action, nonetheless from a corporate action processing perspective (as well as from the *position holder's* perspective) the event can be viewed as containing many interdependent lifecycles.

National CSD A *central securities depository* that holds domestic *securities* and typically facilitates *settlement* of trades in the domestic currency on a *book entry* basis.

Net Income An amount of income following the deduction of tax.

Nil Paid Issued *securities* that represent no *capital value* in the *issuer*. See nil paid rights.

Nil Paid Rights An *interim security* issued during the course of a *rights issue*, which represents the *position holder's* 'right' to purchase additional securities at a pre-defined price from the *issuer*. The nil paid right represents no *equity* in the issuer, and hence is known as 'nil paid'.

Non-Renounceable Not tradeable or *transferable*. See Renounceable.

Non-Tradeable Not tradeable or *transferable*. See Renounceable.

Non-Treaty Where no *double taxation agreement* exists between countries, foreign investors will have *foreign withholding tax* deducted at the standard non-treaty rate. See *Double Taxation Agreement*.

Normal Cum Trading See *cum trading*.

Normal Ex Trading See *ex trading*.

Nostro An organization that holds cash on behalf of its account holder.

Nostro Account The specific account held by a nostro in which cash is held on behalf of the account holder.

Odd Lot Where a standard trading quantity of *shares* for a given *security* exists (known as a board lot), trading in a quantity other than the board lot is commonly known as an odd lot. The cost of trading in odd lots is typically greater than for trading in board lots. See *Board Lot.*

Odd Lot Offer The opportunity for position holders with odd lot holdings, to 'round' their holdings into tradable *lots*. The rounding of holdings is achieved by the issuer offering to sell to the position holder (i.e. the position holder will buy), at a published price, additional securities in order to 'top up' its holding. In some cases the issuer may also offer to buy (i.e. the position holder will sell) those holdings that are less than a lot.

Offer Acceptance The *election decision* that reflects the acceptance of the offeror's *offer terms*.

Offer Close Date The final date of the (takeover) *offer period.*

Offer Consideration The securities and/or cash that the *offeror* pays the *position holder* in exchange for its position in the *offeree.*

Offer Document The legal text issued by the *offeror* that contains the terms of the offer for the *offeree*.

Offer Open Date The first date of a (takeover) *offer period.*

Offer Period The timeframe within which *offer acceptances* can be made. The offer period is defined within the *event terms* by an *offer open date* and an *offer close date*.

Offer Terms The *event terms* applicable to a takeover offer and contained within the *offer document*.

Offeree The target company in a takeover offer. See *offeror*.

Offeror The person(s) or organization making an offer for the *issued share capital* of the *target company*. The target company is known as the *offeree*.

Open Date The first date of an *election period.*

Open Trade A trade for which *settlement* has not yet occurred, whether *value date* is in the future or in the past. Also known as an *unsettled trade.*

Option In the context of corporate actions, the alternatives available to a *position holder* as to how it will participate in an event. For example, the choice between receiving securities and/or cash *resultant entitlements* in a *mandatory with options event.*

Optional Dividend The payment to *shareholders* by an issuer, of *income* in either the form of cash or *securities*. Whether the shareholder receives cash or securities is its choice, communicated via its *election decision.*

Ordinary Shares The standard description of *shares* issued by companies in various parts of the globe, including Australia, India and the UK See *Common Stock.*

OTC Acronym for *over-the-counter.*

Outsourcing The act of moving the management of some or all operational responsibilities to a third party.

Over-Acceptance *Election decisions* to accept the offer that exceed the maximum limit set by the *offeror*. Typically applicable with respect to partial *takeover offers.*

Over-Election Receipt (by an issuer) of *election decisions* in excess of any limits set by the issuer for a given *option,* or the event as a whole.

Over-Election Adjustment The modification made (by the *issuer*) to *election decision* quantities where *election decisions* received exceed any limits set by the issuer for a given *option* or the event as a whole.

Over-Subscription *Subscription decisions* that exceed the maximum limit set by the *issuer*.

Overdue Elections Outstanding *election decisions* from position holders up to and including the *internal deadline date* of the STO, and/or the *issuer's deadline date*.

Ownership Position The accumulated quantity of a *security* owned by a *position holder*. See *position.*

P&L Acronym for Profit and Loss.

Par Currency The currency in which the *par value* of a security is quoted.

Par Value The face value of an *equity security* that reflects the value of equity (or capital) each security represents.

Pari-Passu Latin for 'alike' or 'equally'. In a corporate actions sense, referring to two securities that rank equally in terms of entitlement to dividends; they are described as ranking 'pari-passu'.

Partial Call The repayment of part of the *capital* by the *issuer* to all bondholders prior to the published *maturity date* of a *bond.*

Partial Redemption See *partial call.*

Partial Settlement The exchange of a quantity of *securities* and an amount of cash that are less than the full quantity and cash value of the trade.

Partly-Paid Share A share that has had some but not all of its *capital share value* paid by the position holder (and therefore received by the issuer). The issuer will call the balance of the capital at a later date, at which point the share will become fully paid. See also *equity call.*

Payment Currency The currency in which any cash *resultant entitlements* will be distributed to position holders. See also *entitlement currency*.

Payment Date The date upon which any securities and/or cash *resultant entitlements* are due to be paid to *position holders*. Also known as *distribution date*.

Physical Delivery The actual movement of *securities certificates* for the purposes of *settlement*, outside of a *central securities depository* or other *custodian*. Typically a rare occurrence today as in many financial centres, settlement is effected by *book entry*.

Position The accumulated quantity of a *security*. This term is used to describe any accumulation of securities, including both ownership and locations.

Position Holder The party on behalf of whom the *STO* holds *securities*. A position holder may be a *trading book* or a *custody client*.

Position Holder's Domestic Income Tax Tax deductible from income due to a position holder and payable to a tax authority in the position holder's country of residence.

Predictable Event A corporate action event that is detailed within the *issue* conditions of the security and is therefore predictable, for example *coupon payments* on *bonds*. See *announced events*.

Preference Shares A type of *share* that entitles the holder to a different amount of dividend (in relation to the *ordinary shares* or *common stock*) and, should liquidation of the company occur, the return of the *shareholder's* capital as a priority over ordinary shares.

Preliminary Claim Notice A communication issued to parties with whom an anticipated outstanding receipt relating to an *unsettled trade* has been identified, notifying that a claim will be made if settlement of the underlying trade is not effected prior to the record date.

Preliminary Entitlement Notice A communication informing the position holder of the projected *resultant entitlement* based upon its holding as at the *entitlement date* of the event.

Premium In the context of corporate actions announced data, a 'price' greater than the *par value* of a security, when applied to the *subscription* of new securities.

Primary Market A generic term to describe the issuance of and trading in *securities* that are in the course of being brought to the market place. See *Secondary Market*.

Primary Value Date The earliest date that *settlement* can occur on a new issue of *securities*; also known as *Deferred Delivery Date*.

Priority Issue An offer by an *issuer* (that wishes to raise further capital) to the existing *shareholders* and the public to purchase additional *shares* in the issuer. Existing shareholders are given a priority to apply over members of the public. The offer to purchase additional shares is not transferable or *renounceable*.

Protection The practice of applying *election decisions* to corporate action *claims* from *counterparties* is known in some markets as 'protection', as the *STO* endeavours to protect the counterparty for the requested *resultant entitlement*.

Proprietary Used in the context of securities trading, this refers to those positions held for an organization's own account.

Proprietary Trading Buying, selling and holding *securities* for an organization's own account, not acting as an *agent for investors*. See *Securities Trading Organization*.

Prospectus A document that details the terms and conditions applicable to the issuance of a new *security* and to some corporate action events (e.g. *rights issues*).

Proxy Vote A vote made by a third party (as nominated by the position holder) on behalf of that position holder. Normally relating to resolutions at *issuer meetings*.

Put Call The repayment of *capital* by the *issuer* to a *bondholder*, at the request of the bondholder, prior to the published *maturity date* of the *bond*.

Quarterly Four times a year, every three months.

Rank/Ranking Some equities are issued (for example, as resultant entitlement from a *bonus issue* or a *rights issue*) without qualifying for the next dividend; such securities are distinctly named (e.g. New Ordinary Shares) in order to distinguish them from the ordinary shares/common stock, until such time that they 'rank' the same and merge into a single security. See *pari-passu*.

Rate The cash rate per share to be applied to a quantity of securities to determine a cash *resultant entitlement*. The ratio is made up of two numbers that state the quantity and units of the *entitlement currency*.

Rate Currency The currency in which the cash rate of a corporate action event is quoted.

Rate Re-fixing The determination of the coupon rate for a specified period for a *floating rate note*.

Ratio The quotation of two numbers (as part of the *event terms*) that represents the quantity of the *resultant entitlement* security, relevant to the *underlying security*. A ratio is typically quoted for corporate action events that result in a securities entitlement, such as *bonus issues*, *rights issues* and *stock splits*.

Realized Profit and Loss Actual profit or loss following sales and purchases of *securities*. See *Unrealized Profit and Loss*.

Rebateable Tax Tax (pre-paid) that may be offset against other or later tax liabilities.

Reconciliation The comparison of one set of records to another, typically used to ensure that internal *books & records* agree with *securities* and cash balances held externally at *depots* and *nostros*. Reconciliation is critical in maintaining control of corporate actions processing, as it is for *trading* and *settlement*.

Record Date

- *Equities*: the date at which a company's *share* register is temporarily closed for the purpose of identifying the shareholders to whom *corporate action* benefits, such as *dividends* or *bonus issues*, will be paid. Also known as *books closing date*.
- *Bonds*: the date at which a custodian identifies its account holders to whom *coupon payments* will be made.

Note that for equities and bonds, the recipient of a payment is not necessarily entitled to the benefit (due to settlement failure). See *Entitlement*, *Entitlement Date*, *Ex Date*.

Record Date Entries *Internal entries* passed within the STO's *books & records* on the record date in order to reflect the *resultant entitlement* that is expected to be collected from the *location*; and the resultant entitlement that is to be disbursed to position holders.

Redemption See *bond redemption*.

Redemption Date The date of repayment of *capital* by a bond *issuer* to the *bondholders*. See *maturity date*.

Register The list of holders of a registered *security*, maintained by an *issuer* or a *registrar* acting on the issuer's behalf; this allows direct communication (for example, payments of income) by the issuer with the owners of the security.

Registered Security A *security* where the *issuer* (or a registrar acting on the issuer's behalf) maintains a record of owners of the security; this requires that when securities are sold, the seller's name is replaced by the buyer's name on the register. Typically, *equities* rather than *bonds* are issued in registered form. See *Bearer Security*.

Registrar An organization appointed by an *issuer* of a *registered security* to maintain the register of holders of that security. Also known as transfer agent in the US.

Registration The act of updating the *issuer's* register of owners (of a *registered security*) in order to reflect transfer of ownership.

Registration Date The date upon which the transfer of registered securities from the seller to the buyer is effected within the issuer's *register* of owners.

Regulator An entity that is responsible for the monitoring and controlling of activities within a securities market place, to ensure compliance with rules and regulations.

Regulatory Reporting The provision of information (to a *regulator*) by a *securities trading organization* regarding its trading activity and its *securities* positions.

Re-investment The use of *income* (usually in the form of cash dividends) to purchase additional securities in the issuer directly from the issuer. See *Dividend Re-investment Plan*.

Renounceable Securities that can be relinquished or sold by a holder, and therefore acquired or purchased by a buyer. For some (but not all) corporate actions, *resultant entitlements* in the form of securities are renounceable. See *Non-Renounceable*.

Re-organization The alteration of the capital structure (and possibly other aspects) of an organization. Also known as a *restructure* or reconstruction.

Re-organization Events Corporate action events that re-shape or re-structure the position holder's *underlying securities* position, possibly also combining a cash element. For example a *share split*.

Repurchase Offer See *buy-back*.

Restructure See *re-organization.*

Resultant Entitlement Securities and/or cash amounts resulting from applying the terms of a corporate action event to *entitled positions*, including *ownership*, *locations* and *claims*.

Reverse Split See *consolidation*.

Rights Issue An offer by an *issuer* (that wishes to raise further *capital*) to the existing *shareholders* to purchase additional shares in proportion to their existing shareholding; in order to entice the shareholders to take-up the offer, the price of the rights is typically offered at a reduction to the current market price of the existing shares. The right to purchase additional shares is typically transferable or *renounceable*.

Rights Subscription Period The timeframe within which *election decisions* to subscribe *nil paid rights* to new shares will be accepted by the *issuer*. See *subscription period*.

Rounding (Rules) Regarding fractional securities entitlement, the increase to the next whole number, or the decrease to the previous whole number. See *fractions*.

Safe Custody The holding of *securities* (and in some cases cash) in safekeeping on behalf of the *beneficial owner* of the assets, and the provision of associated services, such as the collection of income payable to the beneficial owner. Also known as '*custody*'. See *custody client*.

Safe Custody Client A client on behalf of whom the STO is holding its securities (and in some cases cash) in *safe custody*. Also known as *custody client*.

Scheme of Arrangement A corporate action event in which the *issuer* issues, to *position holders*, combinations of *securities* and/or cash in exchange for the existing *underlying security*. The purpose, similar to that of a *share split* or *consolidation*, is a *restructure* of the issuer's *issued share capital*.

Scrip Dividend The payment to *shareholders* by an *issuer*, of *income* in the form of scrip (temporary certificates). The scrip represents the issuer's promise to pay a *cash dividend*, at a time when earnings may be considered sufficient to distribute, but cash reserves are being conserved.

Secondary Market A generic term to describe the market place where existing *securities* are traded (as opposed to those securities that are in the course of being brought to the market place, within the *primary market*).

Securities Financial instruments that may be purchased and sold, the most common forms of which are *equities* and *bonds*.

Securities Position The accumulated quantity of an *equity* or *bond* owned by a *position holder*. See *position*.

Securities Trading Organization (STO) An organization that practices *proprietary trading*, involving the buying, selling and holding of *securities* for its own account. When corporate action events arise, the STO will need to assess relevant securities *positions* in order to collect *benefits*, re-structure its holdings, etc. (according to the nature of the event).

Semi-annual Twice yearly, every six months.

Service Level Agreement A legal contract between the *STO* and its *position holders*, and between the STO and the custodian, which defines the level and terms of service that are to be provided.

Settled Custodian Position The quantity of *securities* held in the account of an account holder, at a *custodian*; differences in the settled position and *trading position* are usually due to one or many *open trades*.

Settled Trade A trade for which the exchange of securities and cash between buyer and seller (in order to fulfil their contractual obligations) has been effected.

Settlement The act of buyer and seller (or their agents) exchanging *securities* and cash in order to fulfil their contractual obligation.

Settlement Cycle The standard or default period of time between *trade date* and *value date* of trades, within each market place.

Settlement Date The date the actual exchange of *securities* and cash has been effected; this date is known only after settlement has occurred. (Note that in some countries, 'settlement date' is used to mean the intended date of delivery of securities and cash). See *Value Date*.

Settlement Failure Trades where securities and cash have not been exchanged on *value date* (the *contractual settlement date*).

Settlement Instruction A message issued by an account holder to its *custodian* that requests the custodian to deliver or receive *securities* and/or receive or pay cash on a specified date (the *value date* of the trade).

Settlement Status The condition of a *settlement instruction* reported by a custodian to its account holder; typical statuses are unmatched with counterparty, matched with counterparty, settled, and failed.

Share That which represents *equity* ownership in a company.

Shareholder The owner of *shares* in a company.

Shareholder Eligibility Specific conditions of a corporate actions event that stipulate which categories of *position holder* qualify for participation in the event, or qualify to elect specific options in an event.

Share Capital The total face value (or *par value*) of issued *shares* in a company.

Share Split An increase in an *issuer's* number of issued shares proportional to a reduction in the *capital (par) value* of each existing share.

Short First Coupon A term given to the first payment of interest after a *bond* has been issued, specifically where the elapsed time between issue of the *bond* and the first *coupon payment date* is less than the normal *coupon period* for that bond. See *Long First Coupon*.

Short Trading Position The negative accumulated quantity of an *equity* or *bond* owned by a *position holder*.

Short Value Date A *trade date* to *value date* period that is shorter than the standard *settlement cycle*.

SIS SegaIntersettle AG; the normal place of *settlement* for *bonds* and *equities* traded in Switzerland.

SLA See *Service Level Agreement*.

Special-Cum Trading Trading during the *ex entitlement period*, executed with special conditions agreed between buyer and seller whereby

- the purchaser of a special-cum trade will gain entitlement to the benefit, and
- the seller of a special-cum trade will lose entitlement to the benefit.

Special-Ex Trading Trading during the *cum entitlement period*, executed with special conditions agreed between buyer and seller whereby

- the purchaser of a special-ex trade will not gain entitlement to the benefit, and
- the seller of a special-ex trade will retain entitlement to the benefit.

Special Trading (Cum/Ex) Refer to *special-cum trading* and *special-ex trading*.

Spin-Off The distribution of securities in a subsidiary company, to the *shareholders* of the parent company, without the surrender of the original *underlying securities*. This corporate action event typically involves no cost to the position holder in the parent company.

Standing Election A standing instruction given by a position holder stating its fixed instructions with regard to *election decisions*. For appropriate corporate action events, such instructions will be used, rather than requesting election decisions from the position holder on an event-by-event basis.

Static Data A store of information pertaining to trading companies, *counterparties*, *securities* and currencies which is used in the processing of trades, position management and *corporate actions*.

Static Data Defaulting In the corporate actions context, the automatic attachment of appropriate information in the management of corporate action processing, and the calculation of *resultant entitlements*, according to pre-defined rules.

STO Acronym for *Securities Trading Organization*.

Stock Dividend The payment to *shareholders* by an issuer, of *income* in the form of *securities*.

Stock Record A system of *double entry book-keeping* that accounts on the one side for the ownership of securities (e.g. *trading positions*), and on the other side for their location (e.g. at the *custodian* or with the *counterparty* awaiting settlement).

STP Acronym for *Straight Through Processing*.

Straight Through Processing An objective of *securities trading organizations*, suppliers of communications software, *custodians*, etc., to manage the entire trade lifecycle and corporate actions lifecycle in an automated and seamless manner, without the need for review or repair. The intended benefit of straight through processing is reduced costs and the ability to process high volumes of trades in a secure and risk-free manner.

Subdivision See *share split*.

Subscription The purchase of new securities (by a *position holder*) from the *issuer* as part of a *capital* raising event.

Subscription Close Date The last date upon which *subscription decisions* will be accepted by the issuer. See also *close date*.

Subscription Decision The decision (taken by a *position holder*) as to whether to purchase new securities resulting from a *capital* raising corporate action event, such as a *rights issue*. This is a specific type of *election decision*.

Subscription Open Date The first date that *subscription decisions* will be accepted by the *issuer*. See *open date*.

Subscription Period The timeframe within which *subscription decisions* will be accepted by the *issuer*. This period is defined by a *subscription open date* and a *subscription close date*.

S.W.I.F.T. The Society for Worldwide Interbank Financial Telecommunications; a worldwide organization providing secure message transmission between parties that subscribe to S.W.I.F.T. Message types include *trade confirmation*, *settlement instructions*, *securities* and cash statements and *corporate actions*.

Takeover (Offer) An attempt to purchase by one company, all or part of the *issued share capital* of another company. Also known as *acquisition* or *tender*.

Target Company The company that an *offeror* wishes to acquire in a *takeover offer*. The target company is commonly known as the *offeree*.

Tax Rebate Tax (pre-paid) that may be offset against other or later tax liabilities.

Tax Reclaim The process of recovering tax (whether *foreign withholding* tax or domestic income tax) by or on behalf of the *position holder*, from tax authorities to whom the tax has been paid.

Tender The offer (by an *offeror*) to purchase all or part of the *issued share capital* of another company (referred to as the *target company* or *offeree*). Also known as a *takeover* or *acquisition*.

Trade An agreement to exchange *securities* (for cash or for another asset) between two parties, whether buying or selling, lending or borrowing, etc.

Trade Conditions Information reflecting the specific terms under which a trade was executed, agreed between buyer and seller at the time of *trade execution*. Trade conditions that impact corporate action entitlements are *special-cum* and *special-ex*.

Trade Confirmation A communication of the details of a *trade* from one party to its *counterparty*; various media are used for the communication method. A means of achieving trade agreement.

Trade Date The date the parties to a *trade* agree to trade; the date of *trade execution*.

Trade Execution The agreement to *trade* between two parties, whether buying or selling, lending or borrowing, etc.

Tradeable Able to be bought and sold in the market place, (also transferable).

Trader An individual who buys and sells securities for the account of the *securities trading organization* that employs the trader; one or more traders are typically responsible for the operation of a *trading book.*

Trading The activity of agreeing to exchange *securities* (for cash or for another asset) between parties, whether buying or selling, lending or borrowing, etc.

Trading Book A subdivision of a trading department within a *securities trading organization* in which trading in a specific grouping of *securities* (for example) is conducted and kept separate from the business of other trading books.

Trading Book Position The net sum (by quantity) of all trades in each security, per trading book.

Trading Position A positive or negative trade-dated *securities* holding.

Transformation In the context of corporate actions, the settlement of a *claim* by the 're-shaping' of the underlying *unsettled trade*, where the security, quantity and/or cash settlement value of the trade may alter.

Transformation Date As a result of *transformation*, the original *value date* of the *underlying trade* is typically altered, due to the *underlying security* being replaced by the newly issued security. The market will set the earliest value date (transformation date) for the new security, which will be on or after the *effective date* of the event.

Transformed Trades Trades that have been re-shaped as a result of a corporate action. See *transformation.*

Treaty See *Double Taxation Agreement.*

Unbundling See *spin-off.*

Unconditional The status of a *takeover offer* once the minimum conditions set by the *offeror* have been met. Once unconditional, the offeror is legally obligated to fulfil the terms of the offer.

Unconditional Date The date applicable to a *takeover offer*, upon which the minimum conditions set by the *offeror* are met. This date marks the start of the *unconditional period.*

Unconditional Period The timeframe within a takeover offer, between the *unconditional date* and the *offer close date*, where the minimum conditions set by the *offeror* (for the offer to proceed) have been lifted and no longer apply. The unconditional period follows the *conditional period*.

Underlying Holding The position holder's *entitled position* in the *underlying security* to which the *event terms* will be applied.

Underlying Security The security to which the *event terms* are applicable, resulting in the distribution of *benefits* to *position holders* in that security or the *re-organization* of their holding.

Undersubscription Failure of *subscription decisions* to meet the minimum criteria (e.g. specified percentage of new securities) set by the *issuer*. See *underwriting*.

Underwriting The act of guaranteeing to an *issuer* of *securities* that the issuer will receive the funds it wishes to raise, at the specified time; one or many underwriters will buy any unsold portion of the new issue.

Unrealized Profit and Loss Theoretical profit or loss on a positive or negative *securities trading position* following revaluation of the position. See *Realized Profit and Loss*.

Unsettled Trade A trade for which *settlement* has not yet occurred, whether *value date* is in the future or in the past. Also known as an *open trade*.

Un-Subscribed A position for which *subscription decisions* have not been received by the *issuer*.

Value Date The intended date of exchange of *securities* and cash between buyer and seller. Also known as *contractual settlement date*. (Note that in some countries, the term Settlement Date is used to mean the intended date of exchange of securities and cash).

Voluntary Event A *corporate action event* where participation in the event is based solely upon the decision of the *position holder*.

Voluntary Redemption See *put call*.

VPC Vardepapperscentralen; the normal place of *settlement* for *bonds* and *equities* traded in Sweden.

Warrant A type of *security* entitling (but not obliging) the holder to subscribe to another security in proportion to the number of warrants held, at a fixed price, at or before a pre-specified date; beyond that date, subscription is no longer possible and the warrant expires.

Warrant Exercise The exchange of one security for another security, involving the position holder paying an exercise cost by a specified deadline, to the issuer.

Withholding Tax Tax deducted in the issuer's country of residence, on income paid by *issuers* to investors, whether on *equities* or *bonds*. Investors resident in certain countries may be subject to a lower rate of withholding tax, if the issuer's country and the investor's country have a *double taxation agreement* (or *treaty*) in place.

Write-Off The clearance of a small cash balance on an individual *resultant entitlement* (within internal *books & records*), leaving no cash amount due to or from the *position holder* or *counterparty*.

Zero Coupon Bond *Debt securities* that do not pay interest but are issued at a deep discount and redeemed at their full face value on the bond maturity date.

ENDNOTE: within this Glossary of Terms, certain text has been reproduced with permission from *Securities Operations; A Guide to Trade and Position Management*, ISBN 0-471-49758-4, author Michael Simmons, publisher John Wiley & Sons, Ltd.

Index

Index compiled by Terry Halliday

Printed and bound by CPI Group (UK) Ltd, Croydon, CR0 4YY
23/04/2025
14660969-0002